Advance Praise for

In *Better Off Bald: A Life in 147 Days*, Andrea Wilson Woods [...]
written personal, powerful, and unvarnished rendering of the story of her sister
Adrienne's diagnosis of advanced liver cancer at age fifteen. Adrienne was an
exceptional young woman, strong in her resolve, who refused to stop living her
life despite a relentless disease and an extremely poor prognosis. Ultimately, this
memoir is the story of two strong women—Andrea and Adrienne. Andrea was not
merely a witness to Adrienne's disease; she was a deeply committed, present, and
caring participant in Adrienne's life. It is clear that the fierce, vivacious, remarkable
young woman that Adrienne became reflects the character and strong example of
her sister Andrea.

**—WILLIAM B. COLEMAN, PHD, EXECUTIVE OFFICER
AMERICAN SOCIETY FOR INVESTIGATIVE PATHOLOGY**

Andrea's living and sharing with us her sister's illness and their agony are a
teaching lesson for all of us. It is a wake-up call for us to value what we have.
And if one is to have cancer, we've got to have hope.

**—GHASSAN ABOU-ALFA, MD, MBA, PROFESSOR OF
MEDICINE MEMORIAL SLOAN KETTERING CANCER CENTER**

Better Off Bald is a raw story about two sisters, one a teenager and the other barely
an adult, facing cancer. Andrea Wilson Woods works hard to be the grown-up and
a mother to her younger sister, Adrienne, when the diagnosis of cancer crashes
down on them. Ms. Wilson Woods holds nothing back and delivers a story that at
times feels like you are on a roller coaster ride with these two sisters as they try to
stay on track with life. *Better Off Bald* will jolt you emotionally and hopefully inspire
all medical professionals to do a little better, and all patients to fight a little harder.

**—NICHOLAS BORYS, MD, EXECUTIVE VP AND
CHIEF MEDICAL OFFICER OF CELSION CORPORATION**

Better Off Bald is the beautiful and painful true story of how the author lovingly
shepherds her sister Adrienne through diagnosis and treatment of advanced
liver cancer, striking at far too young an age. I wish for every doctor and medical
trainee to read this book. Andrea Wilson Woods' words bring to vivid life both the
devastation—as well as moments of joy—that flooded these sisters' lives as they
navigated the medical system, faced cancer, experienced suffering and courage,
and held fast to each other.

—JESSE CIVAN, MD, TRANSPLANT HEPATOLOGIST

Better Off Bald: A Life in 147 Days is a phenomenal depiction of the shock, horror, realities, and the humanity of a cancer diagnosis and battle. Andrea Wilson Woods' depiction of her sister's battle with liver cancer is both heart-wrenching and warming. Andrea is as brave as her sister, Adrienne, for sharing their story with such honesty and for her tireless devotion to helping liver cancer patients. Grab a tissue . . .

—HEATHER AMBROSE, DIRECTOR OF ACUTE CARE FIELD
MEDICAL AND PATIENT ADVOCACY; BTG INTERNATIONAL, INC.;
MOM OF GAVIN AMBROSE, STAGE IV BRAIN CANCER SURVIVOR

This exceptional memoir presents a poignant, touching, heart-wrenching and heart-warming recounting of the author's experience caring for her younger sister Adrienne, who is tragically diagnosed with liver cancer at the age of fifteen. Andrea's prose is clear, the story gripping, and the issues relevant for all who have or will experience the catastrophic illness of a loved one. Andrea's story of her sister and her family's journey is one of courage and commitment, told with love and honesty.

—LEWIS R. ROBERTS, MB CHB, PHD, PROFESSOR OF MEDICINE,
MAYO CLINIC COLLEGE OF MEDICINE AND SCIENCE

An awe-inspiring, bare-all account of sisters Andrea and Adrienne Wilson's five-month journey after Adrienne is diagnosed with—and dies from—liver cancer at age fifteen. Intertwined throughout are anecdotes that explain Andrea's obligatory "parent" role, the evolution of their supranormal sibling bond, and how this dual dynamic helped them navigate that journey. Despite the outcome, Adrienne beat liver cancer; Andrea tells us how her hero did just that.

—MARTY SELLERS, MD, MPH, TRANSPLANT SURGEON
AND LIVER CANCER SPECIALIST, EMORY UNIVERSITY

Andrea tells an extraordinary story of courage and persistence important for all patients with liver and other cancers to read. Her strength and hope continue in her perpetual fight against the disease as a tireless advocate for others facing the same devastating diagnosis.

—KABIR MODY, MD, ONCOLOGIST, MAYO CLINIC

The hero of this story—15-year-old Adrienne Wilson—shows incredible strength and courage as she faces a diagnosis of advanced hepatocellular carcinoma with her older sister and guardian Andrea by her side.

—BORIS PASCHE, MD, PHD, FACP
DIRECTOR, COMPREHENSIVE CANCER CENTER,
WAKE FOREST BAPTIST MEDICAL CENTER

Readers can find a measure of comfort in the way Andrea Wilson Woods processes her grief. She avoids being trite, yet her honesty does not come off as harsh. As she did with parenting, she strikes a delicate balance with her words and manages to be both realistic and inspirational. *Better Off Bald* is devastating and heartbreaking, inspiring and edifying. Most importantly, it's real. It's a beautifully written, insightful, page-turning book on how we connect as humans and why life—no matter how truncated—is worth living.

—PACIFIC BOOK REVIEW

Andrea Wilson Wood's memoir of her sister is complex and emotional, raw and honest. *Better Off Bald* tells a captivating story that will have a long lasting impact on any reader.

—INDIES TODAY

Better Off Bald is a story that is thoroughly engrossing and fulfills one of its many purposes: to help readers know a feisty teen who discovered new life while facing its end, moving from being a suicidal, depressed teen to one who figures out how to inject new life into her world and those around her. It's at once sad and inspirational—a story that will linger in the mind long after its conclusion.

—MIDWEST BOOK REVIEW

Even though *Better Off Bald* has a somber ending—as some cancer stories inevitably do—there is a powerful message about both living and dying with dignity. The book's lessons about living life to its fullest, cherishing loved ones, and not giving up are invaluable.

—MANY BOOKS

Better Off Bald paints such a vivid picture of the complexity of cancer, and the real-life challenges of living in the moment. The author captures the reader's heart and attention with clarity and grit. There is so much in Adrienne and Andrea's story that makes you wish you had known them in person and feel like you already do.

—LITERARY TITAN

The [book] places a poignant emphasis on the importance of each fleeting moment. Adrienne's voice is one of powerful, teenage defiance. This memoir/biography is deeply sad with inspirational flashes.

—KIRKUS

Better Off Bald is a realistic memoir about being a caretaker for a loved one with cancer, one that reveals all of the vulnerability that was hidden for the patient's sake.

—FOREWORD CLARION REVIEWS

Better Off Bald is a brutal reading that will move the reader to tears. But even through all the hardship, the memoir is filled with quirky humor and hope as Adrienne's personality and inner strength have her living each day to the fullest and still pursuing her dreams until the end.

—LITERARY PORTALS

An incredible, wonderful, raw and true story of two sisters.

—INTERNATIONAL REVIEW OF BOOKS

better
off
bald

BUILD YOUR **BLISSS**

Build Your BLISSS
1919 Oxmoor Rd Ste 257
Birmingham, AL 35209
betteroffbald.com

Cover Design by Andrea Ho
Cover Photo by Andrea Wilson Woods

PUBLISHER'S CATALOGING-IN-PUBLICATION DATA

Names: Woods, Andrea Wilson, author.
Title: Better off bald : a life in 147 days / Andrea Wilson Woods.
Description: Birmingham, AL: Build Your BLISSS, 2020.
Identifiers: LCCN: 2020901817 | ISBN: 978-1-5445-0561-2 (Hardcover) |
    978-1-5445-0459-9 (pbk.) | 978-1-5445-0460-5 (ebook)
Subjects: LCSH Wilson, Adrienne—(Cancer patient)—Health. | Woods, Andrea
    Wilson. | Cancer—Patients—United States—Biography. | Sisters—United
    States—Biography. | Liver—Cancer—Patients—Biography. | Terminally ill
    adolescents—Biography. | Cancer—Patients—Family relationships. | BISAC
    BIOGRAPHY & AUTOBIOGRAPHY / Medical. | BISAC BIOGRAPHY &
    AUTOBIOGRAPHY / Personal Memoirs | FAMILY & RELATIONSHIPS /
    Siblings. | MEDICAL / Caregiving.
Classification: LCC RC265.6.W5535 W553 2020 | DDC 362.19699/092—dc23

Printed in the United States of America

First printing September 2019

ANDREA WILSON WOODS

better
off
bald

a life in
147 days

For Annah, Jonah, Lola, Madison,
and Shiloh for giving me hope

Before Adrienne

I remember the day Mother and I moved to Birmingham.

As she drove into downtown, Mother said, "There she is Andra. Big B. Our new home."

You named me An-<u>dre</u>-a, not An-dra, I thought to myself. Somewhere along the way, my parents shortened my name. We Southerners like to do that. We either shorten words: gettin,' goin;' combine words: gotta, gonna; or stretch words out with our infamous drawl: Hooowww yallll doinn?

"Andra, you payin' attention?" asked mother.

No but I said, "Yeah."

I looked around. In a few months, my history teacher would tell me Birmingham was nicknamed the 'Pittsburgh of the South' because iron and steel production was the city's major industry during the first half of the twentieth century. It showed. It's not a picturesque place, but that day we watched as two rainbows painted the sky, splashing their colors across the dull gray of the metal buildings.

Mother said, "It's a sign. God's promise."

Promise of what, I wanted to ask but didn't.

Instead, I peered at the skyline, wondering about my new school, my new life. Moving to Birmingham was a chance to start over. My brother and father were becoming a distant memory. I was thirteen years old and for the first time in ten years, I thought I had my mother's full attention. I was wrong. I didn't know it yet, but she was pregnant with my baby sister.

Day 1

When I walk in the door and discover my fifteen-year-old sister Adrienne curled up in a fetal position on her favorite chair, two thoughts go through my mind. *Something is wrong. Adrienne is crying and she never cries. And damn, I'm going to miss my four o'clock workout on the treadmill and another Law & Order rerun.* Adrienne's whimpering pulls my focus back to her.

"Where have you been?" she asks.

I see her hand on her lower right rib. She speaks between choked sobs.

"It hurts. I spent half . . . the day in the nurse's office. I thought about calling you, but I knew . . . had to work. I decided to wait. I need to . . . the doctor, Sissy."

She takes a breath.

"It really hurts."

I know Adrienne is in incredible pain because she has never volunteered to go to the doctor. She hates doctors, especially dentists. She was overjoyed when Medi-Cal (California's Medicaid program) turned us down for her braces. Her teeth are not crooked enough to qualify even though she needs them. According to her dentist, she will develop a nasty cross bite, just like me.

I want to be sympathetic, but I am irritated. I blame Coachella, the outdoor concert my boyfriend John took her to a few weeks ago. Adrienne and John share a love of music so he takes her to concerts. For Coachella, Adrienne saved her money and we matched it so she could see her favorite band, Jane's Addiction. I opted not to go. Twelve hours in the desert with 32,000 people is not my idea of fun.

Coachella, "the best American rock festival" according to *Rolling Stone* magazine, takes place every year at the Empire Polo Field in the town of Indio, which is 140 miles east of Los Angeles. Adrienne and I have driven through Indio many times on our way to visit my dad and stepmother who live in Arizona, but we don't even stop to get gas in that town. Besides Coachella, I wonder what possesses 500,000 tourists to go to Indio each year. It can't be the scenery.

Adrienne described Coachella as a modern-day Woodstock. Being in the front, she was pressed against steel metal bars all day. She wanted to see Dave Navarro sweat. I remember how she devised a way to sneak in a disposable camera. After the concert, John complained his ribs felt bruised. Exactly two weeks ago, Adrienne pulled her shoulder and went to her pediatrician, Dr. Nazzer; he gave her ibuprofen and sent her home. When Dr. Nazzer asked how it happened, Adrienne replied dance class, or maybe it was at Coachella.

I am not a big fan of Coachella.

I tell Adrienne to give me ten minutes. She is suffering but she waits patiently. Never complains. Not even once. Except for the recent shoulder incident, Adrienne has never been seriously hurt before. A few colds here and there. The occasional swollen tonsils, which I assume will need to be taken out one day. Many cavities. Getting her to brush her teeth is a constant battle in our house. She has never broken a bone. She passes her annual physical every year. Why do I make her wait? Am I upset my plans are ruined? Or is it that I don't have sympathy for her if she cracked her rib at a rock concert? And what the hell do I do for ten minutes?

I am harsh about illness and injury. I expect people to be tough. I developed this character trait at a young age. Our mother never took us to the doctor when we were sick. She diagnosed us, gave us medicine, and cured us. She thought seeing the doctor was a waste of time since she was a nurse and knew a cold when she saw it. A sniffly nose was no excuse for missing school. I endured seventeen years of ballet with toenails falling off, shin splints, torn ligaments, and a bruised tailbone. One time my legs were so sore I crawled up six flights of stairs because the elevator had broken. Between Mother and ballet, I learned: pain is a part of life.

We arrive at the Empire Medical Clinic around 3:50 p.m. It is a slow day, and Dr. Nazzer sees Adrienne right away. He assumes her shoulder is still bothering her. Adrienne explains her shoulder is fine now and describes the new pain, which started around noon today. Why does he appear worried? He lifts her shirt to examine her abdomen. He touches it carefully, as if the pressure of his fingers will create holes in her skin.

"How long has this area been swollen?" he asks.

"A few weeks," Adrienne replies.

He gives me an odd look. I tell him Adrienne only showed me her swollen stomach two days ago, but then, it didn't hurt. He must realize

Adrienne, like many teenage girls, is modest about her body, especially around her parents.

I am more concerned she has not gotten her period in a few months, a telltale sign she is either pregnant or something is wrong with her body. I grilled her not too long ago.

"Are you sure that it is not even possible? You and Eli seem serious."
She rolled her eyes.

"I'm serious, Adrienne. You can tell me. I need to know if you didn't take precautions."

My voice trailed off, my mind turning over multiple scenarios and possible solutions.

"Sissy, for the last time, we are not having sex! Sex is gross, sweaty, and dirty. I have no interest in it. Do you believe me now? Can we drop it?"

I felt relief and anxiety at the same time. Adrienne couldn't be pregnant, but why hadn't she gotten her period? And although I am glad she isn't doing it, doesn't she seem to have an unhealthy attitude about sex? Where did that come from?

Dr. Nazzer leaves the room to make a phone call. Adrienne seems to be tolerating the pain well. She stopped crying a while ago. I am convinced she has cracked a rib. I tell myself that's the only thing that makes sense. When he returns, Dr. Nazzer informs us he has called Dr. Brenner, a surgeon at Providence St. Joseph's Medical Center, the only hospital in Burbank. He thinks we should go there, but he wants to arrange it ahead of time. I feel better because I know Dr. Brenner and trust him.

*⋆ *⋆ *⋆

Last summer, after I had a stomachache for a few days, my best friend Anya drove Adrienne and me to the Burbank clinic where Adrienne gets her immunizations. I have medical insurance for Adrienne but not for myself, so the clinic was my only option. John was at work. When the staff refused to see me because they didn't handle urgent care, Adrienne took charge. She tried calling Anya at work. She asked the nurse if she could call a cab for us. Meanwhile, I was shaking all over, lying down on the plastic bench, the security guard's jacket covering me but providing little warmth. Adrienne later told me my skin turned gray, and my lips were purple. I spoke but my voice was a whisper.

Adrienne finally got in touch with Anya, who picked us up and drove us straight to St. Jo's. Dr. Brenner happened to be on-call that afternoon. He performed my emergency laparoscopic appendectomy, aptly nick-named a 'lappy appy.' He inserted a laparoscope, a tiny camera, through a small cut he made below my bikini line. My appendix had already burst—probably while we were waiting at the clinic. The camera helped Dr. Brenner find the various pieces of my appendix, which he removed through my belly button. Sounds disgusting, but it worked.

During my five-day hospital stay, Adrienne amused me by drawing on the whiteboard in my room. She showed my appendix in various stages of life until its surprise death, ending with a tombstone etched with 'RIP, Sissy's Appendix.' Being doped up on Percodan and Demerol didn't stop me from cracking up. Adrienne can always make me laugh.

＊＊

Dr. Nazzer mentions Adrienne needs some tests done. He does not elaborate. Unfortunately, Dr. Brenner is unavailable but another doctor is waiting for us to arrive. You should leave immediately, says Dr. Nazzer. He never gives us any indication what he thinks is wrong, only that it's out of his league. I see the fear in his eyes. Does Adrienne see it too?

5:00 p.m.—the ER is busy. Having a doctor call ahead on your behalf doesn't make a difference. Being seen in this ER is like trying to get a seat at the Burbank Olive Garden on any given night of the week. They don't accept reservations, but you can call ahead and get on the list. What they fail to tell you is it won't matter. You still have to wait your turn.

I call John from a pay phone. He is concerned but can't leave work early. I want to yell at him. This is your fault. Didn't you pay attention? Didn't thousands of people pushing you and Adrienne against a metal railing seem like a bad idea? I hope he knows I will blame him when the doctor says she's cracked a rib. *Can't do anything about it. We'll tape it up. No dance classes until you feel better, young lady.*

I keep checking in with registration, trying to make them understand how urgent our situation is. Even if she can't be seen yet, Adrienne needs something, anything, for the pain. No, sorry. There are only a few people ahead of you, or, it won't be long now. I swear they said the same words to me when I was curled up in a fetal position on this floor, pieces of my appendix already floating around in my body, convinced I would die from the pain. Different staff, same language: rehearsed sympathetic phrases to make the patient, parent, or friend go away.

An hour later, we meet Dr. Lin, who wastes no time in giving Adrienne pain medication. Morphine, I think. She feels better within minutes. After examining her and listening to our story, Dr. Lin fears Adrienne might have bruised her liver and could be bleeding internally. Bruised liver? Bleeding internally? *Goddamn concert. Fucking metal bars.* What was John thinking? I know he couldn't have stopped Adrienne; she is far too stubborn, but I need someone to blame.

Dr. Lin orders a CT scan. Dr. Nazzer said some tests. This is one kind of test. Will there be others? I sign papers as a nurse preps Adrienne for the scan. Something about the use of iodine, which is needed to see the picture. I don't read the fine print.

"Is," the nurse looks down at the chart, "Emma allergic to iodine?"

"It's Adrienne and I don't know. She's never been sick before."

The nurse shrugs.

The test is more important than any potential allergy. I walk beside Adrienne's gurney as she is wheeled down to Radiology. I'm not allowed to be in the room with her. Radiation exposure is bad for your body unless you need X-rays, tests, or treatments. Then, it's okay.

Before Adrienne goes into the room, she leans toward me.

"Hey Sissy, watch it be cancer."

"Bite your tongue," I retort.

I hear her giggling as I watch the door close. I smile.

Adrienne and I continue to wait in a makeshift room in the ER. I call Diana to cancel Adrienne's usual appointment. Adrienne sees her psycho doctor, her words not mine, every Wednesday evening at seven o'clock. Diana is a Marriage and Family Therapist (MFT) who specializes in treating teenagers. Adrienne has been seeing her for almost three years. Although Adrienne has never taken medication for it, she suffers from bouts of depression. Seeing Diana has helped her over the years, and it comforts me she has someone to talk to because I know she doesn't tell me everything.

Next, I contact Anya and her husband Alex. Adrienne considers them her aunt and uncle, and they have always been my biggest support system. Adrienne asks me to call her boyfriend Eli, who has been waiting online for her. He sounds surprised, even scared. I reassure him.

"She was in pain but she's better now. She had a scan and we're waiting for the results. Yes, I'll call you later. Don't come to the ER."

I want to tell him everything will be fine, but I can't make the words come out of my mouth.

Time passes like a snail inching along the sidewalk. The pea-sized ball of anxiety in the pit of my stomach works its way into a golf ball. A nurse checks every half-hour to make sure Adrienne's pain is under control. It is. What do we talk about? Definitely school. Adrienne is worried she won't have time to do her homework. I say nothing. If she is bleeding internally, there will be no school tomorrow.

After several hours, Dr. Lin walks in. I have never seen the color drain out of someone's face before. I thought people used that expression to be dramatic, but I am looking at a man whose complexion, normally beige with an underlying yellowish tinge, is now white. No, not white. Without color. His face is almost translucent. What he is about to say has nothing to do with internal bleeding. It is far worse. He doesn't have to tell me to sit down because I already am. I reach over to Adrienne and grab her hand. Dr. Lin takes a deep breath as he moves closer to us. Working in an ER is supposed to consist of broken bones, chest pains, deep cuts, maybe an occasional gunshot wound. I believe he has never given this kind of news before.

Dr. Lin glances at Adrienne, but then turns to me.

"She has tumors in her liver and lungs."

On an invisible cue, Adrienne and I look at each other and burst into tears.

My mind races. Tumors? What is he talking about? There must be a mistake; it's a cracked rib. She had no pain before today. Tumors? Plural, more than one? How many? I'm afraid to ask. I squeeze Adrienne's hand tighter. Malignant, benign. I associate these words with tumors.

Dr. Lin's voice echoes in the distance.

"We're not equipped to handle this situation."

What does he mean?

I hear myself ask.

"What does that mean?"

He has arranged for an ambulance to transport us to Children's Hospital. Ambulance? Another hospital? I don't understand. Everything is moving too quickly. The world is spinning like the teacup ride at Disneyland. I hate that ride; Adrienne loves it. Faster, faster she always screams while I promise myself I will never go on the ride again. Finally, the teacups slow down; the world comes back into focus. Dr. Lin says he is sorry and walks out.

"I was just joking," says Adrienne, who has stopped crying.

"What?" I ask.

I have no idea what she is talking about. The words ambulance, situation, and tumors are doing cartwheels in my head.

"I was just joking when I said, 'Watch it be cancer.'"

I look at her. I open my mouth to respond, and then, I begin laughing. The laugh originates from deep inside my solar plexus, dissolving the golf ball of stress, pieces of it flying out of my mouth. Adrienne joins in and together our laughter fills the room. The person on the other side of the curtain must think we are bipolar. Only minutes before, we were crying over the news of multiple tumors in two different organs and now we are laughing so hard I think I might cry again. I'm glad no one else is here yet. This moment belongs to us.

John's arrival prompts me to look at the clock. It's past nine. Less than six hours ago, life was normal, or so I thought. A visit to the doctor, a trip to the emergency room, and a CT scan have conspired to turn our lives into pinball-machine balls, as we are pushed and slapped around by forces beyond our control. Last month, I remember telling John that things seem to have settled down in our house. We are getting along better. We have two beautiful, smart, healthy, happy kids: my sister Adrienne and his son Adam. Life is good.

Anya's husband Alex walks in next. He and John discuss what to do with my car while I ride in the ambulance with Adrienne. Nice, safe, practical talk. That's good. Let's all pretend we're not afraid.

The ambulance shows up at ten. The ride itself is uneventful. I expected red lights and a siren, but I guess that's only for emergencies. The EMTs do their best to make Adrienne comfortable. After some discussion, one of them comments she is fifteen going on thirty-five. Adrienne eats up the compliment and flashes a big smile. With teeth. I know she feels good because she rarely shows teeth. A photographer told her to smile big for a school picture one year, maybe it was third grade. When her smile revealed her two missing front teeth, the jerk said, oh, never mind. Some people shouldn't work with children.

✳ ✳ ✳

Without traffic, Children's Hospital Los Angeles is twenty minutes from our house in Burbank. Just over the hill. Out of the San Fernando Valley and into Los Angeles. We used to live in this neighborhood. I knew the hospital was there, but it wasn't part of my existence. It is only blocks away from Barnsdall Art Park, home of the Ragan Art Academy. Adrienne took classes there for many years; she even completed their two-year art program. She was excited when she initially got accepted. At eleven years old, she was too young to be in the program, but her art teachers encouraged her to apply anyway. She submitted a painting she had done on wood inspired by the flowers and trees in the park. It was an atypical piece for her due to the style and subject matter, an Impressionist landscape. The square strokes of pinks, greens, and browns are reminiscent of Cézanne; it's hard to believe a child captured that beauty. Adrienne hated the painting and gave it to Anya, who loves it.

During her second year of art school, Adrienne wanted to quit the Academy. She said the classes were stifling her creative abilities. Too much structure and direction. No freedom of expression. As a parent, it was a tough call for me. I didn't want her to end up hating art, something she had been passionate about since she first held a crayon in her hand, but she had made a commitment. She needed to finish what she had started. I had allowed her to quit ice-skating a few years before. When she was nine, a coach noticed her natural ability. She took classes but when she couldn't master a backwards crossover, she became frustrated. Ice skating lessons don't have an end date, but the art program did. Adrienne resented my decision. Afterward, she swore never to do art again. I waited and watched. Before too long, she picked up a pencil and drew again.

✳ ✳ ✳

I hit my head getting out of the ambulance. It won't be the last time. We are taken to the fourth floor—Hematology/Oncology. Welcome to HEMOC, a nurse says. I struggle to think back to science class. Hema

19

has something to do with blood, but what does Onco mean? I was a good student, but biology was my worst subject. I want to ask someone, but I am afraid of two things: appearing stupid and the answer. A nurse gets Adrienne settled in while Dr. Christina Coleman, the resident on-call, begins hammering me with questions. Most of which, I can't answer.

"I don't know if she's allergic; she's never been sick before." Didn't I just say this to someone else?

"Her father is dead. No, I don't know his medical history."

"No, our mother doesn't live here."

"Yes, I'm her legal guardian."

"She's lived with me since she was eight years old."

"No, I don't know. No. Yes. Maybe? Can I get back to you tomorrow?"

I tell her prior to the abdominal pain, Adrienne's only symptoms were the pain in her shoulder and her lack of a period. Dr. Coleman informs me I need to bring in proof of my legal guardianship as well as Adrienne's immunization records right away. I hope right away can wait until tomorrow. After an hour or so, the interrogation is over.

Dr. Coleman needs to examine Adrienne privately. John, Alex, and I, along with Anya who met us at the hospital, decide to get food. The nurse suggests McDonald's, which is on the first floor. I have never heard of a hospital having a fast food restaurant, and I wonder if this is a new trend in healthcare. We rush downstairs because McDonald's closes at midnight. We get there at 12:02 a.m. We are so tired, hungry, and frazzled, we don't care where or what we eat. However, Adrienne requested a salad. We drive around until we find a Carl's Jr. on the corner of Sunset and Western. They are closing but John and I convince the manager to stay open. We buy our food and return to the hospital. Famished, I eat my chicken sandwich in minutes despite its blandness and lack of mustard. Adrienne barely touches her salad; exhaustion overrides hunger as she falls asleep.

We speak in whispers. We don't want to wake Adrienne. No one says the word. That scary word. If we don't say it, it can't be true.

Step on a crack, break my mama's back. Step on a line, break my mama's spine. I hear my voice as a child chanting this mantra as I walked to school. Sometimes, I broke the rules and stepped on a line to see what would happen. *Cinderella dressed in yellow went upstairs to kiss her fellow. Made a mistake and kissed a snake. How many doctors will it take?* I jumped to the beat of the rope determined to surpass the current record of twenty doctors.

How many doctors will it take? If you exclude EMTs and nurses, we have already seen three. I know what we are dealing with, but I don't mention it. Anya is certain this is all a mistake; Adrienne is on the wrong floor. I want her to be right, but she's not.

I make a list of clothes and toiletries. I write the approximate location of each item so John can find it, or maybe, I tell him where to look. In our relationship, I am the organized one, the administrator, he says. This label makes me feel like a school principal. Does that make John a teacher or a student?

✳ ✳ ✳

"Where's your kid?" asked the small boy.

He stood in front of me on the stoop of our apartment building. He was a pretty child with fine, straight, light brown hair tumbling down his back.

Before I answered, my eyes followed his hand to his father's hand up to his father's face. Oh no! He was <u>that</u> guy. My new neighbor. The one I had wanted to meet. I had seen him yesterday across the hall carrying two bags of groceries. He had not seen me. His curly, dark brown hair was almost to his waist. Too long I had thought, but his toned, athletic legs and tight, round ass were perfect. I felt like someone had reached inside my body and squeezed my heart. Some call it love at first sight. It was more than lust.

Adrienne and I had concocted ridiculous ways I could accidentally meet this man, including asking for a cup of sugar. Only, I didn't cook. Now his kid was talking to me. I was wearing a baggy T-shirt, baggy shorts, and carrying a load of laundry from the basement into the building. I had been cleaning all day; my hair was a nest of dust. Combined with the dried sweat from the heat of early September, I looked fabulous.

"So, where's your kid? Want a Popsicle? Mine is Donald Duck. Dad bought it from the ice cream man. Can I play with your kid?" asked the boy.

"Uh. Sure. Follow me. She's inside."

By the time John and I talked, Adrienne and Adam were engrossed in a board game. John was twenty-eight years old and worked at Bank of America. His son, Adam, was four and the product of a previous relationship. John had Adam every weekend. They had lived up the street prior to moving into our building that weekend. Our children knew each other before we had ever met; Adrienne and Adam had waved to each other as neighbors did. The four of us spent all day together. I wanted to impress this man. He commented on my movie poster puzzles from my two favorite movies of all time: *Gone with the Wind* and *The Wizard of Oz*.

"They were both directed by Victor Fleming. Both MGM. 1939 was a good year," I said in a witty tone I didn't recognize.

I wondered why I was trying so hard. It had been a year since I had been in a relationship. I'd gotten used to the late nights in my tiny kitchen reading at my desk. Adrienne and I had moved into this small studio apartment after being evicted from Highland Terrace because I couldn't afford the rent there. We had gone from two bedrooms, two baths to a no bedroom, one bath. From $950 a month to $475 a month. Located on the eastern edge of Hollywood, Lyman Place apartments had been the only place I had found that didn't check credit. We had lived there for five months. We had a routine. I was lonely but I didn't like change.

When John offered to make dinner, Adrienne said that would be cool before I could protest. After purchasing groceries, John sent me to the liquor store with specific instructions: buy Kendall Jackson Chardonnay. He was making spinach tortellini with Alfredo sauce, Adrienne's favorite.

As I walked the two blocks to Captain Cork's Liquor, I muttered to myself. What am I doing? I don't even know this guy, and I left Adrienne with him. He could be a killer. Lots of Johns are serial killers: John Christie, John Wayne Gacy, No! Adrienne liked this John, which meant he must be okay. I needed to trust her instincts. Trust myself. John and I were supposed to be together.

✳ ✳ ✳

John, Anya, and Alex leave. In Adrienne's hospital room, I curl up in a chair, which is designed for sleeping because it extends out to accommodate your legs, but only if you're short. Good thing, I'm 5'2". I pull out my legal pad and write lesson plans to fax to school in the morning. They will need a substitute for the substitute, which amuses me. I began teaching in after-school programs and later substitute teaching so I could be on Adrienne's schedule, yet neither one of us will be in school tomorrow. I only compose plans for Thursday and Friday. Everything will be fine by Monday.

As I lie down, I think about how much Adrienne and I despise this environment. Growing up, we spent countless hours in nursing homes and hospitals where our mother worked. She insisted we visit her because her girls cheered people up, especially the elderly, who either had no family or had families who wouldn't see them. I danced for crowds of septuagenarians, while Adrienne acted like the adorable toddler she could be at times. Though we gave them brief moments of joy, Adrienne and I could not take away the loneliness we saw in their eyes. I always wanted to leave as soon as possible, as if their sadness was contagious.

Thinking about those isolated old people of the past makes me wonder if all parents stay overnight with their children. I slip my right hand through the metal bars to hold Adrienne's left hand. How many times have I grabbed this hand to give encouragement, to allay fear, to say I love you? I seem to always be to the left of Adrienne. Does that mean anything? As I will myself to sleep, one thought permeates my mind, a stored bit of trivia, probably something my mother told me—benign tumors don't spread, malignant ones do. I hold Adrienne's hand all night long. Day 1 is over.

Adrienne celebrating her 15th birthday
by attending the Rocky Horror Picture Show
© April 2001 (one month before diagnosis)

Day 2

John didn't sleep much last night. I see the lines of worry carving a path around his eyes. He takes over my shift at 8 a.m. so I can go to Burbank High and get Adrienne's books. She is anxious about missing school and doesn't want to fall behind in her classes. I don't call her teachers yet. We don't know anything. But I do, I know. I can feel the diagnosis trying to escape my lips. I push it back down. Once I'm in the car, driving home, I bawl. Once I start, I can't stop. The Mississippi River floods my face, and I have no dam, no way of terminating the tears. I run in the house to retrieve the paperwork requested by the doctor. I also feed our cat, Little Bit. I try to pull myself together by washing my face and taking deep breaths, but I fail miserably.

I arrive at the school, eyes red and puffy, my nerves shot. The school is under construction; therefore, parking spaces are nonexistent. As I prepare to turn on my flashers and risk getting a ticket, I see room behind an SUV. I'm driving John's Honda Accord, which is much bigger than my little CRX. I miscalculate and tap the bumper of the SUV. Great, John's going to kill me even though I barely touched the other car. There is no damage but I do the responsible thing and get out to speak to the owner. She seems pleasant enough and obviously another mother stopping by her child's school that morning. I imagine this tall, older brunette is on the PTA or maybe even the president. She agrees there's no damage as I apologize multiple times, my mind on other things. *How long has it been since I left the hospital? I need to hurry. Need to get back. Can't miss anything.*

I think the whole tap on the SUV's bumper thing is over, so I walk away.

"Wait," she yells, which startles me.

Why is she raising her voice?

"What's your name? Your license number?"

What is this woman talking about? Is she holding me up on purpose? I make a weak attempt at a smile.

"We agree there is no damage. I'm sorry but I'm in a hurry. I have to go."

Maybe the word go sets her off. I'm not sure but she flips out. She demands to know all my information because it is now possible the hitch on the back of her precious, gas-guzzling, environment-destroying SUV is bent. I can't believe this woman. This PTA mom who creates drama to fill the void in her day. Less than two minutes ago, everything was fine and now it's not? Ever since I heard the words 'tumors in her liver and lungs' twelve hours ago, a ball of anger, frustration, and fear has been building up inside of me. I unleash this fury and go for the jugular.

"What is wrong with you? You agreed there's no damage! All of a sudden you want my information? Like this is a hit and run, you're hurt, and I'm walking away from the scene of a crime. I'm in a hurry. My child, who attends school here, is at Children's Hospital and may have cancer."

In my head, I stop speaking. This is the first time I've said the 'C' word aloud and I say it to this angry, horrible woman whose child, I'm sure, is perfectly healthy. I can't think about it. I hear my voice. I am still talking to her. More like talking at her.

"I have to get her books! I have to be back to the hospital by nine because she may have a biopsy today. Do you know what that is? It's a test. It will tell us if she has . . ."

But I can't say it again.

"I'm sorry but I didn't hurt your precious car. Now, I have to go."

I can't believe what happens next. She threatens to call the police. As if she didn't hear a word I said. Maybe she doesn't care. She probably thinks I'm making the whole thing up. I never ask her name or find out who she is. Does she know she is the first person I said it to? Of course she doesn't. How could she?

"Andrea Wilson. California. A-6-0-2-0-8-0-4. Home. 8-1-8-8-4-3-2-7-7-3. Did you get all that? Because if you need me to repeat it or you want anything else from me, you'll have to follow me into the school."

I might have called her a bitch, but I'm not sure. I turn my back, run across the street, and storm inside.

Loaded down with Adrienne's books, I return to the car. The woman and her SUV are gone. Office Depot is on my side of the street. I don't know why but I have an urge to go there, but I don't. Instead, I get in the car, jump on the I-5 South from Burbank, and head toward the hospital. Even though I have no sense of direction, Children's Hospital is easy to find. It's located on the corner of Sunset and Vermont, two major streets in Los Angeles. It's not far from the studio apartment on Lyman Place, where Adrienne and I met John and his son Adam so many years before. *Happier times.*

I doubt John knows it, but I thought about leaving him last summer. I looked at apartments in our neighborhood. Picked up a few rental applications. Called some places in the *Recycler*. The plan was to rent a small one-bedroom apartment, give Adrienne the bedroom, and make the living room into my office/bedroom. It would be tight but cozy. Allow John to see Adrienne whenever he wanted. I had no desire to sever their special relationship.

Adrienne's reaction when I told her I wanted to end my relationship with John surprised me. We pulled up into the driveway and sat in the car. Silent tears fell off her lashes; she wouldn't look at me. I expected her to be angry, not crushed. She looked despondent. I could not give her a father figure and then take him away four years later. Whether they died like her biological father or abandoned her like our mother, Adrienne had already lost too many people. I still loved John, but I didn't like him anymore. I'm not sure I ever did. Adrienne will graduate from high school in four years. Eight years with John. For her, I could stay. I squeezed her left hand.

"Forget I said anything. Let's pretend this conversation never happened. Okay? Don't worry. We'll all be together."

Like the *Recycler* and the rental applications, I threw away my visions of solitude. Adrienne and I have never talked about the moment I almost broke up our family.

I pull into the visitor's parking garage and park on level four, otherwise known as the roof. I check the front of John's car again; the SUV woman has made me paranoid now, but upon careful inspection, there is no sign of the tap. I think if I don't tell John, he won't know the difference. I get into the elevator. The crosswalk to the lobby is one floor down. A sign catches my eye, "Sensitive children should wear masks." It is written in both English and Spanish. Would Adrienne have to wear a mask? Before I can answer my own question, the elevator doors open, and I follow the arrows pointing to the entrance. I pass another sign that reads, "McDonald's: Open during Construction." More construction. First the school and now the hospital. I wonder what they're building.

Before I enter the lobby, there is another sign warning visitors to,

"Please turn off these devices. Cellular phones, two-way radios, and other wireless communication devices can disrupt life support equipment." There are even pictures on this sign. Who designs these signs? Artists? Graphic designers? Is there a whole industry devoted to making these signs in hospitals, one warning after another? I see the designated smoking area, a fenced-in corner that resembles a small prison. I make a mental note to tell John about it. Funny how there aren't any smokers there. If I smoked, I would probably be there now, inhaling one last drag before entering the hospital and facing my child's illness. I wish I smoked.

I walk through the glass doors toward the security desk. All visitors, even parents, must check with security and get a pass. It is a time-consuming process. I shift my weight from one leg to the other, glance at my watch, and silently curse the family in front of me because they don't speak English well. After what seems like an eternity but is probably only five minutes, the guard gives up. Speaking slower and louder to the family didn't work. He hands them a pass.

Finally, the guard asks me, "Name?"

"Adrienne Wilson," I reply without thinking.

He attempts to look her up in the computer and shakes his head at me. "No such person."

"Oh. Try Emma Wilson instead."

Of course, the hospital would have Adrienne listed under her legal first name. I chide myself for making such a stupid mistake. The guard looks at me suspiciously, but before I can explain her first name is Emma but we call her by her middle name Adrienne, he gives me the sacred pass—a bright neon yellow sticker with the room number 404B on it. To avoid waiting in line, I soon learn the trick of recycling these so-called passes even though security switches the color every day.

Security directs me to the giraffe elevators. All the elevators here are named after animals. The giraffe elevators are the main elevators. The tiger elevators are in the ER, and somewhere on the other side of the building, there are even peacock elevators. These animals must have something in common, but I can't figure out what it is. Before I spot the speckled body of a giraffe, I walk through an enormous waiting room where blue butterflies are painted on the walls. I think Adrienne might like them because blue is her favorite color. Another butterfly is on the opposite wall, giant and multi-colored, as well as a huge sun with a smiley face in its center. It strikes me as Mary Poppins-ish. I expect to see Julie Andrews and Dick Van Dyke skipping through the tables and chairs, smiling cheerfully, and singing an inane song, but they are not here today.

My eyes take in the ATM machine, change machine, pay phones, and public restrooms. Four more signs remind people again to turn off their cell phones. I don't have a cell phone, but it occurs to me I might need one now. I arrive at the giraffe elevators; the word giraffe is written in eight languages in case you don't recognize the animal. Inside the elevator, there are pictures and poetry drawn and written by children. I go to the fourth floor—Oncology/Hematology. I know Oncology has something to do with . . . well, maybe I am wrong.

When the doors open, a red, orange, green, blue, and purple rainbow on a bright yellow background assaults my eyes. Adrienne later names this piece of 'art': *A Primary Colors Collision*. I see the artist being told to make it warm, friendly, assure people there is no death here. The air is sterile; there is almost no smell. The lack of smell becomes a scent unto itself. The raw combination of bleach and alcohol overpowers the colognes, perfumes, and soaps of the people running around. A small boy, who looks about three, whizzes by me. He rides his IV pole like a skateboard, giggling as if nothing is wrong with him. I see a small group of teenagers talking in the hall, laughing, joking, pushing each other around.

I listen to the noise—the humming of conversations and machines all around me. Not loud but so constant I wonder how I slept last night. If I close my eyes, I could be in a school. A clean school but just a school. The nurse's station has a whiteboard listing all the children by last name, their room number, and any scheduled tests for the day. Gomez has a CT scan. Tate, a bone scan. Burnham, Ramirez, and Wilson remain blank. No tests today. Not yet anyway. It's early. This is no school.

I walk into Adrienne's room; she is awake but groggy from the pain medication. She doesn't like the morphine because it makes her halluci-nate. No news on her biopsy. Her regular blood test or CBC comes back normal, which perplexes everyone. Dr. Coleman orders a comprehensive metabolic panel or 'chem' panel, a blood test that measures the status of your liver, kidneys, and electrolytes, as well as your blood sugar and protein levels.

Later that afternoon, we meet Dr. No as we like to call him due to his 'no bedside manner.' He is the attending doctor for 4 East today, so he becomes Adrienne's primary oncologist. The good doctor appears to be in his early fifties. Grey hair, glasses. Old school. The antithesis of Dr. Coleman. His bright bow tie clashes with his stiff, formal demeanor. I want to like him, but I don't.

Without any prompting, Adrienne starts her homework. John and I watch TV. In my hurry, I forgot to get us books, a deck of cards, anything to pass the time. We don't talk much. I am afraid if I do, that word will come out again. Does John feel it, know it, the way I do? When he does speak, he tells me he will get us a cell phone later today. We have made too many calls on his work cell phone; he is worried his boss will be upset with him.

Dr. Coleman lets us know Adrienne's biopsy will be tomorrow because surgery is booked solid today. I take this as a good sign. If the doctors were worried, wouldn't they want the biopsy today? Twenty-four hours is a long time to wait. Too much time to think about the question I already know the answer to.

We hear Adrienne's roommate long before we meet her. She is a loud, vivacious African-American teenager, who is on a first-name basis with everyone on the floor from the doctors to the janitors. She is too familiar with this place. Although annoyed by it at first, her constant chatter grows on me. She sticks her head around the curtain and introduces herself. LaQuisha speaks as fast as a roadrunner runs.

"I'm LaQuisha. I'm nineteen. I have sickle cell anemia, which means I get infections a lot and need blood transfusions all the time. I'm usually here for a few days. There are a bunch of us sickle cell kids. I wanna get a job, but who's gonna hire me? I'm always here. I've been in and out of hospitals my whole life. Like my nails? I did them myself. What's your name? I can show you around, Adrienne. I'm gonna make you something. I've got this kit David gave me. Did you get a toy yet? You didn't? Ask David for one. He'll fix you up. How old are you? Really? I thought you were eighteen. Like my nails?"

She comes up for air, smiles, and tells us if we need anything let her know. How can someone who is sick all the time have so much energy? And what is sickle cell anemia? I've heard of it. Isn't it hereditary? Something to do with the genes?

I need to call our mother. I don't want to. She is unpredictable, the kind of person a lawyer never wants on the stand because she speaks without thinking. The nurse in her will give advice; the mother will insist I take it. I pick up the phone and dial the number from memory. I will be short, to the point. Don't give her an opening.

"Hello, Mother. Adrienne is in the hospital. She has tumors in her liver and lungs. No, we don't know. The biopsy is tomorrow."

She gasps, recovers, and then suggests I transfer Adrienne to St. Jude Children's Research Hospital in Memphis. That way, Adrienne will be closer to her 'real family.' I say nothing. I learned a long time ago not to get sucked into an argument, which is always preceded by one of her verbal zingers.

I tell Mother I will call St. Jude's and hear what they have to say, but Adrienne is in no condition to move across the country. Then Mother offers to stay with us. The thought of our pill-popping mother playing nurse to Adrienne makes me shudder.

I remember two-year-old Adrienne, staggering like a drunken sailor, grabbing the TV stand for support, wearing only a diaper. She appeared woozy; her words were garbled. Mother was sitting on the once-white couch watching TV. I had come home from school, and I immediately freaked out.

"What's wrong with Adrienne? Is she okay? We should take her to the hospital."

Mother sighed and looked at me.

"Adrienne's fine. She wouldn't stop crying so I gave her a shot to make her sleepy. She'll be okay."

I picked up Adrienne so she wouldn't hurt herself.

"What have you done? Are you crazy? She's a baby!"

Mother said I worried too much. She was a nurse. She knew exactly how much to give Adrienne. I never thought to ask her what was in the shot. I assumed it was some kind of downer.

After that incident, I saw our mother in a new light. I pretended to be an outsider looking in. When I opened the kitchen cabinets, I found a small pharmacy: pills of every color, shape, and size. The junk drawer was always full of alcohol swabs, surgical scissors, needles, and vials of liquid. After working the night shift, Mother emptied her pockets every morning and dumped the contents into that drawer. Except for the plastic things you put over the outlets, our house was never childproofed.

Then it dawned on me. This wasn't the first time Mother had used a shot to make Adrienne shut up. I made her promise never to do it again. She agreed but she was lying. Addicts always lie. I never caught her again, but after I left home, Adrienne remembered receiving shots of 'vitamins' on a regular basis and falling asleep afterward.

Even though my mind is made up about our mother moving in with us, I feel it is not solely my decision. I hand Adrienne the phone. She eyes me skeptically. Adrienne listens to our mother, looks at me, and then says one word.

"No."

Our mother flies into a rage, her voice emanating from the phone. Adrienne hands it to me, not bothering to cover the mouthpiece.

"You can't let her come, Sissy. I can't talk to her. Make her stop."

I speak over our mother's rant; there is no other way to communicate with her now.

"You can't call Adrienne here. You are upsetting her. You can obtain updates on Adrienne's medical condition by calling my voicemail. The number is 2-1-3-9-4"—

She hangs up.

Eli's parents drop him off after school. It is the first time he has seen Adrienne since she got sick. He seems to be holding it together. Tough kid. He and Adrienne make a list of people she wants him to call. Eli attends Burroughs, the only other public high school in Burbank. He goes to school with most of Adrienne's friends. She asks me to call Nadia, one of her oldest friends, but I can't reach her. I leave a message with a man who must be her grandfather, but he rambles in Russian and hangs up on me. Two for two on the hang-ups today. I need to work on my phone voice.

A tall, attractive brunette walks into the room. She reminds me of a younger, prettier version of our Aunt Tootsie, Mother's oldest sister. Her real name is Laurel, but our oldest cousin couldn't say her name when he was younger, so she became Aunt Tootsie. When she's not forcing children to memorize bible verses or starving herself to death, she's not too bad. Except she always calls Adrienne by her first name, Emma. Mother said I could name my then unborn sister any name I wanted if Emma was part of it. Our grandmother's name was Estelle Emma Green.

Like many Southerners, we have a tradition of naming a child after a living relative. Mother's younger sister is named Francis Sue; her daughter is Peggy Sue. My mother is Myra Jean; I'm Andrea Jeanne, only spelled differently because my mother thought the French version was fancier. The name Adrienne is of Latin origin: the feminized version of Adrian meaning 'of the sea' and 'artful.' Emma is a formality; my sister's name is Adrienne.

Aunt Tootsie's doppelganger turns out to be our social worker, Grace, who exudes kindness and warmth. This woman went into the right profession. She explains to us she handles all sorts of issues from finding financial help for families to getting wigs for kids. As I hand over a copy of my guardianship papers, I inform her I have been Adrienne's legal guardian for almost three years, but she has been in my physical custody for six-and-half years. When Grace asks about our mother, I recount the phone conversation earlier and describe how our mother threatened to come to Los Angeles. Grace suggests we put a block on Adrienne's visitors. If our mother shows up, I will be alerted, and she will not be allowed in without my authorization. Adrienne, John, and I agree to this course of action.

Today's nurse comes in and asks Adrienne, "Is there any possibility you might be pregnant?"

Last night, Dr. Coleman asked the same question; I deferred to Adrienne who said no, of course not. It must be standard procedure to ask every teenage girl this question half a dozen times. Discretion and privacy don't exist in a hospital. Eli averts his gaze and Adrienne manages to get out a "No" as various shades of pink creep up her face. The nurse ignores their embarrassment.

After she leaves, Adrienne declares she wants to put up a sign: "I'm not having sex!" When her pregnancy test comes back negative, I want to feign surprise. *Really? You don't say? Hmm . . . I guess it would be nearly impossible, but Mary did it—although her story is suspect.* Adrienne asks why do they bother asking me if they're going to do a test anyway? I don't have an answer.

The nurse returns with the Numeric Pain Intensity Scale also known as the Wong-Baker FACES Pain Rating Scale. It's a white chart with the numbers 1–10 on it with a face above each number. Number 1 is smiling slightly; however, the other faces become more distressed and contorted as the numbers go up. Number 10 is about to explode. I wonder what's wrong with him.

Adrienne is asked to rate her pain on a scale of 1–10. One is mild, tolerable, slight pain while ten is the worst pain you've ever felt, so bad you think you're going to die. Adrienne states unequivocally when she came home from school yesterday, she was a ten. Like ivy crawling along a trellis, guilt creeps into my veins. Still on morphine, Adrienne is a five now.

The nurse chirps, "Well, I'd say that's an improvement, wouldn't you?"

Her face inscrutable, Adrienne says, "It's not a one, but it's better."

The nurse, oblivious to the sarcasm, smiles and leaves the room.

John buys two new books that evening: *Taber's Cyclopedic Medical Dictionary* and *Gray's Anatomy*. We now have five inches of knowledge to digest. As John pores over the anatomy book, I finger the dictionary: solid green, 19th edition. I find the word on p. 1503. "Oncology: The branch of medicine dealing with tumors." I feel nothing. No fear, no relief.

Later, John says good night and goes to the small kitchen intended for parents. All the amenities of home are there: a refrigerator, microwave, sink, table, and chairs. John sits and reads about the liver and lungs. He takes copious notes, which he will share with me tomorrow.

I lie down on the cushioned window seat, which is a nice change from the foldout chair. My mind wanders back to the autumn day that changed my then thirteen-year-old life forever. It was the day something was different.

$\ast$ $\ast$ $\ast$

Mother and I were having breakfast for dinner at our usual place, The Omelette Shoppe. We went there for the prices. Our standard routine was to count the change Mother had saved during the week. We also checked for loose coins in her purse as well as in the seat cushions. Typically, we scrounged up around six dollars, enough for one meal, which we would split, plus tax and tip if we only drank water. I knew something was wrong when Mother pulled out a fresh, crisp twenty-dollar bill.

"Order anything you want," she said.

I looked at her suspiciously. I couldn't remember the last time I had seen that much money. She had declared bankruptcy recently to get rid of numerous bills accumulated from years of shopping.

She encouraged me to order orange juice, a real luxury. She appeared nervous but her face gave nothing away. When I demanded to know what was going on, she evaded the subject and told me I could have my own omelette—no sharing today. Now, I was seriously worried. Was she sick? Would she die? She was the only person I had in the world. My dad and stepmother seemed light years away; they had recently left Arkansas to move to Arizona. I didn't even know what their house looked like. I refused to order any food until she explained herself. Mother paused and squirmed. She was relieved when the waitress brought my extra-large orange juice. I stared into her hazel eyes, trying to discern what they were hiding.

She swallowed, hesitated, and then mumbled, "I'm pregnant."

Rage and disgust ran laps around my brain. How could a single, forty-one-year-old woman get knocked up? I should have dropped that bomb. At that time, Alabama had one of the highest rates of teen pregnancy in the nation. Mother waited for me to say something.

"What?" and "How could you?" came out of my mouth.

My right hand curled tightly around the tall cool glass of OJ. Mother showed no signs of regret.

"It's Todd's baby," she said, as if that fact was supposed to pacify me.

Todd was her dead fiancé. During the summer, torrents of rain on I-40 had caused his car to flip over. He hit his head and died instantly. Another notch on the bedpost of tragedies in my mother's life. Todd's baby meant she wouldn't consider an abortion. Todd was the love of my mother's life; he was the only person who ever made her happy.

"You've always wanted a sister. Maybe it will be a girl."

I looked down at the table with my head held in shame for the woman in front of me. Beads of condensation reminded me of my full glass of orange juice. I thought about throwing the OJ in my mother's face. I considered walking out of the restaurant. Maybe I did one or both of those things. I don't remember. However, I soon realized a temper tantrum wouldn't kill the little person growing in my mother's stomach. There wasn't enough orange juice in the world to wipe out her baby.

Day 3

You're blue—the most soothing shade in the spectrum. The color of a clear summer sky or a deep, reflective ocean, blue has traditionally symbolized trust, solitude, and loyalty. Most likely a thoughtful person who values spending some time on your own, you'd rather connect deeply with a few people than have a bunch of slight acquaintances. Luckily, making close friends isn't that hard, since people are naturally attracted to you. They're soothed by your calming presence. Cool and collected, you rarely overreact. Instead, you think things through before coming to a decision. That level-headed, thoughtful approach to life is patently blue and patently you!

*—Adrienne's journal entry dated 4/27/01
(Results from "What's your true color?" quiz)*

Today Adrienne will have a biopsy done in the afternoon. A new nurse explains the surgeons will insert a Vascular Access Device (VAD) during the surgery. She gives us a booklet aptly named *How to Care for Your Vascular Access Device.* "The VAD is a soft plastic tube that is used to give fluids like medicine, blood products, and nutrition right into the bloodstream. It is also known as a catheter, port, or central line."

John and I will be taking a class on how to care for Adrienne's central line. The nurse points to a picture and says Adrienne will get a double lumen: two tubes connected to one tube coming out of her chest, below her collarbone. It looks like an upside-down 'Y.' A double lumen port allows her to receive medicine and fluids at the same time. Adrienne will no longer have to be pricked to start an IV, which pleases her because she hates needles.

However, the VAD is not without its problems. The line is susceptible to infections, and it needs daily maintenance to prevent such infections. It must never get wet. Adrienne is no longer allowed to take showers. Before taking a bath, I will have to put the line in plastic, seal it as much as possible, and tape it to her chest. Adrienne's eyes flicker and her chest slumps; this news quashes her spirit.

I look at the picture again and imagine it in Adrienne's chest. The nurse continues talking about this alien piece of medical ingenuity that will become a part of our daily lives. Do all nurses try to normalize this environment? Can't she see how upset we are? Not only does Adrienne hate baths, but now she will be dependent on me to take them. I think about children who must wear casts for broken bones. Casts usually come off in six weeks. Skimming the booklet, my heart sinks when I read, "A VAD can stay in for as long as three years."

Dr. Coleman, who insists we call her Christina, comes in only to ask John and me to step outside. I can't count the number of times I've heard that line on television, but now it's real. Can you step outside? I wonder if anyone ever says no to that question. *No, I can't. No matter what you want to tell me, I have a perceptive teenager who will badger me until I repeat what you are about to say. So save us all some time and say it here. In her room, to her face.* So what do we do? We step outside.

The results from the liver panel are back: Adrienne has hepatitis B and appears to be a carrier of hepatitis C as well. I pretend to know what that means. Christina asks if Adrienne ever had a blood transfusion or if our mother has a history of hepatitis. No blood transfusions and no . . . wait.

"Over a year ago, our mother called and said she had hepatitis B. I didn't believe her."

I don't tell Christina our mother is always sick with some new illness or disease. Even her diagnosis of multiple sclerosis, which qualifies her for disability benefits, is questionable. It never occurred to me our mother might be telling the truth about the hepatitis, or it could have affected Adrienne. Mother said god cured her like he cured Naomi Judd. To me, the alleged hepatitis was another example of Mother's Munchausen syndrome, an artificial disorder characterized by a person feigning illness for attention.

According to Christina, when hepatitis occurs in this country in someone as young as Adrienne, the most logical conclusion is a blood transfusion or transmission from mother to child during childbirth. She says Adrienne has the hepatitis B surface antigen indicating an active, perhaps chronic, infection. Even though Christina isn't attacking me or judging me, I become defensive and repeat my mantra.

"Adrienne has never been sick before, at least, not since she has been living with me."

Okay, there was that time when her tonsils were so swollen she couldn't breathe. It was a Saturday afternoon. I remember because John took my car to work. Our friend Jesse gave us a ride to urgent care, where the doctor gave Adrienne some medicine, and she was better the next day. My mind scrambles to produce more evidence that I am a good parent:

- Adrienne gets a physical every June. I fight to get her thyroid tested since most women in our family have thyroid problems, which are genetic.
- Not only has Adrienne had her hepatitis B vaccination series, but she also had all her childhood immunizations repeated prior to beginning middle school. I tried to get her immunization records, but our mother denied having a copy, and the former school never sent them. Her elementary school in Hollywood let it slide; all they required was proof of a recent TB vaccination, which Adrienne received her first month in Los Angeles. However, the Burbank school district insisted Adrienne redo all her vaccinations.
- Adrienne had never seen a dentist until she lived with me. When she was ten years old, she had a baby root canal and continued to need fillings over the next several years. She hates to brush her teeth, but I make her do it despite the battle that ensues.
- When she was six years old, Adrienne came to visit me in Los Angeles for ten days. She arrived with ringworm all over her body. I took care of it immediately, and she returned home healthy.

Proof does not mitigate my guilt. There's not a better word to describe what I'm feeling right now. Culpability, criminality, sin, wrongdoing, and shame don't suffice. It's guilt. I never got Adrienne tested for hepatitis. I should have believed our mother. I recover from my reverie when Christina tells us to get tested for hepatitis because there's a slim chance we could have been exposed to it. I agree to do it, but I can't think about my own health right now. I need to learn more about hepatitis.

When we return to her room, Adrienne insists on knowing what Dr.

Christina said to us. John and I have an unspoken agreement. We will be truthful with Adrienne about her illness. She may only be fifteen but she is smart, wise beyond her years, and knows bullshit when she hears it. Explaining our choice to be honest with Adrienne will be lost on doctors who have spent years asking parents to 'step outside' so little Bobby, Susie, or Tracy won't hear the prognosis. *Stepping Outside: How to Break the Bad News to Parents* must be a prerequisite course in medical school.

Adrienne asks lots of questions about hepatitis, none of which John and I can answer yet. There must be a relationship between the hepatitis and tumors, but I realize Christina never explained what it is.

"Time to go," a nurse says.

My chest tightens as the tension increases around my heart. I can almost feel my blood pressure rising. Time to go. Time to open up my child. Time to insert a tube in her chest. Time to find out the verdict. Time, time, time.

John and I walk alongside Adrienne's gurney as she is taken to surgery, which is located on the seventh floor. We ride the peacock elevators. I lean over, tell Adrienne I love her, and whisper Tonya Harding in her ear, our family motto for good luck.

One evening, as I was leaving for the premiere of my play *Full Body Massage*, Adrienne ran out of the house and stood next to the front gate. Having spent many years around theatre people, she knew saying 'Good Luck' was considered bad luck. Dancers say 'Merde' (which means shit in French) while actors say, 'Break a Leg.' Her brow furrowed. She smiled.

With a quick karate chop motion in the air, she said, "Tonya Harding!"

I got the joke. She skipped into the house, proud she had made me laugh. Her dry, wry humor is often lost on her peers but never on me.

The massive doors to the OR close with a soft thud. We stare at them. I wonder if John is as scared as I am. There is a woman standing next to us. She must sense our fear because she asks about our child's surgery.

"Liver biopsy," I say, "needed to determine the cause of multiple tumors."

I sound edgy, like a robot on speed.

Noelle tells us her three-year-old daughter Rose was born with a rare, degenerative liver disease; she is on her second liver transplant. Before I can ask about the first one, Noelle goes on. I imagine she has told this story a hundred times. Rose's first transplant occurred when she was a year old, but her new liver failed when someone made a mistake with her medications. *Mistake? Who is the person who made this mistake? A pharmacist? A doctor?* Noelle is so casual about it.

"This time," she says, "Rose is getting a piece of her father's liver."

Both Noelle's husband and daughter are in surgery. I look around; she is alone. I want to hug her, but I don't.

As I walk into the waiting room, I feel better. God, that sounds awful. If I tell John, he will say I am experiencing Schadenfreude. He loves to use big words most people don't understand. *Pleasure derived from the misfortunes of others.* I wouldn't call it pleasure, just appreciation. We have friends here, a strong support system. Adrienne's 'uncles' Jesse and Jared are here along with Anya. We are expecting more people later. When I relate Noelle's story, our friends offer a piece of their livers without hesitation.

"Live donor liver transplants are considered a fairly new procedure," says Anya.

Her mother is a doctor, which automatically makes her one too. It's her most annoying character trait, but in this instance, I drink in the information. She explains the liver is the only organ that can regenerate, which means a portion of the liver can be taken from a healthy, adult donor and transplanted into the recipient. Ideally, the livers in both bodies regain normal function within a few weeks.

We are getting ahead of ourselves. We don't even know if Adrienne is eligible for a transplant, but considering how many livers are up for grabs in this room, I sure hope she is.

The surgery is expected to take several hours. We take turns eating lunch. Anya, John, and I go first. Even though I can't taste the food, I force myself to eat. I need to keep my strength up. I've already lost a few pounds; I can tell because my jeans are looser. Anya's light banter can't shake the sense of doom hovering over my plate. Think positive thoughts. *Guess what? We were wrong! They're not tumors. It's not C . . .* I can't finish the conversation in my head. The black, UFO-shaped cloud won't go away. It stays there, mocking me, penetrating my head with: *Be ready for the inevitable bad news. You know it's coming.*

We go back upstairs to relieve Jesse and Jared so they can eat too. We are Adrienne's posse. United we stand. I know Adrienne is rolling her eyes at me from her deep anesthetic-induced sleep. Oprah's voice resonates from the TV, which is perched up high right below the ceiling. She is supposed to be asking about Nicole Kidman's upcoming film *Moulin Rouge*, but instead she is confirming Nicole is hurt and surprised by Tom Cruise's petition for divorce after ten years of marriage. A few days ago, I would have felt sorry for Nicole. I like her. Now I'm thinking . . . *Divorce? Is that all? Don't worry Nic, you'll move on. Fuck Tom. Your children are healthy; that's all that matters.*

Dr. Jorge, one of the surgeons, walks out of the OR. He reports the central line is in, and the biopsy was a success. Now, the surgical team will look at the tissue sample under a microscope. I can't stand it. He's been in there and has seen Adrienne's liver. Why is he being secretive?

"Does Adrienne have cancer?" I ask.

The words just fall off my lips. I could be asking *do you want a cup of tea?* Same number of syllables, only the former has a desperate nonchalant tone. Yes or no will do. Dr. Jorge says he will return when he has more information. I don't need it. By sidestepping the question, he gave the answer: Yes.

"Can you please step outside?" asks Dr. Jorge.

I hate those words; nothing positive comes after them. Like obedient soldiers, John and I follow him into the corridor. Unlike Dr. Lin, there is color in his face. He expected what he found.

"Your sister has cancer."

My worst fears confirmed. Cancer. I knew what it was all along, but I had not accepted it. I can see the words floating on a banner pulled by an airplane, waving in the wind. Mocking me. *Your sister has cancer. Adrienne has cancer. Kiddo has cancer.* The airplane picks up speed. *YoursisterhascancerAdriennehascancerKiddohascancer.* My eyes wet. My throat closes. My stomach drops.

He continues, "We believe your sister has a type of liver cancer called HCC or hepatocellular carcinoma. It has metastasized to her lungs, which means she is in stage four. It's very serious."

His words are steady; his eyes are not. I see pain, sympathy, but not an ounce of hope. Dr. Jorge can't fix it. Every pore on my face is soaked. Tears flow down, down, dripping off my chin . . . becoming silent drops on the floor. Liver cancer. I have never heard of liver cancer before. Cirrhosis, yes, too much alcohol causes liver damage. What did he say?

H something. Cellular is the second word. Need the fog sucked out of my head. Can't think. Dr. Jorge promises to give us literature about the cancer. He leaves us alone. As I stare at the puddle on the floor, I think . . . he never said her name.

I trudge into the waiting room and pass our friends. I go over to the large window that has a small nook. I sit in it, my knees tucked into my chest. John attempts to comfort me, but I push him away. The grocery store Jons is below us. Many Hispanic women are pushing grocery carts to their cars; young children play around their legs. School must be out because I see older children too—talking, laughing, happy. Normal people with normal lives, they don't know what just happened on the seventh floor of Children's Hospital. This tall building does not exist. Two days ago, I was one of them.

There is Lucky Fashion; I bought one of my favorite outfits there. A black, tight, two-piece skirt set made of rayon with a subtle pattern of light blue flowers. My geisha attire. Adrienne wore it to my friend Marilyn's wedding last year. Although we have different tastes, we occasionally share clothes. At 5'5½", Adrienne is three inches taller than I am. Doctors predicted she would be 5'8"; she hates that she fell short. Shoe size 8. Most clothes size 7/8. One size up from me.

How long do I sit in that window? It seems like minutes to me. John says it was for almost an hour. I don't know. Where is Mimi when I need her? A mean girl in my preschool, Mimi pinched kids for fun. *Pinch me Mimi. Wake me up. I won't pull your blonde ponytail again. Bring me out of this nightmare. Please.*

While I sit in the window, Anya is on the phone with her mother who works at the National Institutes of Health (NIH). When Anya tells her mother the diagnosis, her mother is silent. Dr. Sofia Sárközi always has a scientific, rational, non-emotional approach to life that serves her well in her profession. When her mother says nothing, Anya is surprised and feels her reaction is disproportionate to the situation. She has never known her mother to react that way before.

"It's one more thing, one more battle to win. We've overcome so many different problems. This is just one more problem."

Dr. Sárközi replies, "You will win if you measure winning in terms of having good days and good hours."

"What are you saying? How long is she going to live?"

"Nobody can tell you that. Nobody knows how long anyone is going to live."

After that phone call, Anya calls her husband Alex and tells him to come to the hospital right away. Anya turns around and speaks to anyone who is listening.

"This is war. And it's a war that we're going to have to fight to win."

Her declaration of war brings me out of the window. She is right. It is time to put on our battle gear and start fighting.

Then, I remember, I have to work tomorrow. From May to October, I work as a clown and/or games person for company picnics. Saturdays and Sundays are booked solid throughout the summer. When I started in 1996, I took Adrienne with me to work. She got her face painted, participated in games, and played bingo with the other kids. One time at Silverado Canyon Park, she enjoyed a hayride and saw a litter of newborn piglets at the petting zoo. The catering staff was convinced I never fed Adrienne because they once witnessed her devouring seven hotdogs and three hamburgers within a few hours.

One of my bosses promised Adrienne she would have a job when she turned fourteen. Last summer, she worked as a clown. My clown name is Red; Adrienne named herself Blue, her favorite and current hair color. Making $125 per day, I allowed her to spend $25 while the rest went into her savings account. She has saved $900. Once she earns another hundred, she plans to buy her first mutual fund. John's idea. Her earnings convinced her classmates they should all become clowns. I am proud of her work ethic and her ability to think long-term about her future. Then, it hits me—she can't work this summer.

I never miss work; I can't afford to. I've never bailed out on a picnic. When I had laryngitis, the group found my 'silent clown act' amusing. When a one-inch piece of wood went under my thumbnail, making it the biggest splinter I've ever had, I finished the picnic and went to the ER afterward.

I take John's cell phone into the corridor. When I hear my boss's voice, the words tumble out of my mouth like building blocks falling down. Haphazardly. Everywhere.

"Hi. It's Andrea. At the hospital. No, not me. Adrienne . . . tumors . . . biopsy . . . cancer. Can't work tomorrow. So sorry."

He insists I not worry. He sounds calm; I want to be calm. My boss, our boss, sends Adrienne his best wishes.

When I return to the waiting room, Dr. Jorge gives us papers about HCC. He made copies from medical textbooks. I expected a brochure. He gives us a beacon of hope; there is a slight chance it might be ovarian cancer. Dr. Jorge felt a mass near Adrienne's left ovary so it's possible, especially since one of her only symptoms is lack of menstruation. Ovarian tumors often look like liver cells under a microscope. We will have a definite answer when the pathology report comes back on Monday. He doubts it's ovarian cancer and warns us not to get our hopes up. I see a flicker in his eyes; he wants to believe it's ovarian cancer. A young woman can live without her ovaries.

John and I make a conscious decision to put on a happy face for Adrienne. Not too happy, less she suspects something. We want her to be lucid when we tell her about the cancer. I can't wait to see her. She is the only person in recovery. Still groggy from the anesthesia, she asks about the tumors. We assure her the biopsy went well, and her central line is in place. In two days, we have mastered the *Art of Evasion*, another class taught at med school. The nurses rave about Adrienne's blue hair and dote on her. She seems tickled by all the attention. I manage to steady my voice. How do you tell your sister, who is also your child, she has cancer?

Our friends stay in the fourth-floor waiting room so we can be alone with Adrienne. She gradually wakes up and becomes more alert. Where do I start? John takes over and does most of the talking.

"We're going to be honest with you. We're not going to lie to you or keep anything from you. You have cancer. The doctors believe it is either liver cancer or ovarian cancer. We'll know on Monday. It would be better if it were ovarian cancer but . . ."

I feel the pounding of my heart in my ears. It hurts to hear the word cancer over and over again. Is it necessary to say it so many times? I suck back the corners of my mouth in an effort to smile, but I can't fool Adrienne. Unlike her, when I genuinely smile, I show teeth. I listen to the silence; John never got past the word but.

"What's wrong with you guys? It's not like I'm going to die. I'm not going to die from cancer. So what's next? Chemo?"

God, she's tough. Where does it come from? I feel stupid for crying in the face of adversity when Adrienne responds with such strength and courage. No one had mentioned chemotherapy yet, but like Adrienne, I assumed it came with the territory. I can't count the number of times a female television character has been stricken with cancer. Even if you exclude the medical shows, you will find her. She is always beautiful, wears lots of fun wigs, and most importantly, she lives. How realistic is that picture?

Adrienne is anxious to see our friends so I retrieve Jesse, Jared, Anya, and Alex, who recently arrived, from the waiting room. Anne Geddes pictures hang on the wall here—bright flowers and smiling happy babies. What a façade! The pictures don't cheer me up, but our friends do. If they are upset, I can't tell.

Unbeknownst to me, Adrienne has made plans with them for the evening. At 9 p.m., we are watching *Invader Zim* on Nickelodeon. At Children's Hospital, not only does every room have a television with a VCR attached, but it also has Nickelodeon and The Disney Channel along with the other major networks. Adrienne says the only thing they're missing is MTV.

Eli arrives in time for the show. Two episodes air that night: *Germs* and *Dark Harvest*. In *Germs*, Zim acquires special goggles, which allow him to see germs for the first time. He freaks out because germs are everywhere. In *Dark Harvest*, Zim is sick and sent to the nurse's office. He harvests other kid's organs. He spends most of the episode tracking down a lung. Adrienne can't stop laughing. Everyone makes jokes about tracking down a pair of lungs for Adrienne. Both episodes seem appropriate given our current situation. *Creepy.*

Against my better judgment, I agree to go home with John tonight. I give in to peer pressure. The nurses encourage us to get some rest. They assure us Adrienne will be fine. John reminds me I need clean clothes and a shower. I don't feel good about leaving Adrienne even though she is okay with it. We wait until everyone is gone, and Adrienne is fast asleep. That night is the first and last time John and I leave her alone in the hospital. We feel worse at home, alone together, wondering how she is doing. We fight over nothing and sleep even less.

Adrienne at Marilyn's wedding © February 2000

Days 4 and 5

Ache, pain, stab, throb, thrust, clust, clench, tear, crumble, rebuild, rediscover, light, purple, blue, green, raw finger, numbers, 01136–01044, dull, hallucinating, silver, amber, cottonmouth, voices, inspiration, aura of blinding white, priestess, support, blind faith, acceptance at last, ovarian cancer, liver cancer, cancer? It's ok, everything's ok, nothing is ever worth thinking about, nothing is worth spreading, janes, awareness, early detection, saved, fragile, glass wings, protected, healed, positive, flowing hair, wigs, neat-o-ness, cereal, painted nails, what about toes?, BAC, Filler bunny, constantly full bladder, silly commode, on a scale of 1 to 10—5, constant check-ups, I'm ok, I'm ok, I'm ok, I'm worth believing, gir, Zim, special, happy.

—Adrienne's journal entry dated 5/19/01

At 8 a.m. sharp, John and I arrive at the hospital. We meet Adrienne's new nurse Ronnie, a cheerful, tall, blonde who is obsessed with frogs. She is warming up Adrienne's hot pads, which are wet towels inside of Ziploc bags heated up in the microwave. Adrienne needs three hot pads to be comfortable: on her liver, her lower back, and on her right shoulder. John explains Adrienne likes her towels boiling hot. No one has gotten it right so far; they are afraid of burning her. Ronnie assures John she can do it, but he gives her a doubtful look.

"I'm going to have to prove myself to you," she says.

Her response to John wins me over. I like this woman. She understands us.

Visitors stream in and out all day Saturday. Because LaQuisha was discharged, Adrienne has no roommate for the time being. With the extra space available, the room fills up with close friends. Meanwhile, the fourth-floor waiting room holds more visitors, and even more people are waiting downstairs. Some are having a hard time getting in because they don't know Adrienne's first name is Emma. Others are told Adrienne's room is beyond maximum capacity, and they must wait their turn. Ronnie comments on how lucky we are to have such a good support system.

Anya replies, "There are more of us."

"We're a cult," says our friend Jonathan.

Without missing a beat, Alex comes back with, "Yeah, we even have jackets."

Ronnie laughs out loud. What they don't tell Ronnie is a running joke in our group of friends is your name has to begin with an 'A' or a 'J' to be a member. There are exceptions, of course, like my friend Marilyn, but then, she married her husband Justin so we gave her a pass.

John pays little attention to the people in the room. He is too busy reading and taking notes about the liver in all caps:

LARGEST ORGAN IN THE BODY. 4 LOBES. 5 LIGAMENTS.
   5 FISSURES.
SECRETES BILE, AIDS DIGESTION. UNDERNEATH DIAPHRAGM.
TOO MUCH BILIRUBIN LEADS TO JAUNDICE.
FILTERS OUT BACTERIA IN BLOOD.

Since John is learning how the liver works, I decide to read about hepatitis. I pick up the medical dictionary and open it to the H's. I learn that hepatitis is an inflammation of the liver, and it is transmitted through blood or body fluids. Except for hepatitis A, which is contracted through contaminated water or food. I remember hearing about a hep A scare a few years ago. Something about contaminated strawberries grown in Mexico and later sold to school districts across the country. Los Angeles Unified was one of the districts. I told Adrienne not to eat strawberries at school.

Along with her other immunizations, Adrienne received her hepatitis B vaccination, but since she had been infected years before, it made no difference. Vaccinations are preventative, not curative, and there is no vaccination for hepatitis C. The common ways to contract hepatitis B and C are sex with an infected person, sharing needles, or exposure to contaminated blood—either from a blood transfusion, working in the health care profession, or transmission from mother to child during childbirth.

Dr. Christina's questions make sense now. By eliminating the other options, she concluded our mother did it. Adrienne was born with hepatitis B and C, and no one at the time, including our mother, knew. When Adrienne was born in 1986, pregnant women were not screened for hepatitis. I want to get angry with our mother, but there was no intent on her part, just ignorance. I go back to the book. Reading the next line feels like a punch in the stomach: "Chronic infection (hepatitis B) typically is asymptomatic and may be detected only by blood tests, until it causes late complications such as cirrhosis, portal hypertension, or hepatocellular carcinoma." My hopes for ovarian cancer are squelched.

My nerves are wearing thin. Knowledge is power, but there is such a thing as too much information all at once. There seem to be no concrete answers, just pieces of circumstantial evidence. In my head, I pretend this nightmare is a crime with Adrienne as its victim.

FACT 1: Adrienne has hepatitis B and C.
FACT 2: She must have gotten it from our mother.
FACT 3: It might have been active during her life, but she did not
   display visible symptoms. Therefore, no one was able to diagnose it.
FACT 4: Hepatitis B and C can lead to liver cancer.
CONCLUSION: Adrienne has liver cancer; our mother is guilty.

As a parent, I should have known something was wrong. All those physicals, vaccinations, and thyroid tests and none of it mattered. Adrienne still got sick. Only she didn't get the flu or the chicken pox, she got cancer. The short straw. Why? Why her? Why not our mother? I feel claustrophobic. The people, the noise—it won't go away. They won't go away. My mind stretches like a rubber band until it snaps.

I scream, "Get out. Get out of this room right NOW!"

Our friends look at me in disbelief, but they leave without saying a word. Anya apologizes for my bad behavior as she ushers people out. While they wait outside, Alex and Anya's brother comes up with the idea of building a website so people can check on Adrienne's progress and schedule visits ahead of time. No one wants to see me flip out again. Adrienne names the website *adriennekickscancersass*.

Everyone gives me time to cool off. Two visitors at a time for twenty minutes is the new protocol, which seems reasonable to me. People filter back into the room in pairs. I can breathe now. There were too many people in the room before, but I am also upset because I know this abundance of love won't continue. I remember those abandoned nursing home residents in our mother's care. I know as Adrienne's disease progresses, the visitors will wane. There will be fewer cards, flowers, stuffed animals, and balloons. I scrutinize each person, even our closest friends. How long will they last? I recall my own teenage reaction to hospitals and realize most of Adrienne's peers will not visit again. The first time is a novelty; the second time becomes a reality. No one likes a sick girl. Who will make the cut? I wonder.

At Children's Hospital, parents may visit at any time, and all others may visit from 10 a.m. to 9 p.m. The 9 p.m. rule is not always enforced so it's late by the time everyone leaves. When John and I ask Adrienne if she wants both of us to stay the night, she says no. She sends me home. According to her, I am too stressed out and filling her room with negative energy. I am disappointed but I know she's right. I drive home feeling lost and lonely. In the past, I often complained about not having time to myself. I would finally be alone in the house, and I don't want to be there.

That night is the first time I pray about the cancer. It's hard to pray to an entity you don't believe in. I was raised Southern Baptist, sort of. When my parents were married, they only attended church on Easter Sunday. However, when they divorced, I went to church with my paternal grandmother every Sunday. I went to Vacation Bible School every summer and even Church Camp for an entire week, courtesy of my grandmother. I became 'saved' because it pleased her, not because I felt god calling to me. When I prayed as a kid, god never answered so eventually, I gave up. Today, I consider myself agnostic. I think there's something out there, something beyond this life, but I don't know what it is.

If I pray to god to save Adrienne, I have to reconcile the fact god let this nightmare happen in the first place. Some people believe that god doesn't make bad things happen because he doesn't have that kind of control over our lives. If god does not have control, then how can he produce a miracle? If he can perform miracles, then doesn't it follow that god has tremendous power and should be able to prevent bad things from happening?

Harold Kushner says praying for a person's health has implications that ought to disturb a thoughtful person. If prayer worked the way people think it does, no one would ever die. I agree with him. So instead of praying for the cancer to go away, I pray for something more realistic. *Please god, if you are out there, please let it be ovarian cancer. Adrienne can live without her ovaries, but not her liver. Women survive ovarian cancer. We'll do the chemo, whatever it takes, just don't let it be her liver. She only has one. I'll do anything. Whatever you want. Take my life, just make her okay.* I am desperate. I am bargaining with a god I don't even know exists. Before Adrienne got sick, I believed in karma. Now, I believe in nothing.

✳ ✳ ✳

I always wanted a sister because I don't like my younger brother. I love him but I don't like him. Aidan is different. Special. Everyone remembers him. He was the kid of 100 characters. As Superman, he donned a red cape and jumped off rocks or tree stumps. Becoming Popeye required work: a red baseball cap, a plastic yellow pipe, and one eye shut. I thought Aidan might permanently damage his eye because it never saw the sun, but it recovered in time for his favorite character of all, the Hulk. At recess, he would rip off his T-shirt and growl at the other students. I pretended not to know him. He also followed me around and played Ken to my Barbie.

We have the same parents. When I was nine, I checked our birth certificates because I was convinced one of us was adopted. But no, we are full brother and sister. I was disappointed; I did not want to be related to this weird kid. Like any older sister, I tortured him. I had many opportunities because Aidan walked in his sleep. I would paint his toenails or turn him the wrong direction in the hall so he peed in the kitchen trashcan. He never woke up. My parents said Aidan didn't talk much because I spoke for him, but maybe, he didn't have anything to say.

Like Aidan and me, our parents were polar opposites. *Ding, ding, ding.* I pictured them in a boxing ring: *Solid Gold* vs. *Hee Haw.* Dad was an extrovert who smoked cigarettes and liked rock 'n' roll. Mother, however, was a social misfit who rarely smoked and preferred the tunes of Dolly Parton to Mick Jagger. Dad sometimes smoked pot but never around us. Mother popped pills all the time. Diet pills, she said as I watched her swallow a handful. To my relief, they divorced in 1982. Aidan was seven. I was ten. Dad remarried within a year, which pissed Mother off. She yelled at him over the phone through me; tell your father this and he said tell your mother that. They sheltered Aidan from their fights.

Sometimes being the oldest sucked. Since our mother worked the graveyard shift and slept during the day, she expected me to be in charge of Aidan. I cooked breakfast (e.g., Pop-Tarts, toast), walked Aidan to school, and made him clean his room. When Aidan spilled Pepsi on Mother's new, brown velvet chair, she yelled at me and told me to clean it up. Aidan laughed. I wanted to throttle him. Saturday was cleaning day. I had to dust the furniture, sweep the kitchen, wash the dishes, and take out the trash. Aidan's only job was to pick up his toys off his bedroom floor, which he then shoved under his bed or in his closet. When I complained, our mother said, life's not fair.

For three years, Aidan and I were shuttled back and forth between our parents. We spent every weekend with Dad plus Thursday nights. We were the only kids in our cul-de-sac whose parents were divorced. I was ashamed by their failure and embarrassed when Dad pulled into our driveway on Saturday afternoons to pick us up. Being a child of divorce takes skill. There are rules: Don't have fun at Dad's house. Pretend to hate your stepmother. Tell Dad your bedtime is 9 p.m. even though Mother lets you stay up until midnight reading. Pretend you don't know anything about Mother's love life. And pills? What pills?

My red and green, cloth-covered suitcase had become a part of me until the summer of 1985. Our mother had decided she could no longer live in the same city, let alone the same state as our father. She wanted to move back to her home state of Alabama. Ballet was my passion so when I was accepted into the Alabama School of Fine Arts (ASFA), a performing arts school for grades 7–12, it sealed our fate. Going to ASFA was more important to me than staying near my father, who did not support my desire to dance because it was not practical. He wanted me to be a doctor. However, split legal custody did not allow my parents to take either child out of the state of Arkansas without the other person's permission. My mother dragged me to her lawyer's office many times that summer.

Our parents settled on a strange compromise. Divide the children as if we were property. Mother got me; Dad got Aidan. I don't think my parents thought about how their decision would affect my relationship with my brother. Dad later told me taking Aidan was the only insurance he had that he would ever see me again. Mother compared herself to Meryl Streep's character in *Sophie's Choice*. She would say, your father made me choose between you and your brother, and I chose you as if she had done me a favor. I became the reason she had no connection with her son even though she almost never called him. Dad and I had our regular Thursday night phone call, a habit that continued through college and helped us form a permanent bond. Aidan and I grew apart; we have no relationship.

✳ ✳ ✳

I wake up in the morning feeling rested. More energized. Positive. I make a list of things I have to do: shower, feed cats, go to Office Depot, and go to Anya and Alex's house. I need to use their computer because ours is broken. Then I add, "Eat breakfast?" to the list. Food shouldn't be optional, but eating is not a priority.

Less than an hour later, I'm at Anya and Alex's apartment. Alex surprises me with an English Breakfast Latte and a bagel from Coffeebean. Lack of money forces me to avoid gourmet coffee places so the latte is a luxury; I've never had one before. I take a sip. It's yummy. A week ago, the latte would have tasted the same, but I would not have derived so much pleasure from it. The simple things, like tasting a great tea, mean more to me now. I continue to savor my new favorite drink as I type an email to everyone I know.

Dear everyone:

I am going to be out of the loop for a while. Adrienne got diagnosed with cancer this past Friday. We find out tomorrow exactly what type of cancer it is (either ovarian or liver), and she will begin treatment right away. She is in stage four, and it's bad. I will be spending most of my time with her at the hospital. If you would like to help us in any way or send Adrienne something, here is some contact information:

Children's Hospital Los Angeles
Emma Adrienne Wilson, Room 404B
4650 Sunset Blvd. Los Angeles, CA 90027

Please do not send flowers; they are not permitted in her ward. Please contact my voicemail for updates on Adrienne or to schedule a visit: (213) 941-0617. I'm discouraging phone calls to the hospital. Adrienne needs her rest, and the phone wakes her up. A website is under construction. It will be devoted to Adrienne and her fight against cancer.

Our immediate needs are a laptop. Adrienne would use it to do homework. If you know anyone who can donate an old one, it would be helpful. Do not buy a new one; we're only seeking donations. Minor errands are impossible at the moment. If you live near Burbank and have time to run errands for us, please let us know.

Research: if you have time to research her cancer or research any possible financial aid to parents in our situation, please let us know. I'm not going to be working for some time so we will need some type of assistance.

Thank you. Please pray and be positive. Adrienne sure is! As she said yesterday, "Someone is testing me to see how strong I am. Well, I am strong!"

Love, Andrea

When I arrive at the hospital, I discover Adrienne's pain medication is being changed from morphine to Dilaudid. Although she does not have a full-blown allergic reaction to morphine, it makes her hallucinate and disrupts her sleep. She is groggy but awake. So is John. I want them to see what I bought at Office Depot. I pull out each item and display it proudly: a large whiteboard, a small calendar whiteboard, a set of dry-erase markers, a three-inch black binder, dividers, a three-hole punch, highlighters, pens, and paper.

They look at me. John shakes his head.

Adrienne laughs and asks, "What is all that stuff, Sissy?"

I have a plan. First, I prop up the whiteboard and write with a pink marker 'Messages for Adrienne' on it. She smiles. Her friends will be able to leave her notes where she can see them. I three-hole punch paper and put it in the binder along with the dividers. On a separate piece of paper, I write in three different colors: 'Adrienne's Survival Kit.' I slide the title page into the front sleeve of the binder and hold it up. Adrienne smiles again as she drifts off.

John nods and says, "Good idea."

Even though I didn't get the reaction I wanted, I feel good. Strong. Powerful. I did something. I am not a doctor, but I am going to keep track of every aspect of this disease. I am organized, prepared to fight. For one solid minute, I believe we can win.

Since Adrienne is older, the doctors decide she can have a PCA, which stands for Patient Controlled Analgesia. When she is in pain, all she has to do is click a button, and the medication is released into her IV. A PCA helps the doctors detect patterns and monitor her pain. Initially, Adrienne tries to be brave and refuses to push the button. It aggravates the hell out of me watching her suffer and knowing I can't do anything about it. Only Adrienne can push the button. John and I take this rule seriously as if the medical police are watching and will arrest us at any moment. When I press Adrienne further about pushing the button, she says she doesn't want to become an addict like our mother.

✶ ✶ ✶

Right after Adrienne's eighth birthday, I received a call from Mother, who was in tears. After years of stealing pills from hospitals and nursing homes that employed her, she had been caught in the act. Only it wasn't pills. This time she was shooting up morphine at work. She was fired; her nursing license was revoked. I didn't know what to say. I was sad and disgusted at the same time. Adrienne still lived with our mother, who had always worked. Mother was what therapists call a high-functioning addict. When I mentioned joining a program, she balked saying she didn't have a problem.

Our mother's behavior haunts Adrienne. We come from a family of addicts: drugs (uppers, downers, nicotine), alcohol, food, even lack of food. From our pill-popping mother to our anorexic Aunt Tootsie, our family is a mess. Once in college, I told our mother I had a bad day and was depressed. An envelope full of Halcion arrived in the mail three days later. I took half of one and fell asleep. When I told our mother I flushed the rest down the toilet, she got angry and said I should have sent them back to her. What a waste she said. I was twenty when I realized our mother had a drug problem.

✳ ✳ ✳

What appears to be stubbornness on Adrienne's part is actually fear. I understand that fear. I didn't smoke a cigarette or do any drugs until I was twenty-two. Benson & Hedges Menthol and four lines of cocaine. Except for the occasional cigar, I don't smoke and I never did drugs again, not even pot. Adrienne knows these stories; both incidents happened a few months before she came to live with me. I think she might have tried a cigarette once, but marijuana and other drugs don't interest her. She is what the kids call 'straight-edge.'

I go in search of Ronnie and explain Adrienne's refusal to push the button because of our family's history of addiction. She comes into Adrienne's room and sits on her bed. In laymen's terms, Ronnie explains the difference between taking medication because you need it for physical pain and taking medication because you want it for pleasure. You won't get high from Dilaudid; you will get relief from your pain she says. Don't you want that? Adrienne nods. Ronnie assures her there is a lockout mechanism to prevent Adrienne from getting too much medication within a given amount of time. Adrienne leans over, grabs the PCA, and pushes the button. I exhale when I hear the *click*.

Kirsten, a friend of John's, is driving in today to help us put together a list of questions for Dr. No regarding Adrienne's treatment. Kirsten is the associate director of clinical research at the San Diego Cancer Center and Research Institute. She has her bachelor's degree in physiology and neuroscience with her master's in clinical research. In other words, she is a genius. When John called and told her about Adrienne, she offered to help right away.

While I wait for Kirsten to arrive, John goes with Adrienne to get her first bone scan. The doctors need to know if the tumors have spread beyond her lungs. For two hours, Adrienne must lie on a giant metal plate as another giant metal plate hovers one inch above her body. She can't move. No stretching, no twitching. She can hear though, and John does his best to entertain her with stories about the stupidity of his coworkers without making Adrienne laugh. If she chuckles, the technician reminds her: do not move. When she returns to her room, Adrienne declares the bone scan makes her feel claustrophobic, and it is her least favorite test. She hopes never to do it again.

There are fewer visitors today, and people are sticking to the new '2 in for 20' rule. Jared and his girlfriend Joyce arrive and greet Adrienne by rubbing her feet. Jared's brother Jesse brings Adrienne three wigs in bright colors: red, pink, and lime green. Each wig is cut in the standard pageboy style with thick bangs and blunt ends, the way Adrienne wears her own hair. Adrienne's boyfriend Eli spends most of the afternoon and evening with Adrienne. He does not count as one of the two visitors because he is always here. He brings his *Beavis and Butthead* tapes, home movies from his childhood, and more books and magazines. Adrienne makes each visitor watch baby Eli at Disneyland because she thinks it is hysterical. People come and go, but it is less chaotic than yesterday. With fewer people in the room and a better attitude, I am able to relax.

Kirsten arrives in the late afternoon. John shows Kirsten the notes he has taken so far. She asks more questions and then, she dictates a list to John.

1. Does Adrienne have fibrolamellar HCC (better)?[1]
2. Are the tumors poorly differentiated (bad) or undifferentiated (better)?[2]
3. Did you see nodules in the tumor cells?
4. Did you see broad bands of fibrous tissue?
5. Do the tumors have a fibrous capsule? (No—bad, Yes—good)
6. Are the tumors estrogen receptor positive (bad) or negative (good)?
7. How many cases of HCC have you treated? What are the commonalities?

My brain is in high gear, but I know I can't understand the meaning behind every question. Number seven seems obvious though, and Kirsten explains the first two. I am lost by the time we get to number three. John pays attention and he continues to take notes in all caps on my yellow legal pad.

1 Fibrolamellar, an unusual type of HCC, tends to occur in young women.
2 Poorly differentiated tumors have a poorer prognosis and are more difficult to treat.

At the end of the day, Adrienne gets a new roommate, a four-year-old Hispanic girl suspected of having leukemia. Her parents speak little English. As I listen to the translator through the thin curtain separating the two beds, I wonder how much they understand about what is going on with their daughter and how much gets lost in translation. I can see the worry on their faces; I have to pass them to leave or come into the room. The girl seems lethargic, but when Adrienne puts on her wigs and plays peek-a-boo with the curtain, the girl giggles. Her parents smile and we see the gratitude carving creases in their faces. Some languages are universal; laughter is one of them.

Days 6 and 7

Killer sheep are a very terrifying subject. Not only are they bald and ex-
tremely angry, they are armed and ready to KILL. The first clan of Killer
Sheep were created to seek revenge on the Vikings by a pissed-off Celtic
shepherd. He taught the sheep how to decapitate, torture, verbally assault
(yes, verbal, which means they can speak, too!) and for some odd reason
tickle. The population of Killer Sheep live mostly in Northern Ireland
and the southern parts of the United Kingdom. They are very angry little
animals with no patience and have been known to be very stubborn.

—Excerpt from Adrienne's Killer Sheep short story

Adrienne made her first trip to Los Angeles during the summer of 1992. Although we did go to typical tourist destinations such as Disneyland, Sea World, and the Los Angeles Zoo, we also spent a lot of time on the campus of the University of Southern California (USC). As an undergraduate, I worked at the University Bookstore, and Adrienne came to work with me for several days. She chatted with my coworkers, drew pictures in my boss's office, and ate too much cookie dough out of the freezer. We walked around the campus on my lunch hour as I pointed out specific buildings and talked about the classes I had in them. I didn't realize at the time what an impact those lunchtime tours had on her. When she started first grade in the fall, Adrienne had one long-term goal: to go to college.

Now that I have accepted that I cannot work while Adrienne is sick, I make some necessary phone calls. I call Luther Burbank Middle School to let them know I will be out for the rest of the school year. I call the Burbank Unified district office and turn down a long-term substitute assignment to teach eighth grade English in the fall. Miller Elementary, located in Compton, has offered me a permanent position teaching fourth grade. I call and turn down that offer, too.

For three years, I have worked as a substitute teacher, only taking daily assignments because I needed the flexibility to pursue acting. Last month,

I made the decision to find a permanent job because I wanted to become financially stable and give Adrienne a better life—my acting career be damned. As I hang up the phone, I feel a sense of relief and dread. I don't have to teach now, but I don't have any income either.

My last call is to Rick Carlton, Adrienne's guidance counselor at the high school. We met for the first time three weeks ago to discuss getting high school credit for university classes, the possibility of Adrienne graduating early, and her future college prospects. The meeting was Adrienne's idea. At her middle school graduation last year, Adrienne was one of only three students to win a Creative Writing scholarship to UCLA. She was furious about attending school during the summer saying you mean I'm being punished for being smart? When that argument didn't work, she claimed going to UCLA made her feel like a traitor to USC. Despite her lousy attitude, I made her attend the class. She earned an A.

During the meeting, Mr. Carlton said Adrienne would get credit for attending summer classes at UCLA. Armed with that information, I asked Adrienne if she wanted to take another class this summer. She selected a computer class, and we enrolled her last week. I make a mental note to cancel that class as I dial the number to Burbank High. Mr. Carlton, who asks I call him Rick, is a kind, sympathetic man. He decides to meet with Adrienne's teachers to determine what she needs to do to finish the school year. In the meantime, he needs a letter from her doctor, and Adrienne must continue to do her homework. We agree to talk again later this week.

I ask Dr. Christina for the letter regarding school, and she writes one right away. It reads:

To whom it may concern—please be advised that Emma (Adrienne) Wilson is currently an inpatient at CHLA with no current plans for discharge in the immediate future. It is likely that Adrienne will be unable to complete this school year secondary to her medical condition.

I read the same line three times. No current plans for discharge in the immediate future. It sounds ominous, like a jail sentence. *How much time you got? Three years. Robbed a bank, no bullets in the gun though. How 'bout you? Oh . . . I have cancer. I'm in for life.*

When Dr. No asks us to join him in the consultation room, I know he must have the results of the pathology report. John and I walk into the room with our now favorite nurse Ronnie right behind us. The theme is meant to soothe; there are two impressionist prints with blue and yellow flowers, blue chairs, a table, and a couch. The small TV, VCR, dry-erase board, and boxes of tissue are reminders that parents are brought in here to learn about their child's illness and to hear the prognosis. Even though I am ready to hear the words liver cancer, I still break down when Dr. No confirms our worst fears.

"Your sister has hepatocellular carcinoma (HCC)."

Praying for ovarian cancer didn't do a damn bit of good.

Before the good doctor can put a timeline on Adrienne's life, I interrupt him.

"I don't want to hear numbers. No numbers. Just tell us what it is and what we have to do. Don't you dare predict anything . . . no numbers."

I watch his face digest my request. He already had a number in mind, but he respects my wish and does not say it. I grab the first of many Kleenexes and blow my nose.

Then John begins asking a barrage of questions.

"What other evidence do you have besides the pathology report that Adrienne has HCC?"

With a poker face, Dr. No replies, "Although her liver is functioning normally, her liver enzymes are elevated, which indicates stress on the liver."

Undeterred, John continues, "What is her AFP?"[3]

"1.4 million."

I know that number is too high, but I cannot remember what the normal level of AFP should be. I want to ask but when I open my mouth, no words come out. Instead, I taste the salt from my tears.

Looking at his notes, John asks, "Does Adrienne have fibrolamellar HCC?"

"No."

How can a doctor deliver such terrible news and show no emotion whatsoever?

---

3   AFP or serum alpha-fetoprotein is elevated in 50–80% of people in the United States with primary liver cancer; therefore, it is a good indicator of HCC. For a young female, the normal range for AFP is 6–7 ng/ml.

Given my inability to speak, I like that John has taken charge. He keeps hammering Dr. No with questions.

"I read that well-differentiated tumor cells are good candidates for liver transplants."

"Her tumors are poorly differentiated."

More bad news.

My ears tickle and my face heats up as another wave of tears rush down my cheeks. I need more Kleenex.

"Is a liver transplant an option?"

"No. Since the cancer has already metastasized to her lungs, a liver transplant isn't practical. It won't solve the problem."

Isn't practical? Won't solve the problem? Will anything fucking solve the problem?

I blow my nose again.

And so it goes. Back and forth. A ping-pong match between the knowledgeable, skilled doctor and the newly educated parents, except I'm not helping John. I take a breath, find my voice, and jump in so it's two against one.

I ask, "How many cases of HCC have you treated?"

"Six."

"What happened?"

Please say one of them made it.

"They didn't make it."

Wrong answer.

I reach for another Kleenex. I look at John and admire his dry face. Thank god only one of us is a basket case.

John asks, "Can Adrienne be around her pets? She has a cat and a hamster."

"Yes, but I don't recommend getting any new animals at this time. Also, she must not feed or clean up after the animals, and she must wash her hands after petting them."

Then I remember something I wanted to know.

"Where are the shoulder and back pain coming from?"

"There is a major nerve that runs from the liver up to your right shoulder. Your sister never had a shoulder injury; she felt referred pain from her liver. Her back is hurting because her spleen is enlarged."[4]

---

4 Referred pain is pain that arises in one body part or location, but is perceived in another.

"Oh."

I think things cannot get worse; I'm wrong.

Dr. No adds, "The bone scan indicated a small mass on the back of your sister's neck. It could be another tumor. I am ordering a CT scan of her brain tomorrow to eliminate the possibility of any tumors in that location."

I squeeze the numerous used tissues in my hand. I would make a fantastic sad clown right now with my wet face and red nose. I hesitate before asking my last question.

"Don't you have any good news?

Dr. No looks at me. I study his eyes and I see nothing. No hope, no sympathy, no pity. He seems so detached from our situation. He answers with one word.

"No."

Of course not.

After giving us Adrienne's poor prognosis, Dr. No launches into the quality of life speech. *Quality of Life*—yet another class taught in medical school. He says she can start chemotherapy immediately, but we need to consider Adrienne's quality of life. Since she still feels good, now would be the time to do fun things, like go to Hawaii.

I look at him. I want to yell at him.

Go to Hawaii now? Why? Because she won't be able to later? Why Hawaii? With what money? Do you want to pay for it? If you took the time to get to know your patients, asshole, you would know Adrienne wants to go to Ireland.

I hate this doctor. I hate his cold, impersonal manner. I hate that he suggests we give up and go on a trip instead. I hate that he can't fix this cancer. Most of all, I hate that during this entire conversation, he refused to say Adrienne's name.

With the quality of life speech out of the way, Dr. No gets down to business and discusses his treatment plan for Adrienne. The chemotherapy will be difficult; there is no guarantee it will work. The first course will be a combination of Adriamycin and cisplatin, two drugs that have shrunk tumors in some HCC patients. The side effects are severe: Adriamycin can cause serious heart damage, and cisplatin can cause total hearing loss. Both drugs will knock out Adrienne's immune system. Due to the drugs' negative side effects, Dr. No will only do a maximum of eight chemotherapy sessions at three- to four-week intervals. I cannot stop myself from calculating the numbers in my head.

$8 \times 3, 8 \times 4 = 24–32$ weeks . . . only 6–8 months.

There it is. The dreaded number. At best, Adrienne has six to eight months to live.

I keep my head down as I blow my nose for the umpteenth time. John asks for copies of Adrienne's lab reports and information about the chemotherapy drugs. John and I are strong at different times. We may not be the best couple, but our parenting styles complement each other well. As Dr. No and John continue to talk, I think about Adrienne's attitude: how she joked about it being cancer, how she brought up the subject of chemo before anyone else did, and how she manages to smile for every person who walks into her hospital room.

My tears cease. I lift my head. I look Dr. No in the eye.

"You just don't know Adrienne. Not fighting is not an option."

When Dr. No leaves, we don't go with him. The three of us: John, Ronnie, and I sit in silence. Even though she must have sat in on dozens of conversations like this one, Ronnie's eyes are watering and her nose is sniffling. Ronnie tells us about her sister Brittany, who was diagnosed with leukemia when she was Adrienne's age. Both Ronnie and her mother are oncology nurses, but they couldn't hold it together when a doctor told them Brittany had a few months to live. Brittany refused to accept the diagnosis. She waited two years for the bone marrow transplant (BMT) that saved her life. Ever since Brittany got the BMT, her cancer has been in remission. Brittany's survival gives me a glimmer of hope. As we get up to leave the consultation room, Ronnie says one last thing. She and Brittany call each other Sissy.

We give Adrienne the highlights of our conversation with Dr. No. Chemo will begin on Wednesday. It will last for three days. There are two drugs with many side effects, and he will discuss the details with us tomorrow. We leave out the maximum of eight intervals and the suggested trip to Hawaii. Is omitting the whole truth the same as lying? Maybe. But under these circumstances, John and I don't see the point in conveying Dr. No's sense of hopelessness and doom. It will only anger Adrienne and cause her to dislike him as much as John and I do.

Every Monday, from 2 p.m.–4 p.m., the PAWS (Pets Assisting With Smiles) program visits the fourth floor at Children's Hospital. When asked if Adrienne would like a visit, she responds with an enthusiastic yes. Baci (pronounced Bah-chee), a beautiful black lab, walks into Adrienne's room with his tail wagging and mouth hanging open in a goofy grin. He obeys his trainer and jumps into the chair next to Adrienne's bed. We don't have a dog at home, but Adrienne loves all animals—except sheep. Ever since she wrote a short story about sheep, they have appeared everywhere: films, commercials, billboards, stickers, CD covers. Adrienne claims sheep are taking over the world. She makes me laugh with her outrageous theories. I watch her as she strokes Baci's back; she smiles at the camera. Mouth open, teeth showing. The volunteer writes 'Baci 5/21/01' on the Polaroid picture and hands it to Adrienne. It will be one of the last photos of Adrienne with her hair.

A few hours later, Nadia walks in, sees Adrienne for the first time, and bursts into tears. Adrienne opens her arms to hug her, assuring her everything will be okay. I marvel at this interaction between two old friends, one sick, the other healthy. One strong, the other weak. Nadia apologizes for crying as Adrienne consoles her. Her body may be failing her, but Adrienne's inner strength displays itself time and time again. Where does her desire and ability to set people at ease come from? I wish I could take credit for this gift, but I can't. You can't teach someone to have grace under pressure, to be calm during a storm. Nadia is laughing now, her tears gone; Adrienne has worked her magic.

When Adrienne is napping and John is out of the room, I look at myself in the mirror above the sink next to her bed. To support Adrienne during her chemo, I thought I would shave my head. I take my long, straight, reddish-blonde hair in my hands and sweep it off my face. I imagine myself without hair, but I have a big head and I don't think I would look attractive. Besides, my hair has always been my trademark even if I'm not a natural redhead. I was born with blonde hair, but in various stages of childhood it turned strawberry blonde, reddish brown, dark brown, and medium brown with blonde highlights. I dyed my hair red as a teenager, but now it turns strawberry blonde thanks to the California sun. I remember when Adrienne was in first grade and one of her friends described my hair as 'gold.' Anyway, I am a Lucille Ball/Rita Hayworth redhead; it may not be entirely natural, but my hair is part of my identity. I drop my mane and peer at my reflection. I feel awful but I don't want to cut, much less shave, my hair.

The class *Cancer: A Parent Orientation* is usually held on Thursdays at 2 p.m., but it is moved to Tuesday at 10 a.m. because both Adrienne and Whitney are about to start chemo. John and I meet Whitney's parents at the orientation. Like Adrienne, Whitney is fifteen years old, a freshman in high school, and has a boyfriend. Her cancer was discovered by accident when her vision started bothering her more than six weeks ago. Rhabdomyosarcoma is a soft tissue pediatric cancer with no known cause; it affects 500–700 children in the United States each year. Different cancers, different backgrounds, but as parents, we share the same emotion: fear.

The nurse begins the class.

"The ideal time to take this class is after you have discussed treatment options with your child's oncologist, but before your child starts treatment."

Whitney's parents shake their heads. Whitney had surgery to remove the tumor from her face, but other treatment options have not been discussed yet. Waving off their concerns, the nurse hands each one of us a packet. Each page is divided into two columns: on the left there are black squares with bullet points of information that coincide with the PowerPoint presentation; on the right there are lines for taking notes. Some of the information doesn't apply because Adrienne has few treatment options, but we do learn the lingo of cancer.

- Since chemotherapy affects the body's immune system, a nurse will come to our home twice a week to draw Adrienne's blood to monitor her counts.
- The absolute neutrophil count (ANC) and the white blood cell (WBC) count are the best indication of how much the chemo has compromised the immune system (i.e., is the treatment doing more harm than good?). An ANC below 1000 is considered low. When—not if—it drops below 500, neutropenic precautions, such as wearing a mask, must be taken to prevent the patient from getting an infection.
- Low hemoglobin indicates anemia. If the hemoglobin is 9 or below, a blood transfusion is usually necessary.
- Platelets help the blood clot; if they drop below 150,000, the patient is at risk for bleeding and bruising.

- Neupogen shots can increase the number of white blood cells in the patient's body. I will give Adrienne a Neupogen shot daily.
- If she goes outside, Adrienne must always wear sunscreen, hats with a brim, long pants, and long-sleeved shirts since avoiding the sun is nearly impossible in Los Angeles.
- Adrienne cannot go to the dentist, receive vaccinations, play contact sports, or return to school during her treatment.

While we are in class, Adrienne is prepped for a series of tests. The brain CT scan will be followed by an echocardiogram[5] and a hearing test to establish baselines. Dr. No needs something to compare to when/if the chemotherapy causes heart damage or hearing loss. Since those tests are uneventful, noninvasive, painless procedures, Adrienne does not ask us about them. In less than a week, Adrienne went from a test about the liver in biology class, to tests on her own organs. It's one thing to know what the liver does and how it functions; it's another thing when the function of your liver is being tested. Whether you are taking them or they are being done to you, life is a series of tests. Only now, the stakes are much higher.

Our friend Jonathan comes by to visit Adrienne that afternoon. Jonathan plans to do meditative self-healing with Adrienne. He brings six rocks: two hematites for energy, two types of quartz for healing, an amethyst for spiritual and psychic energy, and a cat's eye for grounding. While meditating, Adrienne is to put all the rocks in one hand, except for the cat's eye, which goes in the other hand. She pulls positive energy from the five rocks and channels her negative energy into the grounding rock, which represents the Earth. According to Jonathan, the goal is to give Adrienne a sense of control; he believes attitude is everything. I am not sure that rocks have healing powers, but Jonathan's visit and meditation tutorial put a smile on her face. It will be one of the only times he sees Adrienne in the hospital.

That evening, Dr. No, along with Ronnie, comes in to discuss the chemotherapy with Adrienne. He explains the two drugs and how they will be administered. Through her central line, Adrienne will receive the first drug, cisplatin, over a six-hour period followed by four hours of

---

5   An echocardiogram is a test that uses ultrasound to show the heart's structures.

fluid to prevent kidney damage. Then the second drug, Adriamycin, will be given over a four-hour period for three consecutive days.

He says, "You will experience nausea and vomiting."

Adrienne nods.

"All of your hair will fall out," he says.

Adrienne nods again.

So far, Dr. No has not told Adrienne anything she didn't expect. He seems perplexed by her casual reaction; Adrienne makes him uncomfortable. If I could remove myself from this situation, I would be laughing right now.

Adrienne remains calm until Dr. No mentions that cisplatin can cause hearing loss. Then she becomes unglued. First, there are tears; it is only the second time she has cried about her condition. Then she gets angry. She states she cannot, will not, lose her hearing.

"What about music?" she asks Dr. No.

He explains her hearing loss would be gradual; she would not wake up one day and be completely deaf. Ronnie makes it worse by assuring Adrienne she can have a hearing aid, and although music would not sound the same, she would be able to hear people speak. They don't get it. She does not care about noises or speech. Not only is she an aficionado of music, but she is also a budding musician.

Adrienne looks at the four of us with a determined gleam.

"I'd rather be dead than deaf."

I want to strangle her. She would rather be dead than deaf? Some people might think Adrienne is a sick teenager who is thinking irrationally, but that's not true. She has her limits and she has drawn a firm line in the sand. I make her a promise; she has control over her treatment. If she experiences any hearing loss, we will stop the cisplatin. Dr. No assures me there are other drugs besides cisplatin, but it has the most promising results. *Is he aware he gave me hope and then killed it in one simple statement?*

Despite his faults, Dr. No comes up with the perfect solution. He asks Adrienne to sign the consent form even though he doesn't need her signature. Like the meditation rocks, the pen gives her a sense of control. She is in charge. Not Dr. No and not me. Satisfied with the outcome, Adrienne signs the consent. Dr. No and I sign it too. Chemo will begin tomorrow morning.

Because chemo damages the hair even before it falls out, Adrienne decides to cut off all her hair that evening. We hope she might have enough hair to make into a wig. John runs to the local pharmacy to buy a razor kit, while I get a Ziploc bag from the nurses. When I tell them about Adrienne's plan, they love it as long as we clean up afterward, and we are careful not to cut Adrienne's scalp. John cuts off large chunks of Adrienne's blue-green hair. He leaves about two inches of hair on her head, which allows us to see the blonde from the original bleaching as well as her dark roots. She makes faces at me as I take multiple pictures with our camera. Then John uses the razor to create four Mohawks on Adrienne's head. I don't know whose idea it was to do a Quad-Hawk, but it looks fabulous on Adrienne. It turns out she has a perfectly round skull. With little hair left, Adrienne's olive-green eyes, prominent cheekbones, and engaging smile become the focus of her face. By cutting her hair before chemo could kill it off, Adrienne has once again gained some control, and she is more beautiful than ever.

GENERAL CONSENT FOR CHEMOTHERAPY A 397552   01136-01044

WILSON, EMMA
CHLA#

DOB APR 8. 1986 SEX F

You (your child) ___Emma Wilson_____ have

(has) a diagnosis of ___hepatocellular carcinoma_____ and

treatment will be given in the following manner: ___Cis platinum____

___+ adriamycin every 3 to 4 wks, Cisplatin on___ ■0840■

___1st day + adriamycin on 1st Thru 3rd___

___days___

Possible side effects: ___Low blood count with risk of___

___anemia, infection, bleeding, hair loss, nausea, vomiting,___

___heart damage, kidney damage, hearing loss, chance of second___

___carcinoma or leukemia___

The reasons for this treatment program, the potential medical benefits and

the risks involved have been explained. You hereby give your consent for

yourself (your child) to be treated in accordance with the above treatment.

Signed _Adrienne Wilson_____ Relationship _Guardian/Sister_

Patient _Adrienne Wilson_____

Witness _____ Date _5-22-01_
                                    01136-01044
Information about this treatment has been provided by:
                              WILSON, EMMA
Dr. _____
                        DOB APR 8, 1986 SEX F
           (Signature)

GENERAL INFORMATION

How to obtain advice: daytime Monday through Friday, 8:30 am to 5 pm,
                                              ■00403■
call area code 213/669-2121. You may leave a message with a secretary and a

doctor will return your call. Evening, nighttime, and weekends or holidays:

call the general hospital number, area code 213/660-2450 and ask for the

on-call Hematology doctor. You may be asked to leave a message with the page

operator and the physician on-call will return you call as soon as possible.

01-17/KR17

Consent for Chemotherapy with Adrienne's signature © May 22, 2001

Days 8–10

*All the joy in my life has some connection to this wonderful city. Yes,
most of LA is horribly disgusting visually, and filled to the rim with
whores, drug addicts, actors and musicians screwing executives to get
their 15 minutes of fame, but within that realm of facades and plastic
exteriors is a wondrous beauty. I can't really describe it, but from my
own personal experience of moving around as a child, Los Angeles
and Southern California in general is the only place that possesses this
greatness. People here are amazingly artistic, and the various mix of
cultures that clash brings a unique feel and vibe to every sub city in LA.
Don't believe me? Just drive down Vermont or Sunset Blvd.*

—Adrienne's journal entry dated 2/24/01
Note: Children's Hospital is located on the
corner of Vermont Ave. and Sunset Blvd.

Before chemotherapy can begin, Dr. No orders a CBC so he will have
another baseline of how Adrienne's body is functioning. Even though
there are acronyms and numbers all over the page, four matter the most:
her white blood cell count (WBC), hemoglobin, platelets, and absolute
neutrophil count (ANC). I am not a math whiz, but I am good at memo-
rizing formulas. The acronyms and normal ranges for the four crucial
counts become embedded in my brain.

Since Adrienne's blood counts are normal, chemotherapy will start
at 10:30 a.m. as planned. Although Adrienne's liver function and AFP
will only be measured every three weeks, her kidney function will be
monitored for three consecutive days throughout her treatment due to
the side effects of cisplatin. Creatinine and BUN (blood urea nitrogen)
are an indication of Adrienne's kidney function. Those numbers are low,
but according to her doctors, it's better to be low than high. Bilirubin
and the liver enzymes AST (aspartate aminotransferase) and ALT (alanine
aminotransferase) show liver function. Her bilirubin is normal, but both

liver enzymes are high, which is normal for liver cancer patients. While John studies the lobes and functions of the liver, I focus on the numbers. I can't say aspartate aminotransferase or tell you what it does, but I know that number is too high, which is not what we want.

A nurse walks in with a paper shirt and pants over her normal attire. With a mask over her mouth, she holds a bag of liquid as far away from her body as possible. There is a skull and crossbones on the label. When she hangs it on Adrienne's IV pole, I stare at it. Are we making the right decision? This woman is dressed as if she is handling a nuclear weapon. I don't know what I expected. The chemo drug is liquid, in a bag, and labeled as poison. We have all agreed to poison Adrienne to stop the tumors that are killing her. I want to yell stop, but we have no other options. To win, poison is the only choice.

✳ ✳ ✳

The bag of chemo reminds me of my own treatment for Graves' disease[6] five years ago. Instead of surgery, my doctor opted for iodide therapy, which is a nice way of saying he used radiation to kill my thyroid gland. I remember showing up at the county hospital, where a nurse came out carrying a large metal container with the same poison sign on it. After opening the container with her latex-gloved hands, she told me to reach inside and get the plastic container. She wasn't allowed to touch it because it was radioactive, but I was expected to. I opened the container (without gloves) to find a small pill bottle holding two large white pills. Drinking a glass of water already prepared by Nurse Do-Not-Touch, I swallowed the radioactive pills. I was not allowed to be around other people's food or children for three days. Adrienne stayed with Anya and Alex while I took some sick days from my teaching and waitressing jobs. I felt nauseated at times, but the radiation didn't hurt. I missed Adrienne though and couldn't wait for her to come home.

✳ ✳ ✳

Short-term side effects of the chemo include nausea, vomiting, hair loss, mouth sores, and low blood counts. Long-term side effects include heart

---

6 Graves' disease is a type of hyperthyroidism caused by an autoimmune attack on the thyroid gland. Thyroid diseases are often genetic and more common in women than men.

damage, kidney damage, and hearing loss. On this first day of chemo, the vomiting worries me most. I know Adrienne can handle it, but I'm not sure I can. As a former ballet dancer, I tried to develop an eating disorder, but I couldn't make myself throw up. The one thing that makes me vomit is the sound or smell of someone else doing so. In college, I was never the girl who held a friend's hair while she regurgitated an evening of margaritas. The first time I heard John vomiting in our bathroom after a night of excessive drinking, I could feel the bile coming up my throat. I vow I will overcome my disgust and sensory reaction to vomiting for Adrienne's sake. I don't know how but I will find a way.

Now that Adrienne has been out of school for a week, cards from her classmates flood her room. Cindy Burns, Adrienne's dance teacher, brings a giant, 3' by 6' yellow banner signed by the Burbank High dance department. We tape it to the wall above the magazine photos of Nicole Kidman in her Moulin Rouge costumes. One class signed a large card with a chicken on it that reads, "Hello, I'm the Get Well Chicken." Another class made homemade cards out of construction paper. Even as the chemo is flowing into her body, Adrienne laughs at both the sincere and inane comments written by her peers. We joke about the spelling mistakes, especially when her name is spelled wrong.

"I don't even know some of these people," she says.

Her comment makes me realize you don't need the right clothes, the perfect skin, or the best body in high school. Cancer can make you popular.

Rick Carlton comes by with good news. Adrienne has been promoted to the tenth grade. She was only three days outside of the twenty-one-day window allotted for medical emergencies. Adrienne is excused from making up the three days' worth of work because her teachers determined doing it would not change her current grades. With A's in French I, Honors English, Health, and Beginning Dance, and two B's in Honors Biology and Geometry, her 4.0 GPA remains intact.[7] Rick suggests Adrienne pass her driver's permit exam and do any other projects requested by teachers over the summer. With schoolwork out of the way, Adrienne can focus on getting well.

Although Ronnie told me not to worry about it, I do think about money, or lack of it. My dad offered to help us so our house bills will be

---

7 Adrienne's weighted GPA; Burbank High School awards more points for honors courses.

paid. The medical bills are another issue altogether. Thanks to a loophole in the system, Adrienne qualifies for Medi-Cal, California's free insurance program. She is considered a minor with no income because as her legal guardian, my income does not count. Through Medi-Cal, Adrienne has Blue Cross HMO medical insurance, but they have already turned us down. The letter dated 5/19/01 is generic and sterile: "Our Utilization Review Analyst has determined that the service(s) requested are not approved because your child is medically eligible for California Children's Services (CCS)."

According to its pamphlet, CCS is "a statewide program that arranges and pays for medical care and therapy services for children under twenty-one years of age with certain health needs," and it may cover "types of serious, chronic, and physically disabling conditions." Adrienne is approved on May 23—her first day of chemo. The turnaround scares me. Blue Cross denied our claim, but four days later CCS approved it. The state never moves quickly on anything. I wish I could say having the financial burden lifted off my shoulders makes me feel better, but it does not. I am scared now more than ever.

As the cisplatin continues making its way into Adrienne's body, John and I learn how to give a Neupogen shot, the one we heard about in our class yesterday. The shots increase her white blood cell count, which helps her body combat the side effects of chemo. Of course, the shot has its own side effects: fever, nausea, muscle aches, and bone pain. When Adrienne learns about this new daily shot that cannot be administered through her central line, she frowns. She hates needles.

"Pay attention in class, Sissy," she says, "and don't hurt me."

Another nurse on the floor is teaching the class; she brings in needles and an orange to practice on. She says the orange most closely resembles subcutaneous tissue, and the goal is an ANC of 5000 or more. First, we have to find a fatty spot on Adrienne's thighs; the quads must be avoided because they have too much muscle. The syringe will be pre-filled, and the dose is based on Adrienne's weight, which will change over time. I assume she means Adrienne will lose weight, but I don't ask her. I focus on the fruit.

1. Keep everything sterile. If the needle or syringe falls on the ground, get a new one. The needle is 5/8 of an inch size 25 or

smaller. I don't know what 25 means, but the needle is tiny. I show Adrienne but she says it's still a needle.

2. Pinch the skin while holding a piece of gauze between the index and middle finger of the pinching hand. With the other hand, push the medicine up until you see a bead at the tip of the needle. Aim the needle down so it forms a 45-degree triangle in relationship to the skin. Insert needle. Release skin as you push the medicine in. Use gauze and apply pressure to the injection site. Put on a Band-Aid but remove within twenty-four hours.

3. Place needles into your sharps container provided by the home pharmacy.

After trying this procedure multiple times, I am ready to give up for the day. The angle isn't right, I keep dropping the gauze, and John forgets to check for the bead. Our teacher seems unfazed by our bungling.

"You'll get it," she says. "It takes practice."

The class feels like a dress rehearsal, only when the show opens we can't make mistakes. Adrienne is an unforgiving audience.

Adrienne makes it through the first day of chemo without throwing up. We are all surprised. I expected vicious vomiting like the one time I remember her being sick as a child. She was two years old, and without warning, chunks of oatmeal spewed out of her mouth. Nonstop for five minutes. Adrienne feels tired but she hasn't tossed her cookies yet. She promises not to pull a Linda Blair on us. Although she loves horror movies, *The Exorcist* spooked her when she saw the re-release last year. The puking didn't bother her so much as the backward spider crawl up the stairs.

"That," she said with a shudder, "was creepy."

At four o'clock in the morning, Adrienne wakes up feeling so nauseated she can't go back to sleep. A nurse gives her two tablets of Benadryl.

Three hours later she says, "Sissy, I'm gonna be sick."

I grab the kidney-shaped bucket and prepare for the worst. I hold my breath so I won't smell anything, and I pretend I can't hear her dry heaves. Then it comes up. Green, like Linda Blair, only it's broccoli and not pea soup.

"Phew," she sighs, "I feel much better."

"That's it?" I ask.

"I guess so," she says.

I peer into the bowl; it looks and smells like broccoli. I smile. I can do this after all.

On Grace's suggestion, I call the Social Security Administration to see if Adrienne is eligible for any type of benefits. A friendly woman named Alice takes my call. I hear the click-click of her keyboard as she types in Adrienne's social security number until she gasps. Then silence. When I ask what's wrong, she says she can't tell me. Instead, she confirms Adrienne's social security number, her residence, and my name and relationship to her. Click-click-click.

"It has something to do with our mother. Doesn't it?"

"I can't confirm that Ma'am," she replies.

Her voice is distant as if she is in shock. "Don't worry," I tell her, "you just did."

Alice urges me to call back next week; she must speak to her supervisor. Before hanging up, she tells me one last thing. She has two daughters; their names are Andrea and Adrienne.

When I hang up the phone, I don't know what to think. I have no way of knowing in a ten-minute conversation, I opened a Pandora's box. I tell Adrienne about the phone call. Like me, she is not concerned about whatever caused Alice to gasp; she is more interested in the names of Alice's daughters. Our names. What are the chances? We entertain the idea of fate. First, Adrienne said watch it be cancer and it was. Then, there's Ronnie and her cancer-stricken sister who call each other Sissy. And now, a stranger named Alice, who has her own Andrea and Adrienne at home. Adrienne is becoming more convinced cancer is her destiny, but I refuse to accept that premise.

✶ ✶ ✶

Unlike most mothers whose children incubate in their bodies for nine months, my life as a parent started on December 19, 1994, when an exuberant eight year old bounded off a plane and into my arms.

The stewardess running after her laughed and said, "You must be her sister, Andrea."

Adrienne chimed in, "Yep. She's my Sissy."

After flashing my driver's license, I took Adrienne to baggage claim. I commented how light one of her suitcases was.

She responded, "Oh. That one is full of my stuffed animals; they wanted to visit you too."

Neither one of us knew it at the time, but Adrienne's two-week holiday visit to Los Angeles would turn into a permanent stay. The day after Christmas, our mother called and asked if I could keep Adrienne for a while. She was tired, ill, and no longer capable of being a mother. She refused to tell Adrienne the news herself. I was twenty-two years old, lived with an alcoholic boyfriend, had little money, and no job stability, but it never occurred to me to say no.

It didn't take long before Adrienne challenged me. Our mother had let her run wild the last few years so Adrienne was used to doing whatever she wanted whenever she wanted. When the staff at a local restaurant sang Happy Birthday to her, she screamed. Then, she melted down like a two year old pitching a temper tantrum, only she was nine. My boyfriend Dan and I carried her out by her arms and legs. I was convinced people were going to call Social Services on us. I could tell by the weary look on his face he wasn't going to last much longer; fatherhood was not on his agenda.

I sent Adrienne to her room, which had been Dan's office. When I walked in to discuss her behavior with her, she was still thrashing her body around, yelling she hated me, and why did I make those people sing to her. I grabbed her arms and pinned her down. I even slapped her forearm to get her attention. It worked.

"You live here now. My house. My rules. You do not make scenes in public. Understand?"

"Oh yeah, I'm moving back to Alabama," she said.

I may have stopped her body from moving, but I couldn't do anything about her mouth.

"I don't like you. I don't want to live with you. I want my mother, and I want to go home!"

I looked into her fiery green eyes and wondered if I should tell her the truth. Mother was caught shooting up morphine at work. She lost her nursing license, and that's why she can't get a job. Or you have no home; no one in Alabama wants you. I said none of those things. Instead, I called her bluff. I released her arms, walked over to the desk, picked up the phone, and dialed 411.

"May I have the toll-free number to Northwest Airlines please?"

Adrienne watched me in silence as I proceeded to make a reservation in her name for a flight out the next day to Birmingham. I pulled out her two suitcases.

"Start packing, kiddo. Are you taking your stuffed animals or should I mail them to you?"

She glared at me, crossed her arms over her chest, and refused to say anything as I walked out of the room.

Meanwhile, I was in the living room hoping I had done the right thing. I knew this moment was a turning point. She had to accept me as her authority figure or this arrangement would never work. I heard her moving around in her bedroom. Shuffling something, slamming something else. What would I do if she packed her things? I waited. It took almost an hour, but Adrienne finally came out. She stared at the ground.

"Okay. I want to stay. Don't send me back."

Thank god, I thought to myself. I don't have the money anyway.

"Here's the deal: I'm your parent first, then your sister, and when you get older, I hope to be your friend. Got it? One more thing, don't ever threaten me again."

"Alright Sissy. Parent, sister, friend—got it."

* * *

Ronnie brings in two baby dolls to teach John and me how to change the dressing on Adrienne's central line. One doll is a white female child with no hair; the other doll is a black male child with a full Afro. How politically correct. Adrienne nicknames the boy the 'Eli doll' because Eli has thick, bushy hair that would stick straight up if he let it. One nurse routinely pulls Eli's hair to see if it's real. Both dolls have tubes coming out of their chests with a dressing of gauze around the exit site. The dressing must be changed twice a week on Mondays and Thursdays. It is much easier than giving the Neupogen shot. The hardest part is remembering all the steps:

1. Remove the old dressing; do not touch it or pull the catheter (i.e., central line).
2. Take the alcohol swab stick (a Q-tip soaked in alcohol) and then clean the catheter site. Start where the catheter comes out of the skin and work outward in a circular motion. Repeat with

second swab stick. Never go back over the same area with the same swab stick.

3.   Repeat step 2 with the Betadine swab sticks. Allow the Betadine to dry for 30 seconds.
4.   Take the 4 × 4 large gauze pads and place over the site to soak up excess Betadine.
5.   Take the 2 × 2 small gauze pad and fold it in quarters; place it over the exit site.
6.   Take out the Tegaderm, a clear adhesive strip. Peel off the back and place the sticky side on the skin. Peel off the frame around the edge of the Tegaderm.
7.   Take a two-inch piece of tape and tear it halfway in the center. Slip the tape under the catheter and overlap the split edges.
8.   Make a loop with the catheter and secure it with tape.

Ronnie suggests we store our supplies in a tackle box to keep them clean and in one location. On Monday, one of us is going to change Adrienne's dressing under her supervision. I nominate myself since I'll be doing it more often than John will, but he insists he gets a chance too.

John has to prove himself as a parent because he feels I get more respect than he does. Also, he needs to be recognized as Adrienne's father because he failed his own son Adam. Several years ago, Adam's mother took John to court and sued him for formal child support as well as legal custody. She had gotten married and had another child; thus John didn't fit into her new perfect family. Until the suit, they had no legal arrangement regarding Adam. John had paid child support every month, usually in cash. Adam had visited him every weekend. Even though Adam's mother lied in court about receiving child support and sending Adam to visit his father every weekend, John backed down and gave in to her demands. Now we only see Adam every other weekend, and John's relationship with him is strained. His constant insecurity is exhausting, especially when Adrienne has stated John is the only father she has ever had.

For her fifteenth birthday last month, John bought Adrienne a bass and an amp. In one month, he taught her major and minor scales as well as chromatic exercises. When her hands blistered, she became excited and showed John.

"That's how you know you're getting somewhere," he said.

She asked John to take her bass home when too many people played it in the hospital.

"You understand," she said.

He did. I wish he would trust Adrienne's love for him. She calls him Johnnee. The brightest spot of John's day is when he returns home from work. Adrienne is usually lounging in her favorite chair and doing her homework. However, when John walks through the door, Adrienne stops, grins, and greets him.

"Hey Johnnee Boy."

The tone in her voice should be enough for him.

END CHEMO—Round 1 is over!

Days 11-13

I've just known this whole time that whatever is meant to be is meant to be. This is a test; a test I can easily ace. I've forgotten how to think negatively, and in 12 days have changed my outlook on life completely. I don't allow any negative people, thoughts, or energy in here. With the support of strangers in the hall, with the loving hug of John or Sissy, or with a touching card from a stranger, I've been able to heal. During chemo, I was sick once. During my stay here, I've cried only for the following reasons: 1. Long treatments of chemo result in the loss of my hearing. 2. I never realized how many people loved me until I was checked into this room. 3. My altar was upset for the second time; of course, I'm over that now. Other than that, I've had no real reason to cry. So I have cancer, and what does that stop me from doing? I haven't felt pain in days. Cancer gave me cheekbones and an excuse to wear a strawberry wig. I get to spend time with my family, which was really rare before this. I'm getting a new bed when I get home. All things positive and light have resulted from the tiny bulbs that have decided to live on my liver and lungs.

—Adrienne's journal entry dated 5/28/01

Beep. Beep. Beep. Although it is a holiday weekend, the floor is quieter, except for the incessant beeps. The infusion pump that delivers fluids into Adrienne's body is always beeping. The first time I heard it, I thought something was wrong. Is there air in the IV? Is she okay? I asked. Now I know the beeps do not mean much; the pump is sensitive. We page a nurse, who comes in and pushes a few buttons to make the beeps stop.

It's too early to know if the chemo shrank the tumors, but Adrienne is feeling better. The Neupogen shots have given her immune system a positive jolt, which increases her energy level. When Nadia comes to visit again, Adrienne insists she get into bed with her.

"Let's see what this thing can do," Adrienne says.

They push buttons, and the bed climbs higher and higher. It's like the glass elevator in *Charlie and the Chocolate Factory*; it just keeps going. I warn them to be careful, but I can't bring myself to say stop. Listening to their girlish giggles gives me a reprieve from this place.

"Look Sissy, we can almost touch the ceiling if we stand on our knees."

Seeing Adrienne smile gives me hope. She looks good and she feels good. The tumors must be smaller now.

✻ ✻ ✻

"Won . . . Too . . . Thwee . . . Fouh . . . Fie . . . Sic . . . Sevin . . . Ate . . . Ninnne . . . Tin . . . Eweven . . . Twelvv . . . Uhhh . . . Hmm . . . Fouhteen . . . Fiffteen . . . Sicteen . . . Sevinteen . . . Ateen . . . Ninneteen . . . Twintee."

"You furgot one Adrinne," said our mother, "the unlucky numba."

Her Southern drawl took up precious seconds on my answering machine.

"Uhh . . . Oh! Thehteen!"

"That's righ. Now say bye to yer Sissy."

"I kin count to twinty Sissy. I learnt it in kinduhgahten. Wif Miss Cahteh. Byyye."

A five-year-old Adrienne counting to twenty on my answering machine in college was the best message I ever got. However, at nineteen years old I was too young to appreciate it. I laughed, played it twice, and then deleted it. In second grade, Adrienne started speech therapy. By the time she began fourth grade at Selma Elementary School in Hollywood, Adrienne had mastered her Rs and lost her Southern accent altogether. I wish I had kept that message. Adrienne was so proud of herself.

✻ ✻ ✻

Both Jared and Jesse are John's childhood friends. I think they all went to church together. Adrienne met Jared three years ago when he returned home after living at a Buddhist retreat. They hit it off immediately. Jared says talking to Adrienne is like drinking from a fire hose; she has too much to say and not enough time to say it. Jesse came along a few months later; he moved back to Los Angeles after graduating from Berkeley. Jesse feels like he has known Adrienne his entire life. They love to pretend to hate each other. Adrienne calls him Mr. Hips. When they come to our house, she demands they rub her feet knowing the reply will be "Get your stinky teen feet out of my face."

Two years ago, Jared was my assistant director for my play, where he met Joyce, one of my actresses. They have been together ever since. They stop in to see Adrienne, who invites Joyce to cuddle with her. I wasn't jealous when Nadia was in bed with Adrienne, but now I am. I suspect Adrienne likes Joyce, an innocent crush. As I watch Adrienne give Joyce a hug, I think why not me? Why can't I hold you? Then I remember, it's not about me. Get over it I tell myself.

As Joyce and Adrienne cuddle, Jared shows off his new look. He shaved his head to show his support for Adrienne, which makes her smile. His act of solidarity lessens my guilt and makes me glad I didn't tell anyone I thought about doing the same thing. After Adrienne touches his scalp in approval, Jared leaves with Joyce to go to our house, which is being cleaned by all our friends this weekend. The best way to prevent Adrienne from getting an infection, according to Ronnie, is to make our house as sterile as possible. Without me asking, Adrienne's posse bands together with one mission: to remove every hint of dust, lint, and odor from our home. I admire their resolve and wonder if they understand the magnitude of this task.

I hate to clean. However, I will wipe up dirt when I see it in the kitchen or bathroom. Dust, however, lingers on my desk for months. Adrienne receives five dollars per week for completing basic chores around the house: doing the dishes, sweeping the floor, cleaning the cat box, and taking out the trash. I relinquished control over her room because Adrienne's therapist Diana convinced me teenagers needed their own space. I shudder whenever I open her door and find clothes blanketing the floor, but Adrienne is also responsible for doing her own laundry now. If she wants to wear dirty clothes to school, I don't stop her.

John acts as if I am his own personal maid. He knows I can't stand it if his things are scattered everywhere. We have lived together for almost four years, and I have picked up his stuff every day. He is far worse than Adrienne, who does not leave her books, clothes, shoes, CDs, jewelry, etc. in the living room. Once I left the dishes in the sink and told Adrienne not to wash them just to see if John would volunteer to do them. I thought he might.

Adrienne said, "Nah, he won't bother. He doesn't care Sissy."

She was right of course. We ran out of forks, spoons, cups, plates, and bowls. When John needed a dish or utensil, he used a dirty one from the sink. Considering we have a dishwasher, I gave up. I resigned myself to living with two slobs who drive me crazy.

Adrienne's friend Sharon arrives with tons of goodies for Adrienne: two Jane's Addiction import CDs, playing cards, and a bass guitar magazine, which John reads. Sharon is a senior but she and Adrienne are in the same dance class. Even though dozens of people have visited Adrienne, she considers Sharon to be the closest thing she has to a friend at Burbank High. She often gives Adrienne a ride home from school, which made me nervous until I got to know Sharon. She is mature and responsible. John barked at her the first time he met her because she parked her pickup truck in our driveway. Sharon is convinced John hates her. I hope Adrienne explained to her it's not personal; he treats all people that way.

While Adrienne and Sharon watch the Tom Green movie *Road Trip*, I sneak down to the gift shop. Last week, Adrienne spotted a snow globe she liked: Pegasus, with his wings spread high above him, is looking down at a male fairy who is staring up at him. Green and yellow sprinkles complement the yellow in Pegasus's garment and the green of the pixie's hat, boots, and tunic. The snow globe plays music I don't recognize. I also buy Adrienne a stuffed animal, a baby killer sheep otherwise known as a lamb. Spending money I don't have feels good, because I get to spoil Adrienne.

It's funny how you remember little things after the fact. The Sunday before Adrienne felt pain was Mother's Day. She and John made a big deal about it. John surprised me with an excellent breakfast: omelette, biscuits, and fruit. Adrienne bought me a pink, scented gel candle for my many baths. The next day Adrienne reorganized her schoolwork because she could never find anything. With her own money, she bought a new folder and spiral notebook for every subject. Then I took her to Sav-On, a drugstore near our house, and purchased a black eyeliner pencil for her because it was on sale. She had wanted one for a while, but makeup was not in our budget. Adrienne wore it the next day—Tuesday, her last full day of school. The last day of normal. Now everything in our lives will be catalogued in my brain as being before or after. Black eyeliner—before. Snow globe—after.

While John reads and I shop, Adrienne and Sharon discuss the benefits of missing the African dance test. Meanwhile, our friends work hard to make our home fit for 'the boy in the bubble.' The boy is a real person; John Travolta starred in the movie based on his life. I don't remember what was wrong with him, but he could not be exposed to germs so he lived in this self-contained environment, sheets of plastic protected him from other people. Our friends pretend Adrienne is the boy, and our house is the bubble.

They begin in Adrienne's room where they remove the dozen or so dead roses hanging from the ceiling and the numerous bottles Adrienne uses for candleholders. Mold has grown inside the bottles, which they nickname demon semen. Adrienne's glass vanity desk, which she calls her altar, is scrubbed to a brilliant sheen. The fake pine pieces surrounding the vanity are soaked in bleach.

Joyce picks up Adrienne's clothes off the floor, strips the sheets from her bed, and does seven loads of laundry. Washing the mattress is too difficult so our friends buy Adrienne a new full-sized bed. All stuffed animals are removed and washed in hot water, but they will not return to Adrienne's room because they gather too much dust. Before leaving Adrienne's room, Jonathan cleanses it. I don't know what that means, but I'm sure Adrienne will like it.

Next, our friends move onto other parts of the house. Anya hires her cleaning woman Cathy to do the bathrooms and kitchen. Alex steam-cleans the carpet and chairs. The wicker sofa is deemed impossible to clean and moved into the garage. Anya and Alex buy a HEPA filter for Adrienne's room, while Jared and Joyce buy us a new vacuum cleaner because our old one broke down under the pressure. Joyce also lends us sheets until we can buy new ones. Every surface receives a generous coating of Lysol. By the time Memorial Day rolls around, our home has become a safe house. Our friends annihilated the germs and Adrienne can enter the bubble, minus the plastic sheets.

We are pleased to discover the PAWS program does not take off for holidays. At 2 p.m. on Memorial Day, a calm black Lab named Vera greets Adrienne. Like Baci, she is trained to jump onto the chair next to Adrienne's bed. Adrienne leans in for her Polaroid picture, scratching Vera under the chin. I compare the photo to the one taken last week. She looks healthier in this one. Maybe it's the Quad-hawk, the big smile, or the effort she made to pet Vera, but there is no question Adrienne seems more enthusiastic now. She says we need to schedule all her future hospital stays on Mondays, so she won't miss a PAWS visit.

Later that afternoon, I receive Adrienne's labs for the three days following chemo: Saturday, Sunday, and today. Except for her hemoglobin, which has dipped slightly below normal, her counts are fine. Better than fine. The Neupogen shot has bolstered her immune system so much that her WBC and ANC have skyrocketed beyond normal range. No wonder she looks so healthy. Like the name of her website, Adrienne is kicking cancer's ass. I love it.

Last week, a hospital volunteer gave Adrienne a chemo cozy, which is a quilt given to all patients who undergo chemotherapy at Children's Hospital. Three women made the quilt the year before. Each square seems to have its own theme: winter wonderland, autumn leaves, pink and purple spring flowers. The quilt comes with pens holding waterproof ink so people can sign it. Adrienne insists anyone who walks in her room autograph her chemo cozy. The comments range from "Kick cancer's behind" to "Hey girl, what's up? It sucks here [school] without you!" to "Keep up your contagious, upbeat spirit." I wonder if those women know how much this quilt means to Adrienne. I catch her rereading the comments at night; the quilt has become one of her most precious belongings.

When we meet Velma, we don't know she has heard about the new oncology kid with the blue hair, which became the Quad-Hawk. In the middle of the night, Velma and some other nurses kidnap Adrienne. Using her mini-Polaroid camera, which produces small self-adhesive stickers, they take pictures. Adrienne sticks them in her journal. There is even a photo of John and me sleeping. I must have been exhausted because the flash didn't wake me up. In every picture, Adrienne is beaming. She may be paler, thinner, and have less hair, but she does not look sick. Unlike Dr. No, nurses like Velma see Adrienne as a whole person; she is more than a kid with supposedly incurable liver cancer.

After writing in her journal, Adrienne asks John and me to read it. I am surprised. She won't even give me the address to her online live journal. She gave it to John months ago knowing he wouldn't bother to read it, but now she wants us to read every word she has written today. Afterward, I hug her and don't let go.

"Stop Sissy," she says, "you're suffocating me."

I think if I can hold her tight enough, I can love the tumors right out of her body.

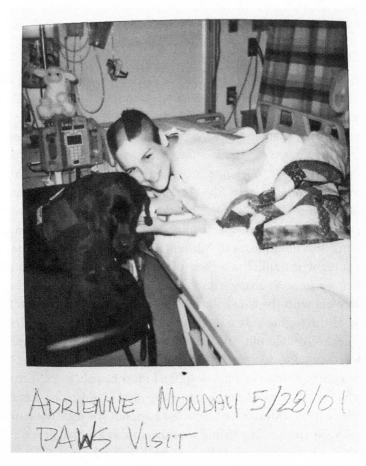

PAWS visit with Vera © May 28, 2001

Days 14–17

TUESDAY–FRIDAY, MAY 29–JUNE 1, 2001

When I was eight, my mother realized that she was extremely mentally and physically ill and sent me to California to live with my sister, who was at that time 22. This is probably the only wise choice my mother has ever made. I believe that by then she realized that I had given up my childhood to raise the fragile, drug addicted, mental case she had become.

—Adrienne's letter to a friend dated January 2001

Going home is scary. We spend the entire morning packing up our things and gathering our discharge materials. A bright yellow booklet with shadows of two girls jumping in the air is labeled "Discharge Instructions." I can picture the publisher discussing the cover art: it must convey happy, happy, happy, because these kids are delighted to be going home. I peruse the table of contents: When to call the Doctor, Taking the Temperature, Giving Medicines by Mouth, Blood Counts, Transfusion Therapy, Going Back to School, etc. Even though it is not in the book, I know when Adrienne's platelets are down, she is not allowed to shave, cut her nails, or blow her nose due to the risk of bleeding. I think Ronnie told us a few days ago.

A nurse gives Adrienne a Volumetric Exerciser and shows her how to use it. This plastic item is designed to "maintain and improve inspiratory volume and respiratory fitness." It is a treadmill for the lungs. Adrienne must do five or more repetitions three times a day. She takes a deep breath and exhales into the mouthpiece; her breath causes the pump to rise in volume by milliliters. To keep it simple, there are marks on the side labeled Good, Better, and Best. She must strive for Best. On her first attempt, she can barely make it to Good. You try Sissy; it's harder than it looks. She's right. I can get between Good and Better, but I feel like passing out afterward. I already know forcing Adrienne to do her lung exercises will be harder than making her swallow a handful of pills.

I have the discharge papers from the hospital's computer in my hand, but we cannot leave yet. We are waiting for Adrienne's prescriptions to be filled by the in-house pharmacy. I read down the list:

- Bactrim—By mouth twice a day: 8 a.m., 8 p.m. Antibiotic to prevent infections. *Is this necessary?*
- Boost—Drink as you want. A nutritional drink like Ensure. Adrienne likes it because it tastes like chocolate milk.
- Lo/Ovral Tab—By mouth once a day: 8 a.m. Birth control to prevent her period from occurring to avoid unnecessary bleeding. *Doubtful. The birth control caused her to have her period.*
- Neupogen shot—Subcutaneously once per day: 8 a.m. Medicine to increase white blood cells. Adrienne says make sure I'm not quite awake yet.
- Nystatin—Swish and swallow four times a day: 8 a.m., 12 p.m., 4 p.m., 8 p.m. Anti-fungal to prevent potential mouth sores caused by chemo. *Easy enough.*
- Peri-Colace—By mouth twice a day/as needed: 8 a.m., 8 p.m. Stool softener to lessen constipation caused by most painkillers. *No problem.*
- Tylenol #3—By mouth every four hours/as needed: 8 a.m., 12 p.m., 4 p.m., 8 p.m., 12 a.m., 4 a.m. Painkiller. *Tylenol 3 for cancer pain? I was prescribed Vicodin after my appendectomy. What the hell?*
- Zofran—By mouth every eight hours: 8 a.m., 4 p.m., 12 a.m. Anti-nausea that is prescribed after Adrienne feels nauseous within days of being at home.

I make a mental note to write Adrienne's meds on the small dry-erase board calendar that I had bought to create our computer schedule. A year ago, my father and stepmother gave us a used computer for Christmas. That same Christmas, Adrienne received her own telephone line. Between the two telephone lines, the computer, and the Internet, we stepped into the modern world and stumbled onto new complications. John, Adrienne, and I were always arguing about whose turn it was on the computer. If Adrienne was instant messaging her friends, I would remind her she had her own phone now and didn't need to talk to them on the computer.

"But it's not the same Sissy," she explained to me.

I attempted to establish a schedule, but John would forget to write his name down and then grumble when he didn't get his time. I finally limited Adrienne to one hour on the Internet Monday through Friday and two hours on weekends. I told John to use the computer when Adrienne was sleeping, and I grabbed time for myself whenever I could. The calendar lay under my desk, dusty and unused. Now it will serve a much higher purpose.

We arrive home in the early afternoon. The house smells of bleach and Lysol. I don't remember ever seeing it this clean before. The living room looks barren without our broken wicker couch. We had two chairs but now one stands alone—beige, suede, and bland. It is in complete contrast with the forest-green carpet, which looks brand new. John spends thousands of dollars on state-of-the-art entertainment equipment. We have the newest VCR, DVD player, 36-inch color TV, surround sound, but he won't chip in a few hundred dollars for decent furniture. Everything we own is donated: secondhand stuff from friends who pity us.

Adrienne is tired, so she settles into her new bed for a nap. We know she can recline, but lying all the way down hurts her back. After arranging her numerous pillows into their new supportive position, I tuck her in and proceed to my office where I find trash bags full of her clean stuffed animals. More of Adrienne's belongings are in the garage, stuff that was not cleaned or was too difficult to clean. I can't go through her things now. I need to set up shop in the kitchen.

After listing Adrienne's medications on the dry-erase board, I lock them up in the tackle box along with the supplies for her central line. Ronnie gave us almost a dozen clamps to put in various locations. The clamps look like small blue scissors; they are used to stop the line from spewing blood, if that should ever happen. I already gave a few to Anya and Alex for their house and cars. I put one in my car, John's car, Adrienne's bathroom, the kitchen, and the tackle box. The clamps are also used when I flush each line, which I must do every morning.

✳ ✳ ✳

When I peek in on Adrienne, she is still asleep. Except for the occasional earthquake, nothing wakes her up. She has always been a sound sleeper. By the time she was six weeks old, she was sleeping through the night. I used to sing lullabies to her even though I am tone deaf. She didn't mind. She would curl her arm around her Minnie Mouse stuffed animal and squeeze it so tight poor Minnie would have asphyxiated had she been alive.

Close your eyes I would say, and then I would begin singing the McGuire Sisters song "Goodnight Sweetheart Goodnight." I learned it after hearing the song in the film *Three Men and a Baby*. After the first verse I would change the words to suit our lives.

"Oh it's eight o'clock at night. And, it's time for you to sleep tight."

Adrienne would be out cold by the third verse.

Nights were easy, but during the day, Adrienne transformed into a holy terror as she entered her toddler years. She had a bizarre cowlick that made her hair stand straight up from the top of her head, which made her look like a devil. Screaming "Sissy" at the top of her lungs was her favorite pastime. Whether she was running through the dance studio, falling on the playground, or standing up on a chair at my high school graduation, Adrienne made her presence, as well as her relationship to me, known to the world.

Her shrieking didn't bother me though unless she was having a temper tantrum in public. One time at the mall, when Adrienne was about three years old, I walked away from her hysterical fit on the ground. I never took my eyes off her, but an old woman berated me for abandoning my poor, helpless child. I lost count of the number of times I said she's my sister, not my kid. With his dark hair and sapphire-blue eyes, my high school boyfriend Bryce was often mistaken for Adrienne's father. He wanted a pin that read, "She's not mine!"

Adrienne spent so much time with my friends and me that she adopted our slang. When she told our mother to chill out man, I laughed so hard I almost cried. She pranced around the house, swinging her hips as she sang Tiffany's remake of *Locomotion* and Lisa Lisa and the Cult Jam's *Head to Toe*. She watched MTV with me when the network still showed videos. For Halloween, she was a punk rocker ala Joan Jett. Even my all-time favorite movie, *The Wizard of Oz*, became one of her favorite movies too.

Bryce would buy Adrienne McDonald's milkshakes and read to her as bribes to give us time alone. Bryce retold the story of *Snow White* to reflect the people in our lives. When Bryce pointed to a particular dwarf, Adrienne would say the person's name: Sleepy = Sissy, Happy = Lisa (my best friend), Doc = Bryce, Sneezy became Sleazy = Jack (Bryce's friend), and Bashful = Shelley (my shy friend). She would point to Dopey and yell that's me! My mother thought less of Bryce when Adrienne told her she was Grumpy.

✳ ✳ ✳

John stays with Adrienne while I run errands. We have not been home for two weeks and we need food. I don't know what possesses me to go to the Burbank Temporary Aid Center. I must have driven by it more than a hundred times over the last four years, but I have never stepped foot inside the place. When I walk in, my nose crinkles at the smell of poverty: government-issued American cheese blocks, roach traps, mice droppings, week-old white Wonder bread, and stale bran muffins.

I want to turn around and run. *This is not my life. I am not homeless. We don't need this food.* But we do. After I explain my situation and sign a form, two women fill up two bags full of groceries. There are dry goods, which have a long shelf life, but there are also rotting bananas, old apples, day-old muffins, and a cake that expired a week ago. Even as I thank them, I vow not to return. Cancer has consumed Adrienne's liver, her lungs, and now our lives, but I refuse to let it take our self-respect.

On Wednesday, we wake up and begin the first morning of our new life. At 7:45 a.m., Adrienne gets out of bed. Two weeks ago today, at this time, she was already at school, but that was before. I have to deal in the now. I wash my hands with the antibacterial sanitizer located next to her supply tackle box. Adrienne sits at the kitchen table watching me lay out the items needed for our first task on a clean paper towel. The two lines coming out of her chest must be flushed with saline to prevent blood clots. A strong flush is 500 units; a weak flush, given if blood has been drawn that day, is 50 units. Like today, most days are a strong flush. If this were a poker game, we would be winning.

First, I clamp one of Adrienne's lines. Using a needle, I pull back the plunger to fill the syringe with saline. If there are air bubbles, a strong tap with my middle finger or a pen gets rid of them. I remove the needle and drop it in the red sharps container. I wipe the cap on the line with alcohol, connect the cap to the syringe, release the clamp, and inject the saline in a steady, continuous motion. Adrienne flinches; she can feel the cold water running through her chest. It doesn't hurt she says, but it is uncomfortable. After flushing one line, I repeat the entire process on the other line.

By 8:15 a.m., we are finished with flushing. I know I'll get faster as time passes, but I fear one day I will master the art of flushing a central line. No parent wants that kind of expertise. Even though I am a good caregiver, I never wanted to be a nurse like our mother, but here I am nursing Adrienne. I look around. Our kitchen resembles an outpatient clinic now, but we are home and that is all that matters.

In the middle of the night, I hear a weak "Sissy" float down the hall. Adrienne is awake and in pain. It hurts to walk she says. I give her Tylenol 3 because it is the only painkiller the doctor ordered. I wait until morning to call our case manager Teresa Granados. We discuss the possibility of switching Adrienne to Dilaudid, the medication she had in the hospital. Less than twenty-four hours later, I call again because Adrienne is experiencing cramping and having small, runny bowel movements. Teresa recommends Mylanta, an easy over-the-counter (OTC) solution.

Although both her gas and joint pain lessen and her energy increases, Adrienne's right ear begins ringing. By Friday, both ears ring, and Adrienne panics.

"I can't lose my hearing Sissy—tell them—I can't."

When I call for a third time, Teresa says keep track of when the ringing occurs. I write down everything in a black spiral notebook that becomes our personal medical bible. Within weeks, I color-code the entries with multiple highlighters: yellow indicates tests, transfusions, blood counts, and changes in meds; orange stands for vomiting; and green means Adrienne is having her period or a chemo treatment. I pick the colors randomly, although I find it strange that I group menstruation and chemotherapy under the same color. I must subconsciously believe they are both forms of torture.

On Friday, I keep my appointment and follow up with Alice from the Social Security Administration. Last week, she gave me her direct line so I could call her back when she had more information. After exchanging initial pleasantries, we get down to business. The cloak of secrecy has come off; for whatever reason, Alice can tell all now. Unbeknownst to me, Adrienne was eligible to receive Social Security benefits when our mother was approved for full disability. Alice explains our mother lied on the application and claimed Adrienne lived with her. For the last five years, she has received a separate check for Adrienne. The current amount she receives as payee is $672 per month.

As soon as I hear the words six hundred, seventy-two dollars, I remember the phone call from our Medi-Cal caseworker earlier this year. She accused me of lying about Adrienne's income; she kept insisting Adrienne was receiving over $600 per month from another program. The caseworker was ready to cancel Adrienne's medical insurance until I begged her not to. I offered to give her copies of my taxes, my pay stubs, anything she wanted. Adrienne is not getting any money I said, there has to be a mistake. I feel like a fool now. Somehow, Medi-Cal discovered our mother's scheme, but they stopped digging after I told them they were wrong. Why didn't I ask more questions? Because I didn't want Adrienne to lose her medical insurance, and I didn't like being called a liar.

All those thoughts fly through my head in under a minute. I don't bother to tell Alice. However, I listen as she explains what the next step is: I have to file a claim to have the payee switched from our mother to myself, which means I have to prove Adrienne lives with me. Alice says school records such as report cards, letters, and awards should be enough. She keeps apologizing for their egregious error, but I don't blame her or Social Security; a large federal bureaucracy can't be held responsible for all the liars in this world. They should have confirmed Adrienne lived with our mother, but they didn't.

When I tell Adrienne about the situation, she replies, "That's Mother."

Is Adrienne wiser than I am for expecting the worst from our mother? She has done terrible things, but I never expected her to cheat her own child. The single tear sliding down my cheek represents the last bit of respect and love I have for our mother. I don't know when or why, but I can see from the look on Adrienne's face she gave up a long time ago. What is the value of a daughter's love? I want to know exactly how much money our mother got at Adrienne's expense. From my rough estimate, it's a minimum of $35,000. I want to shake our mother and yell. *Was it worth it? You lost two daughters for a mere five figures. Don't you know our love is priceless?*

Adrienne & Andrea in
mall photo booth © 1988

Days 18-23

Let's go Blue. We miss you!
Come on Adrienne; get better soon.
So keep it up, and your spirits high
'Cause . . . we believe in you!
We love the way you're always there
To bring—us—smiles.
So go Blue, we're thinking of you!
Just remember, we love you!

—Three Burbank High School cheerleaders on the video

I obsess over Adrienne's lab results. John does, too, but in a different way. Adrienne's platelets have dropped from 272,000 to 113,000 in five days; they are below normal now. John, however, is more intrigued that Adrienne's platelets show his birthday: January 13. He sees his birthday everywhere: on marquees, in commercials, and even on the NASDAQ and Dow Jones numbers when he follows the stock market. I was supportive of his superstition—*you're right honey, it means something*—until he began seeing his birthday on clocks. It is futile to point out to him the time is 1:13 twice a day, every day.

I can't believe John's only comment on Adrienne's labs is his birthday. What about Adrienne's increased risk of bleeding? When I call Children's Hospital, a random oncologist assures me the drop is normal, and the platelets will recover. Within three days, they do. WBC is up. ANC is up. Her immune system is strong. However, her hemoglobin has dropped, which increases the possibility of a blood transfusion. Our bodies are complicated, yet resilient. The first round of chemo barely affected Adrienne's immune system, but the doctors warn me this will not always be the case. The more chemo she endures, the worse it will get.

On Sunday evening, my friend Marilyn asks me to go to a party with her. Both John and Adrienne urge me to get out of the house. I don't want to go, but with three people pushing me, I acquiesce. Marilyn takes me to an all-female season premiere airing of *Sex and the City*, a show I never watch because we don't have HBO. A club in West Hollywood sponsors the event. The local celebrities attending include Jillian Barberie, a weather girl more known for her tight skirts than her meteorology expertise, and Lara (rhymes with Farrah), a local DJ on Star 98.7, one of the most popular radio stations in Los Angeles.

As I sip an apple martini, my first one ever, the crowd mesmerizes me. There are the tacky, trendy outfits. Lara is sporting a leopard-print cowboy hat and a belt buckle with so many fake rhinestones it screams 'Look at my Bling!' Jillian is more subdued in tight pants and her Victoria's Secret water bra that gives her instant cleavage. She has that lollipop celebrity look about her; her head is too big for her body. I hear the chatter and laughter of women all around me talking about the most trivial subjects: fashion, makeup, diet fads. I watch as they give each other that kiss-on-each-cheek greeting that may be sincere in Europe, but is all for show in this town.

For Marilyn's sake, I am a good sport and keep my opinions to myself. I feel stupid for being here. I have nothing to say to anyone because my thoughts are elsewhere. *Did John remember to give Adrienne her 8 p.m. meds? How is she feeling? Will she need more Zofran for the nausea? Does she have nausea?*

I drain the rest of my martini and order another one. Usually two drinks will bring on a buzz, but not tonight. Distraction and worry outweigh the effects of alcohol. From the bar, I can see almost everyone. I hate these people; their biggest problems are finding the right accessories for their designer outfits. To my relief, Marilyn takes me home after I finish my second martini. The night was not a total wash; I did discover a new drink.

※ ※ ※

In a journal entry dated December 4, 1985, I wrote: "Today the most exciting thing happened. I found out the baby is a girl and she is all right." All right meaning healthy. I was worried because Mother took numerous pills during her first trimester to dull her grief. If Adrienne had been a boy, I'm not sure I would have ever become excited about a new sibling. That day, when I found out she was a healthy girl, I changed my attitude toward my mother. I went from being judgmental to being helpful.

At the hospital, Mother's coworkers threw her a baby shower. I folded each outfit with care, mostly dresses, picturing my baby sister in them. The sundress with strawberries on it was by far the cutest. I decided Adrienne would make her public debut in it. I waited in anticipation for Adrienne to become a noticeable bump in my mother's profile. I wanted to see evidence of my sister.

By the spring of 1986, there was no doubt my mother was due any day. She had gained almost sixty pounds, and her stomach was as round as the globe in my school's library. Adrienne was breech, so a C-section had been planned for April 8. Nine days before, Mother grabbed me as she began swaying. Help me to the couch she said, your sister is turning. Afterward, I felt her stomach, finding Adrienne's head, which was the size of a small lemon. Sure enough, she had moved. Mother was excited; she preferred to give birth vaginally because it was cheaper, and her recovery time would be shorter. However, a sonogram the next day revealed bad news. Adrienne had moved, but when she did, one leg got stuck in the birth canal. Dr. Hale, Mother's OB-GYN, was adamant about the C-section now; with Adrienne's leg trapped, there was no other way. I would see my sister on April 8 as planned.

It was a Tuesday. I wore my favorite outfit to school: black stretch pants and my white sweatshirt with panda bears and rainbows on it. Because of a standardized test that morning, we eighth graders missed half of our arts period. I was sitting on the floor of the dance studio, watching the older students execute the adagio sequence in ballet class when an announcement boomed over the speaker system.

"Andrea Wilson, please come to the office. Your mother is in labor. Andrea, please come to the office now. Thank you."

Giggles rippled across the room. Our charter school had fewer than 200 students, so everyone knew my mother was pregnant. I grabbed my bag and ran out the door hearing echoes of good luck and congratulations. They didn't understand. Mother's C-section was supposed to be in the late afternoon; she shouldn't be in labor. Something was wrong.

My mother's cousin drove me to Brookwood Medical Center. My anxiety subsided when we found my mother, still pregnant, ordering people around from her hospital bed. A male nurse explained they had to stop the labor, which started earlier that morning, to make sure the baby was developed enough to be born. Mother yelled something like, developed enough? My C-section is in five hours. I don't think the baby will grow anymore between now and then. Just bump up my surgery and take her out now! I felt sorry for the guy; he looked like a dog with his tail tucked between his legs as he shuffled out of the room.

Since the OR had no openings and Dr. Hale wanted to run tests, Mother's wish was denied, and her labor was stopped. When the male nurse walked back in, I couldn't decide if he was brave or stupid. His announcement the baby was fine barely elicited a glance from my mother. I imagine she was thinking, I told you so. I've been a nurse since before you were born. We never saw him again. Too bad. The verbal sparring made the time pass quicker.

Mother and I played cards, one of our favorite pastimes unless I was winning. At that point, she would accuse me of being too competitive like my father. Since today was special, we didn't keep score. The minutes ticked by as we played countless hands of Gin Rummy. It was almost time.

✳ ✳ ✳

No liver pain since Friday is what I write in our medical bible, but the ringing in Adrienne's ears has continued along with constant nausea. Zofran does not alleviate the nausea, nor does Nystatin stop mouth sores from forming. Adrienne naps daily and experiences low-grade fevers. I wonder if the fevers are a side effect of chemo. Her doctors have no answer; they tell me not to worry. It's a typical, dry Los Angeles summer with temperatures over 100 degrees in the San Fernando Valley. The house we rent does not have central air, just a window unit in the living room. When she's not sleeping, Adrienne curls up in her favorite chair next to the air-conditioning and watches television. I sit on the floor in front of her, monitoring her every minute, except when I nod off from sheer exhaustion.

Tess, the nurse assigned to us by American Home Health, breaks up our morning routine. She arrives every Monday and Thursday morning before 10 a.m. Adrienne likes her and enjoys the reprieve from me. Tess draws blood, flushes the lines, and changes the caps every Monday if I have not already done so. Replacing the old caps with new ones is not difficult to do, but knowing Tess will take care of that task eases my mind. One less thing to remember. Tess earns our trust quickly because she is dependable and competent. We like her. I think she likes us too. She says Adrienne is one of her youngest and most entertaining patients.

Adrienne takes her bath every night after her 8 p.m. meds. I help her by putting her central line in a Ziploc bag and then taping it to her chest. The young woman who didn't want to show me her swollen abdomen a few weeks ago now has to shed most of her clothes before my eyes. Modesty disappears when you are ill. I can tell Adrienne is losing weight. The new Victoria's Secret underwear I bought her last week is hanging off her butt. I figured she was a large since I am a medium, but I didn't think about the potential weight loss. At 138 pounds, she left the hospital five pounds lighter, but she looks even smaller now. She is delighted with her new weight. Before I examine her body too closely, Adrienne kicks me out of the bathroom. She won't take off her now baggy underwear in front of me. She has her limits.

Once an insomniac, I am asleep within minutes of lying down every night at midnight. All those years of dancing, which left me physically exhausted, are nothing compared to what I feel now. The mental fatigue erodes my brain cells; one at a time, they seem to be dying off, unprepared for this emotional journey. I can remember exactly how many milligrams of Tylenol 3 Adrienne has taken in the last week, but I cannot tell you what movie we watched yesterday. With fewer cells, my brain filters data in a new way. It throws out the unnecessary information because it must leave room for the important stuff, the medical stuff. Adrienne's stuff. Only when I sleep do I escape the constant toiling of my mind.

I wake up at 7:55 a.m. to Tchaikovsky's march from *The Nutcracker*. Adrienne bought me this clock for Christmas years ago, but since John hated the noise, I stopped using it. The clock came out of retirement because without a snooze button, it is guaranteed to get me out of bed on time. I wash my hands and retrieve the Neupogen vial out of the refrigerator.

Walking into Adrienne's room with all the necessary props: an alcohol pad, some gauze, a Band-Aid, and the shot, I nudge her awake.

"I'm about to do it."

"Make it quick," she says.

A wipe, a pinch, I'm in, release skin, inject fluid, I'm out. Apply pressure with gauze; slap on the Band-Aid. All done. If she winces, I have performed this task well. A verbal outcry, however, indicates a wrong angle, the injection was too slow or too fast, or some other error on my part.

As her weight decreases, I wonder if there will be enough fatty tissue for the shot. If Adrienne's thighs become too thin or they have too many contusions, I am supposed to use her arms instead. For now, I alternate legs. I know which leg I did the day before by looking at the color of the various bruises, which are forming penny-sized polka dots on her inner thighs.

After the dreaded shot, our day begins with breakfast: one piece of toast, crackers, or a Boost shake, whatever I can coax Adrienne into eating. Breakfast also includes all the 8 a.m. medications, which averages four pills and the requisite swish and swallow of Nystatin. Adrienne spends her day in one of three outfits: her new blue Victoria's Secret nightgown, a light pink pajama top with a loose pair of shorts, or a long dark pink pajama shirt.

We watch television most of the time, but then pore over the mail when it arrives—letters, cards, care packages, and even bibles. Adrienne asks me why people are sending her bibles. I tell her they mean well, but they don't understand a bible does not help her. Sometimes we don't know the sender, or it's someone we barely know like Alex's mother or my first cousin on my dad's side, who is not related to Adrienne at all. Like people flooding her hospital room, I know the mail will subside as Adrienne's disease progresses. People need a happy ending.

Adrienne is excited when two of her favorite teachers, Cindy Burns (dance) and Cybil Bennett (English), stop by to say hello. We didn't know Ms. Bennett had launched a fundraiser at Burbank High. She, along with another teacher, personally donated $500 each. A parent, who wished to remain anonymous, donated a month's rent, $1,250. A student who didn't know Adrienne donated his paycheck of $60, which he said was a gift from god.

Ms. Bennett hands me the money in an envelope; it adds up to just over $3,000. The generosity of the students, teachers, and parents in our community stuns me. Tears well up in my eyes as I say thank you. Adrienne diffuses my astonishment by giving a tour of her room pointing out where the roses used to hang from her ceiling, explaining why she cannot have any more stuffed animals, and showing off her altar with its stones, candles, and chalices as well as her new bed and HEPA filter.

The visit ends with all of us sitting in the living room watching a thirty-minute video made by Adrienne's classmates. During the first segment, three boys, two of whom dressed up in long-sleeved collared shirts and black slacks, are running a mile for Adrienne. They spot the camera after each lap, giving thumbs up and victory signs. Their pace is steady and they finish in six minutes.

"Never give up," they say. "If we can run a mile as fast as we did, you can get better."

Four female students, wearing Groucho Marx glasses with an attached nose, lead the next segment titled: HAY radio or Happiness and You. One girl faces the camera.

She asks, "What animal do you hate the most?"

When a white paper sheep glued to a Popsicle stick dances into the frame, Adrienne bursts out laughing. I had no idea she had shared her sheep theory with her peers.

An energetic blonde dressed in a yellow tank top and jeans leads three other girls in a choreographed dance to The Go-Gos' *We Got the Beat*.

She yells, "I'm doing this for you Adrienne. Dance with us."

As the girls continue to dance and sweat, the blonde smiles.

"Whew," she says.

Much to Adrienne's delight, some male students read *A Midsummer Night's Dream* with terrible accents. Another boy reads lines from a sonnet.

One girl says, "I had fun competing with you because you're so intelligent."

While most of the female students identify themselves by name, few boys do, but Adrienne knows most of them.

There are a few more segments: an incident with an ant walking across the camera lens, a tour of the various bungalows that serve as temporary classrooms until the new school is built, and one boy talking as if he is the wizard Gandalf, the school is Middle-earth, and the students are his subordinate hobbits.

The video ends with a tight zoom on Ms. Bennett, who says, "Keep studying; don't party too much."

Students laugh in the background.

"We would like to see you get into UCLA."

"But she hates UCLA Ms. Bennett," says one student.

"Yeah, she likes USC," says another.

"Oh. Okay," Ms. Bennett says. "USC. Or Stanford. Or Harvard. Or Yale. Don't settle for anything less. We look forward to seeing you graduate with everybody else in a couple of years and seeing you go off to college."

Nadia's mother brought the In-Home Supportive Services (IHSS) program to my attention last week. Our social worker Grace doesn't think we will qualify, but it can't hurt to try. A pamphlet about the program says, "IHSS will pay for services provided to you [the patient] so that you can remain safely in your own home."

The types of services that qualify include housecleaning, meal preparation, laundry, grocery shopping, personal care services (e.g., bathing, grooming), and accompaniment to medical appointments. If it didn't have the disclaimer that only people over sixty-five years of age and some disabled children are eligible, every housewife in America would finally get a paycheck with IHSS as their employer.

It is a long shot. Cancer patients, especially children, are not usually labeled as disabled, which boggles my mind. Adrienne can't go to school, read for long periods, walk more than a block, or do any of her chores. Neither Adrienne nor I say it aloud, but cancer has slowed her down. Is that enough to receive IHSS?

✳ ✳ ✳

Just before 5 p.m., I said goodbye to my mother as she was wheeled into the OR. She arranged it so I could be in the nursery when Adrienne was born, one of the many benefits of being a fellow healthcare professional. A nurse gave me blue scrubs to put over my clothes, made me wash my hands, and then escorted me down a long, wide hallway. I sneaked a glance into each room, seeing one giant belly after another. I had become a thirteen-year-old peeping Tom in search of my mother. The nurse must have noticed my concern because she said it wouldn't be long now. We turned a corner and she left me there. Just wait she said. I was about to meet my sister. I asked myself. Would she like me? More importantly, would I like her? I watched as other newborns arrived. Nope. Not her. Another boy. How long does a C-section take? Are all newborns so... ugly?

Yes, they are. However, when Dr. Hale placed Adrienne in my arms for the first time, I didn't care that she had a big forehead, squishy eyes, and flushed skin covered in dried, yellow crusty stuff. I felt this rush of love jettison through my entire being, so powerful I thought it could knock people down. I would do anything for this kid. For the first time in my life, I understood what the term unconditional love meant. All parents are supposed to have that kind of love for their children, but my parents' love came at a price. I would give that love to my sister Adrienne, who opened her eyes, a deep royal blue, and looked at me. She seemed to be thinking: who the hell are you?

"I'm Andrea—your sister," I said, "and I promise to never let anything bad happen to you. Okay, kiddo?"

She blinked and wailed.

A nurse took Adrienne away from me before I could calm her down. She laid her down on her back and began examining all her limbs and extremities. She tested Adrienne's joints by rotating her shoulders and hips. Up, down, side to side. Soon she had Adrienne's legs in the butterfly, or lotus, position. Knees out, feet together. I thought, wow, this woman is preparing my sister to be a dancer, but Adrienne's voice went up two octaves when the nurse turned her legs out. I wanted to snatch my sister away, save her from the agony of forcing one's body into unnatural positions, but that's when the nurse stopped. She wiped off the crusty stuff with a warm washcloth and handed my new sister back to me.

No longer crying, Adrienne stared at my face. Even the nurse commented on her eyes—how blue, how alert. I knew infants' eyes could change color, especially if they start out blue. Adrienne would end up with the most beautiful eyes in our family. Over a two-year period, her eyes transformed from that brilliant blue to a deep olive green—her father's eyes. Even on her first day of life, Adrienne enchanted me as if she had performed a spell like a genie. Blink-blink. *I love you, kiddo.*

The nurse reminded me several relatives were outside the nursery window wanting a peek at our family's youngest grandchild. There they were: my mother's sisters, Aunt Tootsie and Aunt Sue; Uncle Charles, Sue's husband; and their daughter Peggy, my first cousin. They were waving, smiling, and looking through the thick glass. As Uncle Charles held up his Polaroid camera, the nurse said here let me help you. She held Adrienne up at an almost 90-degree angle so she was now facing the camera. I ran my fingers through Adrienne's thick, black hair, stroking her head, feeling the soft spots where her skull had yet to harden. In the picture, I am looking down. I never took my eyes off Adrienne.

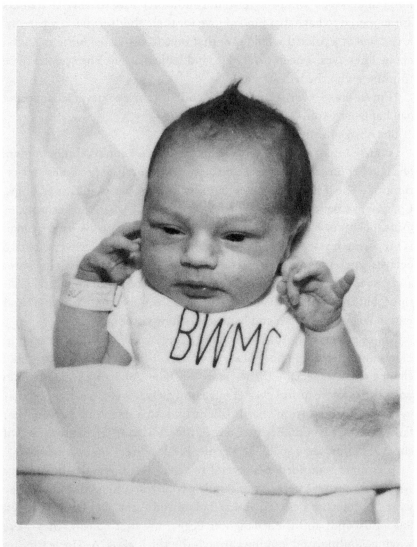

The most beautiful girl!

Adrienne only 24 hours old

Days 24-28

FRIDAY-TUESDAY, JUNE 8-JUNE 12, 2001

*It's comforting to know I **am** alive, not quite rotting as fast as others expect. Do I send out a message of, 'Hey, I can barely survive a cold, let alone liver cancer?' I'M SICK AND TIRED OF COMFORTING YOU PEOPLE. Sorry for the caps. I'm going to hide for awhile and comfort myself. I hope that's 'ok' with everyone.*

—Adrienne's journal entry dated 6/8/01

Century 21 Larson Realty, the management company who handles our rent, calls to let us know the owners have put the house back on the market. The timing could not be worse. The property manager appears sympathetic, but she has to do her job. To protect Adrienne's health, I explain there are guidelines for showing the house. When people enter, they must spray the bottom of their shoes with a mixture of bleach and water. A blue bottle is located on the counter as you walk into the kitchen, the main entrance to our house. Next, they must wash their hands with the antibacterial hand sanitizer. We must be home when the house is being shown, and children are not allowed inside since they pose a greater risk of infection. People may look in Adrienne's bedroom, but they cannot go inside, nor can they touch any doorknobs. The property manager says these restrictions should not be a problem.

I hate moving. When Adrienne and I lived with our mother in Birmingham, we moved four times in five years. Whenever our house/apartment became too dirty, Mother wanted to leave. Some people believe in spring-cleaning; our mother preferred moving in the spring or whenever. She continued her nomadic behavior after I left home. In four years, Adrienne lived in four different cities in three different states. She was in her third school by the beginning of third grade. She completed third grade in her fourth school when she moved to Los Angeles to live with me. Then, we moved and she started fourth grade in Hollywood. I managed to keep her there for fifth grade, too, even though we moved

105

yet again. Before she started middle school, I made a conscious decision to find the best school district in the most affordable neighborhood, so we wouldn't have to move again. We have lived in this house in Burbank for almost four years now, longer than I have lived anywhere else in California and longer than Adrienne has lived anywhere else in her entire life. We can't move.

I consult an attorney to see if we have any rights as tenants given Adrienne's medical condition. John and I cannot afford to buy this house. Even if we could, we don't want to live next to Interstate 5 for the rest of our lives. The asking price is $229,000. The price drops after numerous potential buyers realize the house shakes whenever a semi roars by on the freeway. Eventually, our home will become the cheapest three-bedroom house in Burbank. The attorney researches the issue for weeks. Can we stay here while Adrienne is sick? Do her rights carry more weight than the owners do? No. If the house sells, we will have to move.

Our strong dislike for Dr. No motivates us to seek a second opinion. Kirsten refers us to Dr. Aquino, a liver cancer specialist at UCLA. She heard him speak at a conference, and he impressed her. Getting an appointment is easy; getting the necessary documents together is more challenging and getting the insurance to pay for it is nearly impossible. I sign papers releasing copies of Adrienne's medical files. I pay for a copy of Adrienne's CT scan and bring home the film. Adrienne and I hold it up to the light.

"Hmm . . . looks like dots of lights to me," says Adrienne as she shrugs.

I am stunned by how many dots there are. It looks like it is snowing in her lungs. UCLA requests a tissue sample from the biopsy. More documents to sign. More papers to read. More people to call.

I realize this is the first time I have had full access to Adrienne's medical records. The report on her biopsy states: "15-year-old female, previously healthy who has recently been diagnosed with hepatocellular carcinoma, which has metastasized to the lungs. There is, by radiographic report [CT scan], one dominant liver tumor with multiple smaller satellite tumors." The medical jargon is not lost on me; satellite tumors sound far more threatening than dots of light or snowflakes. I refuse to look at the film or read the biopsy report again. I put everything in a giant envelope and store it next to Adrienne's medical supplies. It taunts me but I resist. Denial sustains me; I cannot let those bulbs of enlightenment destroy my hope.

The ringing in her ears is gone, but Adrienne still suffers from nausea and headaches. Since her counts are up, she can go out in public. John takes her to the movies on Friday night. I opt not to go, which means the movie must be an MTV/teenage/gross humor kind of film. My tastes exclude Tom Green, Ben Stiller, or South Park characters. Adrienne continues her ongoing gin rummy game with John; she is winning.

Over the weekend, she is too tired to go out. We stay in and watch episodes of *Invader Zim* and *Spongebob Squarepants*, whom I mistake for a piece of cheese. Little Bit, Adrienne's cat, scratches her while they are playing. The sight of blood spooks me even though I know Adrienne's platelets are in normal range now. I yell at Little Bit, and she immediately jumps off.

Adrienne says, "She didn't mean to, Sissy."

From that point forward, Little Bit displays extra caution around Adrienne as if she knows her actions might incur my wrath.

Eli spends a few hours a day at our house if Adrienne has enough energy to stay awake. I am talking on the phone when I hear Adrienne and Eli laughing out loud. We have a rule in our house: the bedroom door remains open when a boy is in Adrienne's room. I cover the mouthpiece and yell, "What's going on in there?"

Eli says, "Take a look."

"See Sissy," Adrienne says, "it's finally coming out."

I watch as Eli pulls out a tuft of Adrienne's hair from one of her Mohawks. Both teenagers dissolve into uncontrollable giggles; their laughter is contagious. When I point out Adrienne now has an obvious bald spot, she stops Eli, looks in the mirror, and decides she needs another haircut. I promise to take her to Supercuts later that afternoon.

Adrienne finds out Dave Navarro, her favorite musician, is going to be on *The Tonight Show* on June 18, just weeks after his thirty-fourth birthday, June 7. She and Eli decide to get tickets. Eli calls a friend whose father works on the show.

"I'm in a bit of a pickle," he says.

I call our social worker Grace, who knows Kevin Eubanks because he volunteers for Children's Hospital. She promises to see what she can do. Adrienne and Eli brainstorm other people who might have connections to NBC.

"We're going to milk this cancer thing for everything it's worth," declares Eli.

The words may come out of his mouth, but they sound like something Adrienne would say. All together, they come up with eight tickets and passes to the Green Room before the show. Adrienne's second round of chemotherapy is scheduled the weekend before that Tuesday. She is determined to do well so she can be discharged in time to see Dave.

Teen Impact meets on Mondays at 6 p.m. Their mission is "to improve the quality of life for adolescents and young adults with cancer by providing peer-based group interventions in a safe and therapeutic environment." The group has regular meetings and even retreats. Adrienne is reluctant to attend. She rarely fits into one specific social group and thinks this situation won't be any different. I encourage her to go one time, and she agrees to shut me up.

Before we leave for the meeting, I take Adrienne to Supercuts to fix her hair. We went there when she had lice last year. Super lice, which are resistant to the standard chemicals, invaded her middle school. After spending more than fifty dollars on treatments and two weeks killing the lice, Adrienne needed most of her thick hair cut off to return to school. I remember how the hairdresser looked at us in disgust. The lice are dead, I assured her, but my sister needs some length taken off. Everyone at her school has lice right now. We are not dirty people I said. The hairdresser finally agreed to cut Adrienne's hair to her shoulders, four inches total.

I don't see the other hairdresser, which is a relief because I can't imagine how she would react to this situation. The woman at the cash register sends us over to Mary. I explain to her under no circumstances can the razor touch Adrienne's scalp. She wants her Mohawks shaved off, but she has specific ideas on how her hair should look. Using her middle part as a guide, Adrienne tells Mary to shave off all her hair, but she wants one side to be 1/4 inch longer than the other. I ask Mary if she can do that without touching Adrienne's scalp. She says, yes ma'am. Mary does a beautiful job and receives a much higher tip than the one I gave the other hairdresser the year before.

Like the Quad-hawk, Adrienne's new hairdo serves as a costume. Except for the quarter-sized bald spot in the front, her hair follicles remain intact. Her hairstyle has purpose; it disguises the fact she is sick. She has lost weight and her skin becomes paler each week, but strangers don't know these things. People stare sometimes but I think they stare not because she appears sick, but because she looks different. Adrienne possesses a natural beauty that no plastic surgery in the world can achieve.

Adrienne complains about having a headache as we pull into the parking garage at the hospital. She knows I cannot give her anymore Tylenol for a few hours, but she wants to avoid going to the meeting.

"We'll walk in. If you hate it, we'll walk out," I tell her. "You can show off your new hairdo."

She frowns.

We find Teen Impact in a large room, where chairs are positioned in a circle. Many teenagers have already arrived. We sit in the two chairs closest to the door. A woman opens the meeting by encouraging people to go around and introduce themselves.

"We have some new people here today," she says.

Adrienne glares at me.

Most of the kids have leukemia, and some of them are in remission. An upbeat, sixteen-year-old Hispanic girl has a tumor in her thigh, and her leg may need to be amputated. She sits in a wheelchair to Adrienne's right.

When it is her turn, Adrienne whispers, "Hello. My name is Adrienne."

Some kids respond with an enthusiastic "Hi Adrienne."

The group reminds me of the few Al-Anon meetings I attended many years ago, positive people coping with impossible situations. Do I leave my alcoholic boyfriend? Do I continue treatment even though the tumors keep multiplying?

I smile and look at Adrienne, who runs out of the room in tears. I apologize for both of us and leave too.

Farther down the hall, I find her sitting on the floor, knees tucked into her chest, shaking and crying.

"Don't make me go back. I can't do this," she says.

I pushed her too hard. She does not need or want a support group; I do. I forced my desire onto her; most parents do at one time or another, but unlike our argument over what constitutes a perfect Christmas tree, this time my will incited sadness, not anger.

Between sobs, Adrienne says, "Don't you get it? I can't be around other sick kids. It's too depressing."

"I'm sorry, kiddo. You never have to go back. Let's go home."

As I help Adrienne to her feet, a tall African-American woman approaches us.

"Here," she says as she thrusts a book in my hand. "I just know I am supposed to give this to you. I can't explain why."

I thank her and look down at the small book: *Cancer Bibliography: The best books on cancer—a resource for librarians, oncology nurses, patients and their families.* Four by seven inches with fifty-eight pages, it would be more accurate to call it a booklet. I flip through it as Adrienne and I get on the elevator. The booklet was printed five months ago. To assuage my guilt, I tell myself we were supposed to be here tonight, not to attend the Teen Impact meeting, but to receive this booklet.

Later that evening, John empathizes with Adrienne about the disastrous meeting. He sits next to her while she lies in bed. Every night, Adrienne requests John to do 'hand duty.' He holds her hand as they watch TV in her bedroom, and sometimes she will fall asleep. Tonight, she vents her frustration about being forced to do something she did not want to do. I leave them alone; hand duty is their time together, and Adrienne is too upset with me right now. Instead, I read the booklet and highlight twelve books to buy out of the 109 listed. I feel terrible about what happened, but I can't fix it. I can make up for my mistake by buying books, becoming more educated, and discovering a miracle.

✳ ✳ ✳

Whenever Adrienne and I entered our Highland Terrace apartment, we performed a box-step dance and sang our version of "Hooray for Hollywood."

"Where everyone is crazy and no one's good-hood. In Hollywood-wood..." (I never knew the original lyrics!)

The song and dance was an effort to put on a happy face for her, but I was not doing well. For the first time in my life, I could not hold down a job due to health problems. I slept two hours a night, constantly felt hot, and could not get enough food. I feared I was going crazy. I didn't have health insurance, so I couldn't see a doctor.

Adrienne, then nine years old, needed me, which kept me going. Taking her to school, picking her up, making her dinner, tucking her in, reading to her, and picking up her toys were routines that provided structure. I joined the School Site Council, which gave me another reason to drag my body out of the house. I didn't take it one day at a time; I took it hours at a time. I scraped together one dollar and fifty cents every day for Adrienne's lunch because she had not qualified for the free lunch program yet. Every night, dinner consisted of spaghetti and canned green beans, which Adrienne grew to hate. Friends gave me money here and there for food or gas. Anya's ex-boyfriend once bought us groceries.

I stopped paying the rent, so I avoided the manager who lived on-site. Soon, the phone and electricity were turned off. My father turned me down when I asked for money, so Anya paid our light bill, but we didn't have a phone for months. When I spotted four twenty-dollar bills hanging out of an ATM machine, I hesitated for a second and then took the money to buy food and Adrienne's Christmas present. Knowing twenty-five dollars was the limit, Adrienne picked out a sparkling disco ball that hangs from her ceiling. Unlike the dead roses, it survived the intense cleaning.

Not long after Christmas, I was diagnosed with Grave's disease[8] after Anya insisted I go to County hospital because I appeared to have a stomach flu. With a pulse of 150 bpm lying down, I was immediately admitted and remained there for five days. I met this male nurse, whose shoulder I cried on my last night there.

"I'm being evicted. I have no lights. No phone. No job. My sister is counting on me," I told him. "I've hit rock bottom." I will never forget what he said.

"No, you haven't. When you hit rock bottom, things start looking up. You're not quite there yet."

At the time, I wanted to hit him, but he was right.

My friends urged me to apply for welfare. Surely, you'll qualify they said. You're sick, unable to work. An Armenian caseworker took one look at my skin color, my college education, and my sister, who was not my biological child, before she turned me down. She said not to count on it. Is this rock bottom? I can't even get food stamps.

Less than two months later, I was broadsided by a tan Sedan; the driver, probably uninsured, left the scene. My old Ford Escort, aptly

---

8 Grave's disease is a type of hyperthyroidism caused by an autoimmune attack on the thyroid gland. Symptoms include nervousness, heat intolerance, insomnia, tremors, weight loss, and rapid heart rate.

named Trouble, lost her passenger window and most of her door too. I didn't have a scratch on me, and Adrienne was not in the car. A piece of cardboard replaced the window, which Adrienne loved to jump through even though the car door still opened. That cardboard represented the white trash side of my mother's family I had been running away from my whole life.

I couldn't find a place for us to live because I had no money, no credit, and every apartment manager ran a credit check. I contemplated moving us into a fleabag motel on Sunset Blvd., the kind where you pay a daily rate. I couldn't imagine leaving Adrienne there alone, something I had to do because I got a new job working as a waitress four nights per week. One night at my crappy job, a customer handed me a business card after hearing about my situation.

"Call Sam," he said, "tell him I sent you."

I lied on the application about never being evicted, Sam didn't run a credit check, and we moved into a studio apartment on Lyman Place in mid-April. As I surveyed the two rooms that would be our home for the next sixteen months, I thought—things are looking up.

*   *   *

Nadia's mother drops off a one-inch pile of papers, research she did about HCC as well as Alternative Medicine. As I skim the documents, I think about the concept of rock bottom. I look at Adrienne watching Scooby Doo, laughing her ass off. Her liver hurts again; it feels tight, she says. She almost threw up earlier tonight, and she has another fever, 99.2 degrees.

I think about how little we have seen Adam; his mother uses Adrienne's illness as an excuse not to send him, as if cancer is contagious. Three years ago, a twelve-year-old Adrienne and six-year-old Adam performed for John and me in this same living room. They rocked out to Queen's "Bohemian Rhapsody"—first with solemn faces and then with air guitars. People assume they are brother and sister even though they look nothing alike. I miss him and wonder how much he understands about what is going on.

I have no job. Yet, I have never worked harder in my life. Tears are always near the surface, but an inner core of strength sucks them back down. Things are not looking up. I cannot face what rock bottom will be this time. I lose myself in research: searching for a clinical trial or herbal medicine that will eradicate the tumors, but somewhere deep inside, a part of me knows the truth.

We're not even close to rock bottom yet.

Adrienne's new haircut © June 2001

Days 29-30

*It was the first time I had heard music like that. Everything was so
amazing! The guitar riffs, the drums, the bass, everything! That summer
[1995] was probably the highlight of my life. It was my first time to a
beach (Santa Monica/Venice . . . the best), my first time riding in a VW
van, my first time surfing, and my first time listening (really listening
with both ear and soul) to music. My favorite bands are still the ones I
listened to back in 1995.*

—Excerpts from Adrienne's journals

Wednesday morning Adrienne wakes up in intense pain, a nine she says.
I feel helpless giving her Tylenol 3, but it's all we have. Since we already
have medical appointments scheduled for today, I call ahead to alert
Dr. No about the recurrence of the liver pain. He is not available, but
someone at the clinic agrees to manage the pain with Dilaudid, which
we can pick up at the clinic, until we see the good doctor tomorrow.
Adrienne nods when I tell her this news. Then she crawls into the car,
already exhausted at eight-thirty in the morning.

We check in at Radiology and pick up the contrast drink needed for
Adrienne's CT scan that morning. The drink is the color of apple juice,
but instead of tasting sweet, the contrast has a bitter, metallic taste. Like
drinking liquid copper. Adrienne takes large swigs of it as we walk over
to the clinic, where her lab work will be done.

A nurse calls out "Emma," which means it is Adrienne's turn. We are
tired of correcting people, so we let it go. Adrienne sits in the designated
chair; I stand. I spot the needle right away.

"There's no need to prick her; she has a central line," I say.

On cue, Adrienne pulls the line out of her bra and lets it hang over
the collar of her shirt.

The nurse stares and then states, "I don't know how to draw blood
from that thing."

"Well then," I say, "find someone who does."

The corners of Adrienne's mouth turn up. A slight smile without teeth, but I'll take it.

After a competent nurse retrieves Adrienne's blood from her line, we leave the clinic and walk back over to Radiology. A cacophony of children's voices echoes from the waiting room.

"Great," says Adrienne.

We step over children, who are crying, muttering in Spanish, and making other indiscernible noises. Somehow, two chairs remain empty, and they are next to each other. I pull out a deck of cards; we have our own ongoing Gin Rummy game. Adrienne is beating me, too. After a few hands, she is bored and draws instead. I try to read but the constant clamor breaks my concentration.

Almost an hour has passed when we hear, "Emma Wilson? Please come to the desk."

Making Adrienne comfortable for the CT scan is no small feat. Lying flat is the most difficult position for her to be in for any length of time. The orderly arranges pillows to ease Adrienne's pain. I wish we had picked up the Dilaudid already. Adrienne removes her metal jewelry: the topaz ring my stepmother gave her on a trip to Arizona, the black leather bracelets with silver clasps Marilyn gave her just because, and the necklace with the fairy pendant she bought at Sav-On.

"Okay, I'm ready now," she says.

Whirr. Whirr. Whirr. The machine that resembles the rim of a giant white tire begins turning. I watch from the observation room where the technicians tell Adrienne what to do. I laugh because Adrienne forgot one piece of jewelry, her leather necklace with a metallic sun pendant. I can see it on the screen. The techs say it's okay as they tell Adrienne not to move and to be still. I know from having a CT scan myself Adrienne can see the flashing lights: three orange, one green, and one yellow. Occasionally, the red light flashes too. It's like being stuck at an intersection with a car that died. You can't move, so you watch the lights change. Whirr. Whirr. Wh . . . irr . . . irr. Like a Ferris wheel, the tire gradually slows down before coming to a stop.

✻ ✻ ✻

Whosshh. The roller coaster sailed by us, barely a whisper, lost in a den of giggling children, chatting adults, and shooting carnival games. Adrienne was sporting a pair of oversized pink sunglasses with blue lenses, so I couldn't see her eyes, but I knew she was having the time of her life. We were standing in the Adventure Dome, an indoor theme park inside of the Circus Circus hotel. She laughed as she ran from one game to another, accumulating a collection of useless junk that would always remind her of this trip.

Dan and I took her to Las Vegas after her first Christmas in Los Angeles. While he was the consummate gambler, Adrienne was the wide-eyed eight year old, dazzled by the sights and sounds of Sin City. We walked the entire strip, letting her sip our watered-down, strawberry margaritas from the Frontier hotel. The Riviera, the Excalibur, the Mirage, we saw them all. Adrienne posed in front of a giant sculpture, her hand touching the chin of a tiger, with a young Siegfried and Roy looming over her. The Scarecrow, Tin Man, Dorothy, and the Lion stood in the background, as Adrienne smiled (without teeth) at MGM's *Wizard of Oz* exhibit celebrating the film's 55th anniversary. It was her only trip to Las Vegas, but it stuck with her. From that point on, Adrienne ordered virgin strawberry margaritas almost every time we went out to dinner.

✶ ✶ ✶

"WBC looks good. Hemoglobin is slightly low. Kidneys and liver are functioning normally," says Dr. No.

He has mastered his flat, neutral voice over three decades. It is Thursday, and we are at our official post-chemo, follow-up appointment.

He does not volunteer the most important piece of information—the CT scan results. When I ask, he looks at me with his sky-blue eyes, his best feature.

"No change."

"No change? Nothing?"

"No," he says, "there is no change."

The words hang in the air before falling fast to the ground. No change, which is better than a bad change, but not as good as "the tumors are smaller now" or "the dots have disappeared from her lungs" or "it's a miracle." No change beats me up and then walks away as if nothing has happened. *Fuck you no change.*

The drone of the doctor's voice brings me back to where we are now. He is saying he does not believe the nausea is chemo-related.

"If not the chemo, what then?" I ask.

He doesn't answer. He switches Zofran for Zantac because he worries Adrienne's body will become acclimated to Zofran, thus rendering it useless. I am doubtful an OTC like Zantac is going to stop the nausea with no known cause, but I don't voice my opinion. Dr. No says to check-in tomorrow at 8 a.m. sharp at 4 West for the second round of chemotherapy.

"Can I go swimming?" asks Adrienne. "My sister said I could take surf lessons this summer."

"Out of the question," Dr. No replies as he looks at me. "Public pools have too many germs, and the ocean's waves are too big. She can wade in a private pool if she's careful."

I hate how he speaks to me instead of Adrienne as if she's not there.

One sister discouraged, the other defeated, we trudge to Adrienne's next appointment.

I flip through a *People* magazine, while Adrienne takes her hearing test. The celebrity gossip bores me now, so I am about to put it back on the table when something tells me to look again, from back to front this time. On the last page, I read an article about Shelley Fabares; the actress received a life-saving liver transplant after suffering for two years from an autoimmune form of hepatitis. I glance at the date on the magazine, November 13, 2000. She must be doing well, I think, because if she had died I would have heard something by now. I tear out the article because it gives me hope. Something tangible to hold onto.

✶ ✶ ✶

During the summer of 1995, Adrienne met my male friend Adrian, who always called me 'Ang' as if my name were Angela or Angelina. It was odd, yet endearing, which sums up Adrian's personality. Add flaky to that description. Adrian and I had been coworkers in college, lovers when it suited us, and mostly friends. I liked him from the moment we met because of his name. I told him my sister's name is Adrienne too, but it ends with –ienne instead of –ian. Cool he had said. To me, it wasn't only cool, but a serendipitous sign I was where I was supposed to be and leaving Adrienne with our mother had not been a mistake. Of all my college friends, Adrian was one of the few who accepted Adrienne on her terms as well as my new role as her parent.

I don't know who liked whom first, but when Adrienne met Adrian, they took to each other right away. Not only did Adrian take Adrienne to Raging Waters, but he also took her to the beach several times that summer. Riding in his VW van, they listened to KROC, LA's top alternative rock station. Adrian introduced her to bands I never listened to such as Jane's Addiction, Blind Melon, Stone Temple Pilots, Spin Doctors, Sound Garden, and Nine Inch Nails. Soon, Adrienne was watching reruns of Woodstock 1994 on MTV. Dave Navarro and Trent Reznor became her heroes. Between the dry heat of Los Angeles and salty waves of the Pacific, Adrian planted a seed. With John's cultivation, Adrienne developed a love for music.

Adrian became the big brother Adrienne never had in Aidan, who lived with her and our mother for less than a year after my father kicked him out of his house for threatening my stepmother. Aidan, who got drunk and vomited in Adrienne's bed. Aidan, who shot seven-year-old Adrienne with a BB gun more than one time. Aidan, who hit Adrienne but called it spanking. When I visited for Christmas that year and saw what was going on, I came unglued. Our mother did nothing. I imagine she was too busy working and popping pills to pay attention. Aidan was bigger than me, but I was stronger. I held him by his throat, pushed him against the wall.

I said, "If you ever, ever, touch Adrienne again, I will kill you." I meant it. Adrienne forgave Aidan long before I was able to.

My relationship with Adrian grew more complicated as he spent more time with Adrienne, who began seeing him less as a brother and more like a father. Long-suppressed feelings surfaced. The way to my heart was through Adrienne, and Adrian had a one-way ticket. One night, Adrian babysat for me so I could go on a date with a handsome lawyer. Adrienne, in rare form that night, refused to speak to my date, dropped to her hands and knees, barked like a dog, and bit him. It was my first and last date with the lawyer. Adrienne had a way of weeding out the assholes. Although she never said as much, I think Adrienne wanted Adrian and me to be together, which coupled with my desire for more than a friendship, led to disaster.

After my car died for the umpteenth time, Adrian agreed to take us to my employer's house for a party. He never showed up. He said he forgot.

Then, he stopped wanting to spend time with Adrienne. Since the warm summer days had fallen behind us, I thought it was too cold to go to the beach, their favorite activity. I asked Adrian to go on a game show with me with the sole purpose of winning money in time for Christmas. Had he stuck to our plan, we would have won the show and walked away with $1500 cash. Instead, we lost. I didn't speak to him for a month.

He promised Adrienne his keyboard for her tenth birthday in April. He would stop by Monday he said. She waited up for him, but true to his nature, he never arrived. Tuesday went by, then Wednesday, and finally on Thursday, he appeared—keyboard in hand, full of apologies. Each night he said he would be there and each night Adrienne stayed awake, looking forward to seeing her favorite person. Flaking on me was one thing, but I couldn't stand by and watch Adrian disappoint Adrienne. Too many people had already failed her, especially men. I ended our friendship with a simple letter and banned him from our lives, an action Adrienne deemed unforgivable.

Wearing a shirt that reads, "Choice not chance determines our destiny," Sharon, one of Adrienne's closest friends, walks in our house around six o'clock that evening. I might have agreed with that slogan a month ago, but now I ask myself, who the hell chooses to have cancer? I don't comment on Sharon's shirt. Instead, I lead her to Adrienne's room where Eli and Adrienne are sleeping. Adrienne opens her eyes when she hears my voice, which after years of teaching is always a bit too loud. She smiles at us with sleepy eyes. Like sunshine pouring into a room after opening the blinds, they reveal an alert mind despite her fatigue. I leave the three teenagers alone, comforted by the pitch of their voices: Sharon a soprano, Adrienne an alto, and Eli a bass.

John stomps through the door an hour later, yelling about that damn truck in his parking spot. My efforts to calm him down are useless. He's in full-blown, temper-tantrum mode. Sharon hears his voice, walks into our kitchen, and apologizes to him. Her cheeks flush with embarrassment, as she tries to make herself disappear by pulling her body into itself. Head down, shoulders up, chest contracted, she slinks out the door to move her truck. Her fear goes unnoticed by John, who is too busy checking on Adrienne to give much thought to anyone else.

Sharon returns, mumbling more apologies. I assure her she did nothing wrong. John overreacted. I don't tell her his outbursts are often a reflection of his own insecurities, and that his superiority complex causes him to hurt people's feelings all the time. Once, he commented how ugly this woman on TV was because she had stretch marks on her breasts. He didn't see Adrienne's reaction or realize the impact his words had on her self-esteem. Last year, he gave me speech lessons for Christmas because he believed I spoke poorly, and this deficiency was hurting my acting career. Most of the time John means well, but sometimes, he's just an ass.

The phone rings.

A male voice asks, "Have you seen my daughter Sharon?"

"Yes, she's here. I'm Andrea, Adrienne's sister. You must be Sharon's father."

My attempt at friendly conversation is met with irritation.

"Put her on the phone," says the man I've never met.

Sharon's father is in town for her graduation, which Adrienne wanted to attend, but can't because of chemo. Sharon nods a few times and hangs up.

"Is everything okay?" I ask.

Sharon says, "Yeah."

She is a terrible liar.

After that phone call, the kids stay in the kitchen with John and me. We talk about graduation and Sharon's college plans until she sobs. I try to meet John's eyes, hoping he can read my thoughts, but he averts my gaze.

Sharon thinks this is the last time she is going to see Adrienne.

I want to shake those thoughts right out of her head.

Stop it. Stop crying. Stay positive.

Adrienne consoles her.

"Don't be sad. You can come visit me for Christmas and stay here with us."

I nod my head in agreement, seconding Adrienne's offer, but I am lying. Either I will be too overwhelmed with Adrienne's medical care or there might not be . . .

STOP IT! I scream at the voice in my head.

Stay positive, dammit.

Sharon's cries are muffled now. She offers Eli, who lives less than ten minutes from us, a ride home. The soft thud of the door closing behind them hits my heart. My back to Adrienne, I take a deep breath. I need to refocus my energy. I turn around.

"I'm going to miss her," says Adrienne.

I want to promise her she will see Sharon again, but I can't. We both know tonight was more than an 'I'm going off to college' goodbye. By saying nothing, we speak the truth.

Unable to afford all of the books I want to buy, I narrow down my first purchase from Amazon to four titles: *Everyone's Guide to Cancer Therapy*, *The Cancer Recovery Eating Plan*, *Childhood Cancer: A Parent's Guide to Solid Tumor Cancers*, and the *Physician's Desk Reference for Herbal Medicines*. From chemotherapy to nutrition, I will learn how to battle the tumors. Squash them. Shoot them like the aliens they are. It will be like that old arcade game, Space Invaders. The tumors will hover over me until I push a button—BAM—BAMBAM—BAM. The books are my ammunition; I will kill one tumor at a time and then continue to the next level, only to start all over again.

Tomorrow, Adrienne will begin her second round of chemotherapy. We have advanced to the next level without killing any of the aliens. The bullets didn't work. The tumors seem to have a force field that protects them from the liquid poison. The only button pushed in this game is the PCA when Adrienne is in pain. I can't shoot the tumors; hell, I can't even see them. I picture them as these pulsating, hissing bubbles of skin, but they probably look far less threatening under a microscope.

Watching Adrienne sleep, I see how much suffering her body has endured at the hands of the enemy. She must lie down at a 45-degree angle. She has almost no hair left. Her skin has lost its natural olive tone. She has a tube in her chest, and she has lost ten pounds so far. We didn't know the tumors existed a month ago. A silent war raged in Adrienne's body; her immune system defenseless against an enemy that had already invaded her lungs. The only signs of trouble were the cessation of her menstrual period and the pain in her right shoulder. Liver cancer represents the worst type of adversary: we can't see it, hear it, or touch it—a quiet, invisible predator just out of our reach.

Adrienne, the first summer she lived in Los Angeles © 1995

Days 31-34

I really want to go to West Hollywood and listen to some tapes while driving there. I haven't had a John and Adrienne bonding drive for awhile. I miss those. 5:29 p.m. It worked. [Adrienne talked John into going to Guitar Center.]

And I found the perfect bass! It's a black Fender jazz with a really slim neck and body, plus, the space between the frets is a little smaller so it's easier for me and my tiny hands to play.

—Adrienne's journal entry dated 2/3/01

I go through our usual morning routine on Friday before leaving for the hospital: flush both lines, clean both caps, and give meds. No Neupogen shot this morning due to chemo. Despite taking Dilaudid, Adrienne's headache continues unabated. We don't know what to expect when we show up at Children's Hospital. Will we have to wait even though she has an appointment for the entire weekend? Or will we be welcomed like a high roller in Vegas returning to his favorite casino? Our return falls somewhere in between. We wait but not too long, and the nurses cheerfully greet Adrienne without saying welcome back. They realize no one likes staying in the hospital.

Not long after Adrienne settles in, a five-year-old girl wanders into the room. She has shiny iridescent dinosaur stickers all over her bald head, which she proudly shows off to Adrienne. Her name is Janelle, and according to her mother, she has been fighting leukemia for two years.

"She's always happy," says the mother, puzzled by her daughter's behavior. "Never complains about the treatments."

Janelle points out the bruises that run up and down her legs, a result of too many Neupogen shots.

Adrienne admires the bruises and says, "You've got me beat. I don't have that many yet."

Janelle grins.

I can see how her smile alone gives her mother strength and hope, not unlike Adrienne. We tell Janelle to visit us any time she wants. She beams and skips out of the room, her mother trailing behind her.

＊ ＊ ＊

Meeting five-year-old Janelle reminds me of when a four-year-old Adrienne wrapped her arms around my thigh, the top of her head even with my hips.

"Don't go Sissy," she said.

It was August 19, 1990: the day I left home. The day I moved 2,000 miles away to go to college. The day I left Adrienne alone with our mother. I don't know how Adrienne understood what was happening, but she seemed to know I was going away for a long time. I hesitated for less than a second, but I couldn't stay in Alabama, not even for her.

I unlocked the vise grip Adrienne had on me and knelt down.

"I'm sorry, kiddo. I have to go to college, but I'll be back for Christmas. Don't worry."

Her eyes welled up, but I don't remember a single tear falling down her cheek. Even then, she was a tough kid. I walked out the door and didn't look back.

I said goodbye at our cousin's house in Haleyville, our mother's hometown, which is eighty miles northwest of Birmingham. Adrienne went there often that summer because our mother worked long shifts at the hospital. I wanted to leave home sooner, but according to our mother, I was her property until I was eighteen. So I waited and I planned. I worked full time, saving every penny. I bought my 1988 Ford Escort from our mother. I sold everything I owned, including all my furniture, my television set, and my bed. After attending a three-day orientation in Los Angeles, I returned home flushed with success at having found a job on campus before school even started. There was no stopping me now.

Mother had hoped my new boyfriend Shane, a good ole Southern boy who said, "Yes Ma'am" and "Yes Sir," would convince me to stay. He loved kids, especially Adrienne, whom he called Pumpkin. What my mother didn't know was Shane kept a fifth of whiskey in his glove compartment and believed all women should stay home, raise kids, and keep their mouths shut. He didn't understand the purpose of higher education. He ended our relationship because I chose school over him.

After Shane's departure, Mother stopped speaking to me unless it was necessary. I was leaving Shane. I was leaving Adrienne. Most of all, I was leaving her. She refused to say goodbye to me. I spent my last night at home packing boxes with the help of two friends. I put a cassette in my stereo, the one item I refused to sell, and danced around singing "Funkytown" which may be the quintessential LA song. I shimmied my hips as I sealed a box with packing tape. I smiled as the boxes piled up in a corner. I left the next day on August 19—four days after my eighteenth birthday. It was time to *move on*.

* * *

Chemotherapy has evolved over the years. Along with the Neupogen, other drugs can prevent or lessen the side effects. Most doctors don't give these cytoprotective agents during the first course because they need an accurate assessment of how one's body reacts to chemo. Now, Dr. No is giving Adrienne amifostine; it will protect her kidneys and hearing, which may be damaged by cisplatin. The amifostine flows through Adrienne's IV, into her central line, and makes its way into her body. She appears relieved. She will still be able to hear her music. Her words reverberate in my head: I would rather be dead than deaf.

I leave the hospital when John and Anya arrive because I have to pick up Little Bit from the vet. The pets are my purview. Just as John refuses to wash dishes, he will not lift a finger when it comes to caring for our pets, especially the cats. I should say cat. We only have one cat now. Our other cat Ebony died last December four weeks after our vet performed surgery. Ebony, an all-black cat with twenty-four toes, was diagnosed with mega colon disease, an incurable condition common in male cats. In a few months, Ebony went from twenty pounds down to ten. The surgery was supposed to help him, maybe give him a few more months to live. He was seven years old, young for a cat. Later, our vet said the drug he prescribed Ebony post-surgery was pulled from the market because it caused heart problems. He blamed the drug for Ebony's demise; I blamed him. Now I wonder if I was too quick to judge. As I drop off Little Bit at home, I can't help wondering how Adrienne is doing.

Always ask about potential side effects. While I am navigating the never-ending Los Angeles traffic, Adrienne is vomiting. Over and over and over. John makes a note: "NAUSEA/VOMITING @ 17:50." The amifostine is vicious; everything comes up. Her dinner, her evening meds. By the time I arrive, the worst of it is over, but Adrienne continues to throw up until after nine o'clock. I ask a nurse why someone didn't warn us. She says something about not telling the patient because the doctor doesn't want a psychosomatic response to cause the side effects to happen, like Adrienne wants to vomit. This explanation makes no sense to me. Why tell us about the side effects of some medications but not others? The nurse lacks an answer for that question.

Over a two-hour period on Saturday morning, Adrienne takes meds with crackers and manages to keep everything down. Zofran and Ativan keep the nausea at bay; her lunch of mashed potatoes and more crackers stays in her stomach where it belongs. Children's Hospital has room service like a hotel. There is a standard menu, and the kids can order anything they want whenever they want if they are not on a restrictive diet. I imagine Adrienne will get bored with the menu at some point, but for now, the novelty of room service has not worn off. Ordering food is one of the highlights of her day.

Adrienne is sharing her room with Whitney, whose cancer, which has spread to her lymph system, has diminished after only one round of chemo. Significant progress. I can hear the words through the thin curtain that separates the two beds. I am jealous of Whitney's prognosis. Her doctors sound so hopeful, not like Dr. No. Whitney is doing well even though she has not left the hospital for more than twenty-four hours since we last saw her due to constant infections. Adrienne's body may be more tolerant of the chemo, but her cancer is far worse. I wish we could trade places. Give Adrienne the cancer that responds to treatment. Fuck no change; I want to hear significant progress. What if we never hear those words?

When Adrienne's psycho doctor Diana comes to visit that day, I tell her about my jealousy, outside of Adrienne's room. She explains to me the five stages most people experience when they encounter trauma: denial, anger, bargaining, depression, and acceptance. These stages can occur in any order at any time. I tell her that John is angry, and I have bargained with god. I don't feel sad though. I ponder denial. The meaning of denial, a refusal to grant the truth of a statement, infers that people cannot be aware of their denial. I acknowledge Adrienne is sick. That's a fact and there is evidence to support it. Therefore, I can't be in denial, can I? I don't know. Then, I realize I don't want or need to know. If I am living in denial, it works for me.

✳ ✳ ✳

I was out of town doing an industrial show for two days when I got a call I never expected to get again. Adrienne was in trouble at school, and the assistant principal Mr. Parrino needed to meet with me right away. Three times in thirteen years is a good record, but I would have preferred to keep it at two.

When she was three, Adrienne punched a boy in the face. The preschool couldn't get in touch with our mother, so a teacher called me at high school and requested I pick up Adrienne early that day. I arrived to find her sitting in a small plastic chair in the corner, staring at the wall. The teacher never asked Adrienne why she hit the boy, but I did.

She replied, "He said 'mommies drop off, and daddies pick up. You don't have a daddy.' Then he laughed at me."

I told the staff they needed to speak to the boy and his parents about how there are different types of families. They nodded their heads in agreement. Then I took Adrienne home.

When she was in the fourth grade, Adrienne hit another boy in the stomach for the same reason. He teased her. She was almost expelled from LA's Best, an after-school program that allows students to stay at school until six o'clock. That incident occurred when I was in the hospital doing the radiation treatment for my thyroid condition. Why did these things happen when I wasn't around? Did Adrienne think she could get away with it? Adrienne was grounded and I made her write a behavioral contract, which I posted on the wall near the kitchen.

Also, we discussed other ways she could have handled the situation. I emphasized words were more powerful than fists. The next time a classmate teased her she remembered my advice. Combing through her extensive vocabulary, she stood on her tiptoes and looked the school bully in the eye.

"Carla, you are a hermaphrodite," said Adrienne.

Not knowing what a hermaphrodite was, Carla felt stupid and never picked on Adrienne again. Later they became friends. Flushed with pride, Adrienne told me about the incident as soon as I picked her up from school that day. We laughed together. Brain beats brawn. No phone call that time.

The third time, I arranged a meeting with the assistant principal. Then, I called Adrienne and demanded a full explanation. She sounded contrite but insisted she didn't know she had done anything wrong. Instead of giving her the 'ignorance of the law is no excuse speech,' I decided to wait and see what Mr. Parrino had to say. He knew me well as a substitute teacher, and he was the same man who said I was being too hard on Adrienne when I couldn't find her after school one day.

"She's a good student. Almost straight A's. She can't be that bad."

I was curious what he was going to say now. Adrienne had challenged his perfect grades equals a perfect child theory.

"You see Miss Wilson. We have a policy at this school about profanity," he said.

I know. I work here.

"The students may not use it in any way."

According to Adrienne, she and her friend had been writing song lyrics on the dry-erase board located inside of her locker. An older teacher spotted the word "fuck" and took both the board and Adrienne to the office for defaming school property. I knew this woman. She was ancient, almost retired, and broke students' pencils for pleasure. I was surprised by my reaction; I didn't allow Adrienne to cuss around me. I knew she did but I liked being in denial about it. However, the teacher overreacted in this situation.

The small office became thick with tension.

"Did Adrienne explain what happened and why she wrote that word?" I asked.

"Yes, she did," said Mr. Parrino. "She even cited the first amendment and evoked her right to free speech."

The corners of my mouth turned up, but I didn't squelch the smile in time. Mr. Parrino caught it.

"You don't seem to take this seriously, Miss Wilson."

I used my I-mean-business teacher-voice to hide the laughter bubbling inside of me.

"I do, but I think this was a misunderstanding. Adrienne made a poor choice, and I will discuss it with her. It won't happen again."

Mr. Parrino's face became red. "She violated school property!"

"No, she wrote a song lyric on her whiteboard, which she bought with her own money. It's her property."

"The locker is school property Miss Wilson," he hissed the sss in Miss.

"You're right but can I please have Adrienne's property back so I can return it to her?" I pointed to the whiteboard, where it lay on his desk. He looked ready to throw it at me.

"Fine," he said.

He thought I was one of those parents who allowed their children to run all over them. After that conversation, Mr. Parrino and I didn't speak much. The perfunctory hello, how are you, but that was it. I never got over his inability to separate the difference between an honest mistake and truly bad behavior.

⁂ ⁂ ⁂

Her coughing wakes me up. Adrienne has mucus in her lungs. Every time she coughs, she clutches her liver. A chest X-ray shows no acute changes. While the staff seems unconcerned about her hacking, they are worried about Adrienne's oxygen intake, which has dropped to 93 percent. The norm for most people is 99 percent. They give Adrienne oxygen through a nasal tube, but it dries out her nasal cavity, so she requests a mask instead. The mask makes it difficult to understand her when she talks. However, the oxygen relaxes her, and the coughing subsides.

To control the pain, a nurse increases the Dilaudid in Adrienne's IV from four milligrams to six milligrams. Then she asks me about the amount of Dilaudid Adrienne received during her first round of chemo. I stare at her. I didn't take detailed notes those first two weeks, not the way I do now.

"Where is Adrienne's chart from May?" I ask.

"We can't find it," she says.

"Isn't it in a computer somewhere?"

"No. Children's Hospital is going through a transition period. Not everything is electronically stored yet."

I think about the nurse who yelled at me when I looked at Adrienne's chart. I think about the paranoid looks I get when I write in our sacred spiral notebook. Now the staff is asking to see my notes because they lost Adrienne's chart.

I tell the nurse, "To my recollection, Adrienne was never given more than six milligrams of Dilaudid every four hours as a continuous drip except when she pushed the PCA for acute episodes of pain."

I speak these words, this medical mumbo jumbo, without thinking. I am one of them now, only without the degree. I hate it.

Adrienne tries to swallow her antibiotic, Bactrim, but the large pill sticks in her throat. She throws up again. Looking through my notes, I discover a pattern. Swallow Bactrim; throw up; repeat cycle. Why didn't I notice this before? I see that last night's dinner of Caesar salad, bread, and crackers stayed in Adrienne's stomach until she took her Bactrim pill at 8 p.m. I tell the doctor on-call, and he recommends a liquid form of the antibiotic in the future. Adrienne likes this idea because she believes the pill is too large for her throat, which causes the gagging reflex. Without the Bactrim, Adrienne can keep down her lunch: chicken nuggets and green beans as well as her dinner: a grilled-cheese sandwich and French fries. I don't care her diet today has mostly consisted of junk food. Any calories are better than none at all.

The lamb in the Children's Hospital gift shop is perfect. It is white, fluffy, about eight inches tall, and has the face of a camel, with large brown felt eyelashes hanging over small black beads that serve as eyes. Maybe it is supposed to be an alpaca, but it passes for a lamb. When I turn the plastic key on its back, the tune "Jesus Loves Me" begins to play. I laugh out loud. People stare at me. I don't owe them an explanation; they wouldn't understand anyway. I buy Sweetfeet, which is the name on the lamb's tag.

Adrienne's eyes light up when she sees the lamb.

"You shouldn't have Sissy. We can't afford it," she says.

"It's okay," I tell her. "Wind it up."

The tune is recognizable, but it comes out slowly as if it hurts the lamb/alpaca to produce this piece of music. We laugh, long and hard. *Jesus Loves Me* represents our crazy Aunt Tootsie, and the absurdity of certain aspects of religion. Then Adrienne notices the lamb's head moves from side to side. Its eyes follow us, like the Mona Lisa.

"Creepy," she says smiling.

Adrienne likes creepy.

Monday is the last day of the second round of chemo. Adrienne enjoys her third PAWS visit with Rondo the Keeshond and Vera the black lab, while I ask Dr. No about current lab results and other types of treatment. We stay in Adrienne's room this time.

- Adrienne's AFP has increased from 1.4 million to 2 million. He assures me this is normal. He wants to see a change on the next CT scan scheduled in three weeks. Then we will know if the chemo is helping at all. *Fuck you no change.*
- I ask about radiation therapy. Not an option for liver cancer he says. The necessary dose to be effective is too high for the body to tolerate. *Scratch that option off the list.*
- I tell Dr. No about the articles I've read about HCC in Japan. He dismisses them outright. Their staging system is different, and many drugs used there are not approved in the United States. *So we may have to leave the country to get the right drugs. Fine.*
- Anya's mother, Dr. Sárközi, read a promising study about Pravachol, a cholesterol-lowering medication, used in conjunction with chemotherapy to treat liver cancer. Dr. No agrees to try Pravachol because it can't hurt Adrienne. *He agreed to this because another doctor recommended it. Figures. No MD after your name = no opinion.*

Dr. No leaves. A nurse gives me the discharge papers; there are six new prescriptions. With Dilaudid replacing Tylenol 3 and liquid Bactrim substituting for the pill, that makes three more than last time. Eleven total. Will the number of medications continue to go up?

- Bactrim (liquid)—By mouth twice a day: 8 a.m., 8 p.m. Antibiotic. *Hopefully, it won't make Adrienne sick like the pill form.*
- Boost—Drink as you want. A nutritional drink like Ensure.
- Dilaudid—By mouth four times per day/as needed: 8 a.m., 2 p.m., 8 p.m., 2 a.m. Painkiller. *Tylenol 3 sure didn't work.*
- Lo/Ovral Tab—By mouth once a day: 8 a.m. Birth control.
- Magnesium—By mouth three times per day: 8 a.m., 4 p.m., 12 a.m. A vitamin supplement to alleviate Adrienne's bone aches.
- Neupogen shot—Subcutaneously once per day: 8 a.m. Medicine to increase white blood cells.
- Nystatin—Swish and swallow four times a day: 8 a.m., 12 p.m., 4 p.m., 8 p.m. Antifungal.
- Peri Colace—By mouth twice a day/as needed: 8 a.m., 8 p.m. Stool softener.

- Pravachol—By mouth once per day: 8 a.m. Cholesterol-lowering medication. *Can't hurt Adrienne, may not help her.*
- Zantac—By mouth twice per day: 8 a.m., 8 p.m. Anti-nausea (new prescription).
- Zofran—By mouth every eight hours: 8 a.m., 4 p.m., 12 a.m. Anti-nausea (still prescribed in case Zantac doesn't work).

We leave the hospital at seven o'clock. After her 8 p.m. meds, Adrienne goes to bed early. She wants to be rested for tomorrow. She will see Dave Navarro perform live on *The Tonight Show.* Maybe she will meet him too.

PAWS visit with Rondo & Vera © June 18, 2001

Day 35

I MET DAVE! AND HE WAS A SWEETHEART!

—Adrienne's journal entry dated 6/25/01

Paulina, the caseworker from IHSS, arrives promptly at 11:30 in the morning. She needs to know what I do for Adrienne and how long it takes me to do it, a formal assessment to determine if we are eligible for services. I worry this visit will be a repeat of the welfare office five years ago. However, Paulina seems concerned. She says she will do whatever she can to help us get the maximum amount, but she never says what that is. We sit at the kitchen table as she explains. If we qualify, Adrienne is essentially my boss and will need to sign my timesheet. Adrienne chuckles. I decide not to question the legality of a minor being my employer. Paulina asks numerous questions, each one beginning with how long does it take you to do _____?

Thrilled our roles have changed, Adrienne participates in the meeting. Dishes take at least twenty minutes every day she says. Sissy helps me bathe every night too. She has to tape up my line, which takes a lot of time. I used to give Adrienne an allowance for her chores, now she will give me a salary for doing the same tasks and more. It's like the movie *Freaky Friday* with a sick twist. I remember reading in one booklet the sick child should continue doing his chores to maintain a normal routine. What a joke. Normal left us thirty-five days ago.

A check arrives several weeks later, but since Paulina backdated the application, we were officially approved on June 6. A form printed on legal-size, cheap, carbon-copy paper explains in detail how I spend 73.7 hours per month taking care of Adrienne. The precise breakdown of the tasks amuses me. According to IHSS, each week it takes me:

- 2.33 hours to prepare meals;
- 1.17 hours to clean up after meals;

- 0.83 hours to shop for food, do other errands, and wash clothes;
- 2.33 hours to care for bowels and bladder;
- 1.75 hours to assist with respiration;
- 1.75 hours to feed and dress Adrienne;
- 1.05 hours to help Adrienne in/out of bed, seats, and our vehicle;
- 4.67 hours to bathe and groom Adrienne; and
- 0.69 hours to transport her to medical appointments.

Multiply the total times 4.33 and then add an extra 2 hours more per month for additional domestic services. The person who produced this formula must have been a man. If I could accomplish all those things in 73.7 hours per month, I would be a speed freak, a superhero, or an alien. IHSS pays me less than $250 every two weeks after taxes. Not much but it helps.

Adrienne takes a two-hour nap after Paulina leaves. When she wakes up, she has a fever of 99.5 degrees. No nausea though. We have to be at NBC studios in forty-five minutes. Adrienne looks so tired, but I don't dare suggest we don't go. She is busy dusting her face with glitter powder, and she has already changed into her favorite T-shirt, which has a picture of Ana Voog, a webcam star, on it. Eli shows up wearing Adrienne's old T-shirt, a smiling Mickey Mouse wearing a red suit and matching top hat dancing on top of the words *Walt Disney's World on Ice*. I bought that shirt for Adrienne when she was ten, yet it fits Eli. He's a skinny kid. Eli reminds me of the character Edward Scissorhands, minus the scissors of course but with the same crazy hair. Adrienne loves that movie, classic Tim Burton, her favorite director.

Located on Bob Hope Drive, NBC is less than ten minutes from our house. I pull into the gate; we are on the list along with five other missing people.

"Says here, you have eight guests," the guard comments.

He peers into my CRX, a car that seats two people. Eli lies in the back. I want to joke about the others hiding in my nonexistent trunk by wearing Harry Potter's Invisibility Cloak.

Instead I say, "Sorry about that. There are only three of us."

The guard shrugs.

"Park over there."

He points toward the general parking lot.

"Have fun."

I plan to drop Adrienne and Eli off at the front entrance because I worry the walk will be too long for her. Then, I see a golf cart following me; the driver motions for me to park so I do. He drives us to the studio where we are treated like royalty. The driver hands us off to a page who escorts us to the Green Room, a waiting room for the show's guests. Only no celebrities are in here. Adrienne sits down and sips Gatorade and water, while Eli and I indulge in the munchies. I try to entice Adrienne into eating one of the perfectly ripe strawberries, but she refuses. No appetite. Typical after a round of chemo.

Another page takes us to our seats. Adrienne and Eli sit in the second row, with her in the aisle seat. I sit directly behind her. Our seats are house left, stage right, in front of where all the musical guests perform. Adrienne spins around in the swirly chairs. As the rest of the audience filters in, I make her put on her thin yellow mask. The sign at the hospital says Adrienne has to wear her mask in public, especially when surrounded by strangers. At four o'clock sharp, the show starts.

Over the speakers, we hear Ed Hall's booming voice.

"Tonight, Jay welcomes coach of the world champion LA Lakers, Phil Jackson."

Thundering applause. The Lakers won their second national championship last week.

"And from the new movie *The Fast and the Furious*, actress Michelle Rodriguez."

Who?

"The music of Dave Navarro."

High-pitched screams of delight.

"And now . . . Jay Leno!"

Jay strolls out, shaking hands as people rush the stage. At the last minute, Adrienne runs up, but she doesn't get to the stage in time. The music fades out as Jay steps back to begin his opening monologue.

Jay discusses the recent blackouts in Los Angeles. I've been so focused on Adrienne I forgot about LA's current power crisis. It seems like we have one every year. Like today, the temperature rises to over 100 degrees. People blast their air conditioning. BOOM. Lights out. Burbank has its own power supply, so our lights have stayed on.

Adrienne nods off when Jay talks about the Lakers. LA doesn't have a professional football team, so we hang our athletic hopes on the Lakers and the Dodgers. We get so excited when our precious Lakers win, we throw them a parade. It was yesterday. I love basketball, even the Lakers, but a parade? Jay jokes only the unemployed showed up because who could get off work on a Monday to attend a parade. People laugh.

More jokes and news of the day follow. The first ever Hip Hop Summit occurred, former President Clinton played golf with Jack Nicholson, and Melissa Etheridge admitted in her new book that Brad Pitt, not David Crosby, was the first choice for a sperm donor for her children with her former life partner. Judging by the noise, the audience loves that comment. Who wouldn't want Brad Pitt? He could turn a straight man gay by removing his shirt, or a gay woman straight.

Then Jay says, "According to a new study, 60 percent of doctors lie to their seriously ill patients when they ask how long they have to live."

I sit up and lean in.

"Really want to know the truth? Schedule your next appointment six months from now. If your doctor goes 'Yeah, right' then you know—hey." Jay shrugs.

People laugh. My stomach turns over. With Jay's timing, delivery, and physical gestures, the joke is funny. I would have snickered myself six weeks ago, but now all I can think is—who are these doctors? I look around. Why are people still laughing?

A commercial break. A page asks Adrienne if she needs anything.

"Some matzah crackers would be great," she says.

She feels nauseous. After a segment called Badly Named Products, there is another commercial break. The page brings Adrienne a brand-new box of matzah crackers and a bottle of water. Did someone run to the store and buy the crackers for her? If we were in a restaurant, I would give a huge tip. In most places in Los Angeles, this level of service does not exist.

Phil Jackson walks on stage. He towers over Jay by six inches or more. I knew Phil was a former basketball player, but he does not look that tall on TV. Jay suggests Phil wear all ten of his national championship rings at one time.

"Go out like Mr. T.," says Jay.

Besides reveling in the Lakers' recent victory, Phil is promoting his new book, *More than a Game*. Jay says nice things about it.

The antithesis of David Letterman, Jay radiates optimism and kindness. If he doesn't have anything positive to say about a celebrity's new book, movie, TV show, or album, he doesn't say anything at all. Yet he always finds something nice to say and manages to sound genuine. Makes me wonder if he ever spent time in the South. We Southerners strive to be pleasant people. Adrienne slept during most of Phil's time, but she forces herself to wake up as the prospect of Dave's appearance nears. Musical guests perform at the end of the show.

Unfortunately, we have to sit through Michelle Rodriguez first. Wearing a black denim vest as a shirt and black leather pants, Michelle plops down in the seat next to Jay. I notice the third button on her vest is about to pop because the garment is too small for her. Maybe she is nervous, but Michelle tries too hard to be cool by sniffing her armpits and dismissing her bad behavior in school. We withstand her giggling.

Finally Jay says, "We'll be back with David Navarro."

* * *

John says Adrienne has a Jesus thing with rock stars: Dave Navarro, Chris Cornell, and Trent Reznor. They all resemble the son of god. She discovered their music on her own, but it was John who introduced Adrienne to the rock star who became her god—Freddie Mercury of Queen.

During her first year of middle school, Adrienne tried hard to fit in with others. Her friends consisted of three girls who had known each other since kindergarten. Adrienne was the new kid. She joined spirit squad, a precursor to cheerleading, because they did. She dressed in pastels, collared shirts, and wore khakis because they did. Looking back, I think she let her infamous bangs grow out because her friends didn't have bangs. I could see her struggling to find a balance between her new friends' tastes and her own identity.

Adrienne already knew what type of music she liked, but her friends didn't listen to KROC. She listened to their music, pop music. Her favorite boy band became 98 Degrees, a slight deviation from the more popular Backstreet Boys and NSYNC. John teased her even when I pointed out every decade has its share of boy bands. The Beatles just had more talent and lasted longer. John let the issue go until he heard the popular song "Wannabe" blasting through her speakers.

"Oh no," he said. "Not the Spice Girls. No way."

That's when he introduced her to Freddie.

The obsession developed slowly. She bought Queen albums and videos. She accumulated 140 pictures of Freddie Mercury and taped some of them to her bedroom walls. She joined the Queen International Fan Club. When an extra eighty dollars showed up on the phone bill, Adrienne claimed she didn't know it was an international call even though the club is in London. She took months to pay off that debt with her small allowance. For her twelfth birthday, Adrienne wanted "In Honor of Freddie" on her birthday cake. I didn't see the harm in it. Her favorite songs were "Killer Queen" and "Another One Bites the Dust." She read Freddie Mercury's biography, *The Show Must Go On*. Her devotion to Queen didn't seem unusual for a preteen girl, so I never worried about it. Then, I found the note a few months later, a dry, hot day in August 1998.

During that summer, twelve-year-old Adrienne spent most days at the Boys and Girls Club, while John and I were at work. I had three jobs that summer, so I expected Adrienne to help more around the house. Tired of not being able to see her floor, I insisted she clean her room. She was about to visit our mother in Alabama for three weeks, and she needed to do her laundry and pack. I gave her an ultimatum: she had a week or I would do it myself. Seven days passed, and she did nothing. I marched into her room on the eighth day, trash bag in hand, and sorted through the piles of paper, clothes, CDs, and other junk littering the floor. The note was buried deep. It was one page, typed and single-spaced; the title compelled me to sit down.

SUICIDE NOTE/APOLOGY
I, Adrienne Wilson have committed suicide. I have not been murdered. I have done this as a sacrifice to my only and ultimate god, Freddie Mercury. Let me explain, for almost half a year now I have been a member of a religion that I invented. The god in this religion is Freddie Mercury.

The note continued with what this religion gave Adrienne and how she would like to be cremated with her ashes spread over Freddie's house in London. Halfway through, it became a will stating who should get what. Adam would get her room; I would get most of her artwork.

I don't remember when my body started trembling or when tears started pouring down my face. I do remember my primeval screaming of NO, NO, NO! I called John at work. He didn't believe me at first.

Hysterical, I yelled at him, "Listen to this."

I read most of the note to him until he stopped me.

"I'm coming home."

Then I called in sick. I was supposed to work that afternoon.

Waiting for John, I read Adrienne's journals at the kitchen table. She was always writing in them. I had never invaded her privacy before. Lines jumped out at me. "I am planning my suicide for November 24, 1998." "I am not committing suicide this year, but I will on the same date in whatever year Freddie wants me to." Why do I know that date? Then I remembered. Freddie Mercury died from complications due to AIDS on November 24, 1991. As her obsession grew, the journal entries increased. From a few times a week, to every day, to several times a day. "I'm beginning to frighten myself with my obsession." "Sissy is a hypocritical bitch! I hate her! As much as mom, if not more."

How did this happen? What did I do wrong? What now?

After John came home and read everything, we decided to wait for Adrienne instead of picking her up. She walked home from the Boys and Girls Club in the late afternoon. We were going to confront her, an intervention of sorts. We left the note and her journals on the kitchen table, where she would see them right away. We sat and watched the clock.

I kept thinking; the note never mentioned how Adrienne planned to do it. *Should I remove any razor blades from the house? What about pills?* I thought about the book my best friend and I talked about writing in high school. *101 Ways to Kill Yourself.* Our theory was most people didn't get it right the first time so they should combine methods. Pills and carbon monoxide. Or heroin and a gun like Kurt Cobain. We were halfway kidding. Just crazy teenager talk. Nothing like Adrienne's note, which seemed sincere, purposeful, definite.

Adrienne saw both cars in the driveway so she must have known something was wrong. She walked in nonchalantly.

"What's up?" she asked.

"Sit down," I said, as John remained silent.

I pushed the note across the table.

"We need to talk about this."

First, she feigned surprise as if she didn't type the note. I expected that reaction. In her journals, she stated her greatest sin was lying. Then, Adrienne switched to anger. How dare I go through her things? Finally, she broke down. Sobbing, she admitted it was true. The suicide plan, the religion, and the obsession she couldn't stop. We hugged her. Looking at John, I knew we needed help. This thing was bigger than us.

I grabbed the yellow pages and looked for therapists who specialized in teenagers. Despite the notarized document signed by our mother giving me temporary custody, no one would treat Adrienne because I didn't have legal custody of her. Finally, The Center for Individual and Family Counseling agreed to see Adrienne while I worked on the custody situation. I explained to Adrienne that her first appointment, called an intake, was scheduled for the following week.

Next, I called our mother and canceled Adrienne's trip to Alabama. Adrienne could not get on that plane tomorrow. I feared she would hurt herself since our mother never paid attention.

"An emergency has come up," I said. "No, she can't come out this summer. Maybe later. The ticket will be good for a year."

The ticket expired. Adrienne decided to never see our mother again. I didn't tell our mother what happened because I knew she would blame me. Hell, I blamed myself.

✷ ✷ ✷

Adrienne can't wait to see Dave Navarro sweat. He appears out of nowhere. A hushed silence falls over the audience. The lights bounce off his all-black attire: wife-beater shirt, leather pants, and leather boots. Tattoos cover his arms; most of them are black too. His blue-sequined wristbands, silver chain-link necklace, and white electric guitar complement his black wardrobe and dark features. He sings that he hates his life as the lyrics from his hit single "Rexall" pour out of his mouth.

Dave coaxes his guitar into a riff at the end of the song. He finishes by tossing his guitar behind him, as if it means nothing, on the zebra-patterned rug that covers the makeshift stage.

Rushing up a few stairs to the real stage, Dave sits for his turn with Jay. They discuss cars and motorcycles. Jay asks about Dave's many tattoos.

Dave replies, "I was seventeen and thought I was cool."

Jay wishes Dave a Happy Birthday; it was on June 7. The numbers are tattooed on Dave's knuckles: VI VII VI VII. Jay props up Dave's solo album *Trust No One* on his blue mug and sings its praises. Then, the show ends.

Phil, Michelle, and Dave leave the stage. Jay asked us on a commercial break if we wanted to take pictures with him after the show, so a page takes us on stage to meet Jay. Adrienne looks at me, I nod, and she takes off her mask. A photographer from NBC says smile, an unnecessary request since all of us are beaming. *FLASH. FLASH.* I hope I didn't blink.

Jay asks, "Are you a big fan of David's?"

"Huge!" says Adrienne.

Jay laughs and gives her the *Trust No One* CD.

Then he says, "Oh, so you came to see the cool rock star, not the dorky host, huh?"

Adrienne hesitates because she doesn't want to be rude.

"Well, yeah."

Jay laughs again. "Well hold on a second."

He grabs a page.

"Bring Mr. Navarro out to the stage because a young lady would like to meet him."

I didn't think it was possible for Adrienne's smile to get any bigger, but I swear I can see her back molars now. I silently thank Jay for making Adrienne's dream come true.

Like most celebrities, Dave Navarro is smaller in person than he appears on TV. He is the epitome of the skinny rocker guy with charisma oozing out of his pores. When he first meets Adrienne, she can't speak. I nudge her.

"I'm Adrienne. Remember me? We talked online. I'm the girl who got sick."

Adrienne said she and Dave talked online many times, but I never believed her. I figured she was chatting with someone pretending to be Dave Navarro. I didn't think celebrities took the time to talk one on one with their fans. I was wrong. Dave remembers her.

Eli, Adrienne, Dave, and I pose for the camera. *FLASH.* One more says the photographer. *FLASH.* I notice Dave doesn't smile, but Adrienne does, with and without teeth. As we stand there, Dave rubs Adrienne's back with his right hand. Not in a weird way. It almost seems like a habit. Maybe it's his way of connecting with people. Adrienne doesn't care. Her idol is touching her, comforting her.

"This is for you," says Adrienne.

She hands Dave a letter she rewrote at least ten times.

"I want you to have my talisman too. It kept me going in the hospital."

She takes off her fairy necklace, her good luck charm.

"Ah thanks, but are you sure? I mean, do you really want to part with this?" asks Dave.

Adrienne smiles, "I'll feel better knowing you'll have it."

As she puts the necklace in his hand, she sees the sparkling blue sequins.

"Your wristbands are the same color my hair used to be."

Dave jumps on her comment.

"Here, here. Take them please."

Dave peels off the wristbands, which are wet with perspiration. Adrienne says thank you over and over.

While Adrienne and Dave are talking, I thank Jay and then wander over to the other side of the stage where the band plays. The bandleader, Kevin Eubanks, introduces himself. I thank him, too, since he is responsible for procuring some of the many tickets we got for the show.

"What kind of cancer does she have?" he asks.

I explain what it is and what's happened so far.

Then Kevin asks, "What's the prognosis?"

I hate that question. I look at him. I can feel my throat closing, water rushing into my eyes.

"Not good," I say.

His body jerks; his eyes widen. He looks at Adrienne, who is talking, laughing, standing.

"She's . . . so . . . alive. She doesn't look sick."

I nod.

"I know."

I follow Kevin's eyes. We watch Dave as he hugs Adrienne and gives her a big kiss on the cheek. It must be time to go.

Eli, Adrienne, and I are ushered out of the building through the artist's entrance. I tell Adrienne to put her mask back on as we walk outside. Dave watches while his people load his musical equipment, and a black limo waits for him. A famous collector, Jay's red 1920s Indy Racecar is parked right next to the door. We take more pictures with our own camera this time.

"Sissy, the mask?"

"You have to keep it on," I say with my don't-argue-with-me voice.

I know she is frowning underneath the mask because her eyebrows scrunch together.

"I'm sorry for bugging you for more pictures," says Adrienne to Dave.

"No, it's no big deal. Don't worry. Look, I've got your necklace on."

He even poses for a shot with Adrienne's letter in his mouth.

"Take care of yourself, okay?" says Dave as he gives her one last hug.

Adrienne nods and smiles.

Our limo, a golf cart, shuttles us back to my car. I don't remember talking much on the way home except for Adrienne saying how green Dave's eyes are. I think Eli is jealous because he says nothing. Ever since Dave touched her, Adrienne has ignored Eli. She doesn't mean to; she is caught up in the moment. I don't say that to Eli, but I hope he understands. Adrienne needed today to happen. Meeting Dave did more for her than chemo did. *Fuck no change.* There is a change—in her spirit. Adrienne seems happier, more hopeful. She wants to live.

Adrienne and Andrea meeting Dave Navarro on The Tonight Show © June 19, 2001

Days 36-40

I'm not the same anymore. Nothing is. Nothing ever will be.

—*Adrienne's journal entry dated 6/6/01*

Getting Adrienne's lab results while she was in the hospital proved difficult. I wasn't sure how strong her immune system was yesterday. Being around so many strangers could have been risky, but as it turns out, she was fine except for her low hemoglobin. She is anemic but she won't receive a blood transfusion unless her hemoglobin drops below nine. Despite her high WBC, Adrienne feels lousy. A low-grade fever persists throughout the day. Her pulse is 108–110 beats per minute. She keeps saying something doesn't feel right. I chalk everything up to exhaustion. She didn't rest after chemo; instead, she experienced the best day of her life. Feeling exhilarated must have burned enormous amounts of energy. Adrienne sleeps all day and then she sleeps another eleven hours that night. Jay and Dave wiped her out.

Like most pain medication, Dilaudid causes severe constipation. Adrienne takes Peri-Colace, a stool softener, twice a day, but it doesn't seem to be working. Now I must keep track of every time she poops. One smiley face equals one bowel movement. Adrienne doesn't think my coding method is funny. The goal is one smiley face per day. Stripped of all dignity, I am now stalking Adrienne every time she goes to the bathroom. Before I can even ask, she'll say something like nope, not yet. Fighting the side effects of the medication proves to be as difficult as fighting the cancer itself.

The unnecessary but preventative antibiotic continues to harm Adrienne. Even in its liquid form, Adrienne throws up within hours after taking Bactrim. Cheese quesadilla, Doritos, fruit—it all comes up. There must be an alternative. Aren't there dozens of antibiotics on the market? I call the hospital and the doctor on-call recommends Pentamidine,

144

a medication administered once per month at the clinic. He also prescribes Ativan for nausea and anxiety. Adrienne smiles as I pour the rest of what I consider poison down the sink.

On slow days, when there are no doctor appointments or in-home nurse visits, we measure time around Adrienne's medication schedule.

8 a.m.: Give Neupogen shot, flush lines, change dressing, or change the caps on Adrienne's central line depending on the day. Make breakfast. Give meds. Watch TV. Usually repeats of *Law and Order*, my soap opera *The Young and the Restless*, or cartoons. Adrienne folds her body into the only piece of furniture in our living room: a beige, suede chair. Donated, of course.

12 p.m.: Make lunch. Take more meds. Adrienne naps. I read about liver cancer or do research on the Internet. Sometimes we watch movies in the afternoon. This week we watch the four-hour Emmy-nominated television movie *Me and My Shadow* over several days. Alex got us an advance copy, one of the many benefits of having a friend who works in casting. The film, starring Judy Davis and based on Judy Garland's life, is excellent, but we drift off after a while. Adrienne's head rests on one arm of the chair while her legs hang over the other one. I lie on the floor with my head on a pillow, uncomfortable but too exhausted to care.

4 p.m.: Make snack if Adrienne is hungry. Take meds. Sort through mail. Gifts continue to arrive: cards, books, stuffed animals, and gift cards from Blockbuster, Barnes & Noble, and Virgin Records. A bible arrives every other week or so, usually from someone with good intentions but who doesn't know Adrienne well. The bibles remain untouched in a stack on Adrienne's floor.

The small, worn bible that sits on top was a gift from Victor, an actor I worked with on two occasions. We became friends despite our different religious beliefs. Victor is a devout Christian. John sang and played guitar at Victor's wedding last fall. I allowed Victor to visit because I trusted him. He gave Adrienne his bible explaining how much strength he drew from reading it. Then he prayed over Adrienne. When he raised his hands and began speaking in tongues, Adrienne shot me a look. I was as surprised as she was, but I didn't stop him.

Later Adrienne said, "He scared me Sissy. It reminded me of going to church with Aunt Tootsie."

I feel guilty. I saw the fear on her face and did nothing. That moment taught me something: when people feel helpless, they often do things that make them feel better without any thought to the person in the situation. Victor meant well but praying and speaking to god was for him, not Adrienne. He knew we were not a religious family, but it didn't matter. Victor believed prayer was all he had to offer, and Adrienne needed it.

Some people, like Alex's mother Ellen, use their talents well and give Adrienne cool homemade presents. Ellen made two neck rolls that alleviate pain in the neck and shoulders. The pink satin one has lavender and flax seed inside of it while the blue fleece one contains rice and cinnamon. Heat three minutes in the microwave and experience instant relief. Ellen also sent Adrienne a vaporizer, which purifies her room. Adrienne has two favorite gifts: a small, square blue pillow with a white cat on it embroidered by Ellen and a sticker from a friend that reads, "It's Called THINKING, You Might Try It Some Time."

Adrienne's report card comes in the mail this week. The perfect GPA, a 4.0, is no surprise, but the twenty absences listed for the second semester seem to leap off the paper and smack us in the face.

"Wow. I almost never miss school," says Adrienne.

We ponder the one absence listed for the first semester. Then Adrienne remembers what happened. Someone called in a bomb threat to Burbank High so I didn't allow her to go to school that Friday.

"I think bombs and illness (I can't bring myself to say cancer) are legitimate reasons for missing school," I say.

Adrienne doesn't respond.

Next, we wait for John to get home. I envy how much Adrienne looks forward to his arrival. Spending all day, every day, with me gets on her nerves. I make dinner while John does hand duty. He sits in one of our generic, wooden kitchen chairs, which is next to Adrienne's bed. As I stir the soup in the pot and hear their voices drifting down the hall, I think how we wouldn't even have kitchen chairs if I hadn't bought the dining room set at IKEA with no help from John. He earns three times what I do, but we split our house bills fifty-fifty. John won't spend money on furniture though, except for the TV stand, which he deemed necessary.

8 p.m.: Finish dinner. More meds. Wash dishes. Do cat litter. Watch TV. Prepare Adrienne's bath at nine o'clock. I keep the Ziploc bags and duct tape in her bathroom. I check my email. After bathing, Adrienne

goes online to instant message her friends or to write in her live journal. John works on his music. Some things have not changed at all, except Adrienne brushes her teeth without arguing now. Cancer has not made her less stubborn, but she discovered something recently that makes her want to brush her teeth, a cheap electric toothbrush. Who knew it could be that simple?

"I love the way it feels on my teeth, Sissy."

She peels her lips back and meticulously brushes each tooth. I still can't convince her to floss though, one battle at a time.

12 a.m.: Wake Adrienne up if she falls asleep early. Take nighttime meds. Make her go to bed if she stays up late talking online. Collapse into bed after taking a shower. At the hospital, it's hard to sleep with the bright lights and constant noise, but at home, my brain turns off at midnight and begs for rest. For the first time in my life, I sleep well for nights at a time. I don't remember my dreams anymore, which used to wake me up in the middle of the night or leave me feeling tired the next day. My insomnia started in childhood along with the vivid dreams. Mental fatigue, however, proves to be more powerful than my creative subconscious. I've never felt more rested and more exhausted at the same time. I need sleep the way our mother needs drugs.

No one can find our house. We have an address that doesn't make any sense, 1624 Landis Street. Our house is on San Fernando Road; it's not even on the corner of Landis. We rarely get packages from FedEx or UPS, and one time when our regular mail carrier went on vacation, we didn't get mail for a week. Just when a pizza delivery guy can find our place without directions, he quits, and we have to start all over with a new person. I believe the city of Burbank didn't want to give a residence a numeric address on San Fernando Road because it is primarily a business district. I can't prove my theory, but after living here for almost four years it's easier to avoid deliveries altogether.

As a result, I drive over to Home Health Pharmacy to pick up Adrienne's medical supplies once or twice a week. The workers know my face now; they smile and hand me the large paper bag marked "Emma Wilson." I open it, check the contents, and sign the invoice. When the sharps container is full, I have to bring it here so they can dispose of the needles. An employee usually reminds me they deliver, but I say no thank you. We are lucky. The pharmacy is less than a mile from our house, near the Burbank Animal Shelter where Adrienne and I often go to spend time with the homeless dogs and cats. I can't remember the last time we went there.

I leave the pharmacy and stop by the local liquor store. After buying some soda, I jump into my car, push the clutch, turn the ignition, and shift into reverse without looking behind me. The sickening crunch makes me close my eyes. In an effort to get back to Adrienne, I have hit someone again. The dread rises like bile in my throat. The tears sneak up on me and hide in the corners of my eyes. I take a deep breath and get out of my car.

Even though my heart races, my stomach becomes less knotted when I see the driver and his vehicle. The man is dark-skinned, older, and dressed in worn jeans. His pickup truck appears as exhausted as he is. My voice wavers.

"I'm so sorry. I didn't see you."

"No," he says. "I am sorry. I not see you."

We examine our respective vehicles.

"I see nothing," says the man.

He is correct. Despite backing squarely into each other, our cars suffered from a minor exchange of paint jobs. A few specks of color are the only evidence of our collision.

"My car's fine," I say to him.

"Mine too," he says.

"Okay?" I ask.

"Okay," he smiles.

He hurries back to his truck and drives off. I don't think he has insurance, and I don't care.

Adrienne wakes up on Saturday and feels good. I make her a breakfast shake with the blender we bought solely for this purpose.

"What do you want in it?" I ask.

"Everything!" she says.

She sucks down her fruit shake, which contains cherries, blueberries, blackberries, and strawberries as well as banana, pineapple, ice cream, milk, and Royal Jelly, a natural supplement that boosts the immune system. When she gets her period today, Adrienne rides out the nausea that comes with it. All that natural sugar must have increased her energy because her counts shouldn't be up yet. She likes the shake so much I

148

decide she should have one for breakfast every morning, a welcome addition to our daily routine.

* * *

Money has always been a contentious subject in our family. If my dad had not offered to help us, I would be drowning in debt right now. I hate asking him and my stepmother Ava for money because for a long time they believed I would become my mother—a manipulative, conniving woman who commits fraud as easily as most people tie their shoes. Since leaving Adrienne at home alone was not an option, I would have begged for their assistance, but I didn't have to. Their unsolicited financial aid was the best gift they could have given us.

Three years ago, I called them crying, pleading for help to get full custody of Adrienne. I only waited as long as I did because I never had the money to hire a lawyer, and I knew the older Adrienne was, the more likely her opinion would matter to the court. However, when Adrienne became suicidal and began counseling with Diana, getting legal custody became a top priority. Dad and Ava paid for the lawyer, which cost $1,800. Not a lot of money as far as attorney's fees go, but far more money than I made in a month.

Custody battles usually take place in the jurisdiction where the child currently lives, which worked to our advantage. After a court-appointed inspector interviewed John, Adrienne, and me in our home, she filed her report. I never saw it but we must have passed the test because we appeared in court the following month. Mother never showed up. I didn't expect her to. I am sure Mother claimed she didn't have the financial resources to get to California, but now we know that's a lie since she was getting a check for Adrienne every month. Maybe Mother said her failing health prevented her from jumping on a plane to get her daughter back, but the reason for her absence didn't matter. Due to our mother's abandonment, the court granted me full legal custody of Adrienne.

Days 41-44

*Every fucking moment after this cancer is dead I am going to be alive.
I'm going to every fucking weekend show I can afford. I'm going to
theme parks and swimming pools, taking hiking trips and camping
adventures. I'm gonna mingle with club goers. I am going to be friends
with Mr. Navarro and Jane will play a private show in my living room.
I will be reborn. I will fight this, pills and all, and it will not kill me. I will
be drop dead gorgeous—even if I don't have hair. I will help people who
have to go through this. I will be amazing and impossible to avoid. ALL
OF THIS SHIT IS TEMPORARY, PAIN IS NOT REAL, CANCER DOES
NOT SURVIVE IN ME.*

—Adrienne's journal entry dated 6/28/01

Adrienne's blood counts recover quickly, but the numbers are not as high
as before. In three days, the Neupogen does its job, shooting her WBC
and ANC through the roof. However, her hemoglobin remains low. What
did that nurse say in our parent orientation class?

"If the hemoglobin is 9 or below. Or in that range."

I realize Adrienne will need a blood transfusion soon. I decide not to
ask the doctors about it; the less time Adrienne spends at the hospital
the better.

I receive an unexpected phone call. A producer I know from a previous
job is working on a new version of the game show *Card Sharks*. She offers
me a spot as a contestant. I agree to do it because the grand prize is cash,
up to $50,000. The numbers dance in my head as I think of all the pos-
sibilities: fly to another country to get Adrienne different drugs, travel
to Ireland so Adrienne can see real sheep, hire Dave Navarro to jam with
Adrienne at our house. Maybe even . . . find a cure.

With Jared watching Adrienne, I leave early in the morning to go to
the studio. The production assistant (PA) shows us old episodes of *Card*

Sharks and gives us a tour of the set. Then, we wait. I brought one of my many cancer books to read. Someone asks about the book; I tell him about Adrienne.

"What's the prognosis?" he asks.

My lower lip trembles. *Why do people ask that question? If the prognosis were good, I would have told you already.*

"Not great," I say as I turn back into my book.

By lunchtime, we have not taped a single episode. The PA apologizes. First day she says. Some technical difficulties. By two o'clock, two people from our small group are selected to be contestants in the first taping. We watch on a monitor. Like the card game *War* I played as a kid, *Card Sharks* is mostly luck mixed with a little strategy.

"Is the next card going to be . . . higher or lower?" asks the host.

The studio audience screams, "Higher!"

Winning this game will be the easiest thing I've done all week. All I have to do is count the cards. I'm more competitive than anyone I know.

Mother stopped playing card games with me because she said, "You play too much like your father. Out for blood."

Isn't that the point? To win?

At a holiday party a few years ago, my team demolished the other team in what was supposed to be a friendly game of *Taboo*. Jumping up and down, I taunted the losers.

"We killed you guys. Killed."

No one in that group ever played *Taboo* with me again.

The next two people are called in for the second taping. I watch the clock. Past three. We're running out of time; we were supposed to be done by four. At a quarter till, the PA rushes in.

"I'm sorry, guys. We're out of time."

You've got to be kidding me.

"Out of time?" I say. "I spend the entire day away from my sick child, and all you can say is 'we're out of time'?"

The PA looks contrite.

"Oh, you can definitely come back for the next taping on another day. Don't worry; you'll be on the show."

"You think I would come back and waste another day waiting to be on this show. Forget it. Fuck you for wasting my time."

My shoes slap against the thin carpet as I stomp down the stairs.

I know it's not the PA's fault. She doesn't understand. All I can give Adrienne is my time.

✳ ✳ ✳

Neglect: to give little attention. To leave unattended. The older Adrienne got, the less time our mother gave her. By age six, she ran wild around their neighborhood, playing in the nearby woods, hiding in the gutters, and swimming unattended in the community pool. I taught Adrienne how to swim after seeing a special on a news show, maybe it was *60 Minutes*. With her diaper soaking up every ounce of water, a fourteen-month-old Adrienne kicked her feet and breathed underwater like the show said she would. Since she was a natural fish, I'm sure our mother never worried about her swimming alone. Mother forgot fish swim fast to get away from predators.

Adrienne told me about their neighbor, a man named Mark. He approached her in the swimming pool. He was probably friendly at first. When I pushed Adrienne to describe him to me, all she said was he wasn't too young or too old. He touched her on more than one occasion, and she knew it wasn't right. Playing unsupervised and having a mother who didn't believe her story, Adrienne was the perfect bait for the worst type of predator, a pedophile.

Adrienne didn't tell me about Mark until she came to live with me. She was being stubborn, refusing to take a shower before bedtime. She had practically glued her arms to her side. When my boyfriend Dan innocently helped me pull her shirt over her head, a low painful sound escaped from the back of her throat before Adrienne began wailing at the top of her lungs. Bewildered, Dan backed off and left the room. I held a shaking Adrienne as she sobbed uncontrollably. When I pressed her about her extreme reaction, the Mark molestation story came pouring out of her. At that moment, I wanted to kill two people—first Mark, then our mother.

✳ ✳ ✳

A letter from the Social Security Administration arrives in the mail. Last week, I was approved to be the payee for Adrienne's Social Security check, and the first deposit of $672 will hit her savings account on July 1. Even though the money is legally hers, it doesn't feel real yet.

Adrienne reads the letter. "$672? Wow. We've never had money before."

"It's your money, kiddo, but you can only spend it on food, clothing, or medical stuff not covered by insurance. We have to keep track of every penny."

"You mean I can buy new clothes?" she smiles.

"Yeah, you sure can." I smile too.

Damn mother.

I've sewn the tear in Adrienne's favorite black pants at least two times because I couldn't afford to buy her a new pair. We shop at thrift stores, where Adrienne ducks her head if she sees someone from school. Now if Adrienne needs something, she can get it with her own money.

I should have realized when we got a letter, our mother got one, too, telling her the money train has stopped. When the phone rings a few days later, I am unprepared for her nastiness. She doesn't bother to say hello.

"So ya found out?" Mother says snarling the word "found."

"That's all you have to say?"

"I did nothin' wrong. I got Adrin's money. I was savin' it for her."

"The hell you were. You stole her money. How does it feel stealing from your own daughter?"

"That's my money Andra! My money! I did nothin' wrong."

Then the obscenities begin. Once again, I talk over her, but I doubt she hears my goodbye over her own voice. I hang up.

Adrienne looks over at me from her chair.

"Mother?" she asks.

"Yep."

"Don't worry Sissy. She won't call back."

I nod as I grit my teeth. *Was it worth it, Mother?* I wonder how much our love is worth.

Despite feeling nauseated in the morning, on Tuesday Adrienne wants to get out of the house. First, we go to Victoria's Secret (VS) to buy her a new bra. Adrienne will finally have a nice, expensive bra that fits her properly. The saleswoman helping us seems to ignore Adrienne's almost bald head, pale skin, and hollow eyes. Adrienne explains she needs extra room to tuck her central line into her bra. The woman nods as if she hears this request all the time. Adrienne walks out swinging the characteristic pink VS bag, which holds her new convertible, strapless bra wrapped in pink tissue.

We eat lunch at Crabby Bobs, a local seafood restaurant near the Burbank mall. For the first time, Adrienne and I decide to eat crab legs. We both love crabmeat, but we've never ordered crab legs before.

"What are these for?" I ask when the waitress hands us plastic bibs.

"Trust me, you're gonna need them," she says.

When our food arrives, Adrienne giggles, "How are we going to eat all this, Sissy?"

The oval-shaped platter is filled with mashed potatoes and steamed mixed vegetables with a side of hush puppies. The crab legs lie on top, begging us to eat them first.

"Hold on," says our waitress. "I'll be right back with your bucket."

Adrienne grabs a crab leg and stares at it as butter drips down her bib.

"How do we eat this?" she asks me.

"I have no idea."

I look at the tool between our plates. I remember Julia Roberts' character in the movie *Pretty Woman* when she tries to eat escargot, and it goes flying off the table. I look around. The restaurant is almost empty, but I don't want to make a scene. Then the waitress brings the bucket.

"Uhh . . . look. We've never done this before. Can you show us how to eat crab legs?"

"Oh sure."

The waitress demonstrates how to use the tool to crack open the shell.

"Some people just suck the meat out, but you can pull it out too, like this."

She shows us how the small fork is designed to grab the thin piece of meat. She tells us to toss the shells in the bucket. Adrienne dives in, mastering the art of eating crab legs on her first try.

Even as we're having fun tackling our lunch, I watch her closely. Adrienne has not been in any pain today, but too much food can cause heartburn. I push her to eat some vegetables so she will be able to go to the bathroom later. She knows why I'm doing it, but we don't talk about it. Instead, we relish this moment—eating crab legs together for the first time, making a huge mess on the table and ourselves. I ignore the pain in my heart, caused not by the food, but a deep feeling. *This may be the first and last time. The one and only time. There may be no next time.*

I order more books, more ammunition to fight the faceless enemy.

I choose *American Cancer Society Consumers Guide to Cancer Drugs, Dr. Rosenfeld's Guide to Alternative Medicine*, and *Cancer Clinical Trials: Experimental Treatments and How They Can Help You*. The other books I read taught me what liver cancer was; these books will teach me how to beat it. Kill it. I feel like I'm playing the most important game in my life.

Although not as competitive as me, Adrienne also plays to win. She beat our brother Aidan at Monopoly when she was only ten; he was twenty-one. I was so proud of her. Then I remember the name of her website where I now post updates about her progress. *Adrienne kicks cancer's ass*. Yeah, she's out to win. She's the one who saw a TV commercial for Cancer Treatment Centers of America and wrote down the number, not me. I called but when I discovered both centers were out of state, Adrienne dismissed the idea. She refuses to be away from her family and friends. We must stay in LA she said. Adrienne won't let cancer win. *Fuck you no change*.

Diana visits Adrienne every week even though their therapy sessions have ceased. Whether we're at the hospital or at home, Diana makes time for Adrienne and me. I tell her about Adrienne's low-grade fevers every night this week while Adrienne focuses on our upcoming trip to Arizona. We are leaving on Friday if the doctor says it's okay.

After eighteen months of therapy, Diana seemed certain Adrienne's desire to commit suicide had waned even if she was still somewhat depressed. I asked Adrienne if she wanted to keep seeing her psycho doctor.

"Sure. I like Diana. It's nice having someone to talk to."

So Diana remains in our lives. I remind Diana about the Christmas Tree Incident of 1998. Adrienne and I had a huge fight. I wanted a particular tree in the lot, a tall Noble Fir perfectly shaped like a cone. Adrienne didn't like it, and John didn't care. We finally agreed I would select the tree, but Adrienne would decide how to decorate it. However, when she placed the large round ornaments near the top, I cringed. I corrected her; the round ornaments should go from smallest to largest from top to bottom.

Adrienne snapped at me. "Sissy, we had a deal. I get to do it my way. Now butt out." John backed her up. "You did make a deal. Just let her decorate the tree already."

I hated our tree that year.

The Christmas Tree Incident almost ruined our holidays. Afterward, I asked Diana in one of our few family sessions how we could have handled it better. Her solution was simple. Give Adrienne her own tree for her room the following year. Adrienne loved that idea. I don't know why we didn't think of it ourselves, but sometimes an objective professional opinion is what a family needs.

Now Diana and I laugh about something that once seemed so important. Adrienne didn't even want her own tree last year because she didn't care anymore. At fourteen, she had more important things to do than decorate a tree. Looking back, I can't believe we argued over a damn Christmas tree. So silly. I want that tree now, that stupid tree because it represents normality, stubbornness, and most of all, it reminds me of the way things were.

Adrienne wants to change her hair before we go to Arizona. She has grown tired of the 1/4-inch growth on the left side of her head and the 1/16-inch growth on the right side of her head, complemented by the clean bald patch above her right eye where she and Eli pulled out a chunk of one of her former Mohawks.

Adrienne is always changing her hair, ever since I allowed her to dye it bright red when she turned fourteen last year. She wanted to dye it when she was twelve, but I said no.

"If you want it that bad, you can wait two years," I said.

Not only did I make her wait, but I also mandated she never dye her hair black. I had known too many people who said black never washed out, and it ruined their hair. She agreed to my conditions.

I was hoping she would forget about dyeing her hair, but of course, she didn't. On her fourteenth birthday, she requested a dye job as her present. Adrienne took it one step further though. First, she asked our hairdresser to shave the back of her head up to an imaginary line between the tips of her ears. I almost protested but I had promised her she could do anything she wanted with her hair. I didn't want a repeat of the Christmas Tree Incident.

"My hair's too thick, Sissy. It makes me hot. This way I'll be cooler."

Yeah and you'll have no hair on the back of your head.

Since her hair was dark brown, our hairdresser bleached it first before applying two bottles of Manic Panic red passion semi-permanent color cream. As a bonus, she blow-dried Adrienne's hair and put it in two pigtails.

"Cool. I look like one of the characters from Sailor Moon." (Her favorite animated show when she was younger.)

Her enthusiasm brought a smile to my face even though I knew she would be judged now as a punk kid because of her new Goth, fairylike appearance. If I had told Adrienne my opinion, she would have been thrilled. She loves fairies. However, looking like a Japanese anime character, even a warrior whose destiny is to save the world, does not make the best first impression, which matters despite what people say.

"Let's Nair my head Sissy, that's gotta get rid of the rest of what's left," says Adrienne.

Concerned about an allergic reaction, I do a skin test first. I dab a small dollop of Nair on the bald patch, which is about the size of a fifty-cent coin. We wait the required ten minutes before I wipe it off. Nothing, not even redness.

Adrienne says, "Let's do it!"

I draw her bath and secure her central line in the Ziploc bag before taping it to her chest. Adrienne thinks I should scrub her scalp first to loosen up the hair follicles. Using a bit of shampoo, I massage her head with my fingers doing my best to convince her many stubborn strands of hair to let go. They hold on tight, but Adrienne believes Nair will do the trick. After rinsing her head and using a towel to absorb any remaining moisture, I apply a thick layer of Nair, and we wait again. The smell of Nair reminds me of every bad perm I've ever gotten.

"This better work," says Adrienne. "This stuff stinks."

I wipe off the Nair with a washcloth and rinse Adrienne's scalp again. "Well?"

"You still have hair, kiddo." *You must be the only cancer patient ever who wants her hair to just go ahead and fall out, but it won't.*

"Damn. I thought that would work."

I let the cuss word go even though Adrienne knows I prefer she not use that language around me.

"Keep me in denial," I said to her once. "I don't want to hear it."

I don't forbid her from swearing because then I would be a hypocrite. Driving in traffic, the words coming out of my mouth—move your ass motherfucker—don't set the best example. Moreover, I believe deeming words unspeakable only gives them more power.

Besides, I was thinking the same thing. *Damn. I thought the Nair would work.*

Six-year-old Adrienne when she still lived with our mother © December 1992

Days 45-50

*I love Sedona. Friday—leave for Arizona, hopefully without any compli-
cations. Wee! I can't wait to get to Sedona; it will be so nice and soothing
and perfect.*

—Adrienne's journal entry dated 6/27/01

Friday morning doesn't begin well. After a small breakfast of one Boost
shake and half a piece of toast, Adrienne throws up when she tries to
cough up the mucus in her lungs. We keep a Country Crock plastic container near her at all times so she is prepared when it happens. She's still
no Linda Blair, but the vomiting is more frequent now. If it's going to
happen, it usually does right away, so I watch for signs for up to thirty
minutes after she has eaten. Sometimes she doesn't even feel nauseated;
the food just comes up when she coughs or burps. Thanks to chemo,
which causes the nausea, which leads to vomiting, which results in no
appetite, Adrienne's weight has plunged down to 125 pounds, a loss of 18
pounds in six weeks. Jenny Craig would be jealous.

Adrienne cleans up while I pack the car. We are driving to Arizona
straight from the hospital. Dr. No approved the trip, but we have to go to
the clinic before we leave. I'm afraid he might change his mind. I don't
know what we'll do if he says she can't go. Maybe we shouldn't tell him
about this morning. I suspect he won't care though. Adrienne's low
hemoglobin is a real issue. She might need her first blood transfusion,
which would delay our trip or force us to cancel it altogether. I hope he's
in a good mood. Adrienne needs this trip. So do I.

✳ ✳ ✳

SUMMER 1995
At the first sign of violence, I should have ended my relationship with
Dan. He restrained me during an argument by squeezing my arms so

159

hard I was certain he left bruises. He didn't though. Not long after that incident, he threw a phone at my head. I ducked; the wall suffered minor damage. When he tore the bedroom door off its hinges because I had locked him out, I should have called the police, filed charges, and moved out. Dan was not only an alcoholic but also a mean, violent drunk who lashed out at the slightest provocation.

I never thought much about him hurting me, but I feared Adrienne might get caught in the crossfire. She was living with us when Dan attacked the door, hiding in her bedroom, sleeping I hope. Raising her in a violent home was criminal, but I didn't know how to leave Dan without setting him off. I saw a way out when he almost wrapped his white Ford Ranger truck around a pole at the corner of Highland and Franklin near the Hollywood Bowl. He made it home in one piece; the truck didn't fare as well. Not long after his car accident, we agreed to end our relationship. He blamed me for his drinking. Knowing the relationship was volatile, my dad and stepmother Ava offered to take care of Adrienne for two weeks while Dan moved out. That summer was the first time they met a then nine-year-old Adrienne. Hopping in Ava's old, green, Dodge Dakota pickup, Adrienne learned so much about Arizona in those fourteen days by traveling across the land and experiencing its history.

At Tonto National Monument, Adrienne complained as she and Ava hiked half a mile up the steep hillside. However, once they were inside the two-story cliff dwelling, Adrienne became quiet as she walked through each room, touching the walls of the ruins left behind from the Salado Indians in 1300 AD. She learned the Salado, like many Southwest tribes, abandoned their villages in the early fifteenth century. Ancient people have always fascinated Adrienne. A self-proclaimed Egyptologist by the age of six, she devours books about Egypt, mythology, and religion. By fifth grade, she was reading college textbooks about these subjects. I can imagine her deep reverence for the people who lived in those cliff dwellings so long ago.

With Ava as her tour guide, Adrienne fell in love with Arizona that summer. They went everywhere: the Painted Desert, the Petrified Forest, and more. My favorite picture of Adrienne was taken at Meteor Crater. She is sitting on a rock ledge with her legs crossed, arms outstretched, palms facing forward like she is soaking up the energy of her surroundings through her fingertips. Below her lies the barren desert, above her a cerulean blue sky grazed by white clouds. A slight breeze appears to be ruffling through her hair. Her youthful energy leaps off the picture, bringing life to a deserted land. Adrienne seems ready to take on the world.

Ava took Adrienne on another trip during that first visit. They packed a picnic and went to my father's office to have lunch with him. When a coworker said hello, Ava introduced Adrienne.

"This is Adrienne Wilson."

The woman looked at Adrienne and asked, "And she is . . . ?"

Not skipping a beat, Adrienne replied, "I'm their granddaughter."

After the woman walked away, Adrienne looked at Ava and explained. "It's just easier. She wouldn't understand."

Laughing, Ava agreed. How do you explain to your husband's co-worker this nine-year-old child is his ex-wife's youngest daughter from another relationship, but his oldest daughter is now raising her half-sister, who is visiting you while that same daughter ends a violent relationship? You don't. Even then, Adrienne knew to keep things simple.

I think my dad used to be upset our mother gave Adrienne his last name. Mother never changed her surname after the divorce. When I asked her about it, she replied, "Would you want to go back to bein' Myra Jean Green? I don't like your father, but I'll keep his name."

I believe she gave Adrienne the same name because it was the easiest thing to do. On Adrienne's birth certificate, the boxes for the father's name remain blank. Our mother could have put Todd Dickinson, but she chose not to. I don't know why. Adrienne's paternal grandparents, who live in California, have never been a part of her life. Our mother's parents To-Mama and Papa died when Adrienne was four years old. Considering that Adrienne isn't supposed to be a Wilson, it's ironic my dad and stepmother are the only grandparents she has ever known.

* * *

The doctor at the clinic, turns out Dr. No isn't here today, says we can go, but Adrienne will need a transfusion soon if her hemoglobin doesn't recover. Excited about our trip, we rush over to McDonald's for a late lunch. Adrienne eats a cheeseburger, fries, and one of my chicken Mc-Nuggets plus a Fruit Roll-Up. Big improvement over breakfast. She insists we listen to her CDs in the car so she can quiz me about each song.

"Okay, Sissy. Who's this?"

"Uh . . . Jane's Addiction?" My default answer.

"Noooo! Nine Inch Nails. Trent and Perry sound nothing alike."

She rolls her eyes as she pops in another CD.

"And this is?"

I try to distinguish the voices, but I'm terrible at remembering singers and songs, especially when I don't listen to the same music she does. I think about the bands she likes.

"I got it! Nirvana."

"Nope. Red Hot Chili Peppers. Geez Sissy. You're hopeless."

I laugh with her as she laughs at me. I don't mind losing this game because it keeps her spirits up.

Adrienne continues to test my knowledge of music as our car crawls along the freeway. Two hours later, we are still in Los Angeles. I turn on I-15 North, a big detour that takes us through Lake Havasu. More miles, but the traffic is lighter. The temperature continues to rise even as the sun goes down. By midnight, the heat has leveled off at 100 degrees, same as Adrienne's temperature, which I take whenever we stop for gas. At 2 a.m., ten hours after we left LA, we arrive in Cottonwood, a small town near Sedona. John, who couldn't leave town until after eight o'clock, shows up by 4 a.m. Exhausted, we fall into bed. John lies on an air mattress in the guest bedroom while Adrienne and I claim the bed. As I close my eyes, I think about our other Arizona trips and how this one is going to be so different.

✶ ✶ ✶

WINTER 1996

Adrienne and I visited Dad and Ava at their home near Show Low, Arizona. I say near because they lived in the middle of nowhere. The closest gas station and grocery store were located twenty-five miles away in the even smaller town of Pinetop-Lakeside. After years of living in Phoenix and suffering through its 120-degree heat, Ava and Dad had ventured about 175 miles northeast of the city into the heart of the White Mountains. At 6,400 feet, snow blanketed the land every winter, herds of elk frequented their front yard, and they lived close to the Sunrise Park Resort.

When Dad offered to take us skiing, I jumped at the opportunity. I had only been once before and loved it. Hating the sport, Ava stayed home while Dad, ten-year-old Adrienne, and I set off for Sunrise. Our brother Aidan was also visiting; he tagged along even though he hated skiing too. He became the keeper of our stuff while the rest of us hit the slopes.

Since we had no ski gear, Adrienne and I wore sweatpants and several layers of shirts plus jackets, which we borrowed from Ava. Adrienne donned my black Yale baseball cap. In Aspen, we would have looked like freaks, but at Sunrise, we fit in with the locals, who dressed in jeans, sweaters, and even cowboy hats for skiing.

We had missed the morning ski lessons, so I stayed with Adrienne on the bunny slope while Dad skied some runs. I wanted to make sure Adrienne mastered the snowplow before she tackled the mountain.

She complained all morning about her knees hurting saying, "I can't do it, Sissy."

I knew she could because she had strong legs due to ice-skating, running track, and good genes. On her last attempt before lunch, she managed to stop herself by making a snowplow, the tips of her skis forming a perfect triangle. Pride melted her pain and frustration.

All smiles, she asked, "Now, can I go down the mountain?"

"After lunch," I said.

Together, the three of us rode the ski lift with Dad explaining to Adrienne how to jump off when we got to the top of the easiest run named Spruce Ridge. Now at almost 10,000 feet, Adrienne jumped off the lift like a pro—weight forward, knees bent. When we looked down the mountain, I realized not all green (easy) slopes were created equal. This run was steeper than anything I had ever skied before, and I felt fear crawl into my heart. Before I could remind Adrienne to snowplow, she was hurtling down the run, her skis inches apart.

My dad seemed surprised, too, saying, "Oh my god! I've got to go after her."

He shot off to catch up with Adrienne while I stayed, frozen, wishing I possessed the fearlessness of a child. Although they skied together the rest of the afternoon, I never caught up with them. I never saw Adrienne ski down that mountain.

FALL 1999

The only time Adrienne, John, Adam, and I went to Arizona together was over Labor Day weekend almost two years ago. Dad and Ava had moved back to the state after being gone for some time. We went to Jerome, a hippie town tucked into the hillside and home to many local artists. We visited a ghost town named Haynes, which boasted a population of 304 people in 1901 during the height of the gold rush. Adrienne and I decided to explore an old house in the town, ignoring the signs that read, "Don't go beyond this point. Rattlesnake area."

My father became agitated. "Girls, didn't you read the sign?"

"We'll be fine Dad," I said.

John threw his hands up in the air and stormed away.

"They play by their own rules," he said to my father.

I smiled. Like the sign, Adrienne and I ignored them and walked through the house, touching the wood and marveling at how the structure was still standing after so many years.

FALL 2000

Last September, Adrienne and I trekked out to Arizona, without John. I don't remember why he didn't come with us. With her newly-dyed bright-blue hair, Adrienne wanted to go to Arizona before she started her first day of high school, the Tuesday after Labor Day. We cheered on horses at the Prescott Downs racetrack, hiked through the red rocks, and spent time doing nothing.

The highlight of our weekend, however, was an innocuous trip to Wal-Mart. When Ava, Adrienne, and I walked out of the store, we saw this heavyset woman loading groceries into her SUV. Rolls of cellulite burst out of the woman's too-tight short shorts revealing red pimples so large we could see the pus oozing out of them from ten feet away. Speechless, we looked at each other.

Then Adrienne said, "That—is so—wrong."

The three of us laughed so hard we could barely stand up straight. Tears poured down my face. I knew we shouldn't be laughing, but sometimes the truth is too funny. We couldn't wait to get home to tell my father.

✳ ✳ ✳

Saturday morning I set up shop. I had emailed Dad and Ava in advance about our needs during our visit: clean house, clean counter space, and a clean dog. I put the tackle box along with Adrienne's other medical supplies on the counter. My dad watches me as I lay the bottle of saline, needle, syringe, and alcohol pad on a paper towel.

"What are you doing?" he asks.

Adrienne yawns as she sits down at the kitchen table. She pulls out the double lumen from her pajama top—the two lines dangling against her chest.

"Flushing her lines."

I explain the process as I attach the needle, withdraw the saline, dump the needle in our Sharps container, and wipe the cap with alcohol.

"I have to make sure there are no air bubbles," I say.

I thump the syringe with my middle finger and examine it closely.

My dad's face reveals nothing; he is the most stoic man I know. He watches though. I wonder how he would have reacted if he had seen me give Adrienne her Neupogen shot ten minutes before in the bedroom.

Ava flutters around the kitchen asking Adrienne if she wants anything to eat. Adrienne nibbles on toast. Her eyes droop but she wakes up when Sophie, Ava and Dad's terrier mutt, comes over wagging her bushy tail. Adrienne leans down and scratches the top of Sophie's head while giving her a piece of toast.

Sophie was a puppy when Adrienne went to Arizona for the first time. Adrienne and Sophie would walk on the treadmill together until Sophie would lose her footing and slide off. Giggling, Adrienne would pick up Sophie, and they would start over again. Six years later, Adrienne adores Sophie and looks forward to seeing her.

This visit is different though. Too tired to play with her favorite dog, Adrienne lies on the couch and watches MTV2, a network we don't have on our cable at home. She drifts in and out of sleep the rest of the afternoon.

On Saturday night, Adrienne spends time writing in her live journal online, but afterward she can't sleep. I give her fifty milligrams of Benadryl around midnight. She once had a negative reaction to it in the hospital, but the nurse administered the medication through Adrienne's IV. Given by mouth, she normally doesn't have any problem, except for tonight. Her muscles twitch and she feels jumpy.

John talks to Adrienne to distract her while I call Children's Hospital. The doctor on-call recommends Ativan to counteract the Benadryl, which takes six hours to wear off. I don't remember when I picked up the prescription for Ativan, but I find a bottle of it in Adrienne's tackle box. The label reads PRN meaning take as needed. Well, she needs it now. I give Adrienne the small tablet—.75 mg—before she lies down in bed.

Sleeping next to her, I feel Adrienne's body thrashing around, her legs jerking, forearms twitching. Two hours later, I give her more Ativan. I make a mental note to add Benadryl to her increasing list of allergies. Adrienne falls into a restless sleep by 5 a.m. I opt not to wake her for her morning meds. Since I was the one who gave her the medication that kept her up all night, the least I can do is let her sleep in. The meds can wait.

The constant balancing act with Adrienne's medications reminds me of a seesaw. The trick to playing on a seesaw is both people must be approximately the same size or else it doesn't work. Sitting up high in the air with your legs hanging down because you are smaller than your friend defeats the whole purpose. If that same friend jumps off quickly, you come crashing down, your rear end sore from the force of the wood hitting the ground.

Too much Benadryl, crash! Give Adrienne Ativan to help her body recover. Get back on the seesaw. Keep it straight. Balance the meds. No more extreme ups or downs until Adrienne has diarrhea twice on Sunday afternoon from too much Peri-Colace. The seesaw loses its equilibrium again. Not quite a crash this time, but a definite thud on the ground. An easy fix though: cut back on the Peri-Colace. I want to stop and pull Adrienne off the damn seesaw, but I can't. I have to find the balance. Keep the balance.

I believe we all have a place that resonates with our soul. Whether it's a country, region, or city, our heart connects with the land, and we know we belong there. My place is the Santa Ynez Valley, just east of Santa Barbara. Driving through the rolling green hills, full of vineyards and orchards, I feel a sense of calm. I imagine living there on a small ranch, growing my own grapes, making my own wine, riding my own horses, and eating blackberries straight off the vine.

My dad always jokes, "To my daughter Andra, there are only two places in America: Los Angeles and New York. Then there is the great wasteland in between."

He doesn't understand. Even though I love big cities, they don't bring me peace. Adrienne gets it. She loves Los Angeles and wants to stay here for college, but she also wants a house in Arizona one day, somewhere near Sedona. Adrienne savors the dry land with its red rocks and spiritual vortices. She desires an acre of Arizona desert for hell-raising bonfires. Since hiking is out of the question, Adrienne wants to go shopping in Sedona during this trip, but I'm not sure if she will have enough energy to do so.

In her Honda Prelude, Ava speeds down Highway 89a, the road between Cottonwood and Sedona. The drive can take up to an hour, depending on traffic. Ava picks the perfect time to go, late Monday morning. Not in the mood to shop, I stay home with Dad. Ava and Adrienne arrive at the Sedona Center, an outdoor plaza with shops, galleries, and restaurants, twenty minutes after they leave the house.

Adrienne looks for her favorite store, the one with the alien face in the window. Ava finds it and together they walk upstairs. Adrienne buys presents for her friends. One gift, an Indian-style cuff with a buckle and blue bands, she chooses to keep for herself.

As they leave the store, Adrienne says, "I have to sit down. I can't go any farther."

When she reaches the bottom of the stairs, she sits on a nearby bench.

"Are you okay?" asks Ava.

"No," says Adrienne. "I don't think so. I don't feel good."

"Can you make it back to the car?"

"No, I don't think so."

"Will you be alright here while I go get the car?"

"Yeah."

Ava races back to the car. She jumps in the Prelude, shifts in reverse, and pulls out of the parking lot. She reaches Adrienne by driving onto the sidewalk. Exhausted after forty-five minutes of shopping, Adrienne naps for four hours when they come home.

After days of feeling nauseated and tired, Adrienne wakes up on Tuesday morning looking more like her normal self. She wants to return to Sedona to finish her shopping. We grab lunch at Sonic, a restaurant we love but don't have in Los Angeles. Adrienne drinks their famous strawberry lemonade and noshes on fries.

We get on the highway only to discover traffic has stopped due to construction. More construction. We can't seem to get away from it. We move a few feet. We wait five minutes. Then, we progress another ten feet. We wait. We finish our lunch in the car. We move again. Forty-five minutes goes by, and we are no closer to the red rocks of Sedona.

"I'm getting tired, Sissy," says Adrienne.

"Do you want to go back?" I ask.

"Yeah, let's go home," she says referring to Dad and Ava's house.

The disappointment in her voice stings me like a bee. *Goddamn construction; it's everywhere. Children's Hospital. Burbank High. Highway 89a.*

I want to tell her we'll get there eventually, but I don't. I see her pale face and her drooping eyelids, and I know she needs to lie down. I wait for the car ahead of me to move forward a few feet before making an illegal U-turn across the highway. As we drive back to Cottonwood, I crush the thoughts in my head: *Will yesterday be her last trip to Sedona? Did I miss another opportunity to spend time with Adrienne? Goddamn construction.*

Adrienne loving Arizona © summer 1995

Days 51-52

Greetings from Sedona,
I warn you in advance that this letter might end up being a bit long.
Driving out here made me come to terms with what's going on in my life
right now. Hell, what else can you do in a car for ten hours but think?
You have been an amazing influential force and source of inspiration
for me. If it wasn't for you, I don't think I would be this far along, alive,
in my cancer. It was always a dream of mine to meet you. I achieved
that dream. If nothing else, I succeeded in that. If I can achieve one of
my greatest dreams in life, what makes me think I can't defeat cancer?
I now have the strength and courage to fight this. I have the mindset to
keep myself positive in this hellhole. Before this, I kept thinking about
how I could lose my hearing, and how I would rather die than live life
deaf. Music is the bane of my existence. With your advice, I have been
keeping myself in the moment and have forgotten all consequences of
chemo. I'm a happier, healthier person thanks to you. Thank you again
Dave. I don't know what else to say or do to prove my gratitude.
With Love and Admiration, Adrienne

—Adrienne's letter to Dave written in her journal, entry dated 6/30/01

We left Arizona yesterday morning, which was the fourth of July. Coming home, the drive only took eight hours. I promised John we would be back in time to see fireworks; we have a perfect view of the city's annual show from our house. However, he didn't bother to come outside and watch them. Adrienne peered up at the sky for a few minutes before going in; she was feeling light-headed and had a low-grade fever again. I felt empty as I watched the fireworks dazzle the sky, reminding me of Adrienne's various hair colors over the last year: red, purple, blue, and then blue again. The doctors won't let her dye the stubble that clings to her scalp, but they have given her medicine labeled with a skull and crossbones.

This world makes no sense. Unable to muster up any enthusiasm, I go inside too, the fireworks already forgotten.

✳ ✳ ✳

When the red faded, Adrienne's friends nicknamed her 'Matchstick' and 'Flame' because her hair was yellow, orange, and red, much like a lit match. Two months later, the night before her middle school graduation, Adrienne dyed her hair again. She chose purple, which ended up looking mostly brown mixed with lavender since she did it herself. She cut her bangs in the shape of a rainbow and wore a long-sleeved, black lace dress from Hot Topic. One of her teachers wasn't pleased, but the school told the students they could wear anything they wanted as long as they complied with the dress code. For girls that meant: no spaghetti straps, no bare midriffs, no skirts more than three inches above their knees, and no open-toed shoes. Adrienne looked more Goth than ever, but she followed the rules so no one could stop her from wearing what she wanted.

As an honor student, Adrienne sat in the front row on the stage. Behind her, the other students were seated alphabetically. Besides the UCLA Creative Writing Scholarship, Adrienne won the President's Education Award for outstanding academic achievement; the California Junior Scholarship Federation (CJSF) Honor Award for academic excellence; the Outstanding Portfolio Award for her eighth grade writing portfolio, and the Pathfinder's Triple 'A' Award for maintaining A's in English, History, and Science. Every time Adrienne got up to receive an award, I cried. The CJSF award also came with a medal, which lay on top of the black lace of her dress. John and I beamed; we must have been the proudest parents in the audience that day.

Teachers, students, and parents flooded the front lawn after the ceremony. People approached me; some I knew others I didn't.

A chorus erupted around me. "I had no idea." "You must be so proud." "That kid is smart." "You did good."

I protested, "I didn't do it. Adrienne did. Congratulate her."

They wouldn't listen to me nor did they acknowledge John, who was standing at my side. I didn't understand why they seemed surprised by Adrienne's success until I caught sight of her, laughing with her friends, her purple hair gleaming in the sunlight. I laughed too. These people, some of whom were parents of Adrienne's friends, had thought she was stupid, or a slacker, or both. They had judged her based on her appearance. *You proved them wrong, kiddo. You shattered that stereotype today. That's my girl.*

✱ ✱ ✱

I wake up feeling anxious while Adrienne is downright grouchy. I ignore her crankiness, but I know if she were well, I would have told her to get over it. Maybe she is as nervous as I am. Today we meet Dr. Aquino, the liver-cancer specialist referred by Kirsten. We should have gotten this second opinion weeks ago, but the health insurance held us up. I don't expect a miracle; I only want some hope. A miracle would be nice though.

Dr. Aquino runs the gastrointestinal clinic at UCLA Medical Center, a hospital famous for its liver-transplant program. Compared to Children's Hospital, the waiting room's décor is bland: beige walls combined with flowered wallpaper. With only adults occupying the chairs that line the perimeter of the room, the noise is minimal. Adrienne sinks into a padded chair, adjusting her body weight to find the most comfortable position.

"It's quiet here," she says, "I like it."

Ignoring the avocado-pit of anxiety in my stomach, I read my list of questions again. I will be firm. Confident. We need straight, honest answers. As I glance around the room, I notice people looking at Adrienne; she is the only 'child' here. I see empathy in the eyes of other caregivers: spouses, friends, siblings, and children of the ill; we share a mutual understanding. We feel helpless.

After more than an hour, Adrienne and I are escorted into an examination room. We speculate about Dr. Aquino. What will he look like? How will he treat us? How much experience does he have? The door opens and all I can think is first impressions matter. With dark hair and dark eyes, he stands at medium height. He is younger than I expected, older than me, but much younger than Dr. No. He possesses an air of reserved pleasantness, like someone who is wary of making new friends but open to the possibility. We exchange a few niceties before I get down to business.

"Do you mind if I ask you some questions, Dr. Aquino?" I ask.

"Go ahead. I see you have a list," he smiles.

I smile back.

"How many HCC patients have you treated before, and have you ever treated a ped?"

"Well, we see about six cases per week in all stages of disease, but no, I have never treated a pediatric patient before."

I do the math in my head, over 300 cases a year.

"Do you mind speaking to our family friends, Kirsten, who referred you, and Dr. Sofia Sárközi, a doctor at NIH?"

"Of course not. Let me ask you—both of you," he looks at Adrienne and me. "What are your expectations?"

Damn. I didn't expect him to interrupt me. Is this a test? If so, what's the right answer?

I glance at Adrienne before speaking. "We don't expect a miracle."

Yes, we do.

"No numbers. No predictions of . . ." I can't even finish the sentence. "We want you to treat the cancer, which we know isn't typical for a ped. At Children's, the doctors don't seem open to trying other therapies because Adrienne's a minor."

"Fair enough," he says. "Adrienne, your age will be an issue in most clinical trials, but there are exceptions."

Adrienne nods as a smile appears on her face. Dr. Aquino used her name and spoke directly to her.

"Will the statistics about HCC affect how you treat Adrienne?"

"Statistics are just numbers that serve as a rough guide. I don't believe they're relevant once you start treating the individual patient. I believe attitude is important; a person must be willing to fight. There is evidence that the immune system and the brain are connected. Also, I want my patients to understand their disease and know all of their options."

Did someone give this man a script? He's saying all the right things.

"I don't like staying in the hospital," says Adrienne.

"I don't know anyone who does," replies Dr. Aquino. "We can make sure you are home as much as possible."

I look into the doctor's eyes. "Okay. Tell us what you would do differently."

"Since the standard protocols of chemotherapy have been administered with no success, I would recommend a treatment that combines Xeloda, another chemotherapy drug, with interferon alpha, a drug that stimulates the body's own immune system to fight the disease. Xeloda can be administered orally, and interferon is a shot given in the arm three times per week. In both instances," he looks at Adrienne, "You can stay home."

"Really?" asks Adrienne.

"Yes," he replies before turning back to me.

I nod my head as I gnaw on the corner of my lip. Didn't someone tell us about interferon before? It sounds familiar.

"Can you spell Xeloda?" I ask.

Adrienne smiles, "Sissy, it's almost like Xiola. That's my hamster," she says to Dr. Aquino, who nods as if all of his patients have pet hamsters.

"Of course."

I chuckle because Adrienne, the world's worst speller, is telling me how to spell a drug that begins with the letter X. After I finish taking notes, I extend my hand to Dr. Aquino.

"Thank you for your time; you've been very helpful. I will follow up with you after I talk to Adrienne's health insurance."

Maybe we can transfer her care to UCLA.

"If you have any questions, just call," he says. "Adrienne," he extends his hand to her, "it was a pleasure."

"Sure, nice to meet you."

"Dr. Aquino, one more thing," I say.

"Yes?" he asks.

"We'll need copies of all of Adrienne's medical records. Labs, reports . . . everything. Is that a problem?"

"Not at all," he replies before walking out.

"I like him," says Adrienne, "He didn't talk down to us."

"I like him too, kiddo. I like him too."

Adrienne wakes up on Friday morning with a temperature of 100.3 degrees. Since we are spending most of the day at the hospital, I don't call Dr. No. She has three tests scheduled for today: a hearing test, a CT scan, and an echocardiogram, and she will get the stitches removed from the opening Dr. Jorge made when he inserted her central line. We will also visit the clinic so she can get her labs done. Neither one of us is looking forward to the long day ahead of us.

Today, I will tell Dr. No we want to change oncologists. It's too soon to transfer to UCLA, that will take weeks to sort out with the insurance, but in the meantime, we want someone else. A doctor who understands us. A doctor who believes in possibilities. A doctor who has hope.

Of all the tests Adrienne is continually subjected to, the echocardiogram is by far the easiest one, both physically and mentally. Adrienne does not have to lie flat on her back like she does for a CT scan, and she does not worry about her heart failing the way she worries about losing her hearing.

Even though I know the chemo can cause heart damage, I don't torture myself with the impending results like I do with the CT scan. For some reason, I connect Adrienne's spirit with her heart; I can't imagine one working without the other. Her spirit is strong; her heart must be.

I soon realize the naiveté in my thinking a few minutes into the echocardiogram. The technician glides the device over Adrienne's chest, just above her heart. I watch the monitor as the most important muscle in Adrienne's body beats quickly but steadily like the thumping of an excited dog's tail against linoleum when its owner walks in the door. Then, I see the technician frown.

"What's wrong? I ask, feeling my shoulders as they harden like steel, my body becoming rigid, unmoving.

"I cannot say," says the man whose name I never bothered to get.

"What is it?" my alto-pitched voice turning into a shrill.

Adrienne looks at him, but she is too tired to respond.

"What do you see?"

"I cannot say."

"Do—you—see—something?" I ask as I squeeze Adrienne's hand without thinking.

"Ouch. Watch it, Sissy."

Adrienne yawns and closes her eyes.

"You must discuss the results with," the man glances at Adrienne, "her doctor."

He says her doctor with such finality I can feel an invisible door slamming in my face. *Thanks asshole for giving me something else to worry about. Thanks a lot.*

Our 1 p.m. appointment with Dr. No does not fare well either. The nurse ushers us into an examination room right away, but then, Adrienne falls asleep as we wait over an hour for the good doctor to show up. I know he must be busy with another patient, but I cannot help feeling frustrated with him, the technician, the hospital, and the cancer. With

Adrienne asleep, I have no one to talk to, nothing to stop my thoughts as they run awry.

Is Adrienne's heart okay? What will the CT scan show? Please let her hearing be normal. Who am I talking to? God? No. No god would allow this to happen. Who then? What am I going to say to Dr. No? How will I fire him?

My thoughts come to a screeching halt when the door opens and a nurse walks in. Adrienne stirs, opens her eyes, and wakes up.

"Let's take a look at your line," says the nurse.

Adrienne removes her shirt but leaves her bra on, as I help her put on a gown. The nurse removes the dressing.

"Looks good. We can go ahead and remove the stitches."

Who are we? Why do people say 'we' when they mean 'I'?

Adrienne winces as the nurse cuts the black threads that appear stronger than fishing line. Snip-snip.

"One more."

Snip.

"There. All done."

The nurse puts a new dressing over the insertion point.

"You can put your shirt back on. The doctor will be with you shortly."

She leaves the room, closing the door behind her.

Adrienne looks weary.

"That hurt, Sissy."

"I'm sorry, kiddo."

"What time is it?"

Adrienne never wears a watch.

"After two," I reply.

"I wanna go home."

"I know," I nod in agreement, "me too."

I promise her I will talk to Dr. No as quickly as possible. I'm sure he will appreciate my efficiency since I'm probably one of his least favorite parents.

On some level, I understand how he must feel. As a teacher, I've had my share of pain-in-the-ass parents, the ones who always grate on your nerves because they constantly bug you about their child's education. They call you during your lunch. They call you after school, or worse they call you during school while you're teaching their kid. Usually their child

175

is failing, and they want to know what they can do about it. I always want to say YOU cannot do anything. Your child needs to do the work.

Am I one of those parents now? Is that why Dr. No acts the way he does? No, I tell myself. It's not the same thing. Kids can work harder to improve their grades, but Adrienne cannot make her liver work—can she? Is there a crazy mind-over-matter Scientologist-type treatment we haven't tried? *STOP!*

The Serenity Prayer pops into my head. I see it etched on a small plate glued to a piece of wood lying in a drawer, one of the few references to religion in my childhood home. "God grant me the serenity to accept the things I cannot change, the courage to change the things I can, and the wisdom to know the difference." All I can think right now is fuck god.

Dr. No interrupts my internal rant against god when he walks in and asks how Adrienne is doing. His bowtie is especially bright today; it screams happy but his face says otherwise. The test results are not back yet, so we discuss the myriad of side effects Adrienne has been experiencing since the second round of chemo ended: more nausea, more vomiting, some headaches, less constipation, and no pain since June 25. He seems unmoved by her lack of pain so I repeat myself.

"She's had no pain since June 25. No Dilaudid."

He nods.

I realize now is the time to tell him. Just say it. *Why is this so hard?* I look at him.

"We want to switch oncologists. You are not a good match for our family."

For a moment, I see his soul, as if someone opened the blinds, which reveals a flash of regret and sadness in his eyes. Then he blinks, and the blinds close, his blue eyes back to neutral. I wonder if Adrienne saw his response. *Why do I care about his feelings? So the man has a soul, so what?*

Dr. No nods again before speaking, "I'll speak to your case manager Teresa. I'm sure she can find someone more . . . suited to you and your sister."

Say her name dammit. A-dri-enne. Treat her like a person. This time I'm the one who nods while anxiety over a new doctor and relief over getting rid of Dr. No chase each other in my brain. Relief tags anxiety and wins the game. Any doctor is better than Dr. No. We never have to see him again.

We arrive home. Both of us are exhausted by the long day. Adrienne changes into her shorts and pajama top and watches television. I read my new book *Everyone's Guide to Cancer Therapy*. I find the section on the liver and read.

"What Causes It: Hepatocellular carcinoma most often develops in damaged livers. Long-standing infections with either hepatitis B or hepatitis C virus often precedes it and is therefore seen as a significant risk factor."

Finally, Adrienne is a textbook case. Fifteen years of living with hepatitis. I never got her tested. I didn't know.

I think about how I have never been able to envision Adrienne as an adult. It's stupid but it has always bugged me. When she was a baby, I dismissed the thought, but as she got older, I wondered: *Why? Why can't I see her all grown up?* Then I remember something Adrienne said to me a few months ago, before this madness ensued.

"I believe you're psychic, Sissy. You should read this."

She gave me a book about developing your psychic energy. I only read it to humor her. *What if she's right?*

- The night before it happened, I sensed John was going to lose all the money he had invested in a tech stock, and I don't know a thing about the stock market. *Coincidence.*
- My dreams often come true. *Doesn't that happen to everyone?*
- I knew Adrienne would live with me one day even before our mother's mental state deteriorated. *A logical conclusion given our mother's age, drug addiction, and parenting skills.*
- I've had an unnatural fear of cancer since my early twenties— right about the time Adrienne moved in with me. *But I'm the one that's supposed to get cancer.*
- I have always known I would outlive everyone I love—even Adrienne, but she's supposed to be fifty-something and I'm supposed to be seventy-something—or so I thought. *No. I can't be psychic. That's ridiculous.*

"What's the prognosis?" asks Adrienne.

"Huh?"

Her question grants me a reprieve from my own mind and its questions.

"The prognosis? What does the book say?"

"Oh. Yeah."

I read the sub-heading, "Advanced Disease." I hesitate but I can't lie to Adrienne. She might pick up the book and read it herself. I keep my voice steady as I read aloud.

"Advanced Disease: The tumor involves all lobes of the liver and/or has spread to involve other organs such as the lungs, intra-abdominal lymph nodes, or bone."

I stop.

"What else, Sissy?"

I continue.

"Standard treatment: No standard therapy is known to prolong survival."

I can't look at Adrienne as I read the final line.

"Two-Year Survival: Less than five percent."

My throat constricts as I swallow the lump in it. I feel water rushing to my eyes as I bite the dry skin off my lip. I look at Adrienne.

"Well, it didn't say zero percent. I'll just be one of the less than five percent who survive."

Adrienne smiles at me.

The glass is half-full for her. Being honest with her was the right choice. Her boundless optimism squashes my tears. I return her smile.

"That's right, kiddo. You will."

However, the words don't ring true.

Adrienne laughs as something on TV amuses her. She doesn't seem to notice my trepidation.

I close my eyes and try to imagine Adrienne as a healthy twenty year old strolling through a college campus, but I can't see the picture. I see the pieces scattered like a 1000-piece jigsaw puzzle in a box, but I can't make them fit together to form the whole. *Why can't I see her in the future? Was the irrational cancer fear a warning I didn't heed? I believe you're psychic, Sissy. No, I'm not. I can't be. Not this time.*

Adrienne marching in her middle school graduation. © *June 2000*

Days 53-58

A pulse of 108. Over 120 is a hospital call for me. I've nearly gotten used to the sterile white walls and fluorescent lights. "How is Whitney?" "She had a nosebleed that wouldn't quit; it led to urinary tract infections, bleeding double hickmens, and a collapse. Well, see you Tuesday!" Right . . .

—Adrienne's journal entry dated 7/7/01

The pain returns where it all began—in Adrienne's right shoulder. Maybe if I hadn't bragged to Dr. No yesterday about the pain being gone, Adrienne's shoulder wouldn't be hurting this morning. I give Adrienne 2 mg of Dilaudid. I get out the extension cord and plug in the heating pad so she can use it on her shoulder while she watches TV. I make a notation on the whiteboard where I keep track of Adrienne's medicine schedule. "Pain back. Gave 2 mg Dilaudid 8 a.m. Try Q6."[9] Eight milligrams total for today.

On Sunday, the pain continues like an uncontrollable wildfire. I write, "Pain worse. Try 4mg Dilaudid Q8." Now, we're up to 12 mg. Adrienne has a temperature of 99.3 degrees, but Tylenol does nothing. Her pulse fluctuates between 108 bpm–120 bpm. Her next round of chemo is a week away. I'm not sure her body can wait that long. I'll ask when we go to the clinic; Adrienne is scheduled for a blood transfusion tomorrow.

During her first hospital stay, Adrienne's blood was typed A positive. It seems fitting an honor-roll student would have A positive or A+ blood. I know one has nothing to do with the other, but it makes it easy for me to remember. My blood type is A negative, and my cumulative grade point average in both high school and college was an A-. I cannot give Adrienne my blood; it's not good enough, it's not compatible. Once again, I can't help her.

---

9   Q is short for quaque, which means "every" in Latin. Q8 means give every eight hours.

Monday morning begins.

"I don't feel well, Sissy."

"How's the shoulder?" I ask.

"Between a 2 and 3."

A happy sigh escapes my lips. Adrienne's pain has lessened. I give her only 2 mg of Dilaudid along with her other morning meds. She drinks juice but refuses a piece of toast. A little nausea caused by swallowing pills on an empty stomach doesn't compare to chemo-induced nausea. My relief is short-lived, however, when Adrienne grabs the plastic Country Crock bowl and throws up all six ounces of the juice. Somehow, the pills stay down. She sighs and shakes her head.

I look at my watch, half past eight. We have less than two hours to get to the hospital. I think about The Bangles' song "Manic Monday." That song was spot on. I wish it were Sunday except I don't. Yesterday, Adrienne was in more pain. I'll take the vomiting over the pain any day. Why am I debating these issues? What kind of reality are we living in? At what point did we acknowledge, adapt, and accept these circumstances? When did this become normal? It's not a manic Monday. For us, this is Monday.

The blood-transfusion suite, as I like to call it, is a large white room filled with a half dozen beds, television sets, and IV poles. A nurse brings a pint of O positive blood, the universal donor. After Adrienne is hooked up to receive the blood through her central line, the same nurse brings her pills. Adrienne looks at me with one eyebrow cocked.

"What's that for?" I ask.

"Oh," the nurse replies, "some people need pre-meds before the transfusion. To help them relax."

I can read the 'no' on Adrienne's face.

"I think we'll skip them and see how it goes. Adrienne has had enough pills for one morning."

"Okay."

The nurse shrugs her shoulders and puts down the paper cup containing the pills so she can begin the transfusion.

"Just relax. Here's the remote so you can watch TV."

As she leaves, the nurse closes the curtain around the bed to give us privacy. Within fifteen minutes, Adrienne closes her eyes and falls asleep. I take the remote out of her hand and turn off the TV. I watch the blood as it flows from the bag through the plastic tube, which is connected to her line. Who donated this blood, I wonder. Was it a man or woman? Someone young or old? I say a silent thank-you.

The transfusion takes almost three hours. When Adrienne wakes up, I notice how her face is flushed with color. I didn't realize how pale she had gotten until now. Her red cheeks make her appear healthier.

I ask, "How ya doin, kiddo?"

Adrienne yawns.

"Little sleepy, but I feel better."

"You look good."

Adrienne grins and yawns again.

Her smile fades when Dr. No pulls the curtain back. He clears his throat. Adrienne and I say hello. Our greeting to him feels strained. Unnatural. *Why is he here?*

"I have her test results," he looks at me.

My breath catches in my throat.

"Heart is normal."

I exhale. *Damn that technician for scaring me.*

"The CT scan shows no change."

This time no change falls into place like a block in the video game Tetris. No change fits perfectly between my expectations of no worse and no better. *Fuck you no change.*

"AFP has decreased to 1.7 million."

That's an improvement.

"Hearing shows a slight loss at higher tones in the right ear."

Adrienne sits up. "What? A loss?"

"It's minor," says Dr. No. "A human cannot even hear at those higher tones."

"No more, Sissy."

"Adrienne . . ."

"No." She crosses her arms over her chest. "I will not be deaf."

"We'll talk about this later."

Adrienne grimaces.

"Thank you Dr. No for giving us the test results."

"Of course. Teresa should be in soon to discuss the arrangements."

He makes it sound like we're planning a funeral instead of changing physicians. Dr. No walks out leaving the curtain open.

"Sissy, you can't make me take that chemo again."

She is referring to cisplatin, the one drug that could cause her to lose her hearing permanently.

My head hurts from digesting the good news along with the bad news.

"We'll talk about it later, Adrienne."

I can already tell by the look on her face the discussion is closed.

✶ ✶ ✶

If there is one trait Adrienne and I share, it is stubbornness. When we disagree and go head-to-head with each other, even John gets out of the way. A few years before the Christmas Tree Incident, we battled over her fifth-grade science project. The year before, Adrienne had won first place at her elementary school's annual science fair competition, and she was determined to win again. However, on the day the students were to present their projects to the judges, Adrienne and I were leaving town to visit our mother for spring break. Her teacher Mr. Snyder offered to videotape her presentation so she wouldn't be disqualified. He told Adrienne to describe her project in detail, explain why she chose that project, and to relax, to smile, and to be herself.

Adrienne stood in front of me in our tiny kitchen in our studio apartment. I insisted she practice her presentation before Mr. Snyder taped her the next day.

"Hi. My name is Adrienne Wilson. For my project, I created a battery by using electrical currents."

Adrienne looked at her notes.

"I chose this project because I like electricity . . . and it was hard to do."

"Okay, honey. Try again. Smile and relax. Say the title of your project first. Tell us why it was hard to do."

I was remembering what Mr. Snyder had said and imagining what the judges wanted to hear.

"Hi. My name is Adrienne Wilson. Sissy, I can't do this!"

Adrienne whined. I hate whining.

"Yes, you can."

I stressed the word <u>can</u> even though I meant <u>will</u>.

"You have to since you won't be there in person. Try again."

"My project is . . . is . . . about electricity," Adrienne whimpered.

She looked at her notes again to find the words and then up at me.

"I don't wanna do this, Sissy. I hate public speaking."

"You have to do this or you'll be disqualified. Now Adrienne, Mr. Snyder gave you a chance to stay in the competition. You're not going to blow it. Do it again."

The "I can't"-"You can" war went on for two hours ending with me throwing my hands up in the air and Adrienne dissolving into tears. Despite numerous attempts the next day, she never successfully presented her project on camera. Mr. Snyder gave up too. Adrienne didn't place in the science fair that year, which was a shame since her project was by far one of the most complicated and interesting ones in the competition.

Looking back, I wish I had changed our flight and risked our mother's wrath. The irony is, even though she hates public speaking, Adrienne would have been fine in person. The harder I pushed her, the harder she pushed back. When she makes up her mind about something, whether it's I can't talk on camera or I won't take that drug, Adrienne does not change it.

I've learned my lesson though. This time I won't push. Even though a part of me wants to shake her into submission and scream this drug could save your life! You're going to take it, dammit! I will not do it. I do not understand, but it's her life, her body, and therefore, her choice.

✳ ✳ ✳

After the successful transfusion, Adrienne receives her first Pentamidine treatment, the antibiotic that replaced Bactrim. There are no pills to swallow, no liquids to drink; instead Adrienne inhales the Pentamidine for about forty minutes. She cannot talk during the treatment so when I ask how she's doing, she nods and gives me a thumbs-up.

Adrienne finishes inhaling the Pentamidine, and we return to her assigned bed to wait for Teresa. She doesn't keep us waiting long. I ask about two other doctors we have met at Children's, but neither one of them specialize in liver cancer. Teresa recommends Dr. Marco; he goes by his first name because no one can spell, much less pronounce, his last name.

"He is the chair of the Liver Tumors Disease Strategy Committee for the Children's Oncology Group. Plus, I think you and Adrienne will like him," she says.

We agree to meet him the day after tomorrow. I wonder what Dr. Marco has heard about us, but then I realize I don't care.

That evening, I sit down to write an email to the editor of our local newspaper, the *Burbank Leader*. I cannot remember whose idea it was to contact the paper, but someone suggested it. I bite my lip as I watch the cursor blinking on the screen. Even though I have heard the term pitch letter before, I don't know how to do it so I write from the heart. I introduce myself and Adrienne; give basic facts such as her age, her interests, and her diagnosis; and I explain our desire to make more people aware of HCC, a common cancer worldwide even if it is considered rare in the United States. As I skim the email, certain lines jump out at me: "light of my life," "she's a fighter," and "an old soul who touches everyone who meets her." As I press send, I feel that someone will call us. I mean, how could they not write a story about Adrienne?

The day before we are to meet Dr. Marco, Adrienne lies in bed with pain infiltrating her body from all sides. Her head hurts, her shoulder aches, and her back spasms due to pressure caused by her now-enlarged spleen. I give her 2 mg of Dilaudid around 3 p.m. As her pain increases, I first increase the frequency of the medication, from every four hours to two hours to one hour, and then I increase the amount, giving her 6 mg of Dilaudid at midnight so she can sleep in peace. She has consumed a total of 14 mg of Dilaudid for the day, the most since her last round of chemo. I wonder what, if anything, Dr. Marco will say about her pain. Is it a sign? Is Adrienne getting worse? Are the tumors spreading? How can we make the pain go away?

As soon as Adrienne wakes up, I give her another 6 mg of Dilaudid so she can make it through our appointment with Dr. Marco. She keeps asking about Dr. Aquino at UCLA, but I tell her to be patient since Medi-Cal has not approved the transfer yet. I never had time to conjure an image in my mind of what Dr. Marco would look like so when he walks into the examination room, he does not fail to meet any expectations. He appears younger than Dr. No, and he volunteers he is originally from Brazil, which I would not have guessed given his light complexion.

First, I ask him about Adrienne's increased pain. Dr. Marco lapses into a monologue about stable vs. progressive disease without answering my question. As soon as he finishes speaking, Adrienne wastes no time telling him what she wants.

"I don't want to be on cisplatin anymore. I'd rather be dead than deaf."

I can't wait to see how he responds to her.

"We can try amifostine with the cisplatin to help lessen any potential hearing loss."

He hasn't read her chart yet.

"We already tried that, Dr. Marco," I reply. "As you can tell, Adrienne isn't happy with the result. Plus, the amifostine made her very sick. There must be other drugs."

"Of course. Carboplatin and etoposide are two other possibilities, but carboplatin can hurt the kidneys," says Dr. Marco.

"Are those chemotherapy drugs?" I ask as I write down the drug names phonetically in my spiral notebook.

"Yes. Since your sister is tolerating Adriamycin well, we can give her dexrazoxane, a cytoprotective agent, before administering the treatment." *Good, her heart will be protected now.* "I recommend replacing cisplatin with ifosfamide; it causes bladder damage, but another cytoprotective agent, mesna, can help minimize that side effect, and well, the bladder isn't a vital organ like your kidneys."

Adrienne blanches, but I can see her mind turning over the possibilities: keep my hearing and kidneys; lose my bladder. She nods.

I scribble notes as fast as I can. Dr. Marco treats me like an equal, and I don't want him to think I can't keep up. *Thank god, I bought that Consumers Guide book. All these drugs will be listed there.* I ask, "What about Xeloda?" remembering the discussion with Dr. Aquino.

"Xeloda converts to 5-fluorouracil, or 5-FU, in your body; it has no proof of efficacy with liver cancer."

I nod, not because I agree with him, but I already know that Xeloda is a derivative of 5-FU. I read about it after the appointment at UCLA.

I push harder. "Have you used Xeloda before?"

"No, but I'll be happy to look up some studies for you."

I say, "Fine," even though I suspect he will find studies to support his position.

Dr. Marco continues, "Thalidomide has proven successful in increasing appetite, weight, and lean body mass in cancer patients."

"The drug that caused birth defects?" I ask him believing I must be wrong.

"Yes. The very same."

"Oh. Okay."

I write down thalidomide wondering when it came back on the market.

"What about Epogen? I read it can treat or even prevent anemia caused by chemo."

"We can try it; it has proven effective in many cases."

Wait a minute. I just suggested a drug, and you said okay. If it is such a good idea, why didn't Dr. No prescribe it before?

Adrienne interrupts for the first time since she got her way about the cisplatin. "My bones and muscles ache. What's causing that? And I'm always nauseous. Nothing helps."

Dr. Marco replies, "We should check your calcium and magnesium. You might need supplements. We'll schedule a quick blood test before you leave today."

"Can we continue the Pravachol?"

"I don't see why not; it's not hurting your sister." Dr. Marco looks at Adrienne. "You know, we could try Marinol for your nausea."

"Marinol?" Adrienne and I ask the question in unison.

"It's the medicinal form of marijuana."

I voted for that bill to pass in a state election years ago. I never thought it would affect us though.

"I shouldn't say this, but smoking the drug is better. Many people have no response to the synthetic form."

Adrienne laughs.

"You mean I can take pot—legally?"

"That's what I'm recommending," says Dr. Marco.

I don't know how to respond.

"You said smoking it was better . . . but I wouldn't even know where to get it."

Adrienne laughs harder and says, "I can think of a few people."

Dr. Marco smiles.

"Well, I can't help you there, but we'll try the pill first and see how it works for you. I'll have Teresa call you later today to follow up with our conversation."

He looks at Adrienne.

"I'll see you soon," he says before walking out.

"I can't believe I'm going to take pot! All those times I said no at school, and now I get to take it and see what the big deal is."

I see Adrienne's shoulder blades jut out as she hunches over, still chuckling over the recent turn of events.

187

I feel myself smiling.

"I can't believe it either, kiddo. I've never tried pot; you'll have to tell me what it's like." *If Marinol helps you gain some weight, then I'm glad I voted for it.*

An old college friend Nicole calls to tell me she is in town. She wants to take me out to lunch tomorrow to show off her new baby, Sarah, whom I've never met. I was a bridesmaid in Nicole's wedding three years ago. Adrienne attended as a guest. Nicole knows Adrienne is sick, but she seems surprised when I explain I can't have lunch with her.

"My life is different now," I tell her. "I can't just jump up and leave anymore, but you are welcome to come by the house."

Nicole finds a reason to say no. Still wanting to see her, I suggest she visit us at the hospital next week saying how much Adrienne likes company during chemo. Nicole doesn't respond, but I feel her apprehension through the phone line. Part of me wants to say your precious baby girl can't catch cancer, but I don't. Nicole is a mental healthcare provider; I shouldn't have to tell her what she already knows.

Nicole and I have been growing apart for years. She moved to the East Coast after graduation and converted to Christianity. Living in Philly didn't hurt our friendship much; Nicole becoming a Christian and believing I was a sinner doomed to hell, however, did. Then Nicole says it, one of those stupid utterances people offer when they don't know what else to say.

"God only gives you what you can handle."

My jaw drops. I mumble goodbye and I hang up.

Of course, I come up with the perfect response later that evening.

I wish I had said, "By your logic, Adrienne got cancer because she and I are strong people, who are given tests in the form of diseases that might kill them. So if Adrienne and I were weaker people, she would be healthy now."

I want to show Nicole how irrational her statement is, but she never calls me again.

Days 59-61

I am on a different plane when I dance. All my troubles and problems disappear for that one brief moment. In my head, I see myself growing wings and spiraling again and again, letting all my headaches and stress vanish through my body and its movements. I feel graceful and beautiful, even if I'm not technically amazing. Dancing has a hidden factor that I cannot describe in words, that hits a nerve and just lets everything flow within me. It is almost as if I am cured from something when I am dancing, but I am not quite sure what I have been cured of once I stop.

—Excerpt from Adrienne's essay for dance class

Today Adrienne has her first appointment with Nina, a licensed R.N. and a practitioner of Alternative Medicine. We met Nina on the last night of Adrienne's first round of chemo. I trust her because she is familiar with Adrienne's illness, and she approaches it holistically, an attitude Adrienne and I both appreciate. We don't know what to expect, but the ninety-minute session consists of massage and meditation. I doze off waiting in the lobby even though I normally don't fall asleep sitting up. A rejuvenated Adrienne emerges, almost glowing with serenity as if the war in her body has agreed to a cease-fire. Energetic and pain-free, Adrienne asks how long it will take to get to the mall.

We are on a mission to find the perfect dress for a benefit being thrown in Adrienne's honor. The Stage Door Theatre in Agoura Hills is donating tonight's proceeds from their production of *The Seven Year Itch* to Adrienne for her medical care. The owners offered to produce the affair because I had previously directed and acted in two shows there. The unexpected generosity of acquaintances helps balance out the sting of comments from supposed friends.

As Adrienne and I soon discover, the best time to go prom-dress shopping is during the summer. She spots a full-length, royal blue, sleeveless gown with a tank style top and an A-line bottom. The dress fits well. While it is too large in places where Adrienne continues to lose weight, it doesn't constrict her abdomen, which remains swollen by her liver and spleen. At 80 percent off, we can afford the twenty-dollar dress. Adrienne also buys a black-studded belt for herself and a Polaroid camera for Nadia's birthday. We complete our shopping excursion with shakes and fries at Johnny Rockets, our favorite mall food. Watching Adrienne munch on fries like any typical teenager, I think how today is almost perfect.

Adrienne invites Eli to attend the benefit with us. We take John's car; of course, Adrienne rides shotgun. Fiddling with my camera, I tell her to look back at me. Even though her olive eyes are half-closed, she appears fully awake, as if she knows something we don't. I cock the camera at an odd angle.

"Hurry up, Sissy."

SNAP. Adrienne yawns. That picture will be gorgeous.

Many people attend the benefit, which raises nearly a thousand dollars. Actors I worked with in the past show up, as well as close friends like Anya, Alex, and Anya's brother, who happens to be in town. Adrienne tells me afterward she feels guilty for falling asleep during the play, but I tell her not to worry about it. Everyone is happy she is well enough to be here.

We take many pictures after the show, and friends groan every time my camera freezes.

But I love my ten-year-old 35 mm Minolta and refuse to buy a new one.

"Wait. Wait. Hold on. I've got it now," I say more than a few times.

Formerly camera shy, Adrienne strikes a pose in her new dress and points to her head, where she applied body glitter earlier that evening.

"My new look," she says.

I smile. She has the confidence of a runway model. The atmosphere is festive, and I realize I haven't felt this relaxed in a long time.

The local newspaper *The Acorn* interviews us, and I can see John grimacing because the reporter pays little attention to him. John thinks people don't ask his opinion because they don't understand his role in Adrienne's life. He doesn't realize his constant frown, his stiff arms, and his penetrating eyes don't make him the most approachable person. He's different at home, away from strangers. I wish they could see what Adrienne and I do. John loves her like a father.

I wake up at 1:30 a.m. to faint cries.

"Sissy . . . Sissy."

I find Adrienne in the bathroom trying to poop.

"It's right there, Sissy. I can feel it."

I give her Peri-Colace with an orange juice chaser. All modesty aside, Adrienne allows John to hold her hand while I grab our trusted notebook. I look for the smiley faces. Yesterday, no, day before yesterday, no. *Oh god. That can't be right.*

"Well, when was the last time?" asks John.

I meet Adrienne's eyes. She must know. I feel like I'm ratting us both out to the school principal.

"According to this," I wave at the notebook, "last week." *Damn that Dilaudid. Damn me for not realizing. For not asking.*

"What? I thought you were handling this!" John raises his voice.

"Don't fight," Adrienne whimpers. "What are we going to do?"

John squeezes Adrienne's hand.

"Hang in there, kiddo. We'll figure something out."

Our immediate solution is to wait. Constipation is not usually life-threatening. Thirty minutes later, Adrienne has a small bowel movement and releases some gas, but she still cannot move. Time to call the hospital.

The doctor on-call prescribes MiraLAX. I rush to the one pharmacy near us that is open twenty-four hours to pick it up. Despite the urgency, a miscommunication between the hospital and the pharmacy causes a delay. John and I attempt to ease Adrienne's anxiety and pain by joking about Danny Glover in *Lethal Weapon 2*. Hey kiddo, at least there's no bomb under the toilet, but even she isn't laughing now. *Damn. Where's that prescription?*

Adrienne takes the first dose of MiraLAX at 3:15 a.m. The doctor said we would see results right away. We are more hopeful. We allow thirty minutes to pass before declaring the MiraLAX a complete failure. We call the doctor back, and he says Adrienne needs to be admitted to the hospital right away. He doesn't realize Adrienne hasn't moved in three hours; her legs are numb. She can't stand up on her own, and John and I can't lift her without help.

I call 911 and explain the situation without getting hysterical. I explicitly request paramedics with pain medication due to Adrienne's condition. The operator assures me she will send the appropriate team to our home. I wait outside to flag them down since no one can find our house. John sits with Adrienne doing hand duty.

When the paramedics arrive, I apprise them of the situation, but they are reluctant to give Adrienne anything at all. I fly into a rage and scream at the top of my lungs.

"You have to help her. She can't move. I told the 911 operator all of this! Please, help my baby!"

John rushes outside and tells me to go in the house. He will handle it. Tears stream down my face; I know part of my anger is misdirected. I'm mad at myself because I could have prevented this problem from happening. I should have asked Adrienne about going to the bathroom; she's not one to volunteer that information. People love to tell fart jokes, but nobody likes to talk about their own shit.

I don't know what John says to them, but the paramedics agree to give Adrienne nitrous oxide to relax her. Even though Adrienne doesn't want two strange men to see her stranded on a toilet, trapped by pain, she is open to any option that will end her misery. Adrienne inhales the invisible fumes, and within minutes, the laughing gas eases her suffering enough for the paramedics to lift her to a standing position. I quickly pull up her panties. They carry her to the stretcher, and I climb in the ambulance for the short ride to St. Jo's wondering if Dr. Lin, *she has tumors in her liver and lungs,* will be there.

By a quarter after four, I am signing the familiar pink "Patient Rights and Responsibilities" form. Dr. Lin isn't working. Instead, we meet the affable Dr. Wallace, who gives Adrienne Dilaudid for the pain and Ativan for her increasing anxiety. Her blood tests are normal. The doctor on-call from Children's Hospital wants Adrienne transferred there immediately, but we decide to stay at St. Jo's. Adrienne likes Dr. Wallace and if she is only constipated, I am sure he is more than capable of handling the matter. Sometimes the doctors at Children's Hospital act as though no other doctor is competent when it comes to their patients. *He's not curing cancer; he needs her to poop.*

John and I stay in the room while Dr. Wallace prepares for the dis-impaction, the removal of feces in the rectum, by doing an initial rectal exam. Despite the enormous amount of medication, Adrienne's eyes water.

"It hurts."

I soothe her with words since I am unable to touch her. Adrienne allows us to be nearby, but not so close that we might see anything. I feel helpless.

I see Dr. Wallace shaking his head. He tells Adrienne he's finished and covers her up. Then he walks toward us.

"I don't feel stool in the colon, but there appears to be a mass. Perhaps a teratoma," he says.

Damn. I didn't bring the medical dictionary.

"A what?" I ask.

"A type of tumor. I'm going to call Children's. I think she should be transferred now."

Minutes later, a nurse hands me a pen and a new white form to sign, a "Patient Transfer Summary and Acknowledgment." Someone else already filled in the boxes. I notice under diagnosis Dr. Wallace, or perhaps a nurse wrote, "constipation, possible rectal mass." According to the paper, Dr. Feinstein is receiving the transfer; I'm relieved the doctor on-call will not be there to say I told you so.

Two months ago, we didn't even know the disease ravaging Adrienne's body existed. I want to go back to the 'before' when things seemed normal. Our lives were by no means perfect, but now this black hole called cancer is using its gravitational force to suck us in deeper every day. Even light cannot escape a black hole, and isn't that what hope is: that clichéd light at the end of the tunnel. As we travel from one fluorescent-lit emergency room to another one over the hill, I long to see Adrienne walking. Outside. In the sunshine. A momentary coldness creeps into my heart as the black hole says to me . . . you may never see that image again.

We wait for hours in the emergency room because the oncology ward has no beds available. John and I take turns getting breakfast in the cafeteria. When I show up, I see the cook behind the counter.

"Two eggs, sunny-side up?" he asks.

I nod.

"Haven't seen you in a while."

I nod again because I am too tired to speak. I don't tell this nice man I am not supposed to be here today, the third round of chemo starts next week. I don't tell him how sad it makes me he remembers my order. He senses my reluctance and asks the person behind me what he wants.

I glance at the stranger over my shoulder. *Just wait, if you spend too much time here, he'll memorize your order too.*

Adrienne finally has a CT scan at 3:30 p.m., but the results are far from conclusive. Dr. Feinstein reads the results as normal with some stool in the rectum. The radiologist concedes there is no abnormality, but he sees lots of stool in the colon. When Adrienne's oncologist Dr. Marco arrives, he comes up with a different conclusion. He agrees stool is present, but he is concerned about what appears to be a pouch in the rectum, possibly an abscess.

What the hell? I don't know whom to believe. At least they all agree Adrienne needs to go to the bathroom.

Since the rectum is a perfect host for bacteria, oncologists are careful about administering any medication anally because cancer patients cannot afford to have infections. Although reluctant to do so, Dr. Marco prescribes a suppository, and Adrienne has a bowel movement twenty minutes later. If I had known it would be that easy, I would have given her a suppository myself at home. When I ask about the teratoma, Dr. Marco says we will discuss it next week after he reviews Dr. Wallace's notes.

Feeling hungry for the first time in twenty-four hours, Adrienne eats a salad and falls into a deep drug-induced sleep. Anya and Alex bring us clothes, toiletries, and videos from the house. John and I watch *Jurassic Park*. As we begin to watch the sequel *The Lost World*, Adrienne wakes up experiencing intense cramping that leads to diarrhea. I help her walk to the bathroom next to her bed, but she shuts the door in my face. I can do it, Sissy, she says. *Poor kid. She's had enough humiliation to last a lifetime.* I don't note the diarrhea with happy faces in the notebook since it is not the desired outcome.

The doctors and nurses are befuddled. The suppository should have worn off so they speculate the diarrhea might be a delayed effect of the MiraLAX. *Somehow, I doubt it.* Even though Adrienne feels nauseated too, she's still hungry and attempts to eat a few French fries.

"I need to throw up, but I can't," she grumbles.

The doctors hope Adrienne's regular dosage of Dilaudid will counteract the diarrhea and constipate her. *Here we go again, the seesaw factor.* At 10:30 p.m., the nurse administers Ativan through Adrienne's central line; she falls asleep within fifteen minutes. They hope her stomach will settle down overnight.

The next morning, Adrienne insists on going home because we have tickets to the ballet that afternoon. Since her bowel movements have ceased and we are going to return tomorrow for her chemo, Dr. Marco agrees to let her go home. He discharges Adrienne at 9:15 a.m., and only one item appears on the list of medications—Milk of Magnesia for constipation, 15 mL, PRN. Adrienne now has thirteen prescriptions.

⚹ ⚹ ⚹

Watching Adrienne and Sharon kick up their heels to the Andrews Sisters' tune "*Boogie Woogie Bugle Boy*," I couldn't help but smile. I held the video camera as steady as I could during Adrienne's first dance performance three months ago. I had practiced all week during the rehearsals until I had her routine memorized. I knew when she and Sharon would veer away from the group to perform their partner sequence. I zoomed in on them to capture their close-up. Adrienne's blue ponytail whipped through the air as she spun into a pirouette, and Sharon's ponytail brushed her bottom as she jumped into splits. Even though they were in the Beginning Dance class, their group's infectious energy had the crowd cheering.

I had always wanted Adrienne to love dance the way I do, but I never forced it on her. Our mother enrolled her in dance class when she was three years old. She figured if one daughter liked to dance, the other one would too. With her sullen expression and rouge on her cheeks, Adrienne looked like a sad clown the night of her recital. Our mother never made her dance again.

Adrienne showed interest in gymnastics. Mother paid for tumbling lessons and swimming lessons, but those extracurricular activities stopped when she was fired. When I taught gymnastics at a local park in Hollywood, Adrienne participated in my classes. In exchange for teaching one day per week, Adrienne attended the summer program free excluding the cost of the weekly field trips. The following year, I taught the dance drill team at Adrienne's elementary school, and they won an honorable mention for creative choreography at the citywide competition. On the way home, Adrienne cried on the bus because the team didn't place. Given the fact I was hired two months prior to the contest, I was proud of the girls. They did their best, but I couldn't console Adrienne. She thought she could have danced better.

* * *

Putting the last thirty-six hours behind her, Adrienne focuses on what she's going to wear to the ballet. She puts on her new pink fairy shirt along with her new blue jeans that look like different sections of denim sewn together, giving the jeans a patchwork feel to them. She completes her ensemble with her new belt, her favorite blue-jelly bracelets, and black eyeliner. She rubs more glitter on her head to make it sparkle. As I take pictures, I try to elicit a smile, but she gives me a parents-are-lame look.

As I had hoped, the editor of *The Burbank Leader* called, and a reporter interviewed Adrienne and me a few days ago. Today, a photographer shows up to take Adrienne's picture, which will accompany the story the paper is publishing next week. As I watch the photographer snapping away, I know the precise moment when he captures his perfect shot. Adrienne is putting on mascara; her eyes are wide open and she is peering into her mirrored closet door. **SNAP!** The photographer shoots her reflection as the mascara wand brushes her long eyelashes. I stand back near the bedroom door and wonder what Adrienne is thinking.

After the photographer leaves, Adrienne asks me to help her with her foundation.

"I look so pale, Sissy."

The regular beige color she uses for her olive skin is too dark now, so we apply my foundation, a shade of ivory.

John walks in and out of Adrienne's room and asks every few minutes, "Are you sure this is a good idea? You just got home, kiddo."

She gives him the same look she gave me when I tried to take her picture. She's going to this ballet, no matter what. I bought the tickets months ago. The truth is I want to go too.

Adrienne ended up taking dance in high school by accident. Thrilled she was able to choose from a variety of activities for her P.E. credit, a class she had always hated and almost failed in elementary school, she signed up for golf. However, when she came home with the list of the items she would need to begin, I told her she had to choose another class. We couldn't afford to buy even a used set of golf clubs, and she didn't know if she liked the sport. I suspect she chose golf because she wanted as little aerobic activity as possible. She didn't want to change the rest of her schedule, so Adrienne chose the only other P.E. class that fit into that time slot—Beginning Dance.

The first semester she complained a lot about how clumsy she was and how she was never going to get it. When she landed a spot in the fall dance show, she refused to participate, citing stage fright as her excuse. Halfway through the school year, she liked dance more. Upon arriving home, she asked me questions such as how do you spot when you turn, Sissy? Or how can I improve my extension? I hid my enthusiasm for her growing love of dance, but I was secretly thrilled we shared a passion. She and John had music; now, she and I had dance. When she came home and told me she was doing the spring dance show and she was auditioning for dance the following year, I hugged her. I suggested we take ballet classes together that summer to help her improve her technique, and she loved the idea.

Adrienne wanted to see Sylvie Guillem perform after watching the ballerina execute an incredible modern dance piece titled *Wet Woman*. The short clip aired on television along with an interview with Sylvie, who was preparing to choreograph *Giselle*, a full-length classical ballet.

"Can we see her, Sissy? Pleeeaaassse."

I was as entranced by Sylvie as Adrienne was and seeing a ballet together seemed fitting given our summer plans.

In the past, I had taken Adrienne to see *Grease* and *Riverdance* for her eleventh and twelfth birthdays respectively. I loved taking her to see shows. It was becoming a tradition until she asked for cash on her thirteenth birthday. Lucky for us, Sylvie was performing with the La Scala Ballet at the Orange County Performing Arts Center. I splurged and bought the best tickets in the house: Orchestra, Row A, Seats 3 and 4.

"Sissy, look at what you did!"

Frustrated, Adrienne peers at herself in the mirror attached to the passenger seat visor in my car.

"What?"

I glance over briefly, but I turn back to keep my eyes on the road. We left the house five minutes ago, and we are about to get on the freeway.

"My makeup! It's uneven," Adrienne pouts.

I sigh and look at the clock on my dashboard. We still have time to go home and correct it; I didn't bring the foundation with us.

"I'll fix it. Don't worry."

I pull into the liquor store parking lot to turn around and go back the way we came. When we arrive, John freaks out.

"What's wrong? Did something happen? Are you okay?"

He looks at Adrienne.

"I need to fix her makeup John. Relax."

Adrienne trails me into her bathroom where the light is far better than in her bedroom where we originally did her makeup. I even out the foundation as best I can, filling in the places I missed and blending with a light touch of powder. I notice ivory is too dark for Adrienne's face. I suspect she is anemic, but I don't mention it.

Ten minutes later, we are back in the car again and on our way to Orange County. We attend the preview lecture about *Giselle*, which tells the history and story of the ballet. A peasant girl Giselle falls for a prince, but when she finds out he is betrothed to another, she goes mad and dies. In the second act, Giselle enters the land of the Wilis, spirits of young women who were betrayed and died before their wedding day. She ends up saving the prince from the Wilis, who try to kill him by literally dancing him to his death.

As we settle into our front row seats, I squeeze Adrienne's hand, "I am so glad we came, sweetie."

She nods as her attention focuses on the stage. Not only did Sylvie Guillem choreograph this modernized version of *Giselle*, but she also plays the lead role, a concept similar to an actor directing and starring in the same film. Adrienne and I are both disappointed by Giselle's mad scene, the climax of act one. Sylvie's choreography doesn't incorporate the strengths of her talent; she seems to be playing it safe.

During intermission, I ask Adrienne how her pain is. She missed her Dilaudid at 2 p.m., and given what happened on Friday night, I only want to give it to her when she needs it. She says she feels fine. Distracted by our conversation, Adrienne is unable to dodge out of the way when a little boy comes zipping around the corner with a chocolate ice cream cone. The top of the scoop brushes the bottom of Adrienne's new shirt.

"Damn!"

I tell her we can get it out, but I'm not sure. The stain will probably set before we get home.

We return to our seats. As the Wilis begin their famous dance to exhaust the Prince to his grave, Adrienne leans over.

"Sissy, it hurts."

"What?" I whisper.

"My side. My liver."

"Hold on."

I fish around in my bag for the Dilaudid. *Stupid—I should have given her some earlier.* I give Adrienne four milligrams while I look for water. *Where is that damn water bottle? I always carry water.* Meanwhile, the selfish part of me is sorry I am missing the most interesting part of the entire ballet, but it's my fault.

"I'll be right back."

I rush into the lobby to buy water, but I'm dismayed when I see all the vendors are closed. I see a woman counting money and think maybe it's not too late.

"May I buy some water?"

"We're closed."

"I know. Look, I just need one bottle."

The woman stares at me as if I'm an idiot who didn't hear her the first time. Time to play the C-card.

"My child has cancer. She needs the water to swallow her pain pills."

The woman says of course and insists I take the water bottle; she won't let me pay for it. I sneak back into the show. Adrienne takes her medication. The Wilis' dance is over. Giselle is dead and the prince lives happily ever after.

On the way home, Adrienne falls asleep in the car. That night she has a low-grade fever, and her pain worsens. She breaks it down for me: right lower rib—8; back—7; right shoulder—8; and liver—8. I get the feeling this next round of chemo is not going to be as smooth as the last one. I dread going to the hospital tomorrow, almost as much as Adrienne does.

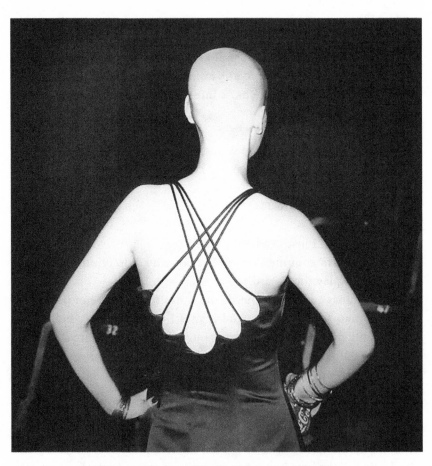

Adrienne showing off her new dress at the benefit.

Days 62-67

I dont know what im feeling i don't know if i want a leash straining my course of breathing right now fantasy world seems so much more peaceful if i was happy i wouldn't have to escape reality i don't think i was built for certain things im no trophy what if a cloud the mind the last thing i need is a dip back into depression that's what created them in the first place maybe ive been here this entire time distraction::sigh::i don't know i don't know

—Adrienne's journal entry dated 7/3/01

We check into the hospital at 9 a.m. The nurses already have a nail polish remover pad for Adrienne. We both laugh but there is something disconcerting about the nurses remembering Adrienne always wears nail polish, like the cook who knows how I like my eggs. *We spend too much time here.*

Adrienne takes the blue nail polish off her middle finger and then attaches the monitor that tracks her heart rate, respiratory rate, and pulse. I find it ironic that two layers of nail polish can prevent a sophisticated piece of machinery from working. Despite all the drugs, Adrienne's nails keep growing; they are long, healthy, and strong, unlike her body.

Before long, Dr. Marco arrives. Though Dr. Wallace suspected Adrienne might have a teratoma, Dr. Marco explains there are three reasons why she doesn't have one. Teratomas are masses that would have shown up on any CT scan. Cisplatin, the chemo drug Adrienne refuses to take again, should have shrunk any teratomas; those tumors respond well to that drug. Adrienne's symptoms do not match a diagnosis of a teratoma.

I should have known better. Part of me needed Dr. Wallace to be right: Adrienne has a teratoma, which is more treatable according to my books. I read all about teratomas last night. I didn't pray for it the way I prayed Adrienne had ovarian cancer instead of liver cancer. Instead, the elusive teratoma became my beacon of hope.

Dr. Marco delays chemo because he is still concerned about the possibility of an abscess in Adrienne's rectum. He starts Adrienne on two different antibiotics and says he will have a gastroenterologist (GI) look at her CT scan from this past weekend. As the attending physician this week, Dr. Feinstein attempts a rectal exam, but it proves to be inconclusive because he has to stop when Adrienne cries. I see she has hemorrhoids now, and I wonder what caused them. Then, I remember the silly smiley faces I draw in our spiral notebook whenever Adrienne has a bowel movement. There has only been one smiley face during the past three days. Given that amount of constipation, of course she has hemorrhoids. When no one can mimic Dr. Wallace's findings, they are dismissed.

A weird rash has erupted on Adrienne's back. Its appearance reminds me of ringworm, only it is straight, not round. The nurse scrapes a sample of it for testing and applies topical ointment. When I ask several doctors how Adrienne got a fungus on her back, they don't know the answer.

As they do every Monday, PAWS visits the entire fourth floor. Adrienne leans over and smiles for her picture with Vera, the black lab. Her face is almost paler than the white gown she's wearing, and her eyes are sunken into her head. The volunteer sees Adrienne is sicker than usual and keeps the visit short. I thank her for coming by, and I watch the Polaroid picture develop. With a tired smile, a wan Adrienne stares back at the camera. Even Vera looks sad and today is only the first day of this hospital stay. *Great.*

That evening, I simmer when Adrienne still hasn't gotten her PCA. She receives Dilaudid through her IV now, but Dr. Marco ordered a PCA earlier that day so the doctors can assess Adrienne's pain more accurately. We also requested an oxygen mask hours ago, instead of the usual nasal tube, but Adrienne doesn't have one yet. When her 8 p.m. meds are late, I finally lose my temper and ask to speak to the house supervisor. Keeping my voice calm, I tell her what we need as I check off each complaint in my notebook, not bothering to hide my notes from her. In many ways, a hospital is no different from any other business; one has to speak to the right person to get things done. Within fifteen minutes, our needs are met.

Adrienne sleeps in fits. The pain wakes her up. Every time I hear the *click* of the PCA machine, I know she is hurting, and I cannot fix it. The kid who had so few colds I can count them on one hand now lies in a hospital bed, unable to sleep, with heavy narcotics in her body that seem to be doing no good. I remember one time when I let her stay home from school because her head cold had reached its peak. We cuddled together on the couch, drank hot chocolate, and watched as a Los Angeles jury pronounced O.J. Simpson 'not guilty' for the murders of his former wife Nicole Brown Simpson and Ron Goldman. We both gasped.

Then, a pensive nine-year-old Adrienne asked, "How can something like that happen, Sissy?"

"I don't know, kiddo."

How could something like this happen to you now? I don't know.

"Sissy, come look at this!"

Adrienne summons me into the bathroom the following morning to examine her pee, which has turned burnt orange, beautiful for a sunset, ominous for a sick girl.

"Don't flush it. We'll have the nurse look at it."

Despite its tint, Adrienne's urine shows no traces of blood and the analysis is normal. Even her CBC is normal, revealing no infection thus rendering the antibiotics useless. Her bilirubin is high, which might have caused her urine to change color, but no one will give me a definitive answer on that issue either. *Argh.*

The GI agrees with Dr. Marco's recommendations: a contrast enema and an X-ray of the pelvis. However, one doctor agreeing with the other does not guarantee immediate results. Like our first ER visit and Adrienne's biopsy surgery, you must wait your turn. I sense Dr. Marco's frustration when the GI department delays Adrienne's tests, but I am relieved when he fights on behalf of Adrienne. Behind the hospital doors in this land of medical bureaucracy, his words carry far more weight than mine do. Dr. Marco explains the situation is urgent: Adrienne's chemo is on hold until the tests are done. With that argument, the GI and other departments cooperate. Done that afternoon, the pelvis X-ray shows stool in the colon, but not the rectum.

Meanwhile, Adrienne continues to push the button on the PCA, pumping more Dilaudid into her body to assuage her increasing pain. The more medication she receives, the more constipated she becomes. However, I'm less worried about any blockage at this point and more worried about her getting the nutrients she needs. She hasn't kept food down all day.

Like the California wildfires, there are so many hot spots in Adrienne's body right now; the doctors don't know which one should be treated first. They are focused on what happened over the weekend, and now there's the orange pee, the funky rash, and the constant nausea. What about the cancer pain, which desperately needs the chemo that was supposed to start yesterday? I never ask that question, but it burns inside of me, my own personal fire, waiting to be put out.

Instead of pain waking her up tonight, Adrienne's nausea and subsequent vomiting wake us both up at 3 a.m. We had not been sleeping long. The attending physician gave Adrienne a magnesium citrate laxative at 2:15 a.m. in preparation for the lower GI enema in seven hours. At least two-thirds of it comes up, and I worry Adrienne will not be ready for the test. I find out later the magnesium citrate was not necessary, and I want to hurt that physician for interrupting Adrienne's sleep and for making her sick. I decide not to tell Adrienne she didn't need it.

While John goes with Adrienne to Radiology for the contrast enema, I gather my toiletries and go to the "Parent Sleep Room and Shower Area." To get there, I walk to the end of the 4 West wing, where I pass the big steel doors to the Bone Marrow Transplant (BMT) unit. Every time I see those doors, I think how much worse it could be for us. At least, we don't have to wear protective gear and masks to see Adrienne. *But people survive bone marrow transplants, don't they?*

After bypassing the BMT unit, I open a fire exit door; a sign above it reads, "Keep door closed." I pass stairs that lead somewhere and then go through yet another door, which lands me into a white corridor that connects to another building, where the parent room is located. With two restrooms, two showers, four locked sleep rooms, and a washer and dryer, it has all the amenities of home, except for its antiseptic smell, lack of loofahs, and tubes of toothpaste with missing caps.

I always expect to see another parent here, especially since BMT parents get priority (they are not allowed to sleep in their children's rooms), but I haven't yet. I know some stay at the Ronald McDonald House down the street, but I need to be closer to Adrienne. Others don't stay at all. I felt awkward at first, walking around with my bag and towel, navigating the maze, I even got lost twice, but I'm used to it now. The housekeeper smiles when she sees me and sometimes gives me extra towels. I shower as quickly as possible; otherwise, I will lose myself in negative thoughts, as Adrienne would say.

John and Adrienne return. When I ask her how the test went, she frowns. John waits until Adrienne falls asleep for a mid-morning nap before telling me how horrible the contrast enema was.

"Kiddo was in so much pain. I just wanted to take it away."

The enema causes diarrhea, which counts as a bowel movement although it's not ideal. When Adrienne wakes up, the doctor gives her Lasix to help her urinate. She also begins her first dose of Epogen, the drug that should improve her anemia.

Dr. Feinstein examines Adrienne that evening. He tells us the culture from the rash proves it is not a fungus, but a kind of unknown skin infection they will treat with antibiotics for forty-eight hours. I ask if we can start chemo tonight, and he hesitates.

"She'll feel better once she has chemo," I say.

John and I plead with him.

"Okay, but we're going to watch for mucus in the lungs after the treatment is over."

I love how doctors call chemo 'treatment' when it's actually poison. Any treatment that kills healthy cells should be questioned, not that we have any alternatives.

A few hours later, a nurse covered in scrubs brings in the poison, and we discover the timing of the Adriamycin is different. When I ask the nurse why, she summons the doctor. Most nurses are wary of John and me. Apparently, our reputation precedes us. One of the few nurses we like, Helen, told us what other staff members said.

"The kid is great, but the parents—watch out! They ask too many questions. They are too involved, and they are too needy."

I don't care what they think. Besides, these same people asked me about Adrienne's PCA dosage last month because they lost her chart. And we ask too many questions? *Right.*

At 12:20 a.m., Dr. Feinstein explains there are different protocols for different combinations of drugs. A lower dosage of Adriamycin is given in conjunction with ifosfamide (instead of cisplatin—the "I'd rather be dead than deaf" drug). Since Adrienne is receiving dexrazoxane to protect her heart, the Adriamycin will be administered much faster than before, but still in twenty-four-hour increments. I thank Dr. Feinstein for his thoroughness. All John and I want is to understand the process.

The following day, Dr. Feinstein delays Adrienne's chemo because her urine is not clean enough, meaning it has not separated from her stool. Even though I wanted chemo to start last night, I don't ask why this non-separation issue matters. At least Adrienne is going to the bathroom; the Milk of Magnesia is doing its job. One fire out, another one breaks out.

A nurse takes a culture of a white spot in Adrienne's left nostril, another unexplainable skin abnormality that appeared overnight. I don't understand why these problems are popping up, especially considering how good chemo has been for Adrienne's skin. In two months, the pimples on her face, the benign cyst inside her mouth, and the warts on her hands have all disappeared. The poison has improved harmless skin conditions, but it has not reduced the cancerous tumors inside her body. How ironic.

That afternoon, we meet Dr. Howdy Doody, a tall redheaded man, who specializes in neuropathic pain.[10] I like him immediately because it seems important to him John and I comprehend what is going on in Adrienne's body, or at least what his theory is. Without being condescending, he speaks to Adrienne.

"Do you know that the nerve sends signals to the brain that there is pain?"

She nods.

"Well, your brain has memory of that pain, and your body pays attention to your pain."

She nods again.

I fervently take notes.

"The drugs we give you address the signals from the nerves. We're going to switch you from Ativan to Valium; it might help you relax more."

Then Dr. Doody tilts his head toward the door and eyes John and me. We follow him outside. Adrienne appears too tired to care.

"Don't ask Adrienne about her pain anymore. Let her bring it up."

"Why not?" I ask.

---

10 Neuropathic pain originates in the nerves themselves rather than in other damaged organs that are innervated by them.

"You don't want to reinforce the acute nature of a chronic illness."

"So by asking her if she's in pain, her brain may process that information and believe she feels pain, even if her body doesn't, because her brain remembers it?"

"Something like that. Just let her bring it up. I think the Valium will make a big difference too. Let me know if you need anything else." Dr. Doody shakes our hands, says goodbye, and walks away from us. *I like him. Why have we never met him before?*

Adrienne begins the first day of her third round of chemo at 5:20 p.m. She receives dexrazoxane followed by Adriamycin for fifteen minutes, then ifosfamide for one hour followed by mesna, which will protect her kidneys, for three hours. At 8 p.m., she takes her first dose of Valium as well as her first Marinol pill. I marvel at how the small brown round ball is synthetic marijuana. Adrienne smiles after swallowing it.

"I can't wait to tell my friends I'm taking pot—by prescription!"

I laugh. If it works, she can tell the whole world. *Please let it work. You can't lose any more weight, kiddo. Fifteen pounds is enough.*

I hear moaning on the other side of the curtain. Adrienne's roommate is eight-year-old Veronica, who has been diagnosed with neuroblastoma that started in her stomach.[11] She had surgery to remove the tumor and now she is undergoing chemotherapy. Unfortunately, her body is not tolerating the treatment well, and she is experiencing all the possible side effects including sores in her mouth and rectum. Her constant whining grates on everyone's nerves. I should be sympathetic, but Veronica has a better chance of survival. I looked it up. I call a nurse to help her and go back to sleep. *Poor kid. She needs her mom right now, not some stranger.*

Adrienne wakes up hungry. She devours her breakfast, and I prepare for it to come back up by grabbing the kidney-shaped bowl, but then a remarkable thing happens. It doesn't. By noon, Adrienne wants Buffalo wings for lunch, and she eats almost an entire plate by herself. Friends drop by to visit, and Adrienne tells funny stories, but by far the most entertaining thing is watching her laugh at her own jokes. John and I look at each other.

"Does she seem . . . ?"

"A little loopy. Yeah," he answers.

---

11 A pediatric cancer of the sympathetic nervous system.

"Do you care?"

"No."

John and I smile. Adrienne is stoned but she feels no pain. She keeps food down, and she appears relaxed and happy. *If this is the side effect of pot, why wasn't she on it sooner?* The doctors are not as nonchalant about Adrienne's condition. They don't give Adrienne any more Valium for the rest of the day, and they consider lowering the dosage of Dilaudid. I nod my head in agreement, as long as they don't take away the Marinol, I won't argue with them.

Adrienne seems to be retaining fluid so another dose of Lasix is given that evening. With the effects of the drugs waning, a more coherent Adrienne complains.

"I feel like I have to pee all the time, Sissy. And it burns when I stop."

I tell the nurse, who suspects a urinary tract infection (UTI), but the urine analysis is negative.

I suggest a bath might make Adrienne feel better. She likes that idea. Gathering several towels, clean clothes, and soap, we walk down the hall. Adrienne pulls her IV pole beside her to the bathtub room. When I close the door behind us, I think we can pretend we are at home, only this bathroom is smaller and doesn't have a toilet. I help Adrienne step into the tub, where she sits for fifteen minutes. The hot water relieves some of the burning sensation, and she feels better when we return to her room.

However, Adrienne receives more Lasix at 1:50 a.m., and she stays up most of the night going back and forth to the restroom. She tries her best not to disturb Veronica, whose bed she must pass to get to the bathroom they share. By morning the burning sensation is gone, another fire that came and went.

Today is the third and last day of this round of chemo. Of course, things don't go as smoothly as we would like. The phlegm in Adrienne's chest has the doctors concerned about pneumonia, but a chest X-ray is negative. She has no fluid in her lungs. Adrienne continues coughing throughout the day, and I become disturbed when she spits blood out of her mouth. The doctors assure me the blood and cough are not coming from Adrienne's lungs, which they treat with Albuterol to open up her airways.

John brings copies of the *Burbank Leader* to the hospital. Adrienne made the front page. The headline reads, "Burbank High sophomore is 'one tough cookie.'" The reporter used my quote about Adrienne, which sounds cheesy in retrospect. Except for some factual errors, the article is good and I show it to everyone on the floor. Adrienne rolls her eyes as she coughs for the umpteenth time today. She hates it when I brag too much, but she does like the picture of herself. My favorite part is the end.

"No matter what has been thrown her way, Adrienne has big plans for the future. 'I'm looking forward to going to college to study zoology and religion,' she said."

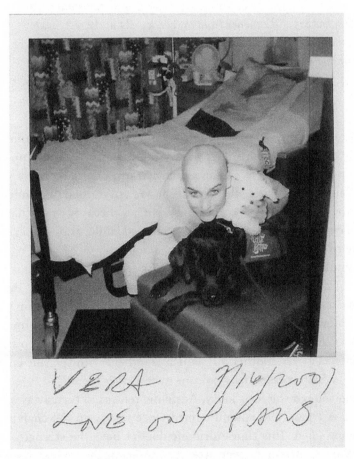

PAWS visit with Vera © July 16, 2001

Days 68-72

My sis is cool with surf lessons and says she'll drive me down to Venice every weekday that I don't have classes [at UCLA]. So I can surf, and she can run, and we'll bring Eli, who will sit and laugh his ass off at me trying to surf. Oh, I'll be working as a clown again this summer, and I'll spend $25 of the money from my check and put the rest into my investment fund and yeah, this is gonna be awesome. Why can't it be summer yet?

—*Adrienne's journal entry dated 2/3/01*

The attending physician comes up with a simple explanation for Adrienne's constant cough: mucositis, which is an inflammation of the mucous membrane. He explains medications, especially those used to treat cancer, often cause this condition. We are warned Adrienne might be more prone to mouth sores now since her throat is irritated already. He relays this information with a concerned smile, as he prescribes yet another respiratory treatment at 5:30 a.m.

I should be relieved. Adrienne doesn't have pneumonia, but I can't help thinking how much worse she feels this time around. These so-called curative measures are killing her. Most of the time I don't blame the doctors, they are only doing their jobs. However, when one pill is given to counteract the side effects of another pill, which is to stop the side effects of yet another pill, which is to help with the side effects of chemo, which is essentially poison—where does it end?

Even though she feels lousy, Adrienne refuses to turn away a PAWS visitor. A friendly Keeshond named Onee jumps on the chair next to Adrienne's bed. This time Adrienne doesn't have the strength to lean over and pet the dog or even attempt a smile for the camera. Looking at the Polaroid afterward, I am encouraged to see more color in her cheeks, but dismayed at how far her collarbone juts out now. Spending every minute of the day with her, I don't always notice how much she has changed, but photos don't lie. She looks miserable and a happy dog can't cheer her up this time.

Round three of chemo may be over, but Adrienne must be weaned off the PCA and the continuous IV drip before we can go home. Every afternoon someone from pain management lowers the amount of Dilaudid in the IV, but increases the amount available in the PCA. Dr. Marco and our case manager Teresa drop by each day to encourage Adrienne to push the button so they can determine the proper dosage of pain medication for her upon discharge.

I count down as if I am personally launching a rocket into space. Monday: 180 mcg to 150 mcg. *Good.* PCA increases from 125 mcg to 175 mcg. *Two steps forward, one step back.* Tuesday: 150 mcg to 75 mcg. *Even better. Almost there.* Valium given in IV instead of by mouth. *Another step backward.* Wednesday: at approximately 12:30 p.m., the doctors stop the continuous drip of Dilaudid. After ten days in the hospital, we are clear for takeoff. *We can go home soon.*

Adrienne and I develop a new pastime in the hospital. We watch Dr. Phil on Oprah every Tuesday afternoon at three o'clock. We both like Dr. Phil because he calls things as he sees them. We also try to catch Montel Williams every day; Adrienne likes the way he handles screwed-up teenagers. She thinks his honesty is refreshing. After her success with meeting Dave and Jay on *The Tonight Show*, she insisted I write Montel a letter because she wants to meet him in person. I mailed the letter last week, but we haven't heard anything yet.

Adrienne has the pleasure of meeting Nurse Bitchy before I do. I step out to use the restroom down the hall since parents are not allowed to use the one in the patient's room. During the five minutes I am gone, Nurse Bitchy walks into Adrienne's room and takes away her oxygen mask. She tells Adrienne she needs to use the nasal tube instead. Adrienne explains she doesn't like the sensation, she prefers the mask, but Nurse Bitchy overrides her objections and walks out.

When I return and find out what happened, I summon Nurse Bitchy to Adrienne's room.

"Can you explain to me why you gave my sister the nose tube?" I don't give her time to answer. "You do realize at fifteen, she is old enough to articulate what she wants and why."

Nurse Bitchy glares at me. She spits out a curt "Yes."

"Is it possible you didn't understand Adrienne's explanation?" I can feel Adrienne smiling behind me. *Stupid bitch. You messed with the wrong family.*

"No. I . . ." Nurse Bitchy sputters.

"Then get my sister a new oxygen mask. Now. Then get me your supervisor."

Nurse Bitchy turns around.

"One more thing." She looks back at Adrienne and me. "You will never be my sister's nurse again."

Nurse Bitchy slams the door behind her—at night—when children are sleeping. *Why is this woman working in pediatrics?* I file a formal complaint that evening with the floor supervisor. We never see Nurse Bitchy again.

I meet Veronica's father, and I wonder if he heard the heated exchange. The curtain separating the two beds is for looks only; sounds permeate the thin material, which is why we hear Veronica crying at all hours. Her father stays at the hospital during the week, but he often roams the halls at night unable to sleep due to his normal graveyard job routine. Veronica's mother visits on the weekends with their three other children. They are kind people juggling an impossible load. When she's not keeping me awake, I feel the sorriest for Veronica, who often has no one at her bedside.

Maybe Veronica is the most honest one of all, letting her pain out, telling the whole world how much her illness sucks. Sure, doctors and nurses don't like crybabies; they want their patients to be strong, tough, the way I expect Adrienne to be. The staff may not like John and me, but most of them love Adrienne for who she is—a smart, passionate, funny, and yes—strong, young woman.

However, these past two weeks have wrecked her enthusiasm. Am I setting the bar too high, again? Only this time, I'm not asking for straight A's. I'm not saying make smart choices: don't smoke, don't drink, don't do drugs. Now I'm subconsciously telling Adrienne: stay the same. Don't let cancer change you.

Since our friend Jared is unemployed, he tries to see Adrienne every time she is in the hospital, day or night. John and I both trust him to be on top of things. When we're not in the room, Adrienne will ask Jared, okay, they're gone. How am I really doing?

He tells her what he knows, but with the caveat, he's not an oncologist. Although he doesn't have children of his own, Jared had a similar experience with his father, and he knows being honest, especially with a sharp teenager like Adrienne, is the only way to keep her trust. I am not privy to their conversations, like Adrienne's live journal, she needs her own space away from me, even with our friends.

During one of these visits, I walk in to find Jared massaging Adrienne's calves, which are wasting away as her body has consumed its own muscle mass. To an outsider, the scenario may appear odd, but Jared has training in massage, and I can see the effects his touch is having on Adrienne. Her respiratory rate has decreased by half. She is now in the normal range of 12–20 breaths per minute. The coughing is sporadic now, allowing her to rest more. She opens her eyes when she hears me talking to Jared about my observations. Smiling, she says she doesn't hurt much either before she closes her eyes again. An idea dawns on me; I need to ask about physical therapy.

I waste no time and put in a formal request. The next day, a physical therapist (PT) shows me exercises I can do with Adrienne at home. Her main concern is the continuing atrophy of Adrienne's legs, which will eventually make it difficult for her to walk. The PT demonstrates the main exercise. She pulls Adrienne's leg out straight in front of her. Then she lifts it in the air at a 90-degree angle and holds it there for five seconds. She then bends Adrienne's knee and pushes it into her chest and holds again for five seconds. She says to repeat the exercise several times for both legs as well as reverse the direction. When I tell her I'm a former dancer and Adrienne enjoys doing yoga, she recommends other stretches we are both familiar with that will strengthen Adrienne's legs as well as her lower back. I mentally add physical therapy to our daily list of activities.

Adrienne has not been outside in ten days. She feels slightly better after receiving a blood transfusion, which I knew was coming after seeing her lab results. After the pain management team stops by to discuss the details of her discharge and the last bit of an anonymous donor's blood pumps its last drop into her body, Adrienne asks if we can get out of the room for a while. I can't say no, even I miss what constitutes as fresh air in Los Angeles.

I secure a wheelchair from a nurse and tell her I'm taking Adrienne on a short journey. I've learned not to ask permission around here.

I wrap a blanket around Adrienne and then cover her with her chemo cozy quilt. Grabbing her IV pole, I put it between the wheelchair and my body, holding onto it and one handle with one hand while my other hand grasps the other handle. Sometimes Adrienne holds the IV pole to the side while I push, but she huddles under the covers today. We make a brief stop at the gift shop in the lobby, but people stare.

"Let's go outside, Sissy."

We sit in front of the hospital, away from the smoking section, away from the happy lobby, away from everyone. At first, I make conversation.

"You're going to be discharged tomorrow, sweetie."

"We'll see. What if something else happens?"

She doesn't look at me. She stares at the cars driving down Sunset Boulevard. I can't tell her nothing else will happen when it seems like everything that could possibly go wrong during this round of chemo did.

"John will be here in a while. You guys can watch a movie. He can do hand duty."

"Yeah."

I stroke her left cheek with my right hand.

"Are you warm enough?"

"Yeah. Look Sissy, I don't want to talk. I just want . . . to be."

"Okay."

We sit there in silence, breathing in the unusually chilly July air, watching the traffic, listening to the honking horns, swimming in our thoughts. I am surprised at how much I missed being outside. I wouldn't classify Adrienne or myself as outdoorsy types; my idea of camping includes a toilet that flushes, not a port-a-potty, but we both love nature. We have hiked in the Verdugo Mountains near our house, on trails off Angeles Crest Highway and off trails in the Red Rocks of Sedona. We believe snow is meant for skiing. We like the smell of the salty breeze that wafts off the waves of the Pacific. *I didn't take her to the beach often enough.*

I look at Adrienne; her eyes are closed. I think about the time when I chaperoned a school trip to Universal Studios. In charge of five teenage girls including Adrienne, we laughed when they said to us you don't look like your sister, but then you do look like your sister.

Adrienne knows she looks more like her father than our mother. However, I can't count how many times people have said you two seem so different, yet you're so much alike.

We have different tastes in music, films, and clothes except for anything black and white, but we are more alike than I ever realized. Adrienne's friends confuse inner character with outer appearance. I feel the familiar tickle of my ears, the water creeping toward my eyes. *I can't let her see me cry.*

"Ready to go in, kiddo?"

Adrienne yawns. "Sure, Sissy."

I reposition the covers and grab the IV pole. As we head toward the giraffe elevators, something else occurs to me. I don't remember ever pushing Adrienne around the hospital in a wheelchair before. She always walked. One teardrop slides down my cheek, but I wipe it away with the back of my hand before Adrienne can see it. *I must stay strong. She needs me.*

I don't know if it was the fresh air, but in the middle of the night, I wake up to find the Adrienne I know and love—strong, stubborn, and spirited—meticulously coloring a fuzzy velvet poster with special markers. I glance at my watch.

"What are you doing up at two o'clock in the morning?"

"Coloring a poster for David," she says as if she is attending a scheduled art class.

The famous David, who procures toys, stuffed animals, jewelry-making kits, and art sets for the children, dropped one off the night before. Adrienne felt so lousy I figured she would either do it at home or not at all.

"Do you need to work on it right now?"

She looks at me, and I see that determined gleam that I know so well. She nods.

"Do you mind if I sleep?"

"Nope. But look at how I colored the kittens. I want to make it perfect for him."

With my eyes half open, I glance at the poster, and say, "Go to sleep soon."

"Uh, huh."

"I mean it."

Slumping back down on the pullout couch, I throw the blanket over my head. We're going to be out of here tomorrow. Adrienne is ready to go home and her body is too.

Early on Thursday morning, a woman from pain management drops by to review Adrienne's medications. Given how many new prescriptions Adrienne has, I can understand why the doctors want to make sure I understand how to administer them. I scan the documents. I read "Dilaudid, 1 mg, Q6."

I say, "You're kidding, right? Four milligrams for the entire day? That's not realistic."

The woman must know my reputation because she doesn't argue with me; she says there must have been an error in the calculation from the amount given in the IV to the oral dosage.

Five hours later, our case manager Teresa pages the attending doctor, who agrees the quantity of Dilaudid is too low. By the time he adjusts the amount, another five hours has passed. The discharge papers say 15:20 as our official escape time, but they fail to consider the amount of time it takes for the in-house pharmacy to fill all the prescriptions, which total fifteen now. I'm not even counting the Pentamidine treatment (the general antibiotic that replaced the nasty Bactrim) Adrienne receives once a month in the clinic and the Epogen, which will be administered by Adrienne's home nurse Tess on Mondays. As I scan the list, I frown when I realize seven out of fifteen medications are new. Granted some of them replaced others that were not working, but I wonder if the list will continue to grow with each round of chemo.

- Bacitracin Topical Ointment—Apply every six hours/as needed to mysterious back lesions. Antibiotic to prevent bacterial infections.
- Boost—Drink as you want. A nutritional drink like Ensure.
- Decadron—Taper schedule: Give 4 mg every six hours (day 1); give 4 mg every twelve hours (day 2); give 2 mg every twelve hours (day 3); give 1 mg every twelve hours (day 4); give 0.5 mg every twelve hours (day 5). Corticosteroid hormone to treat nausea caused by cancer chemotherapy. *Crazy.*
- Dilaudid—Give 4 mg by mouth four times per day/as needed: 8 a.m., 2 p.m., 8 p.m., 2 a.m. + 1 mg every four hours for 'breakthrough' pain only.[12] Painkiller.

---

12 Pain that comes on suddenly for short periods of time that is not alleviated by patient's normal pain management.

- Elavil—By mouth once per day: 8 a.m. Antidepressant. *Adrienne told the doctors staying in the hospital is what made her depressed. Does she need this pill at home?*
- Lo/Ovral Tab—By mouth every eight hours until menses stop for at least two consecutive days. Then every twelve hours for two weeks. Then once per day. Birth control. *When are the doctors going to realize they cannot control Mother Nature?*
- Magnesium plus Protein—By mouth three times per day: 8 a.m., 4 p.m., 12 a.m. Vitamin supplement.
- Marinol—By mouth four times per day: 8 a.m., 2 p.m., 8 p.m., 2 a.m. Cannabinoid to stimulate appetite and reduce nausea/vomiting. *Prescribed pot—but hey, it works.*
- Milk of Magnesia—By mouth once per day. Stool softener to lessen constipation. Stop if diarrhea occurs. *Permanently replaces Peri-Colace since it didn't work too well.*
- Neupogen shot—Subcutaneously once per day: 8 a.m. Medicine to increase white blood cells.
- Nystatin—Swish and swallow four times a day: 8 a.m., 12 p.m., 4 p.m., 8 p.m. Anti-fungal.
- Peridex mouthwash—(1/2 strength)—Swish and spit four times a day: 8 a.m., 12 p.m., 4 p.m., 8 p.m. Antimicrobial to reduce bacteria in the mouth. *In case of the unseen, but predicted mouth sores.*
- Pravachol—By mouth once per day: 8 a.m. Cholesterol-lowering medication.
- Valium—By mouth three times per day/as needed: 8 a.m., 4 p.m., 12 a.m. Benzodiazepine tranquilizer to reduce anxiety. *Replaces Ativan.*
- Zantac—By mouth twice per day: 8 a.m., 8 p.m. Anti-nausea. *No more Zofran.*

PAWS visit with Onee © July 23, 2001

Days 73-79

Back home for now. Six days overdue at the hospital. They ignored my coughs of blood. Strange bleeding, pussing wounds on my back. I hurt from coughing so much. They didn't even know what IV amount to put me on. Sent me home with legal pot, Valium, and Dilaudid, which keeps me asleep all fucking day. I really want to go shopping. Next time I go, it's Sissy, Eli and me. I'm getting Xiola another cage. I feel guilty for having clothes and money I want. I'm not used to it yet. Oh well. Bye.

—Adrienne's journal entry dated 7/31/01

Last night, Adrienne needed four milligrams of Dilaudid for pain and another two milligrams two hours later for breakthrough pain. I gave her another six milligrams at midnight because I never wake her up for the 2 a.m. dosage. After nibbling on a piece of toast this morning and taking her morning meds, she goes back to bed. Adrienne sleeps all day long. I peek in on her every half hour or so like a nervous new mother who is afraid her newborn will stop breathing. The difference is I don't recall ever being this scared when Adrienne was a baby.

The first time I took Adrienne on an outing, she was only five days old. Our mother said Adrienne was too young, but I wanted to show her off. To whom, I don't know; our mother didn't speak to her neighbors. I dressed baby Adrienne in a strawberry-print frock. The red complemented her then jet-black hair. I placed my awake, yet calm, sister in a simple secondhand umbrella stroller. I strapped her in and covered her with a light blanket, which she pushed away. I am convinced some traits are genetic because Adrienne was stubborn from birth.

During the first few months of Adrienne's life, I lived at the dormitory at school while Mother lived in a basement apartment next to the Birmingham Zoo. I came home every weekend though, especially after Adrienne was born since our mother didn't have to pay me to watch her.

On a typical Saturday, I pushed Adrienne in a stroller toward the zoo explaining all the animal sounds we heard along the way. I picked up leaves, let her tiny fists crush them, and blew the bits out of her hand before she put them in her mouth. I pointed out the kudzu, a climbing woody vine, indigenous to Japan that covers nearly every tree in Alabama. Most of the time, I just talked to her; those regular walks became our time together.

Three months later, Mother moved us all into an apartment across town. I like to believe those weekend outings during the early months of Adrienne's life influenced her. Of course, she couldn't understand what I was talking about at the time, but she loves animals and has such an appreciation for nature.

When I must look to the past to feel like I did something right, that tells me how uncertain I am about my decisions in the present. *Am I giving too much Dilaudid? Too little? Do I wake her? Do I not?* I don't even want to think about any choices I may face in the future.

Adrienne wakes up at 4 p.m.—just in time for her mountain of meds and good news in the mail: the Make-a-Wish Foundation will grant her wish. Adrienne wanted to see Dave again, and she figured the foundation was her best shot. Since she is drowsy, I read the letter to her.

"We are happy to inform you that Emma [her legal name] has been medically qualified to receive a wish."

Adrienne replies, "Cool. I'm going to make a list. Oh, and we need to tell them to call me Adrienne."

I read the types of wishes that cannot be granted. I warn Adrienne they don't grant wishes involving firearms, and she gives me that closed mouth, almost smile as if to say right Sissy, I want a gun. It takes a lot to make her laugh these days.

As Adrienne ruminates over her wishes, I am stuck on the words medically qualified. Is that Make-a-Wish's official euphemism for terminally ill? On their website, the organization uses the term life-threatening medical conditions. Of course, I knew Adrienne would qualify, but . . . no, I cannot think about it.

I want to write the foundation a letter and ask for a wish for myself. I wish I could walk in the house and see Adrienne sitting outside her bedroom door, giggling with her girlfriend Lori, after their wrestling in the hallway left a hole in the wall. I remember Adrienne's astonishment I didn't kill her because it was an accident.

I wish I could substitute teach for one of Adrienne's teachers again, and have to tell her to shut her mouth because she thought she could talk because Sissy was teaching class.

I wish she would ask me to take her and her friends to *The Rocky Horror Picture Show*, and this time I wouldn't say no, I'm too tired, ask John.

Even though my desires are not on their list of exclusions, the Make-a-Wish Foundation cannot make my wishes come true. They are not able to make things the way they were, and that is my ultimate wish.

Adrienne refuses to take her Valium, barely eats dinner, and stays awake long enough to take her 8 p.m. meds. Then, she falls asleep again with John doing hand duty. He stays in her room with her for a few hours, as he does most nights, watching television with little or no sound. I leave them alone so they can have their time together, while I read my books or do research on the Internet, the only weapons I have in my arsenal.

I cannot focus though. I wonder how couples survive this thing. John and I have had sex once since Adrienne's diagnosis, and for the first time in our relationship, he's not complaining about our sex life or lack thereof. Neither one of us cares, or at least I don't. I picture us sitting in a car at an intersection in the middle of the night. The world feels empty like right after a storm ends. The darkness presses down on us, and we see only a red stoplight blinking: on, off, on, off, on, off. We can't turn the car around and go back where we were, but we can't seem to move forward either. The red light taunts us: stop, go, stop, go, stop, go. But we remain stuck. I crack the window for fresh air.

Adrienne sleeps most of the weekend, but finding a comfortable position is difficult. The normal 45-degree angle provided by her numerous pillows puts too much pressure on her enlarged spleen. Lying flat is out of the question. I try to convince her to sleep on her stomach, but despite taking two to three birth control pills a day, her menstrual period continues unabated, and the cramping is too intense. Since we seem to have no other options, I rearrange Adrienne's pillows, place a heating pad under her spleen, and give her pain pills around the clock. She drifts in and out of sleep, once more resting on her back. By Sunday evening, Adrienne says she is still tired, but feeling much better.

Adrienne's barely spoken since we've been home so I'm relieved when she nags me about the Montel letter the next day.

"How come we've haven't heard anything, Sissy?"

"I don't know, kiddo."

"Did you tell him I want to meet him? Did you tell him about my cancer and everything that's happened?"

"Yes, yes I did. I even sent pictures—remember?"

"No. I don't. That seems like a long time ago now. Can you read me the letter again?"

"Sure."

Excerpt from the Montel Williams letter written on July 10, 2001:

I know of an extraordinary teenager who wants to meet you. Her name is Adrienne Wilson, and she is my sister. Adrienne is fifteen years old, and she just got diagnosed with cancer two months ago. Adrienne has been in my care since she was eight years old. I know she is not the first teenager with cancer nor will she be the last, but she is a very special person who has touched many lives—especially mine. Many people think she is lucky to have me, but the truth is I'm lucky to have her. She is the light of my life, and despite her illness, she has never given up hope or lost her optimistic spirit. She's a fighter, and she's been fighting battles her whole life.

We hope by coming on your show that we can accomplish a few things:

- make people more aware of this type of cancer [HCC] and encourage them to be tested for hepatitis,
- find more oncologists who are familiar with this cancer and have had some success,
- meet a survivor of HCC (the statistics are just terrible),
- and of course, meet you.

"Okay, that sounds good enough. I want to work out now."

"What?" I can't believe what I'm hearing.

"Sissy, I have no ass meat. My calves are disappearing. I need to work out. I'm going to walk on the treadmill for twenty minutes."

"No, you're not."

I'm wondering if Adrienne's Monday dose of Epogen had caffeine in it when Tess gave it to her this morning. I know it's supposed to help her anemia. Hell, it was my suggestion, but there's no way a drug can work that fast. I feel a negotiation coming on, and Adrienne learned how to haggle from the best—me.

"You can walk for ten minutes at a slow speed."

She grins.

"Fifteen?"

"Ten. Final offer and we do your physical therapy afterward."

"Okay!"

She plugs in the treadmill, and it comes to life after being dormant for over two months. Adrienne holds onto the rails and walks. I watch her in amazement.

The last time I worked out was the last normal day of our lives—May 15. I had been training for a marathon. When I received a flyer in the mail from The Leukemia and Lymphoma Society, I joined their Team in Training marathon program to raise money for cancer research. I thought the flyer was a sign I needed to conquer my fear of cancer and I should do something I thought I could never do—finish a marathon, all 26.2 miles of it.

I raised over $2,000, but I never ran in the San Diego marathon because it happened the first Sunday in June. I hadn't trained in weeks, and I didn't want to leave Adrienne for an entire day, especially our first weekend home from the hospital. Like many goals in my life, running a marathon fell off the list, along with pursuing my acting career, and getting a permanent teaching position. None of those things matter now because they cannot make Adrienne well.

I am so lost in thought that I forget to keep track of time.

"How long has it been, Adrienne?"

"Uhh . . . twelve minutes."

"Stop! Now."

"Okay, okay. Look, Sissy. I went one-third of a mile."

"That's great. Now let's stretch you out."

I proceed to do the exercises the physical therapist taught me in the hospital. I massage Adrienne's calves, too, because I don't want her to be sore tomorrow. All women in our mother's family are blessed or cursed with shapely legs, even the ones who don't exercise at all. Now Adrienne's legs look like they belong to other kinfolk, as Southerners would say. Any fat she had on her thighs has disappeared. Her body is attacking what's left—the lean muscle mass. She's no stick figure, but Adrienne's physical appearance has deteriorated. I need to weigh her soon. *God, I hope the Marinol puts some meat on her bones.*

I usually call the lab the day after the in-home visit to get the results of Adrienne's blood tests. I can't believe it when I hear the outcome from yesterday's blood draw. I ask the technician to repeat the results as I write them down. Those numbers cannot be right. For god's sake, Adrienne exercised yesterday for the first time since she's been sick. How can those numbers be correct?

The lowest her WBC has ever been was 3,000—low, but still in four digits. Now it's 800? With an ANC of 112, the doctors might hospitalize Adrienne; I can't let them do that. We just got out of that place. And her platelets are 7,000? From six digits to four digits, that's a huge drop. With her hemoglobin still below eight, it seems like the blood transfusion in the hospital made no difference whatsoever.

Someone will call us soon. If they want to admit Adrienne in the hospital, I can refuse. If they want us to come to the clinic for a platelet transfusion, because she must need one, then fine. I wonder if the doctors can do both the blood and platelets on the same day. Probably not. I look over at Adrienne who is reading Lois Lowry's *Gathering Blue*, an assigned book in preparation for Honors English in the fall. She's not going to be happy about returning to Children's Hospital so soon, even for a blood transfusion, which they will definitely do.

The hospital called. We arrive the following morning. Our case manager Teresa told us to be prepared to stay all day. This time, Adrienne will receive two units of blood since one wasn't enough to boost her hemoglobin last time. When I ask about the platelets, Teresa says she'll talk to Dr. Marco, but he didn't mention it to her. Platelets bounce back faster, so as long as Adrienne doesn't bleed she will be fine. How comforting.

A nurse brings over two units of donor-directed blood.

"You're one lucky girl," she says. "This blood is specifically for you."

Adrienne and I look at each other, and then I remember how everyone we know seems to have the same blood type as Adrienne, except for me.

"I think Alex donated blood for you weeks ago."

"You mean I'm getting some of Alex's blood into my body?" asks Adrienne.

"Yep."

"Ooo. That is so . . . weird."

The nurse laughs at Adrienne's bemused expression.

"It's kinda cool though too. Like he's part of me."

I wish Alex could hear her now; I doubt he realizes how much his donation of A-positive blood, weird and cool, means to Adrienne.

I watch TV and read while Adrienne studies the materials for her driver's permit exam. Her health teacher taught the course during the last few weeks of school. When her peers were learning which direction to turn the wheels when parked at a curb, Adrienne was undergoing her first round of chemo. If she learns the information and passes the test, the high school will not make her repeat that portion of the class. Unfortunately, the California Department of Motor Vehicles handbook is far from stimulating, and Adrienne soon falls asleep.

∗ ∗ ∗

In the spring of 1996, I bought my 1987 silver Honda CRX at the Los Angeles Public Auction. While people can examine the engine and interior of the cars before bidding begins, they are not permitted to drive the cars. The CRX was in fair condition except for two things: it was a manual transmission—something I failed to notice, and the car wouldn't accelerate past 55 mph on the highway.

Even though the first car I learned to drive, our mother's Toyota Celica, had a stick shift, I had not driven one in eight years. Re-teaching myself to drive a manual transmission with ten-year-old Adrienne sitting in the passenger seat, sighing every time the car stalled, grated on my nerves. Each sputter of the engine made an impression on her.

"I am never learning to drive a stick!" she declared within a few weeks. "Ever!"

I couldn't blame her; one time it took me twenty minutes to back out of a driveway.

The only cool thing about our new used car was she thought it looked like the one from the *Back to the Future* movies. I laughed when she told me. My CRX was no DeLorean. When we discovered my car couldn't drive fast without shaking violently, I told Adrienne our car was like an old woman.

"That's it Sissy. We'll call her Dolores."

The name stuck even though the acceleration/vibration problem was repaired.

Though Adrienne likes Dolores, she refuses to learn how to drive her. When she gets better, she wants John to teach her how to drive his car, a Honda Accord with an automatic transmission. I don't allow myself to think about the possibility she may never drive a car. She just won't drive my car.

✳ ✳ ✳

The blood transfusion makes a difference this time. I don't know if it is the quality of Alex's blood or the quantity, but Adrienne's hemoglobin rises from 7.9 to 11.0. Though her platelets are still far below normal, her immune system is strong enough for her to face the public. She wants to go shopping tomorrow, and we're planning a trip to Medieval Times this weekend with Adam, whom we haven't seen in ages.

Now I understand what Anya's mother Dr. Sárközi meant when she talked about measuring winning in terms of good days and good hours. When Adrienne's counts are up and she feels good, like her old self, we are winning on those days. When I see her white blood cell count has increased to 6,000 in three days, joy floods my heart for what is the smallest of victories. Adrienne—wanting to go shopping; reading for school; studying for her driver's permit; laughing at the TV show *South Park*; instant messaging her friends online; going over her allotted time on the computer; talking too long on the phone with her boyfriend; arguing with me—these activities are all triumphs because they represent normal teenage behavior. Each one is a sign. We are winning. *Fuck you no change.*

Days 80-83

☺☺

*I love music. I love dancing. I love sunshine that doesn't make me too
warm. I love the rain. I love jumping into puddles. I love drawing on my
arms. I love Eli. I love Perry Farrell. I love glitter. I love big headphones.
I love my blue hair. I love hairless arms. I love the shape of a female back.
I love fashion photography. I love bus drivers. I love fast computers.
I love doing high kicks.*

—Adrienne's journal entry dated 3/15/01

After another massage appointment with Nina, Adrienne asks to go to
the local animal shelter. Before cancer, we visited the dogs and cats all
the time. The overly-cautious-your-immune-system-crashed-three-days-
ago parent in me wants to say no, but my rational mind takes over and I
agree. Besides, I carry hand sanitizer in my purse, and animal germs are
less threatening to Adrienne than bacteria from people.

If the employees working at the front desk recognize us, they pretend
not to. Adrienne and I walk down the long corridor lined with pens on
each side; each cell has one or two dogs in it, most containing Pitt Bulls.
We don't have a dog yet, but we want one, but our tastes are different.
Adrienne likes the Bichon Frise, a fifteen-pound dog that resembles a
white powder puff. I hate small, yippy dogs. For years, I have longed for
an English Mastiff, a true gentle giant that weighs approximately 200
pounds. Adrienne refuses to have what she calls an overgrown slobber
machine near her stuff. We don't argue about what kind of dog to get because our lease doesn't allow one, and John doesn't want another animal
in the house. A cat and a hamster are enough.

At the end of the hall, we turn to go into the Cat Room, where a
chorus of meows greet us. As Adrienne passes a cage, a giant black paw
reaches through the metal bars, and Adrienne feels a tap-tap-tap on the

back of her hand. She turns around and says "look Sissy," in the voice of a child who has seen a ghost, but is not scared.

Inside of a cage, two sleepy black cats lie together, spooning one another. The smaller one, on the inside, is the rascal that hit Adrienne. We step forward and press our faces closer. We count six toes on each foot. Their large yellow eyes stare back at us, and the smaller one's pupils are so dilated they resemble black marbles. He, especially, seems to be communicating with Adrienne as he continues his playful paw banter without moving any other part of his body.

"They, no, he looks like Ebony," says Adrienne. "Can we get him? Pleeeassse Sissy."

I don't know what to say. The last thing I need is another animal, another responsibility, in the house. I can barely remember to clean the litter box these days. John may be a terrific father, but he is useless when it comes to pets. A kitten needs shots and sterilization. How will Little Bit react? She's had the house to herself for over seven months.

"I'll think about it."

"Great. That always means no."

"Not necessarily."

"He reached out and touched me, Sissy. It's a sign."

I sigh. "We'll ask about him, but I'm not promising anything."

Adrienne skips down the corridor to the lobby. At the front desk, she describes the two cats. An employee says they are both male; they were found together outside, and they are believed to be from the same litter despite their size discrepancy. Both kittens are up for adoption on August 10, a week from today. I thank the woman and tell her we might be back next week.

Adrienne smiles.

Adrienne talks at warp speed the minute the door shuts behind us.

"I think my cat is Bombay, but maybe his brother has more Siamese in him, that would explain why he's longer and leaner. His face is skinnier too. Anyway, doesn't Marinol look just like Ebony? He was Bombay. Are there black Siamese cats, Sissy? Can you believe they both have twenty-four toes like Ebony? Marinol is the perfect name."

Great. She has already named the cat. I interrupt her even though I can't remember the last time she was this excited about anything.

"Okay, I'll bite. Why Marinol?"

"Because," she rolls her eyes at me as if it should be obvious, "he's so laid back, like he's high on something. Like me, when I take Marinol."

I laugh because only Adrienne would come up with that.

"Adrienne, I never said yes."

"But Sissy," she cocks her eyebrow, "Marinol is the best."

I know that expression—that I-just-made-you-laugh-so-you-can't-say-no-now look.

I want her to be happy, but we don't need another cat, especially one that is the spitting image of Ebony. I can't deny that Marinol, no, that kitten, touching Adrienne was eerie as if he knew his only chance of getting out of jail was by using his best assets: his giant paws, not a loud voice that blends in with the crowd.

I need to make someone else the bad guy.

"If both John and Dr. Marco say yes, then you can have the kitten."

There's no way they will both say yes. No way.

Adrienne squeals.

"I can't wait to tell Eli about Marinol."

"They both have to agree, Adrienne. Don't get your hopes up."

"Don't worry, Sissy. I won't because they will."

After eating lunch, we pick up Eli and shop at Ross, where Adrienne buys several shirts and skirts. Then we go see Tim Burton's remake of *Planet of the Apes*. I am paranoid about movie theaters. They are ripe with germs, but Adrienne has wanted to see this film ever since she read Tim Burton was directing it. As we settle into what appear to be the cleanest seats available, not that dirt is visible in dim light, I think about how important seeing this movie is to Adrienne.

Adrienne likes most of Burton's films except for *Mars Attacks*, which she thinks is too silly. However, she was thrilled when she read Burton grew up in Burbank and based the neighborhood in his film *Edward Scissorhands* on his hometown. She was more delighted when she discovered she and Burton shared the same biology teacher, Mr. Hines. Adrienne asked her teacher about Tim Burton a few months ago. A firm believer in paper, Mr. Hines kept all his grade books from the time he started teaching. With Adrienne supplying Burton's age, he soon found the appropriate year.

"Ah yes. Timothy Burton. Very average—a C student, I'm afraid. Not like you," he said.

"Mr. Hines, do you have any idea how famous he is? How good his films are?"

Mr. Hines chuckled.

"No. But I seem to remember he liked to draw a lot."

Adrienne gave Mr. Hines a brief biography on his former average student; then, she recommended her favorite Tim Burton movies. I wonder if he followed her advice. Adrienne can be persuasive when she wants to be.

Adrienne shakes her head and sighs as the end credits roll up the screen.

"That wasn't good. He sold out. I never thought he would, but he did."

I don't think the film is that terrible, average I guess, but I can see how disappointed Adrienne is in one of her heroes. Eli agrees with Adrienne; he doesn't like it much either.

"Maybe the original is better," I offer to cheer up Adrienne.

"That's my point, Sissy. He never should have done a remake. He sold out."

After dropping Eli off at home, I change the subject to the one thing I don't want to discuss.

"You can ask John about Mari—the cat—when he gets home."

Adrienne perks up.

"That's right. He'll say yes."

That famous quote, "Never assume. You'll make an ass out of you and me," is something I should have learned by now. After five years with John, he surprises me. He says yes, of course Adrienne can have a cat. I remind Adrienne her doctor has to agree too.

She says, "I know, Sissy. You told me, like, ten times already."

I wait until Adrienne is in bed before confronting John.

"You weren't supposed to say yes. Why did you say yes? You hate pets."

"How could I say no to her right now?" he replies.

Then I realize John would give Adrienne anything she wants because he cannot give her what she needs—a new liver, her old life back. Part of me wants to strangle him for being unpredictable and another part wants to hug him for making her happy.

"I'm the one who's going to take care of it."

"I'll help out," he says.

We both know he's lying.

The next day Adrienne sleeps all morning in anticipation of our big night out to Medieval Times. I allow her to get a manicure and pedicure that afternoon. I explain to the Vietnamese manicurist in detail about how low Adrienne's platelets are and how platelets help our blood clot, but I realize I've gone too far and it has nothing to do with any language barrier. I need to drop the medical jargon and get to the point.

"Look, she can't bleed. Just be extra careful, okay?"

"Yes ma'am. I be careful. Don't worry," she replies. "What color you want?"

Adrienne points to the bright blue polish, of course.

The woman may not understand why she needs to be cautious, but I can see from the way she takes her time she comprehends something is wrong. Later when I share my thoughts with Adrienne, she laughs.

"Gee Sissy, don't you think my bald head and pasty skin gave her a clue?"

I know she's right. The woman probably labeled Adrienne a sick girl when she saw her, but people should never assume.

Adrienne begs me to stop at Junk for Joy, one of the coolest second-hand stores in Burbank. She does not have anything in mind, but when Adrienne sees a large pair of blue Monarch butterfly wings, she has to have them. Because Adrienne loves fairies, she has always wanted a pair of wings. About two feet in height and diameter, the wings attach under her shoulders with a wide piece of ribbon.

"Can I get them, Sissy?" she asks as she twirls around.

I want to say how impractical the wings are; how cumbersome they must be, and how heavy they will feel after a long stretch of time. But like John with the kitten, I cannot say no. Adrienne appears so young in the wings, like a child who has never known pain. Like a child who has never experienced three rounds of chemotherapy. Like a child who has never had cancer.

"It's your money, kiddo. You want them, you buy them," I tell her.

Whooping with glee, Adrienne purchases the blue butterfly wings for less than fifty dollars.

An expensive dinner extravaganza, Medieval Times transports one back to the eleventh century to witness a tournament while eating a four-course feast served by wenches and serfs. Both Adam and Adrienne always wanted to go, Adam to see knights joust and Adrienne to experience the antics of the Middle Ages, but John and I never had the money before. Now I do not let not having the money stop us from doing anything Adrienne wants to do. For an additional ten dollars per person, I buy the Royalty package, which comes with preferred seating, commemorative programs, cheering banners, and free admission to the museum.

Before cancer, I would have balked at spending over $200 for one evening of fun, but we no longer live in the past—the before. We live in the after, no—the present with cancer, and on a subconscious level, I am aware of how hard I am trying to make each day special for Adrienne. *We will go to Medieval Times tonight, and we will have fun, dammit.*

In less than two weeks, I will turn twenty-nine on my birthday. Women my age are supposed to hear their biological clocks ticking, but I don't. Instead, a cancer clock, *Adrienne has been sick for eighty-one days,* pulsates throughout my body, as it tracks the numbers: How long has it been since we left normal? How many rounds of chemo? How many times has she thrown up? How many good days? Bad days? How many meds? How? How? How? How? I prefer the how questions because I can answer them with real numbers: quantitative evidence as the doctors would say. However, I find no answer exists for the hardest question of all: why Adrienne?

When Adrienne exits her bedroom, I gasp. She appears so ethereal with her blue Monarch butterfly wings and blue bobbed wig Marilyn bought for her. I'm looking at a blue fairy from another world. Adrienne is also wearing her brand new blue tie-dyed shirt from Ross along with a blue scarf tied around her neck. On another person, so many shades of blue would be overwhelming, but Adrienne manages to pull off the monochromatic style. I grab my camera and take many pictures of her and Adam, who also opted to wear a shirt with blue in it, a coincidence I believe. I smile behind the lens as they make goofy faces at me. For a few seconds, things are back to normal.

Despite buying the Royalty package, we have to wait in line with everyone else. I notice people staring at Adrienne, but I see no pity in their eyes, no poor sick girl. They appear intrigued by her presence. Even I feel Adrienne's aura, as it moves through the crowd soothing people like an unseen, but welcome, mist on this hot summer evening. The steel rod of tension in my shoulders loosens, and I breathe a sigh of relief. This evening will be perfect.

Before going to our seats, we enter the Torture Museum, which scares Adam. John escorts him out while Adrienne and I walk around. We comment on the various apparatuses that prove just how medieval the Medieval Times were. After seeing many devices including the famous Judas Chair covered with spikes that pierced human flesh, Adrienne and I agree the guillotine was one of the more humane forms of torture because death was quick in most cases. My eyes linger on the exhibit as we exit. *Is cancer just another form of torture?*

We sit in a giant stadium, where King Alfonso and his daughter Princess Esperanza introduce themselves. They tell us how the knights will display their courage, strength, and chivalry in many different tournaments. Each section of the arena is dedicated to one knight, and our job is to cheer him to victory with our voices and banners. Our knight's colors are red and yellow, which Adrienne and I take as a good sign, USC colors.

To my dismay, the feast begins with bread and soup without a spoon. When I ask for one, Adrienne groans.

"They didn't have utensils back then, Sissy. You're supposed to use your hands."

She demonstrates by picking up her bowl and sipping her soup. I play along until the main course arrives, a choice of roasted chicken or spare ribs with an herb-basted potato. We Southerners may eat chicken with our hands, but I am not eating a potato with one. Our kind wench of a waitress brings me a fork. Adrienne rolls her eyes as she noshes on her ribs. I don't care how square she thinks I am because I am too busy mentally noting how much food she is eating. The Marinol has increased her appetite, and she hasn't complained about feeling nauseous yet. *Keep it down. Please keep it down.*

Despite his lucky USC colors and our loud whooping (except for John who doesn't believe in showing any kind of vocal enthusiasm), our knight loses during one of the earlier jousts. For a brief second, I am frustrated even though I know we are watching a carefully choreographed show. I tell myself the winner is predetermined like the wrestling matches on television our grandfather Papa loved so much.

Gotta watch me wrastlin.' Move Andra, ya blockin' the tv. Get outta the way now, ya hear.

I told Papa once the matches were fixed, but he wouldn't hear of it. As we do tonight, he continued to cheer on his favorite wrestlers, not wanting to believe his dedication had no bearing on the outcome.

I feel an epiphany coming on, but I push it away. Cancer is not a game; it's a disease. Loud clapping brings me back to the present as King Alfonso thanks us for joining him this evening. I slap my hands together to a staccato rhythm only I can hear. *If cancer is not a game, why are we fighting to win?*

After the tournament, we join the mob in the lobby to obtain autographs and pictures. We each take a photograph with King Alfonso, except for John of course. Adam waits in line to have his program signed by the knight who won the tournament and who is by far the most popular man in the room. I give the kids twenty dollars each to buy a souvenir. Adam chooses a sword while Adrienne purchases a purple cone-shaped princess cap with gold-sequined trimming along the brim. I am surprised by her choice. Usually, she doesn't go for anything purple, but she explains she doesn't plan to wear it; she just thinks it's pretty.

Outside Adam exclaims, "That was the best night of my life!"

This time even John laughs along with Adrienne and me. Those innocent words mean more to John than Adam will ever know. John wants Adam to like him so much, but he has a better relationship with Adrienne than he has with his own son, due mostly to proximity and access. John not only sees Adrienne every day, but he also spends time with her. John thinks by giving Adam the best night of his life, he will score points, but he cannot change facts. Adam lives with his mother over thirty miles away, and we see him every other weekend, even less since Adrienne has been ill because his mother refuses to switch weekends. *What a bitch.* Tonight though, we are a family again, the four of us, the one J and three A's, and it feels good.

Part of my new armor to fight the enemy is making Adrienne a fruit smoothie twice a day. I spoke to Dr. Marco and Nina about herbs I read about in the *Physician's Desk Reference.* They agree in small doses the herbs cannot hurt Adrienne, but Dr. Marco does not believe they will help either. Nina is more optimistic. Using a blender, I mix carrot, orange, and banana juice with one capsule of milk thistle, one capsule of cats claw, and fifteen drops of astragalus: all herbs that aid liver function. In the evening, I use the same juice with one crushed caplet of a hepatic cleanse, a sort of multi-vitamin for the liver. Adrienne loves the smoothies and says she cannot taste the herbs at all. Another bonus is the smoothies are loaded with healthy calories, and if Adrienne's body can tolerate them, she will gain some much-needed weight.

Adrienne at Medieval Times

Days 84–89

My sister does [expects me to be strong all the time]. Or at least she wants me to be. Just because she won't accept the idea of me becoming weak or dying. Ah, but I feel like giving up at this point. And I know I won't or can't, but I want to.

—Adrienne's journal entry dated 8/11/01

Adrienne wakes up with a runny nose and a slight cough. Even though her blood tests yesterday confirmed her immune system was healthy, she caught a cold from someone over the weekend. The exposure to people at the movie theater, the shopping mall, and Medieval Times was too much for her body. Now I realize I cannot rely on the blood tests alone to determine when Adrienne can interact with the public. The Neupogen shot I give her every morning artificially boosts her immune system. While the medicine does increase her white blood cells, it is not natural. Adrienne's body is not producing them on its own. The Neupogen serves as a Band-Aid to a much bigger problem; chemotherapy kills the cancerous as well as the healthy cells. Even with highly elevated WBC and ANC levels, Adrienne's body was not as protected from germs as I thought it was. I should have known better.

At eleven o'clock, Adrienne and I arrive at the Children's Hospital clinic for her pre-chemo checkup. Near the elevators, we run into five-year-old Janelle and her mother, who has tears in her eyes. I don't know if I should ask what's wrong since we have only met once before, but I feel I must.

"Is . . . is everything okay?"

Janelle's mother nods her head.

"Yes . . . yes. It . . . it's gone. No more."

I hug this woman I barely know as a tinge of jealousy shoots through my body.

"I'm so happy for you."

I look at Janelle as she skips around in circles. She seems oblivious to what must be the best news her mother has ever heard.

"That's wonderful Janelle."

She smiles and continues humming a tune, but somewhere in those chocolate-brown eyes, I sense an understanding—no more shots, no more clinic, no more hospital, no more cancer.

"We come back. Six months," says her mother.

I smile while my brain shouts. *Six months? She must be cured if she doesn't need to come back for six months!* Adrienne and I wave goodbye to Janelle and her mother as they walk into the elevator and the doors shut behind them. I cling to hope. Children can be cured. People do survive. *But Janelle had leukemia—not liver cancer. It's not the same.* I want to hear come back in six months, but then I remember that awful statistic, "two-year survival less than five percent."

Fuck you less than five percent.

We do not hear come back in six months, you're cured. Instead, Dr. Marco chides me for not tapering Adrienne off the Marinol sooner.

"Starting today, give it every eight hours. Tomorrow, every twelve hours, and then, one time the following day. She never should have stayed on the Marinol so long."

"The discharge papers didn't say anything about decreasing the dosage over time, or I would have done it."

I cannot tell if he believes me or not. I wish I had those papers with me so I can prove either he didn't order the drug to be tapered off or someone made a mistake doing the paperwork. *I didn't do anything wrong.*

I agree to reduce the Marinol and wonder how it will affect Adrienne's appetite. Her weight is holding at 125 pounds, 18 pounds less than before. I do the math in my head. On average, Adrienne is losing 1.5 pounds per week. I wonder why no one seems concerned about that number. When I express my concerns about her weight, Adrienne changes the subject, sort of.

"Speaking of Marinol," Adrienne says, "Dr. Marco, can I have a new kitten? He's half Bombay and half Siamese and all black with six toes on every foot, and he's mellow. I named him Marinol. Isn't that cool? Pleeassee."

Come on—say no. I can't take another responsibility.

Dr. Marco laughs but stops when he sees the look on my face.

"Umm . . . well, I suppose so—as long as you don't get scratched, and you don't handle the feces in any way."

Damn. I can't believe we're getting another cat.

Adrienne cheers. "Don't worry, Sissy cleans the cat litter now, and I'll be careful with his claws 'cause our other cat did scratch me—by accident. There was some blood."

"Very little," I say, although I can see Dr. Marco is losing interest. Why did he have to add one more thing to my plate? Because it makes Adrienne happy. He can't cure her, but he can give permission for a pet.

"Okay, time to examine you." Dr. Marco presses Adrienne's abdomen several times. "Hmm . . ."

"What? What is it?" I bite the corner of my lip.

"Well, don't get too excited, but the liver feels smaller horizontally now, but that's based solely on my touch. The CT scan after the next round of chemotherapy will tell us more."

I feel hopeful. Adrienne's liver is smaller. Maybe? Possibly? Doctors hate using definitive terms.

"Any news about her AFP?"

"1.4 million," Dr. Marco replies with a straight face.

Great, we're back to where we started. From 1.4 to 2 to 1.7 back to 1.4 again. Dr. Marco agrees Adrienne has a cold, but her lungs are clear, no signs of pneumonia. He warns Adrienne.

"Remember . . ."

"I know," Adrienne sighs. "Be careful."

"Right. You can blow your nose, but not too hard. We can't have a nosebleed."

I know what he's really saying. The bleeding might not stop with her platelets down to 69,000.

"What about the coughing?"

"Her lungs are clear, so I'm not worried."

"But she's coughing up green mucus."

I wish Adrienne could demonstrate on demand. This situation reminds me of when I take my car to the shop because it's making a noise only it stops once I get there.

"If she can't stop, coughing that is, call me. I wanted to start the next round of chemotherapy on Thursday, (Adrienne's jaw drops), but her platelets are still too low."

Good. We just got out of this place.

"If all goes well, we'll begin on Monday."

Dr. Marco doesn't see Adrienne smile as he walks out. We don't want her platelets to be low, of course, but they just bought us more time at home.

"Hey kiddo, you're getting your kitten. You won."

The corners of her mouth turn upward and I see teeth.

"Yep! Told ya. When can you pick Marinol up, Sissy?" she asks.

"On Friday, he's available for adoption. I'll go as soon as they open."

In case she got her way, I had memorized the date: Friday, August 10. I will go to the shelter and bring Ebony's twin home.

The next two days trudge by as Adrienne waits for her new kitten, and I try to balance her meds. Ride the seesaw. As I taper off the Marinol, Adrienne's nausea increases, and she vomits what little she eats: juice, Top Ramen, and sometimes crackers. I give her Zofran for the nausea even though we both know it doesn't work for her as well as Marinol. I eliminate the hepatic cleanse in her evening smoothie when I realize she wakes up two mornings in a row feeling ill. She continues drinking the morning smoothie since it is the only nutrients she can keep down, and it doesn't make her feel any worse or better.

Adrienne suffers from severe headaches, but her liver stops hurting so I decrease the Dilaudid. As a result, I worry less about constipation now. Every day has a happy face signifying one bowel movement. With every small victory, there seems to be a setback. With less Marinol in her system, Adrienne is more awake and now has insomnia, which allows her to spend more time reading. She has a book report due at the end of the summer for her honors English class. Except for the emails exchanged between Adrienne's teachers and me, she and I haven't talked about school much. However, with Back-to-School commercials blaring from the television, we cannot ignore the topic forever. I have no idea how we are going to manage school, but we will figure it out, but not now, maybe after chemo.

The night before I am supposed to pick up Marinol at the shelter, Adrienne calls me into her room. John is already there doing hand duty.

Adrienne wants to talk. She asks questions about the past, about our mother, our grandparents, and even her father.

"What was she like, Sissy, before she was sick?"

I think before answering. I conjure up early memories of our mother, and I remember a picture my father must have taken when I was seven or eight, before the divorce, long before Adrienne. My mother, brother, and I were playing on the front lawn of our house in Arkansas. Aidan and I were laughing as Mother tickled us. Her long, straight, auburn hair whipped through the air as she smiled. I love that photo because it is proof our mother was once a happy person. Adrienne never knew that woman.

"I'm going to tell you what I know and what I think, okay?"

Adrienne nods and squeezes John's hand. I lie down next to her on her bed.

"There was a time when Mother wasn't sick, and by sick I mean an addict. She was never a PTA mom, but she supported everything Aidan and I wanted to do. She drove us to his karate and my dance lessons. Before the divorce, during the summer, we spent every weekend swimming in the public pool at Ben Garen Park, in the giant pool at Lake Ft. Smith, or at Kerr Lake in Oklahoma."

I stop and look at Adrienne. Her eyes resemble the pools of water I am talking about, but she nods for me to go on.

"According to my dad, Mother started taking diet pills when I was about eight years old, and her increasing addiction to them is what ended their marriage. She also brought home pills from the hospital—dozens of bottles. After working all night, she would empty her pockets in the morning and dump alcohol pads, scissors, surgical tape, syringes, and vials into what we called the 'junk drawer.'"

Adrienne interrupts me.

"I remember that stuff. She gave me vitamin shots. They made me sleepy."

I cringe as the image of little Adrienne, the drunken sailor, flashes through my mind. *Goddamn you mother. How many times did you drug her as a child?*

"She gave me a flu shot once, too, but I never let her do it again because it hurt too much. You know, I thought it was normal that our house looked like a pharmacy, but I didn't know any better."

Adrienne laughs. I laugh. John does not laugh. I hold Adrienne's other hand.

"When I left, Mother made bad choices, and things got worse, which is why you came to live with me. She is a prescription drug addict, but that does not excuse her emotional neglect of you."

I squeeze Adrienne's hand.

"I'm sorry you didn't get any of the good years because there were some."

I watch two silent tears slide down Adrienne's sharp cheekbones, chiseled by chemo.

"It's okay, Sissy. It's good to know she wasn't all bad."

I suck back my own tears as our mother's mantra echoes in my head: Life isn't fair, Andra. You're right, mother. You never gave Adrienne a chance to know that once upon a time, you were a decent mother.

"Tell me about my dad."

Adrienne has heard this story before, but I don't mind repeating it. Part of me wonders if I should be worried she is asking these questions now: this journey to the past and her desire to process the truth. Adrienne and I don't usually talk about this stuff. *Why now?*

"As you know, your dad was the only man who ever made Mother happy. Maybe the only person. I don't know where they met, but they fell in love immediately. Within weeks, your father moved into the house. I hated him. I hated that he made Mother laugh. I hated that she paid more attention to him than to me, but I didn't understand. He was always nice to me, your dad, never tried too hard."

I look at Adrienne and John. Her eyes droop but she nods for me to continue.

"When he died in that car accident, Mother said her heart felt like ground-up hamburger meat. She took pills, mostly downers. Then, she discovered she was pregnant with you. We were worried about how you would turn out. Then you popped out: screaming, healthy, and normal."

I stop at the word normal. If only the doctors had tested Adrienne for hepatitis at birth. If only we had known all these years, we would have monitored her liver. If only our mother had not given her hepatitis either during childbirth or with tainted needles during the so-called vitamin shots. If only I had made the pediatrician test Adrienne for hepatitis last year. I don't say any of my thoughts aloud, but they plague me. The if-onlys in life can kill you.

Adrienne yawns.

"You have your father's eyes, kiddo."

The corners of her mouth turn up, but she seems too tired to deliver a full grin.

"He would have been so proud of you Adrienne."

I want her to know she can let go. There has to be more beneath those few tears released tonight.

"It's okay to be sad. It's okay to cry. I don't expect you to be strong all the time. It may appear that way, but I don't. I love you and John loves you. We all do. You're amazing. I'm so proud of you."

Adrienne, I need you to keep fighting—for me.

As I am about to spin yarns about our grandparents, I realize Adrienne has fallen asleep. I will save those stories for another day because we have plenty of time, or so I tell myself. Watching her breathe, I see it's not too slow or too fast. Her respiratory rate appears normal. I hope she dreams about a better reality.

I lie in bed thinking . . . How can I explain to Adrienne she is the best part of my life? The best part of me. That anyone who knows me or meets me for the first time finds out about her because all I talk about is Adrienne. How can I tell Adrienne being her parent has been the most rewarding aspect of my life? That I cannot, will not, lose her. Not now. Not yet.

Who will go with me to the Topanga Canyon haunted house on Halloween? Who will stain the entire bathroom blue with hair dye? Who will argue with me I have seen that episode of *Law & Order* when I think I haven't, but she is always right? Who will ask me to proofread her paper so "it's perfect because I need a 4.0 to get into a good college?" Who will insist I watch the USC vs. UCLA football game with her because "you should have school spirit" even though we don't like the sport? Who will test me on music I don't even listen to and expect me to know all the answers and then roll her eyes when I don't?

I don't know what caused the seed of panic to grow inside of me. Was it Adrienne's AFP count, which although lower, had returned to the beginning, as if we have been wasting time? Was it her platelets, which took so long to bounce back, delaying chemo? Was it the fear of school beginning? Was it watching Adrienne sit on more and more pillows like the princess on the pea because she has no ass meat? Or was it

Adrienne's numerous questions about the past and people who are dead or should be?

I fear her desire to know more about our mother. Adrienne seems to be reconciling her feelings toward Mother. Perhaps even forgiving her. But Adrienne wouldn't do that unless she were *nonononono*. We are fighters. We are survivors. Adrienne is kicking cancer's ass, right? If that is true, then why is an unbearable anxiety fluttering through my body? I recall the last time I felt this sensation. When we were evicted from the Highland Terrace apartment, I was desperate for money. Now, I need so much more than money can buy. Such a tired cliché, but wait, I think, maybe money can buy something. Not a cure perhaps, but what about other treatments? In other countries? I must find out what else is out there. Explore all our options. Because we Wilson sisters don't give up. We fight until we win.

Even though I don't want him, today Marinol the cat will come home, and he will make Adrienne happy. I arrive at the Burbank Animal Shelter ten minutes before they open. I pace outside as I wait for someone to open the door. Another woman shows up, and I worry. What if she wants him too? What happens then?

We walk inside together. When the employee behind the desk asks what can she do for us, the woman and I reply at the same time.

"We're here to adopt a cat."

Shit. There are not many kittens back there.

The employee shrugs, gives us paperwork, and says if we want the same cat, there will be a drawing since we arrived at the same time.

Bullshit. I was here before her, and I have to bring Marinol home. No other cat will do. He chose Adrienne.

I panic until the other woman mentions a tabby. My shoulders drop as I sigh. I'm being ridiculous. What were the odds we wanted the same kitten? Don't most people think black cats are unlucky? I pay $40 for Marinol and take him to the vet for his shots.

Unfortunately, Marinol is not mellow because it's his nature. The vet diagnoses him with severe dehydration caused by the kitty flu. Another $160 later, armed with specific fluids and antibiotics, I bring Marinol home. Adrienne dotes on him while Little Bit, our other cat, eyes the newcomer with suspicion. Despite being sick, Marinol talks nonstop and explores his new home with reckless abandon.

I don't like Marinol because he looks and acts too much like our old cat Ebony, but Adrienne couldn't be happier with the new addition to our family. He can't take away her pain or her nausea, but Marinol, like most pets, provides emotional comfort. Adrienne tells him how she feels, and he listens. He even replies, meowing at the slightest provocation. Watching them together, I know getting him was the right thing to do, even if I am reluctant to accept him.

Baby Marinol

Days 90–93

I kinda brought this upon myself. A lot of stuff happened in my early youth, and I repressed it for years and I think that's what caused it [cancer] for some reason. I just have a gut feeling about it. I've been going through a breakdown now, because I'm trying to let go of everything that happened and forgive the people that caused it. I don't think the chemo is doing its job; so I'm turning to anything I can to start healing. It's hard letting go of the forest, stream, bb guns, brothers, and abandoned mothers. It's all I've held onto these past six or seven years and now I need it all to gently fade. I don't want a huge explosion, just something soothing, you know? Something calm. I learned a lot about her. It explains a lot of what happened to me and why. It doesn't excuse it, but at least there's some sort of reason now. "She was too old, too sick, and she had a drug problem."

—Adrienne's journal entry dated 8/11/01

John goes to work as Adrienne and I leave for Children's Hospital. This week she begins her fourth round of chemo. We are both apprehensive. We don't want to be stuck there for two weeks. Even though her nausea continues, Adrienne's pain has lessened. Her liver does not hurt anymore, only her joints.

We run into our case manager Teresa on the first floor in the Mary Poppinish butterfly waiting room next to the Giraffe elevators. After exchanging hellos, she comments.

"Wow, you guys have a lot of stuff there."

I follow her eyes. I'm dragging a portable luggage carrier that holds Adrienne's overnight bag, my duffel bag, my purse, and another bag with Adrienne's quilt, pillow, fan, and other items. For the first time, I will not have to make another trip to the car.

I laugh and say, "Yeah, we've got it down to a science now."

Teresa nods as her eyes narrow before she turns away. I ponder her reaction. I am proud I have finally figured out how to organize our stuff, but then I realize how sad it is I know exactly what to pack now.

I watch our feet as we walk toward the elevator. Adrienne shuffles along at a much slower pace than ever before. She says her ankles hurt. I match her gait even though her legs are longer than my own. I can keep up with her now. I hate it.

The nurse takes one look at Adrienne and insists on weighing her immediately. She has lost six pounds since the clinic appointment last week. As I tapered Adrienne off the Marinol, her nausea increased, her appetite decreased, and her weight dropped. Having a cold didn't help either, as we discover Adrienne is also dehydrated.

"Just like Marinol," says Adrienne.

The nurse looks confused while I stifle a laugh.

"The name of her new kitten—Marinol."

"Like the drug?" asks the nurse.

"Yep. 'Cause he's mellow," Adrienne replies.

Now we all laugh, but the moment is short-lived when the nurse tells us chemo will start tomorrow. Because Adrienne weighs 119 pounds now, the chemo orders must be changed, as they were based on her previous weight. Adrienne also needs to be rehydrated, twenty-four hours of nonstop fluids. When the nurse leaves, I wonder why couldn't Adrienne stay on Marinol? It helped her. I never thought I would be someone to tout the benefits of marijuana, but without it, Adrienne's body suffered.

Six pounds in six days. Twenty-four pounds total since we began—what should I call it—this unexpected trip ninety days ago. How many rounds of chemo did Dr. No say she could endure? Eight, I think. I'll have to check my notes. If Adrienne keeps losing weight at this rate, she won't make it. The chemo, not the damn cancer, will kill her.

I meet Adrienne's roommate, a ten-year-old named Leila. She lies in bed awake, but motionless and silent. In broken English, her mother tells me their story. Leila was diagnosed with rhabdomyosarcoma (the same rare cancer Whitney has) before she was three years old. At that time, she had tumors in her stomach and her pelvis. The cancer returned when she was seven. Now, three years later, Leila with her vacant brown eyes and thick curly, brown hair waits for the doctors to determine how they are going to beat it this time.

I recognize that glint of determination in the mother's eyes, but I wonder if she can see her child the way I see her. Ten years old, eleven surgeries, countless chemo treatments, Leila has endured too much. She is, of course, behind in school and will have lifelong medical issues. *What kind of life has she had?* As I close the thin curtain separating two girls, one full of life the other devoid of it, I make a promise to Adrienne without telling her. If I see that dead look in her eyes, I will stop treatment. No matter what.

The highlight of the day, like every Monday on the Oncology ward at Children's Hospital, is the PAWS visit. A standard black poodle named Raven trots in to meet Adrienne. Rondo, the Keeshond, is also with the volunteer, who asks if she can take digital photos of Adrienne with the dogs for an upcoming presentation for the doctors and nurses. According to the volunteer, the nurses suggested Adrienne would be a good candidate because she likes the dogs so much we schedule her chemo treatments to fall on Mondays. I sign a photo release, as Adrienne smiles for several pictures. The volunteer promises someone will send me copies of the photos. In the meantime, she gives me the Polaroid picture that shows Raven sitting stoically on the bed, and Adrienne nuzzling her cheek against the dog's ear.

✳ ✳ ✳

This time last year, I was packing for a redeye flight to Birmingham for my ten-year high school reunion, which was four days after my twenty-eighth birthday. Since I didn't have a party, I only asked for one gift. I wanted Adrienne to take pictures with me at the mall, those cheap pseudo-glamour shots that kids her age got all the time. I figured I could take a bunch of photos with me to show off Adrienne, as well as give pictures to Mother and other family members, whom I planned to see as well. Adrienne, however, did not want to have her picture taken with me, her uncool, older, sister-parent. The night before my birthday, we discussed the matter.

"I'll do it if you pay me," she said.

"What? That's extortion. What about doing it for my birthday?"

"I already got you something. Besides, I can't be seen at the mall . . . with you."

"I take you to the mall all the time."

247

"Yeah, but we don't like hang out together. Or get our picture taken."

I knew she was messing with me, but I was going to have to give her something to make it worth her time.

"How about five dollars?" I suggested.

"Sheesh. How about twenty?"

"Absolutely not. No way. All I'm asking for is an hour of your time. I can't believe you won't take a picture with me and . . ."

She interrupted me, "Okay, okay."

"Ten is my final offer, Adrienne."

"Fine. But we have to go as soon as the mall opens. None of my friends will be up that early in the morning."

"Fine."

✳ ✳ ✳

What a difference a year makes. With Adrienne hydrated, chemo will begin on Tuesday as planned. The doctor on-call orders Marinol, Decadron, and Zofran—preemptive measures for the predictable nausea and vomiting. He also has a nurse administer Lasix when he sees how puffy Adrienne's body is. I almost feel better when I see the expert ride the same seesaw I do. Not enough water? Let's pump her full for twenty-four hours like a hot air balloon. Oops—now, she has too much air, need to let some out to bring her back down to 'normal' only no one seems to know what that is anymore.

Adrienne and I watch Dr. Phil on Oprah. She pesters me about Montel Williams again asking why they haven't called. I don't know what to tell her. Who knows if Montel even saw the letter? We were lucky with *The Tonight Show* and the Make-a-Wish Foundation. Adrienne reviews her list of wishes, which she has rewritten several times.

1. A private concert at the Whiskey Go-Go performed by Jane's Addiction with 45–50 of my friends there.
2. Front-row tickets to the Jane's Addiction concert in LA in October.
3. More information about my father and his past.

We met with our wish coordinator Becca last week, and she is supposed to call us soon. I have little doubt Becca will be able to contact

Dave Navarro. Getting in touch with a celebrity is easier than finding out information about a dead man who never knew his daughter.

On the morning of my birthday, Adrienne wakes up with fluid in her chest, probably another episode of mucositis. At least no one suspects pneumonia this time. Even though it isn't necessary, the doctor gives Adrienne oxygen to relax her. When he leaves, I also give her Valium. I know I should request the meds through the staff when we're in the hospital, but it takes too long, especially with an attending physician who barely knows Adrienne's medical history. A nurse returns with Cepacol, an OTC throat lozenge, as if it will make everything better. Adrienne sucks on it, but claims the numbness lasts for only minutes. She continues to cough, and her throat hurts.

✷ ✷ ✷

The night before our mall trip, Adrienne used a different brand of hair dye to color her hair blue. She wanted it to look perfect since school was starting soon. Unfortunately, she managed to dye her entire bathroom, her sheets, and her skin blue too. I was livid when I saw her bathroom, which happened to be the main one in the house. Together, we began bleaching the sink and bathtub right away, undoing the damage before the dye set in.

I didn't give her skin much thought until John came home, took one look at her, and said, "What's up Smurf?"

Adrienne wailed, "Sisssssssy, I told you it looked bad. What am I going to do?"

"Cover it with makeup. Besides, it will fade before school starts. Now scrub."

I pointed to the bathtub with its stubborn ring of blue clinging to the porcelain.

"But Sissy."

"But what? We're cleaning this mess first, and then we will worry about your . . . sort of bluish face."

Adrienne gave me that you-don't-care-about-my-feelings look and went back to work.

✷ ✷ ✷

"Sissy, look at my arms."

249

Despite the Lasix, Adrienne appears puffier than ever. When I show a nurse, she agrees and decides to weigh Adrienne. 133 pounds. Adrienne and I look at the scale.

"That can't be right," I say, "she was 119 two days ago."

"All fluid," says the nurse, "I'll see the doctor about ordering more Lasix."

"Now that's what I call water weight," says Adrienne as she crawls back into bed. "No wonder I feel so bloated."

I shake my head. Fourteen pounds in two days. Is that safe? Can't too much water be a bad thing? Can't it dilute the blood or something? I decide not to bring it up with the doctor. If all goes well, Adrienne has one more day of chemo. We might go home as early as tomorrow evening. I don't want to mess up that chance for us by questioning the doctor's decision. For Adrienne to be discharged, we need his consent. In hospitals, doctors have the power. Patients don't.

Anya and Alex drop by and surprise me with a piece of birthday cake as well as a tray of sweets for the nurses and staff. I don't know why I didn't think of doing that sooner. Nurses are like teachers, underappreciated and overworked, yet paid more. Before long, people peek their heads in to wish me happy birthday. I appreciate the gesture, but I'm thinking about last year when I dragged Adrienne out of bed, paid her the negotiated ten-dollar fee, and took her to the mall at ten o'clock in the morning. Before we left, I helped her cover her skin with foundation and powder to diminish its Smurf-like appearance.

Not long after we left the glamour shot place, I exacted sweet revenge, albeit accidental. We bumped into one of Adrienne's closest friends, Lori, who was surprised to see Adrienne shopping so early. As she marveled at Adrienne's new blue hair, I made sure to tell Lori Adrienne and I had our picture taken together. Adrienne jabbed me in the ribs with her elbow, but in a playful way. As I had suspected, she was not as embarrassed as she had pretended to be. She even kept some pictures for herself while I took most of the wallet-size prints and distributed them to friends and family as planned during my trip.

Savoring my last bite of cake, I miss that blue bathtub. I would trade Adrienne's now translucent skin for seeing her as a Smurf again. Her blue-green hair remains in a Ziploc bag in a drawer at home. I wish I had found someone to make a wig out of Adrienne's own hair for free.

I put the word out in several emails, but I never heard back from anyone. I imagine the free part is the reason because I know people who know someone who could do it.

"Happy Birthday, Sissy. Sorry we had to be," Adrienne gestures, "in here."

"It's not your fault, kiddo. Not a big deal."

"Still kinda sucks."

Lying on the bed, Adrienne looks me in the eye. I can't lie to her.

"Yeah. It kind of sucks. But the cake was good."

Adrienne almost laughs but stops herself. Laughing can trigger a coughing attack, and she's tired.

"Night, Sissy."

"Goodnight, sweetie. Love you."

I wait for an I love you too, but she is already asleep.

The dry coughing wakes me up. I glance at my watch as I walk toward the bed half-asleep—3 a.m. Adrienne holds one hand over her mouth, while the other clutches her ribs. When the nurse offers another throat lozenge, I want to throw it at her. Can't she hear the gurgling in Adrienne's chest? Can't she see Adrienne spitting up blood?

The doctors have only speculated about the cause of the mucositis; they believe either it is a side effect of the chemo or the tumors in Adrienne's chest are making it harder for her to breathe. I prefer the former theory. No matter what the cause, no one seems to be able to offer a cure for the coughing itself.

I sit on a chair and hold Adrienne's hand, as she hacks for almost two hours. Finally, her body exhausts itself, and she falls asleep again around a quarter after five. I curl back up in the window seat, which I've decided is not as comfortable as the foldout chair. The benefit of being near the window is we are farther away from the door, which constantly opens and closes, and closer to the bathroom, which means less walking for Adrienne. However, unlike the chair, the seat is too far from the bed. I can't sleep next to Adrienne. I close my eyes. *Please let us go home tomorrow.*

By noon, Adrienne's fourth round of chemo is complete. Since the pain medication was given by mouth (instead of through the IV) this time, Adrienne and I know there will be no issues of weaning her off a machine or calculating the correct dosage to take at home. We wait.

When the attending doctor comes in to discuss Adrienne's discharge,

I want to jump up and down on the window seat and tell the world. Four days! Four fucking days, and we're going home! I don't, of course, because then the doctor might have me committed. The only thing Adrienne needs to do before we leave is have another Pentamidine treatment because someone realized it's been more than a month since she's had one. Fine, no problem. One antibiotic-inhalation procedure at 2 p.m. We'll be there.

Like last time, the discharge papers read 15:20, but unlike last time, we are out of the hospital ten minutes later at 3:30 p.m. I don't know if the doctor called the pharmacy in advance, or if we have fewer prescriptions to fill since we still have some at home. I look at the papers and count the meds. Fourteen! One less than last time. The Decadron and ointment for the mysterious, yet now disappeared, rash are out, but I see the Zofran is back.

- Boost—Drink as you want. A nutritional drink like Ensure.
- Dilaudid—Give 4 mg by mouth four times per day/as needed: 8 a.m., 2 p.m., 8 p.m., 2 a.m. Painkiller.
- Elavil—By mouth once per day: 8 a.m. Anti-depressant.
- Lo/Ovral Tab—By mouth once a day: 8 a.m. Birth control.
- Magnesium plus Protein—By mouth three times per day: 8 a.m., 4 p.m., 12 a.m. Vitamin supplement.
- Marinol—By mouth four times per day for two consecutive days after chemo: 8 a.m., 2 p.m., 8 p.m., 2 a.m. Appetite stimulant and anti-nausea.
- Milk of Magnesia—By mouth once per day. Stool softener.
- Neupogen shot—Subcutaneously once per day: 8 a.m. Medicine to increase white blood cells.
- Nystatin—Swish and swallow four times a day: 8 a.m., 12 p.m., 4 p.m., 8 p.m. Anti-fungal.
- Peridex mouthwash—(1/2 strength)—Swish and spit four times a day: 8 a.m., 12 p.m., 4 p.m., 8 p.m. Antimicrobial.
- Pravachol—By mouth once per day: 8 a.m. Cholesterol-lowering medication.
- Valium—By mouth once per day/as needed: 12 a.m. Anti-anxiety.
- Zantac—By mouth twice per day: 8 a.m., 8 p.m. Anti-nausea.

- Zofran—By mouth four times per day for two consecutive days after chemo: 8 a.m., 2 p.m., 8 p.m., 2 a.m. Anti-nausea.

I almost whistle as I drive us home, but my inability to stay on pitch irritates Adrienne. Thoughts, more numbers, roam around in my head. Four days of chemo. Fourteen meds instead of fifteen. No liver pain. Those must be good signs, right? What if it's an illusion and things are only getting better before they get worse? NO. I will be positive. We are going home. Adrienne can play with Marinol. We will have a good weekend.

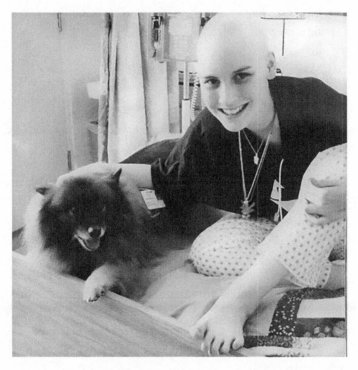

PAWS visit with Raven © August 13, 2001

Days 94–98

Top ten reasons to live:
1. Eli
2. Jane's Addiction
3. The beach
4. Sleep
5. Learning/Expanding
6. Meeting new people
7. The Internet
8. Public buses
9. Cheese
10. Helping others

—Adrienne's journal entry dated 2/5/01

When I am not reading books about cancer, I am on the Internet searching for . . . something or someone, quelling the desperation. I think about what Adrienne said. I'll just be one of the less than five percent who survive. One of my books quotes that statistic, but I haven't found a survivor, yet. I need to find one, just one person who has beaten Stage IV liver cancer. Maybe not having another CT scan after the third round of chemo caused my anxiety to heighten, but then again, I don't think I could have heard 'no change' again without punching someone out.

I emailed Dr. Bernie Siegel after I finished reading his book *Love, Medicine, & Miracles*. When he replied the same day, I felt like a movie star. His words inspired me:

> "People are not statistics, so have her [Adrienne] go for it [other treatments]. Seek the help you need. Alternatives [are] available too, if doctors give her no hope."

What I didn't tell Dr. Siegel, or many other people is, I have been looking at alternative treatments. I contacted The Center for Holistic Life Extension through its website ExtendLife.com. With such an optimistic name, I expect an upbeat, over-the-top sales pitch to my query about their services. Instead, I receive a sobering, honest reply from the founder Dr. Luis Velazquez.

"Ms. Andrea W.
Thank you for your email. The situation of your sister is advanced. In stage IV, we can't help you. Only we can give her a good quality of life. Hepatitis C and the tumors in her lungs and liver makes difficult the treatments. Thank you."

A doctor in Mexico who runs a clinic that uses non-FDA-approved drugs and unorthodox therapies tells me he can't help. He can only give good quality of life, the same words Dr. No said in that horrible meeting that feels like forever ago. Only when I swallow do I realize how dry my throat is. Adrienne does not need to know about this email. I tell myself we couldn't have afforded the treatments anyway. Medi-Cal wouldn't have covered it. Hell, I've been arguing with them about transferring Adrienne to UCLA for over six weeks. I reread the email. I find comfort in the doctor's imperfect grammar, as if he is not a capable physician. I can't handle his truth so I dismiss his credentials and close the email. But I don't delete it.

"But Sissy, water is boring."

"Drink it."

"It has no taste."

"You'll get used to it."

"What about my blue Powerade?"

"You can drink that too as long as three-quarters of the sixty-four ounces of your daily intake of fluids is water."

Adrienne rolls her eyes, but sips the glass of water as she nibbles a piece of toast.

Now I not only monitor every time Adrienne throws up, every pill she ingests, every pain she feels, every stool she produces, but I also track the amount of fluids she drinks, something I should have done all along. I will not allow her to get dehydrated again. Our first day home after chemo, Adrienne drinks fifty-four ounces of fluid that includes mostly water, as well as blue Powerade, a fruit shake, and half a can of Boost. I don't realize it until I write it down. When did Adrienne stop drinking soda? I always limited her consumption to one can per day, so she never drank a lot of it unless we went out to dinner, but when did she stop and why am I sad about it?

I continue my trek through Mexico and email the International Bio Care Hospital located in San Diego, California, and Tijuana, Mexico. I receive an automatic reply; a doctor will contact me soon. Within twenty-four hours, Dr. Jose Henriquez sends me a polite, professional email with a subject line that reads, "Buenos dias Doc, Lo molesto con otro email, thanks, Juan." I know enough Spanish to recognize, "Good morning, Doc. With other email." I wonder what "lo molesto" means and suspect molesto must be the verb in the sentence, but don't care enough to find out.

Although he doesn't push his services, Dr. Henriquez does list all of the treatments the hospital provides including diet, detoxification, immune regulation, and specific anticancer therapy with daily intravenous infusions of laetrile, vitamin C, DMSO, taurine, butyrate, glutathione, antioxidants, vitamins, minerals, enzymes, live-cell therapy, etc. While he states his team is having good results even with terminal patients, he adds, at the end of the email, he has not had too many cases of HCC. I wonder if he inserted that line as a disclaimer. *Don't get your hopes up.*

I know we cannot afford Dr. Henriquez's three-week intensive program. I am also suspicious of the Bio Care Hospital when an obvious competitor that offers similar treatments already told me their alternative therapies would not help Adrienne. I finally received the reply I expected, and I need to tear it apart too so I won't feel defeated.

"This [HCC] is a rather unusual disease in USA, especially in a 15 y/o girl." *DUH.* "There may be some associated factors such as Hepatitis B or C; cirrhosis, etc." *Does he honestly believe I don't know this information?*

If I rip apart the character of every physician or the content of each email, then I can claim a victory. We are not moving forward, but we are not stepping backward either. No cha-cha here. *Remaining stagnant—no change—status quo—is acceptable. When did I lower my standards?*

At the Staples Center, the crowd screams as Depeche Mode launches into one of their biggest hits *Personal Jesus*. Anya obtained floor seats for Adrienne hoping she would want to go to the concert. Even though her counts tend to peak immediately after chemo, making it safe for her to go out in public, Adrienne decided not to go tonight. Instead, she asked Alex, not a huge Depeche Mode fan, to take her place. When Alex sees how many stairs without handrails we have to walk down to get to our seats, he comments.

"I would have had to carry her down."

I nod, he's right.

So there we are, the four of us, Anya, Alex, Eli, and I standing in front of our floor seats. Unable to see anything in front of me due to my short stature, I look up. I like the song, but I have never paid attention to the lyrics before. Even as I move my upper body in time with the music, I find the whole situation ironic. Here I am staring at the ceiling of an arena, dancing to a song about finding my own personal Jesus, and I stopped praying because no one was listening.

I catch Anya's eye and smile. Part of me is having a good time and she needs to know that, since this concert is also a belated birthday present for me. I focus on the beat and try to ignore the guilt I feel for having fun while Adrienne stays home with John. Yesterday, her heart rate escalated to 138 bpm. Her temperature rose to 99.7 degrees, and her esophagus burned. When I left tonight, those symptoms had disappeared, but the pain and nausea continued despite Dilaudid and Marinol around the clock. John and Adrienne pushed me out the door insisting I go to the concert and have fun. I miss them.

Since his first email was so positive and he got back to me right away, I contact Dr. Bernie Siegel again asking if he knows of anyone who has survived liver cancer. He replies he knows of a few people, but

"The diagnosis is less important than the attitude of the patient from the standpoint of exceeding expectations. I know how helpful it is to speak to other natives who have the same thing, but I am not seeing many people right now. One physician in our group for a year has [had] the same thing and has chosen alternative therapies based upon her needs and beliefs as well as what she heard from oncologists."

Other than natives striking me as an odd word choice, I can't find anything wrong with his email. I wish I could meet him, talk to him, soak up his energy, but he is not speaking in California anytime soon. I wonder if the physician with liver cancer chose other therapies because her oncologists said, hey, let's be honest, we both know chemo won't work. Or maybe it's what her doctor didn't say that made her choose a different route. Either way, she's been living with liver cancer for a year, only I don't know what stage, which makes a huge difference.

I don't live for baseball, even though it's one of my favorite sports, but I do like the three strikes, you're out rule. With one strike left, I once again look for answers south of the border and discover the Oasis of Hope Hospital in Tijuana, Mexico. Their motto "First, do no harm" reminds of a line from one of Adrienne's poems, "If it harm none (including yourself) do what thou wilt."

I call the hospital's toll-free number, and a woman assures me a doctor will return my message. When a well-spoken clinical oncologist named Dr. Soto calls me back within hours, I am shocked. I grab a pen and a legal pad and prepare to take notes.

Dr. Soto listens as I describe Adrienne's condition and current treatments in detail. Then he says lots of research suggests cancer cells cannot survive in the presence of oxygen. He would saturate Adrienne's blood with oxygen and give her laetrile, shark cartilage, vitamins including A and C among others, and enzymes to enhance her immune system. The oxygen theory and shark cartilage are new to me, but the other therapies sound like what Dr. Henriquez listed in his email. Dr. Soto doesn't sound like a charlatan; however, I do pay closer attention when he mentions the hospital also provides chemotherapy in some cases.

"Have you heard of Tegafur? Bristol-Myers Squibb, an American company, makes it."

"Uh. Maybe."

I write down the name of a drug that sounds familiar. Who talked about it before? Was it Anya's mother? I don't remember.

Dr. Soto continues. "Tegafur is a derivative of 5-FU."

I interrupt, "like Xeloda?"

"Yes, but it's different. We would try Tegafur along with the other therapies."

I know as soon as he says it the drug isn't legal in the U.S. yet.

"And how . . . I mean, will . . . ?"

The words stick in my mouth as if I'm eating a peanut-butter sandwich.

"Given your sister's age and how advanced her disease is I don't believe we can do much for her, but any clinical improvement is a good sign."

"Right." Three strikes, we're out. "Well um . . . thank you for your time and the information."

I'm in such a hurry to get off the phone I forget to ask what Adrienne's age has to do with anything. Shouldn't youth be an advantage? I look up Tegafur and find UFT is the generic name of the drug. Under FDA approval, it reads, "This is an investigational drug for cancer treatments." Like a bolt of lightning, the meaning of Dr. Soto's words strikes me. An investigational drug is tested in clinical trials, and I suspect one must be a legal adult, eighteen years old, to participate in those procedures.

Every time a door opens even a crack, it slams into my face, knocks me to the ground, and reminds me I picked the wrong one like on the game show *Let's Make a Deal*. When the winning contestant makes it to the final round, she chooses a door to claim her grand prize: a new car, a room filled with fancy furniture, or a booby prize like a lifetime supply of a generic product no one would want. When am I going to pick the right door? Are we out of doors?

Without an IV pumping water into her 24/7, Adrienne's weight plummets back down to 120 pounds. Her liver feels tight so she can only lie on her left side. If I touch her shins, she flinches from the pain. When she says my bones ache, Sissy, she reminds me of an old woman with osteoporosis. From behind, watching her walk is like seeing a doll come to life learning how to use her limbs for the first time. Each step is careful, purposeful, and she often grasps at the wall for support. I offer to help but she refuses. Like me, Adrienne is too proud and too stubborn. As she eases her thin figure into the living room chair to watch television, I retreat to my office to do research.

The breakthrough happens without warning. I am reading my daily dose of PubMed searching for clinical trials involving liver cancer when I discover a series of abstracts. Words leap off the computer screen . . .

HEPATOCELLULAR CARCINOMA with BONE METASTASIS.
Oral administration of UFT. 63-year-old male patient. Six months
MASS in the left chest wall ELIMINATED. Rare case.

HEPATOCELLULAR CARCINOMA with portal invasion and right
adrenal gland METASTASIS. 79-year-old female. Treated by low
dose UFT. CT scan revealed <u>marked contraction</u> of the primary
liver tumor and right adrenal metastasis. AFP was REDUCED.
This case RARE.

Rare? Liver cancer itself is not rare. There must be more success stories.
I type hepatocellular carcinoma and UFT into the search box again determined to find other results. When I read . . .

Almost complete DISAPPEARANCE of METASTATIC pulmonary
tumor and REDUCTION of the MAIN HEPATIC MASS in HEPA-
TOCELLULAR CARCINOMA treated with UFT. 61-year-old female
patient.

the words blur together . . .

HEPATOCELLULAR CARCINOMA with REDUCTION of primary
tumor and DISAPPEARANCE of MULTIPLE LUNG METASTASIS.
56-year-old male. Administer UFT orally as an outpatient. After
seven months, the primary hepatic lesions were DECREASED in
size, and metastatic lesions of lung were COMPLETELY ELIMI-
NATED with REDUCTION of AFP level.

my heart beats faster . . .

Complete response of a massive HEPATOCELLULAR CARCI-
NOMA with LUNG METASTASIS to UFT. 77-year-old male.
DISAPPEARED COMPLETELY. Administration of UFT appears
PROMISING for the treatment of HCC and can be used SAFELY,
even with patients in poor general condition.

and then I find them . . .

Advanced HEPATOCELLULAR CARCINOMA with LUNG and
BONE METASTASIS treated by orally administered UFT. 52-year-
old male. Several months later, liver tumor and metastasis had

almost DISAPPEARED. <u>Maintained a good state of health for four years now.</u>

survivors.

Advanced HEPATOCELLULAR CARCINOMA with LUNG and SPINE METASTASIS treated with combination therapy of IFN-alpha and UFT. 44-year-old male. Complete resolution of all lung nodules. <u>Patient was working full-time and showed no evidence of tumor relapse.</u>

HEPATOCELLULAR CARCINOMA with BONE METASTASIS responded to oral administration of UFT. 61-year-old male. Seven months later, AFP was 3,997 (from a high of 111,683) and REDUCTION of TUMOR was shown on CT scan and Ultrasound. Right upper arm pain diminished. <u>The patient is presently still alive.</u>

Until I see a drop of water fall on the keyboard, I don't even realize I am crying. I touch my face. It is soaked. As the printer churns out each page, each person who had stage IV liver cancer and survived, I weep. Hope floods back into my body, and I welcome it because I need it the way our mother needs her drugs, the way some people need a god. I feel reborn as the papers pile up in the printer feeder; my faith restored by UFT, a miracle drug doctors cannot yet explain.

Yesterday, Dr. Soto mentioned UFT, and I cannot believe the timing is a coincidence. He must not know about these case studies in Japan. These people all had metastasis like Adrienne, some in multiple organs. The printer sputters as the cartridges stop moving signifying my print job is complete. I pick up the half-inch pile and read every abstract to note the commonalities. Male or female, all the survivors are Japanese, they are over fifty years old, and they were treated with a combination of UFT, either orally or intravenously.

I grab my chemo-drug book to look up UFT again. UFT is a combination of Ftorafur and Uracil. The former metabolizes as 5-FU, a common chemotherapy drug, while the latter is an amino acid that enhances the effect of 5-FU. Since Uracil is what makes UFT different from other derivatives of 5-FU, I imagine it as a wonder drug that a doctor must have stumbled upon by accident. I see him or her wearing a lab coat peering down the lens of a microscope observing cancer cells and placing a drop of an amino acid into the mix to see what would happen. To his or her surprise, the doctor realizes Uracil has strengthened Ftorafur and together they have stopped the cell from growing like Batman and Robin outwitting the Joker. The doctor will become famous for creating the next superhero in the war against cancer.

My rational mind acknowledges UFT still presents a problem: it is not an approved drug and getting Adrienne into a clinical trial may be impossible. Flying to Japan is out of the question; at least we could have driven to Mexico. However, the hope has rejuvenated me in a way I never expected. The abstracts are my bible, and in UFT, I have found my own personal Jesus.

The news of Adrienne's labs from yesterday dampens my spirits. I ask the nurse to repeat the last number.

"Zero?" I ask.

"Zero," she confirms.

No immune system. Nada.

I call the property manager and tell her she cannot show the house for a few days. She tries to mask her frustration with concern, but she fails. I never tell her how many prospective buyers seem spooked by the sick girl in the house, as if Adrienne is contagious. The owner can always throw us out before the house sells, but I can't worry about that right now. By law, she must give us thirty days' notice, so we should have a home through September.

After I hang up the phone, Adrienne insists on walking on the treadmill. I argue with her.

"You have no immune system!"

"I already drank more than sixty-four ounces of fluids today," she counters. "I won't faint."

"You need a blood transfusion to give you strength."

"I need my muscles back to get stronger," she replies.

"Ten minutes. That's all."

I give in because I don't want to waste time fighting with her. *Time—I hear a clock ticking.*

I watch in amazement as Adrienne walks, the frail doll from yesterday now a determined young woman confident of each step. How can she exercise with no immune system? Where does that strength come from? As I return to the abstracts and cancer books, I realize being able to walk on the treadmill gives Adrienne control the way my research gives me hope. She needs to find power wherever she can because we are living in a somewhat powerless situation.

We never discuss it though—our attempts at commanding cancer. We bully it, suppress it, drown it, ignore it, and conquer it—any way we can.

Andrea & Adrienne © August 15, 2000 (Andrea's 28th birthday)

Days 99–104

11:59 pm: weeeeeeeeeeeeeeee Guess what? Make-a-Wish called Dave up and he instantly knew who I was! His manager knows about me! HE TALKED TO HIS MANAGER ABOUT ME!!!!!!! He was like: Oh! I know Adrienne. I met her at Leno and we talk online a lot. How about she comes to one of my rehearsals to hang out and enjoy a sort of show/ concert? EEEEEEEEEEPPPPPPPPPPPP!!! The girl from Make-a-Wish said that EVERYONE she called up wants to make something happen for me. ☺ I feel so loved. ::blush:: He wants me, haha ;-) giddy giddy giddy I get a blood transfusion tomorrow. Blah. There's a chance that my central line might have to be taken out and a new one placed in surgically on the other side. BLAH. I got a fever last night of 100.1. Highest yet. Was two minutes away from going to the hospital. I've got a new doctor, and I actually like him. Even if he did show up three hours after he was scheduled to. ☹ I gotta go write a thank-you letter to Dave for remembering me. ::laughs:: I have no life, and I only have 300 white blood cells. Oh well. All's good in the end.

—Adrienne's journal entry dated 8/23/01

I am so worried about strangers coming into our home and making Adrienne sick, it never occurs to me I am susceptible to germs too. The same cold Adrienne caught at Medieval Times moves on to my body when it's finished with her. To avoid giving Adrienne the cold again, I obsessively wash my hands with both antibacterial soap followed by antibacterial hand sanitizer until they are red and dry. I even consider wearing gloves when I flush her central line. What I fail to realize is the bacterium is airborne, and if it wants to infect Adrienne, it will find a way.

That evening, Adrienne complains her central line hurts. I examine it, as well as change the dressing. When I remove the gauze, I see the skin around the entrance site of the port is swollen and red, warning signs of an infection. I apply Neosporin on the area to ease her discomfort until I can ask our home health nurse Tess about it tomorrow morning. Adrienne and I know if the site doesn't improve within a few days, Dr. Marco will schedule a surgery to remove the line and then reinsert it on the opposite side of her chest. I hope the Neosporin attacks the unseen germs with the same vigor Adrienne has when she walks on the treadmill. The last thing she needs is another surgery.

When Tess looks at the site the next day, the redness has faded to a dark pink and the swelling has decreased. She agrees it might be the beginning of a minor infection, but it seems to be improving. I blow my nose a few feet away as Tess cleans the area. Watching her, I see how close her face is to Adrienne's chest when she flushes the lines. I ask Tess if it's plausible I infected Adrienne with my cold, if the germs leaving my mouth as I exhaled attacked her skin. Tess says Adrienne is vulnerable to any bacteria, especially near an open area such as the entrance of the central line. *I'm an idiot. Adrienne has no immune system, and I was breathing all over her.* Seeing the blanched look on my face, Tess assures me not to worry. The site looks better. She tells me to wear a mask every time I change the dressing until my cold is gone and to continue with the Neosporin. Adrienne says thanks a lot, Sissy. *Breath. Why didn't I think about it?*

On Thursday, Adrienne and I sit in the waiting room of UCLA's pediatric clinic. Dr. Aquino referred us to Dr. Fenn, a pediatric oncologist. Apparently, the insurance will approve the transfer if Adrienne is treated as a pediatric patient. If this meeting goes well, Adrienne will start her next round of chemo at UCLA with Dr. Fenn listed as her primary oncologist, although Dr. Aquino will make the decisions regarding treatment. Another doctor, a hepatologist, will monitor Adrienne's liver at all times. I already like UCLA's team approach to Adrienne's care. She will have three doctors working together to figure out how to make her well again.

Since her immune system is severely comprised, Adrienne wears a mask, the same kind I wear when I change the dressing on her line. She shouldn't even be out in public, but the appointment was scheduled weeks ago. Because the fourth round of chemo was delayed, the timing of everything has changed. Her counts should be up by now, but they're not. Her WBC has dropped to 300, and her ANC is still zero. We sit as far away from small children as possible and hope for the best.

An hour goes by. Then another. The receptionist keeps apologizing. Dr. Fenn is running behind today. I want to yell but I don't. This doctor had better be outstanding because this delay is ridiculous. Finally, we are sitting inside an examination room, which makes me feel safer because everything is sterile. Our cell phone rings. I forgot to turn it off, and our Make-a-Wish coordinator Becca Goldberg gives us the good news. Dave Navarro not only remembers Adrienne, but he would also be happy to make her wish come true. Moments later, Dr. Fenn walks in.

Still flushed with excitement, Adrienne greets him by exclaiming in a singsong voice.

"DAVE Navarro KNOWS who I am! DAVE Navarro KNOWS who I am!"

Not missing a beat, Dr. Fenn mimics her tone.

"WHO is DAVE Navarro?"

"I can't believe you don't know who he is."

Adrienne bursts into giggles and explains the phone call, her wish, and meeting Dave Navarro on *The Tonight Show*.

I watch as Dr. Fenn listens attentively to Adrienne; he acts as though understanding how important Dave Navarro is to Adrienne is key to knowing her as an individual, not just another patient. I like him already and we haven't even discussed her treatment yet. Adrienne can't stop smiling, but she finally stops talking about Dave long enough for us to focus on why we are here.

"How many cases of HCC have you personally treated, Dr. Fenn?" I ask him.

"About five to seven, although it's not uncommon to work with another oncologist when a child"—he looks at Adrienne—"or a teenager has an adult form of cancer."

"I've been researching an investigational drug called UFT. What can you tell me about it? Do you think it's an option for Adrienne?"

"I've heard of it. I will definitely speak to Dr. Aquino about it since he will be determining the best course of treatment for Adrienne."

"I've already spoken to Dr. Aquino about this issue, but it's important to me I receive all copies of Adrienne's lab work and any other medical records. Will that be a problem?"

"Of course not. Just tell our receptionist Janet what you need, and give her a fax number."

I look at Adrienne who will later tell me Dr. Fenn is her new favorite doctor ahead of Dr. Aquino and even Dr. Marco, of whom we have both become quite fond.

"Well then. What do we do next?"

Dr. Fenn smiles. He sensed our silent sister communication. He passed our test. We are transferring Adrienne's care to UCLA.

"We will speak to Children's and arrange to have another CT scan there or here to see if there's been any progress. I would think everything will be finalized by the end of the month."

Adrienne and I thank Dr. Fenn as he leaves. He was worth the wait, I think to myself. He gets Adrienne. I replay the scene in my head: *DAVE Navarro KNOWS who I am! WHO is DAVE Navarro?* He responded to Adrienne in the same enthusiastic manner she evoked without being condescending or mocking her. He must spend a lot of time with teenagers. I wish we had found him months ago, but now that we have, I'm not wasting another minute at Children's. I will tell Dr. Marco about our decision at Adrienne's clinic appointment on Monday.

True to their word, UCLA faxes over Dr. Fenn's clinic notes regarding our first meeting with him. The main section reads, "Emma is a delightful 15-year-old who was diagnosed with hepatocellular carcinoma after her initial presentation with right upper quadrant pain. She is doing reasonably well. She has had significant weight loss, which makes it uncomfortable for her to sit for any length of time. She has had no jaundice, no ascites,[13] no encephalopathy.[14] By the report, her synthetic function of her liver has remained very good in spite of chronically elevated liver enzymes."

I love how he calls Adrienne delightful, and I am comforted by the words reasonably well and very good. I also feel better reading the list of things Adrienne could but does not have: jaundice, abdominal fluid, and brain dysfunction. I remember how one nurse yelled at me for reading Adrienne's chart at the hospital a few months ago. Funny how some healthcare providers don't realize parents gain not only knowledge from reading their children's medical records, but also, in many cases, some

---

13 Accumulation of fluid in the abdominal cavity
14 Generalized brain dysfunction marked by varying degrees of impairment of speech, cognition, orientation, and arousal

much-needed encouragement. We are not looking for the bad stuff; at least, I'm not. I want to find that beacon of hope amidst the medical mumbo-jumbo. As I file the clinic report, one thought leaves a footprint on my brain: Dr. Fenn finds Adrienne to be delightful.

EMAIL
Subject: Hepatocellular Carcinoma
Date: 8/23/2001
To: OCCC@cc.nih.gov

Dear NIH,
Are there any current clinical trials for Hepatocellular Carcinoma and the drug UFT? How about HCC with Tegafur alone? I've only found one trial done in the US in the last five years with UFT; can you please send me more information? Thank you.

Sincerely,
Andrea J. Wilson

Adrienne's school counselor Rick Carlton and I have been emailing for several weeks figuring out what classes she can take in the fall, who will be her teachers, and how her work will be monitored. Originally, Adrienne was enrolled in six courses for her sophomore year of high school: French II, Algebra II, Honors English 10, Honors Chemistry, Honors World History, and Advanced Dance. Since physical activity isn't possible, Rick and I have already agreed she will drop dance and make up that class later. Due to the lab component of chemistry, Adrienne may have to take a different science course. Rick isn't certain yet which teachers can help me home school Adrienne. I am prepared to teach English and history if the district provides me with the materials, and Anya has offered to teach French if necessary. Adrienne hasn't said much about school. I imagine the formerly dreaded math homework, her least favorite subject, will seem easy compared to cancer.

Because Adrienne's hemoglobin is hovering around 7.4, we go to Children's Hospital on Friday so she can receive a blood transfusion—two bags this time. I look for Dr. Marco because I would rather tell him the news today about the transfer than wait until Tuesday. I want him to be the first one to know. Since he's not around, I don't say anything. I ask a nurse to examine Adrienne's central line, which is still sensitive to the touch, but looks much better. To be safe, she has a doctor prescribe a short-term antibiotic. We spend almost the entire day at the clinic with Adrienne sleeping through the transfusion. I try to nap too, but I cannot.

I remember as a toddler how Adrienne refused to let our mother brush her hair for an entire week until Mother cut it into a short bob. Now she has no hair at all. Adrienne was so active and limber, she would crawl out of her crib every night without hurting herself and sleep on the floor. Now she can't sit comfortably much less take dance class at school in a few weeks. An excerpt from an essay I wrote for a college application flashes through my head,

"With fourteen years between us and the circumstances of her birth, I couldn't see how I could possibly love her. When I saw her for the first time, I couldn't believe how beautiful she was. Loving her was not a problem at all."

I watch as a stranger's blood infuses Adrienne's face with color like someone putting blush on her cheeks from the inside out. *I love you so much, kiddo. Maybe too much, if that's possible. Please don't leave me.*

That evening I call American Home Health to speak to someone about Adrienne's platelet count, which is at an all-time low of 21,000. I thought she would receive a platelet transfusion at the clinic today since she is at an extreme risk of bleeding, but I guess her hemoglobin is a bigger concern. A nurse named Brooke assures me although 21,000 is very low, the doctors are probably waiting to see if Adrienne's body will recover on its own. If not, she should get a transfusion.

At some point, our conversation goes beyond blood counts, and Brooke reveals her younger daughter had an inoperable brain tumor and passed away. I don't know how to respond except to say how sorry I am. As Brooke continues to talk about her daughter, I marvel at the warmth that emanates from her voice. She must be sad, but I can't hear it. Instead, she focuses on the years her daughter had.

I want to tell John I feel good after talking to Brooke, but I know he won't understand. I'm not sure I can explain my reaction. This woman, a virtual stranger, must be devastated after losing her daughter, and yet, she manages to exude such positive energy. I can't imagine being her, having to carry that burden. Brooke is a wonderful person, but I hope never to share her experience. *A brain tumor is different. Adrienne is different.*

Saturday and Sunday come and go with a mix of low-grade fevers, right-quadrant pain, and hard stool (good) that creates a cut in Adrienne's rectum (bad). John and I write these notes down along with the sixty-four ounces of fluid on Saturday and the seventy-two ounces of fluid on Sunday. We give Dilaudid for the pain and Milk of Magnesia for the constipation. We do not dole out Tylenol for the fevers since they remain below 100 degrees. We encourage Adrienne to rest as much as possible because Monday is going to be a long day.

I wake up two hours earlier than normal and give the Neupogen shot in Adrienne's thigh while she's barely awake. With her legs becoming thinner each day, I will have to use her arms soon as an injection site. When I change the dressing of Adrienne's central line, I find a dry scab at the opening of the port, which is still red and sensitive, but not oozing any fluid. The antibiotic seems to be working. I administer the Epogen and flush Adrienne's lines. She eats breakfast while I pack a bag with stuff to keep us busy throughout the day: books, magazines, videos, CDs, CD player, and a deck of cards. We rush out the door at 7:45 a.m.

Forty-five minutes later, after dodging through rush-hour traffic, Adrienne lies flat, the most painful position for her, as a giant rectangular-shaped plate hovers over the length of her body for a bone scan. From motion to stillness, from noise to silence, the change is abrupt, but we are used to leaving the world behind us when we walk through those hospital doors.

From Radiology, we go to the clinic where we run into Dr. Marco, with whom we have an appointment tomorrow. I see no reason to wait until then to tell him the news. Firing him is much harder than firing Dr. No. We didn't like Dr. No; we like Dr. Marco. We didn't leave Children's before; we are leaving now. I practiced what to say, but when I speak, it comes out all wrong.

"You know, if you had been Adrienne's oncologist to begin with, maybe we wouldn't be leaving . . ."

Adrienne nods.

"We have to go somewhere that will treat her cancer and not just look at her as a pediatric patient."

Dr. Marco tells us he used to be at UCLA and explains why he came over to Children's Hospital, why he feels they are better equipped to treat Adrienne, but I can see he's grasping. He cares. He doesn't want us to leave. I feel torn about our decision for one moment, but it passes like an involuntary blink. I am doing what's best for Adrienne; I cannot be concerned about hurting a doctor's feelings.

"Thank you for everything you've done. I would appreciate it if you would make this transition as smooth as possible."

His shoulders drop as he replies, "Of course."

He says he will cancel our appointment with him for tomorrow, but we need to stay today. The lab rushed the blood tests completed a few hours ago. According to Dr. Marco, Adrienne's hemoglobin, now 9.6, is still too low. She needs another transfusion, only one bag this time. When I ask about her continued low platelet count, Dr. Marco makes no plans for a transfusion. I don't argue with him; there's no point now. The best news is Adrienne's immune system has bounced back in time for her Make-a-Wish day tomorrow. With normal WBC and ANC counts, she can meet Dave Navarro again, and even take off her mask for pictures.

Day 105

EMAIL (condensed)
Subject: Adrienne ranting once again ;)
Date: 8/28/2001
To: Dave Navarro

Today was honestly one of the best days of my life. I cannot describe in words how incredible of a person you are. I have never
before met someone who was so wise, down to earth, intelligent,
talented, and humorous. Throughout most of my childhood, you
were that one string of hope that held me together after years of
abuse from my mother. I do feel strange telling you that to me
you are a dear friend. It's sort of like walking up to a stranger and
saying the same thing, but then again we are no longer strangers
to each other. When you said that we don't have to go through
contacts to hang out or talk, were you serious? That kind of threw
me into shock, and again, in a good way :)

You are a truly beautiful person. Your kind is rare in this world.
You are a true gem—worth being cherished.

Thank you for giving me hope.
Until we meet again, -=Adrienne=-

*P.S. Sorry if I talked your ear off today or got in the way of things that you
needed to get done.*

One of the best days of Adrienne's life begins with a routine echocardiogram at Children's Hospital; it is her last test here, her last appointment.
We arrive early, eager to complete the task so we can go home and get
ready for her big day. Adrienne is already upset about having less than an

hour to get dressed and do her makeup. I pay little attention to her heart thumping on the screen, but the technician notes her pulse rate is high.

"Oh that," says Adrienne. "I'm seeing Dave today. He knows who I am."

She smiles. The technician shrugs, which makes me chuckle. Adrienne is too excited to notice he has no idea who Dave is.

Despite the time crunch, Adrienne wants to go upstairs and say goodbye to the nurses on the HEMOC ward. Feeling weak and wanting to save all her strength for later today, she requests a wheelchair. I find one and as we enter the giraffe elevators, I realize I will miss them. I never found out why giraffes, tigers, and peacocks were chosen for the elevators as themes. When the elevator doors open at the fourth floor, the artistic work assaults my eyes. I won't miss it or the overabundance of primary colors that attempts to hide the suffering here. I will, however, miss certain people.

We run into Helen, one of our favorite nurses. I taught her how to tie her ballet shoes; she told us what others said about our family. Her ditzy demeanor made us laugh while her competence and caring impressed us. When Adrienne tells her today is our last day, Helen nods. I told her weeks ago about our desire to transfer to UCLA. She is not surprised, only saddened by the news. She leans over and hugs Adrienne who is chattering away about meeting Dave. Goodbye and good luck Helen says. I hug her too.

We look for Ronnie, whom we haven't seen in a while, but who got us through those first two weeks of this madness with her kindness and her advice. Ronnie, with her frog-designed scrub tops and perky manner, reminds me of the Reese Witherspoon character, only taller, from the *Legally Blonde* trailers that keep running on television. Attractive, smart, and funny, Ronnie is the total package. We know more about Ronnie's personal life than we do about some of our so-called friends. She's married to a fireman. Her sister Brittany survived cancer, and she wants babies in a few years. Ronnie isn't working today.

Then, there's Velma who still talks about the time she kidnapped a wide-awake Adrienne in the middle of the night while John and I slept on the window seat barely big enough for a small child, much less two grown adults. After taking pictures with Adrienne's Polaroid camera, which produces mini-adhesive prints, the nurses signed them.

Velma wrote, "Thank you for letting me take care of you. Keep in touch. Fight hard," like USC's motto "Fight on." Velma is off today too.

We say goodbye to a few more familiar faces, nurses whose names we can't remember. We continue waving until the elevator doors shut. As the car drops down four floors to the lobby, I feel a sense of relief. Here on the seventh floor, the surgical ward, we found out Adrienne had cancer. Here we heard 'no change' more than once. Here I prayed in a chapel to a god who doesn't exist, couldn't help, or didn't listen. I push the wheelchair faster. The doors open.

We zip through the Mary Poppins area with its "no cell phone" sign and the smiley face on the wall. I wheel Adrienne past the giant plastic palm trees and the huge fish tank named "Guppywood," and wonder if the children playing on the oversized cubes are siblings of sick patients. We go around the security desk, home of the sticky, colored passes. I look at the huge panel on our right where Children's Hospital "acknowledges its special friends." I glance at hundreds of names etched in frosted glass. We exit and I see the dingy smoking area. I remember the time I caught a surgeon smoking on the roof of the parking lot. Then, I spot the sign that greeted me when we started this journey, "McDonald's: Open during Construction."

I point it out to Adrienne.

"You know something, kiddo? I will be okay if I never eat another McDonald's French fry."

"Well, I still like their McFlurrys," she says. "When I'm hungry."

Adrienne has already decided to wear her blue dress today, the same one she wore for the benefit. Last night, she painted her fingernails and toenails the exact same shade of royal blue as well as drew intricate designs on her hands with a black Sharpie marker. From far away, she appears to have tattoos; she likes it when people make that mistake. After the foundation disaster on our way to the ballet last month, she decides to wear none this morning. Instead, she applies blush to her cheeks to give her otherwise pale face some color. She rubs glitter on her bald head and even brushes her teeth without being pestered. She slips on a necklace, a pendant with glitter in it, and asks how she looks. I tell a white lie.

"You look perfect, sweetie. Just beautiful."

She looks stunning except for her shoulder blades jutting out of her back, showing how thin she has gotten. Then, there are the purple-red circles behind her eyelids revealing a new kind of fatigue. And her face is so white except for the cheekbones where blush attempts to cover the truth. Two blood transfusions and she has no color in her face. I can't remember a time when I was darker than Adrienne, but now I am.

"Look Sissy, there it is," Adrienne points to the black limousine parked in our driveway.

I push my worries aside when I see Adrienne smile. Her enthusiasm is contagious.

"John, they're here," I yell even though he hates it when I shout in the house.

He walks out wearing a long-sleeved white crew shirt and blue jeans. I'm wearing a black rayon button-up shirt and matching slacks. John looks ready to drink beer with his buddies while I am prepared to teach school. Adrienne is the only one dressed appropriately for such a special day; she looks like a princess who is attending her first formal ball. I hope we don't embarrass her in front of Dave. She'll never forgive us.

I don't know if I feel better or worse when I see our wish coordinator Becca dressed more casually than us. She's wearing turquoise cropped pants and a cotton top with an intricate design along with high-heeled sandals. Becca reminds me of a typical Southern California woman. She keeps her body in good shape. Her skin has seen too much sun. She wears clothes that are not age appropriate, yet she always manages to look good. I note her necklace matches her pants. I used to hate women like her, women with too much money and too few worries, but Becca has been kind to us, and she helped make this day possible, even if Adrienne already knew Dave.

After Becca takes pictures of us, we begin our day. The air-conditioning is a welcome relief from the dry heat outside. Adrienne explores the interior of the limo. She accepts a Coke when Becca offers her one, but she doesn't finish it. Instead, she talks about where we're going for lunch because she is the only person who knows anything about the place. Adrienne loves watching the Food Network. *Iron Chef* is one of her favorite shows, and she saw a review of a restaurant called The Standard. Today, we are eating lunch there, The Standard on Sunset.

"You're going to love it," she tells us.

Knowing her, I have no doubt.

The first thing I notice about our destination is the sign is upside-down, a signal The Standard is anything but standard, which turns out to be the hotel's slogan. When we walk through the sliding glass doors, we immediately see two spherical, translucent chairs with white cushions hanging from the ceiling.

Adrienne squeals and plops into one saying, "Aren't these cool?"

I agree and sit in the other one, which is comfortable. We twirl around for a few minutes while Becca finds out whom we're supposed to meet for lunch.

John walks through the lobby and says, "Hey kiddo, check this out."

John points at a full-length vitrine behind the registration desk where a lifelike female dummy lies nude with one arm draped across her breasts and her knee crossed over her body so nothing is revealed.

"She's bald, just like me," says Adrienne, "but she's not real—is she?"

"No . . . she can't be. She looks . . ." *I'm not sure.* "Too perfect. And who could lie still that long?"

All three of us laugh as we stand there on the white terrazzo. Any other day I would feel hopelessly out of place, but not today. We fit in among the potted cacti that line one wall and the floor-to-ceiling white shag carpeting that lines the opposite wall, where brown suede chaises provide the perfect spot for people-watching. The whole place, with its light vs. dark interior and plush vs. stark vibe, reminds me of the battle we've been fighting for the last 105 days, good vs. evil. Change vs. no change.

We walk into The Standard's 24/7 coffee shop.

"Check it out, guys," says Adrienne.

She points to two clocks labeled "Here" and "There." Neither one is on the correct time. I take a picture of this phenomenon. I don't know why I expected a fancier place; I should have known Adrienne would be attracted to something funky, smart. Between the blue ceiling and the blue Formica tabletops, I feel like I've been transported back to the 1950s living among Smurfs. Adrienne loves it though, especially when she realizes she can see Sunset Boulevard from our booth. With such retro hip décor and a prime location, I expect outrageous prices, not that we're paying for lunch, but I am surprised when the average price for a sandwich or salad is about twelve dollars. Unfortunately, Adrienne and I can't find anything on the menu we want to eat. Her stomach can barely tolerate food these days, and as for me, I'm too picky as John likes to remind me.

After bringing out odd-size glasses and pouring Smart Water into them, I explain the situation to our waiter, who offers to bring out the chef Marc Urwand. I don't want to cause any trouble, but he insists it's no problem.

"One other thing," I ask, "can you tell me how many ounces of liquid that glass holds? I'm guessing seven."

He gives me a puzzled look but says sure.

"I need to know how much water she drinks every day. It's important."

He nods and goes to retrieve the chef.

Chef Urwand, who insists we call him Marc, asks Adrienne what she likes.

"Well, I love pasta—especially tortellini, but I hate spaghetti."

"Hmm . . . well, I have some fettuccini, would that do?"

"Sure." Adrienne shrugs her shoulders.

I can tell she's not hungry.

"What kind of sauce?"

"I love Alfredo sauce, but I dunno if that would taste good right now."

"How about I mix up an olive oil-based sauce with some shrimp. Do you like shrimp?"

"I love shrimp!"

Adrienne will eat most of the shrimp and pick at the pasta.

"Do you mind adding some vegetables?" I ask.

Adrienne frowns.

"For me—we'll split the meal; it sounds wonderful."

"Of course," says Marc, acting as if we're royalty. He leaves as our waiter returns, confirming the glass holds exactly seven ounces of fluid.

"How did you know that?" he asks.

"A good guess," I reply, feeling a weird mix of pride and sadness that seven was the right answer. How can I explain to him eyeballing a glass and knowing its precise volume capacity is one of the many rare talents you develop when your child has cancer?

After lunch, a young African-American woman wearing sleek black slacks and a pink spaghetti-strap top that hugs her upper body offers to give us a tour of The Standard hotel. Jeanette begins by telling us the futuristic seats we encountered upon our arrival are Eero Aarnio bubble chairs. I nod and smile as though I know who this Eero person is; I guess he or she is a trendy designer who is known for weird but comfortable chairs.

277

We cross the lobby and enter the Cactus Lounge, which displays a large photomural of California's Joshua Tree National Monument. Through this lounge lies the pool, surrounded by an electric-blue Astroturf deck. Adrienne loves the pool deck, telling Jeanette blue is her favorite color as she spins around to show off her dress. Even the ping-pong table is a shade of blue, lighter and brighter than the deck although that doesn't seem possible. The pool almost seems out of place: the chlorine affecting the natural color of water giving it that familiar blue-green tint, the exact color of Adrienne's hair before chemo. I glance at Adrienne's head and say we should go back inside; she cannot be in the sun too long.

Before showing us an actual room, Jeanette takes us into the Lounge, a cocktail bar closed during the day, but a hot spot among the 'in crowd' at night even though it's been open only three months. With a maximum capacity of 115 people, the Lounge is intimate, yet spacious. Adrienne comments how cool it is to be in a bar at her age, and we all laugh. Jeanette runs down a list of celebrities who frequent the bar including musicians.

"And Dave Navarro had a surprise birthday party thrown for him here."

Adrienne swoons.

"What? No way! I'm going to see him later. He's the other part of my wish."

"Well, he often eats at the coffee shop too," Jeanette replies.

"Really? How cool."

While Adrienne relishes the fact that she and Dave like the same place, goosebumps crawl along the back of my neck, another weird coincidence although not as odd as some of the others. Nevertheless, what are the chances of Adrienne picking the one place where Dave had his birthday party two months ago and eating there on the same day she is seeing him? Once again, this journey feels planned, but not by us, and the outcome is out of our control. I hate that feeling.

Our last stop on the tour is a look at an actual room in the hotel.

"Wow. Those are some curtains."

I would never have them in my home. How tacky.

Jeanette replies, "Yes, those are Andy Warhol print poppy drapes; we had to get permission to use the design."

Upon hearing the pride in her voice, I keep my opinion to myself. The white walls display no art, but the giant mirror and large screen TV make up for the bareness, and the silver beanbag chair in the corner adds flare.

"I want to stay here, Sissy," Adrienne says as she walks around and examines the stereo.

My first thought isn't *we can't afford it*, but instead it's *you couldn't sleep on that platform bed*. Jeanette shows us the unique mini-bar stocked with sake, energy drinks, licorice, animal crackers, Rice Krispie Treats, Oreos, Vaseline, and scented candles.

Adrienne smells a candle, "Oh . . . patchouli, my favorite."

"You can have it," says Jeanette.

"Are you sure?" I ask.

"Of course."

Adrienne thanks her and seems tickled by the souvenir. Before we leave, however, Jeanette gives us more gifts: a complete press kit full of photos, articles, and two T-shirts with the hotel's logo. We take pictures outside of the lobby with Jeanette, the waiter, and Wes, the guy who offered to let Adrienne into the Lounge, despite my protests about her age, any time she wants to show up.

As we wait for the limo, I take a picture of Adrienne talking to John. She has her right hand on her forehead as if she's hitting herself or blocking the sun and her left hand on her hip. She's smiling—with teeth. Later, she decides that photo is her favorite picture of herself because she looks like an elegant mannequin. I'm happy she sees what everyone else has known all along. She is beautiful—with or without hair. *But it took being bald for her to see it.*

As the limo pulls into the rear parking lot of a nondescript building, I realize I've driven by this area of Hollywood more than a hundred times. I ask John if he knew this place was a rehearsal space, and he shakes his head. We walk through a small foyer into the heart of the building, a soundproofed area complete with a stage. Except for a half-dozen folding chairs, a white leather sofa is the only place to sit. Tonight, Dave is leaving for Boston to launch his solo tour for his new album *Trust No One*, and we are privileged enough to watch the final rehearsal. He and his band are going to perform the entire set for Adrienne, her own private concert.

We spot Dave immediately, but wait by the entrance while Becca talks to the professional photographer, provided by Make-a-Wish, who will take pictures of Dave and Adrienne. When a shirtless Dave sees Adrienne, he walks over and hugs her, apologizing for his nonexistent perspiration. I imagine how giddy Adrienne must feel receiving a kiss on the cheek from someone she has worshipped for years. I might have fainted if I had met Prince when I was her age, and if he had kissed me, maybe never washed my face again. However she's feeling, Adrienne maintains her composure as Dave invites her to sit down and talk to him.

"Remember these?" she asks.

Adrienne shows Dave the blue-sequined wristbands on her forearms—the ones he gave her at *The Tonight Show*.

He laughs and says of course. Sitting on his knees in front of her, you would think Adrienne was a queen with a royal subject kneeling before her, except for the large cup of Starbucks coffee next to Dave's knee; it ruins the fairytale.

Adrienne presents Dave with a framed picture, a sketch she drew of his face. I know how nervous she is, how many times she started that drawing only to begin again, afraid he wouldn't like it. He looks at it and peers up at her.

"Thank you."

The words feel heavy as if they are weighed down by sincerity. Judging from the earnest look on Dave's face, he means what he says. Not wanting to make too much out of the moment, Adrienne gives Dave another present, a unicorn snow globe she bought at Children's Hospital, an engagement gift for him and his fiancée Carmen Electra. He makes a joke about being with Adrienne and Carmen now and she laughs.

Although we meet Dave, for the most part John and I watch the conversation between him and Adrienne. We don't want to intrude, but we do remain close by in case Adrienne doesn't feel well. Seeing Adrienne talk to Dave like an old friend makes me think at least one good thing has come out of this experience, and it's more than a teenage girl meeting her favorite rock star. Though she knew his flaws, Adrienne always put Dave on a pedestal. He could do no wrong. I believe it's good for her to see him for who he is, not only for what he does.

I hear him asking about her health and what hospital she's transferring to, and he sounds concerned. Then Dave introduces her to his band. The bass player—another Dave—is also bald and within minutes, he and Adrienne are discussing the benefits of baldness: how little time they need to get ready to go somewhere, how good they look in hats, and how they spend no money on hair products. After many laughs, the band sets up for one final rehearsal.

As their biggest fan in the audience, Adrienne walks toward the leather couch with her disposable camera. Dave's manager appears out of nowhere.

"No pictures!"

I beg him, swearing they are for us when Dave steps in.

"It's okay," he says. "She can take pictures."

The manager mutters something about signing a privacy/non-disclosure agreement, and I promise him we'll sign anything if Adrienne can take pictures. He leaves to get the paperwork.

When the show starts, I pay more attention to Adrienne than the music. Although I do snap photos of the band playing with my 35 mm camera, I have more fun taking pictures of Adrienne as she clicks away. She never takes her eyes off the stage even when she's not looking through the camera lens. I worry the pictures won't turn out well because it's dark in here. Someone turned down the house lights so the full effect of the stage lights could be seen, but I know Adrienne won't care. If she can see even a shadow of Dave playing on stage, she will be happy.

Adrienne with Dave Navarro © August 28, 2001
Photo courtesy of Sara Corwin

Days 106–110

Parents: In my eyes Sissy and Johnny, truly Myra and Todd.
An email in Adrienne's Waiting to be Sent folder

As he does almost every day, Eli calls Wednesday afternoon and wants to come over and spend time with Adrienne, as well as hear about her Make-a-Wish day, I presume. She turns him down saying she's not feeling too great and doesn't want to talk. I'm not surprised because she's been tired and grumpy since she woke up; she's still exhausted from yesterday. That evening, they are talking on the phone when Eli tells her she was a monstrous bitch earlier in the day. Adrienne slams the receiver down, hanging up on him.

The noise is so loud John and I hear it from the living room. We ask her what happened, and she tells us everything. When her phone rings, I have this flashback to the film *Frankie and Johnny* when Nathan Lane's character says, "Excuse me, Johnny, I've got to hang up. We're expecting a call from you any minute." However, I shouldn't joke right now and John grabs the phone before I do.

John unleashes his rage.

"You have blown it with our family."

He lambasts Eli for his behavior with a string of expletives. Then he finishes.

"You better not fucking call here again."

He hangs up.

I count in my head. One. Two. Three. The phone rings. John reaches for the phone and mutters.

"Unfuckingbelievable."

I snatch the phone away from him.

"I'll handle it this time."

I motion for him to walk away.

Adrienne watches this entire scene play out and makes no effort to stop us. She seems happy to let John and I, her strict and protective parents, fight this battle for her. However, I know Eli won't stop calling until he talks to Adrienne. No matter what John and I think of him right now, the fight is between them. Reining in my own anger, I tell Eli to hold on.

"Do you want to talk to him?" I ask Adrienne.

She sighs.

"I guess so."

I hand her the phone and close her bedroom door, leaving it open a crack so John and I can hear her if she gets upset. Although, something tells me she has the upper hand in this conversation.

John and I don't talk about what Adrienne and Eli are going through. He doesn't agree with my decision to allow Eli to speak to Adrienne again so we have nothing to say to each other. Despite our five-year anniversary next week, our relationship is tenuous. He thinks we're going out to dinner because I want to, but I suggested we celebrate because the books I've read recommend parents and siblings of the cancer patient should resume their normal activities. I am trying to reconnect with John because he is a wonderful father to Adrienne, and I can't imagine how we could have gotten through this experience without him.

As I think about my reasons for wanting to close the chasm between John and me, I wonder about Adrienne and her relationships with people. Although she talks online to friends, few of them visit now. Lori, who had been out of town for weeks, has returned but Adrienne hasn't mentioned getting together with her. We will see Nadia on Labor Day, but Adrienne doesn't seem excited. Are her friends staying away or is Adrienne keeping them at a distance?

Eli has remained by her side all summer, but lately, she has pushed him away and complained about his clinginess. He has always needed her more than she's needed him, an issue we've discussed many times, but she seems more frustrated now. I suspect the bitch comment will be a turning point because once you say something cruel to someone you love, it can never be unsaid. I can't forgive Eli right now because even if she was acting bitchy, we should cut Adrienne some slack. None of us knows how she feels, emotionally or physically. While I don't condone rudeness, Eli was out of line. However, I don't think an apology will be enough for Adrienne.

Two hours later, Adrienne walks out of her room.

"We broke up. We're going to stay friends. He'll pick up his stuff in a few days."

She says these sentences as if she's stating the weather. Today will be dry. Hot. Sunny. I ask if she's okay and she shrugs.

"I guess so. Whatever."

She pauses and then smiles.

"Dave loves me."

Under normal circumstances, she would be devastated. However, we live in a different world, and I can see she's not faking. While she may be sad, she's not suffering a traumatic loss, perhaps because she saw Dave yesterday or because she must focus on getting well, but whatever the reason, she seems fine with her decision.

The following day, with the relationship drama over, I pay closer attention to Adrienne's body. She appears even thinner than she was during her last round of chemo. Knowing she has a doctor's appointment tomorrow at UCLA, I decide to be proactive and find out what she weighs now instead of being surprised at the clinic.

"Step on the scale, kiddo."

I look down.

"Well?" she asks.

"Shit. 115 pounds. You weigh less than I do now, and it doesn't look good."

"Yeah, no ass meat. No calves. Got no muscle left."

I can't think of a witty comeback because she's right. Looking at her, I can't see any muscle mass left on her body, only pale skin clinging to bones. I calculate: four pounds in two weeks. She can't afford to lose more weight. *How many times have I told myself that?* The shock reminds me I need to email our resident experts—Sofia and Kirsten—about UFT, the drug I am convinced will save Adrienne.

EMAIL (condensed)
Subject: Adrienne
Date: 8/30/2001
To: Sofia, Kirsten, and various doctors

I wanted to ask both of you your opinion on something. What do

you know about the drug UFT? (Trade name: Tegafur & Uracil)
I know it is not currently legal in the United States. I've found
several cases (I know it's not a majority but at least it's anecdotal
evidence) of people in Japan who were in Stage IV HCC and
UFT made their cancer go into remission. (Don't want to use the
word "cured.")

- What is the difference between drugs like Xeloda & UFT? They are
  both derivatives of 5-FU and both given in an oral form. I don't
  understand why one is legal and one is not.
- Why is UFT not legal in this country but legal in most other countries in the world?
- How come there are not more clinical trials with UFT & HCC
  given the Japanese results? I found only one study done several
  years ago in Chicago. Then I found two Phase 1 trials (currently
  looking for patients), but one is for rectal & colon cancer only;
  the other is for any solid tumor cancer.
- What is your opinion on the Japanese studies? I found all of my
  information on Pub Med so I'm assuming it's legitimate. I know
  Dr. No said that the Japanese "stage their cancers differently,"
  but all of the people I found who did well on UFT had metastasis
  in their lungs, bones, or glands. One man even had metastasis in
  his lungs & bones!

I would appreciate any information you can give me. Also, we are
officially at UCLA as of tomorrow.

I never would have guessed termites would save us from having to
move, at least temporarily. Some people were interested in buying the
house; they even made an offer on it a few weeks ago. Before the deal
was finalized, they dropped by with their real estate agent to examine
the property. The potential owners asked questions about the house's
history with termites. I didn't lie or exaggerate, but I thought the nasty
varmints might buy us more time. Yes, termites ate out the insides of the
living room walls a few years ago. Last year, another species tumbled out
of the bathroom plumbing overnight; they were living in the pipes. Did
the property manager forget to tell you? I smiled as the agent frowned.

She shook her head at her clients and ushered them out the door. The deal fell through, but the management company is still pressuring us to move by the end of September. They have another house for rent in Burbank and suggest we look at it.

The place is a dump. By the looks of it, the former tenants, who were evicted, must have been drug dealers. John and I discover a high-intensity lamp in the garage that seems ideal for growing pot. We also notice that in every closet of the four bedrooms, long nails are spaced about three to four inches apart. The same setup exists in the garage too. John says that's how they dried the bud. I don't ask how he knows that. I don't want to know. We even find empty vials we throw away in the bins outside.

Besides the obvious signs of illegal activity, the house is filthy. The once light-blue carpet (at least we think that was the original color), only five months old according to the property manager, is now moldy brown. A dark oily stain measuring $1' \times 1'$ has seeped into the kitchen linoleum as if someone left a car engine there. Trash litters the floor; we have to push it aside with our feet. I try to imagine us living here, but I can't. We don't have much of a choice though. We don't have time to look for a place to live. I make a list of all the things the owners need to do before we can move in, starting with new carpet.

Since John and I don't care, we agree Adrienne can choose the color. We are not surprised when she examines carpet samples and picks a deep royal blue. When John protests, she argues it's better than the forest green we have now, and we said she could pick any color she wanted. He shuts ups and she wins. When we move, the house will have brand new blue carpet.

The daily injections of Neupogen cause Adrienne's immune system to bounce back with incredible resilience. Though there is no guarantee, she did catch a cold before, the shots act as a suit of armor against invisible germs. I read on the Internet anywhere from 40–60 percent of cancer patients die from infections due to a suppressed immune system caused by chemotherapy. Adrienne has already suffered from one cold, and that was one too many. I feel relieved her counts are high on the day she has to visit the hospital, a place full of sick people.

Although we have been to UCLA twice now, we have never been to Radiology before. I'm not surprised to find it on the ground floor, the same as Children's Hospital. I keep meaning to ask someone why every hospital I've ever been to puts the Radiology department on the bottom level; there must be a logical reason. I ruminate over the possibilities during Adrienne's CT scans of her pelvis, her abdomen, and her chest. Maybe it has something to do with the radiation waves needing to be grounded. I ask Adrienne because she's better at science than I am, but she rolls her eyes and says, I don't know, Sissy.

Maybe a long time ago someone realized standardizing the location makes it easier for the patient to find the department. No, engineers don't think that way. Maybe I'm reading too much into what is simply another coincidence. No, I don't believe in coincidences anymore. I'm not sure I ever did.

Since Adrienne feels well and she can spend time in public, we meet Anya and Alex for dinner at a local restaurant, the same place where Adrienne threw that embarrassing temper tantrum so many years ago. Adrienne sips tea and orders soup. I remember how she used to love the macaroni and cheese here; now it's too rich and creamy for her delicate digestive system. I notice the busboy looking at Adrienne, but she either doesn't see him or chooses to ignore him until he speaks to her. He raves about her baldness.

"Wow. It looks great. How bold," he says as he gestures toward her head. "I love that you shaved your head. What made you decide to do it?"

I want to stop his gushing because I know he does not realize the truth. Unlike most cancer patients who undergo chemotherapy, Adrienne has not lost her eyebrow hair, and the hair follicles on her head never fell out. Her appearance often throws people off, especially when her hemoglobin is up, like today, and she has color in her cheeks. I hold my breath waiting for the zinger that must be coming.

Adrienne looks the busboy in the eye.

"I have cancer."

The poor guy blanches, almost drops the dishes in his hands, and scurries away.

Adrienne turns her eyes back to us and picks up her soup spoon.

"He won't be back."

Maybe we shouldn't but we all burst into laughter, not at the guy's obvious humiliation, but at Adrienne's ability to handle herself in any situation. To think we worry about her so much, yet she didn't need us to scare away a potential suitor. Throughout our meal, we never see the busboy again, but he would have gained Adrienne's respect, and perhaps admiration, if he had continued to bus our table. Like me, she appreciates people who stand up to her.

EMAIL
Subject: Adrienne
Date: 9/1/2001
From: Sofia

UFT may be better for hepatocellular carcinoma than the other compounds. One can get it from Mexico (maybe). It appears to me that these substances are VERY toxic. In tablets, it is less toxic than in IV injection form. The issue is not "legal" or "not legal." Many foreign manufacturers find U.S. FDA approval too expensive. They may not want to compete on the U.S. market either. The Japanese results have just been published. It takes several years for other studies to follow the first report. Please let me know when I can talk to Adrienne's new oncologist.

Have a nice Labor Day.
Love, Sofia

For our fifth anniversary, John and I decide to have dinner at Gladstones, a seafood restaurant in Malibu. We ask his aunt, a licensed health-care provider, to watch Adrienne while we're gone. During dinner, John and I talk about Adrienne and Eli. John laughs when I tell him about the incident with the bus boy the day before. We discuss how little we have seen Adam this summer due to Adrienne's hospital stays and Adam's mother's refusal to be flexible about the visitation schedule. In fact, we cover many topics except for the scary ones. We talk about the transfer to UCLA, the miracle drug UFT, and the new chemo regimen that starts next week, but we avoid any reference to how thin Adrienne is or how pale she looks. We don't say the tests may show, yet again, there is no change, no improvement. We don't acknowledge our relationship has improved because we need each other in a way we never did before. We eat, we laugh, and later we even make love. The whole evening feels like an act we must perform to convince ourselves everything is normal.

Adrienne's favorite photo of herself; she thought she looked like an elegant mannequin.
Make-A-Wish Day © August 28, 2001

Days 111–117

I feel as though there is no hope left in me for myself and that's never good, especially now. I want to be IN school, I'm not sure why because I hate the place, but I want to be there.

—*Adrienne's email to a friend dated 9/4/01*

When children lose their innocence, I am saddened because they don't get it back; once it's gone, it's gone. I wonder if Adrienne can remember a specific moment in her life that ended her childhood. Was it when Mother's neighbor molested her in the community swimming pool? Or when our brother repeatedly shot her with his BB gun? What about when I moved away to go to college? Did that event cause her to grow up too fast? Even though she's fifteen now, I want to protect her, make it all better, and the slow realization I can't is causing me to lose any faith I may have had.

I remember this silly question someone asked me once about having superhero powers: would you rather be able to fly or be able to be invisible? I choose neither. Instead, I want to be a superhealer. I want to make Adrienne well, healthy, whole again so she can go to school tomorrow, jam at rock concerts, dance at the prom. As I watch Adrienne climb into the car, her pale skin glowing in contrast to the bright reds and greens of yet another fairy shirt, I think how she looks like a ghost wearing clothes. Having lost 20 percent of her body weight, she seems like an impression of her former self until she speaks, then I know she's all there.

On the way home from Anya and Alex's house, Adrienne remains quiet. We attended their Labor Day barbeque, although I don't remember Adrienne eating much. She seemed happy to see Nadia, but when they spoke about school starting, Adrienne became silent. I don't know why I picked that moment to take a picture. A beaming Nadia in a bright tie-dyed shirt looked right at the camera while Adrienne hugged a pillow to her chest and averted her eyes. I can only guess she was thinking about not being able to go to school. She claims to hate that place, but I know she wants to be there. Home schooling won't be the same, another thing I can't fix.

The following morning I do my best to pretend everything is normal, but it's impossible to ignore the chatter of kids outside as they walk to school. Everyone is excited on the first day, even the delinquents. Adrienne peers through the blinds and watches them for a few minutes; silent tears slip down her cheeks. She sighs, turns on the TV, and slumps in her chair. Although most of her subjects have been determined, Honors Chemistry has been dropped in favor of Honors Physics, I cannot start home school with Adrienne yet because I'm waiting on books from the district and the unofficial go ahead. A more formal meeting will happen soon to determine Adrienne's individual educational plan or IEP. With nothing to do, Adrienne mopes around all day, even reading *The Fellowship of the Ring* doesn't cheer her up, despite the fact she is looking forward to the film's debut in December.

A few days later, we have a much-anticipated appointment at UCLA. The CT scan results are in, and I know something is going to be different this time. I feel like I've been holding my breath and waiting to exhale. I feel tingly, as if my whole body just woke up from being numb and I need to jump around to ward off that needle sensation. I pace in the waiting area. I tap my foot when I sit down. I pick my cuticles until they bleed as Adrienne and I sit in the exam room. Finally, Dr. Fenn walks in.

"Well?" I ask.

"There's been a change."

For half a second, my heart soars like a young bird finding its wings, taking its first flight, racing through the air. Then I look into his eyes, and my brain connects the words to the look on his face. My heart stops, forgetting to flap its wing, and falls to the ground, landing with a loud THUMP. *There's been a change.* Those words were supposed to be good. I've waited so long *for a change.* I guess I wasn't specific enough in my wish. I wanted a positive change—fewer tumors, smaller tumors, no tumors. *There's been a change.*

"It's . . . not good?" I ask.

Dr. Fenn shakes his head.

"No. I'm sorry. They're worse."

I know the 'they' he is referring to are the tumors. I glance at Adrienne, but I can't read her expression. She seems neither happy nor sad. Then I realize, she's not surprised. Dr. Fenn goes on to tell us Adrienne's AFP count has increased to 1.6 million, another blow. Forcing myself to sound more positive than I feel, I ask him if he has any good news. When I hear the words come out of my mouth, a sense of déjà vu comes over me and then I remember the last time I asked a doctor that question, the answer was no.

"We have the results from the tests at Children's Hospital. The echocardiogram is normal. The bone scan still shows a lump on the back of the skull, but it hasn't grown."

I nod. I should be relieved that Adrienne's heart is functioning normally, and the mysterious mass has remained the same size, but all I can think is how four rounds of chemotherapy did nothing but make Adrienne miserable.

"I do believe the cytotoxic chemotherapy drugs are doing more harm than good, and it's time to switch to drugs that affect the cell's behavior as you previously discussed with Dr. Aquino."

I nod again. When I ask Dr. Fenn if he received my email yesterday regarding UFT, he admits he hasn't read it yet. I tell him about the studies on PubMed, but he refers me to Dr. Aquino who has already decided to start Adrienne on Xeloda tomorrow. Dr. Fenn mentions a colleague of Dr. Aquino's may contact me about a clinical trial, and I can ask him specific questions about UFT. After a handful of new prescriptions and an appointment tomorrow for a brain scan, we leave UCLA—changed, but not the way I expected. *Fuck you change.*

When we get home, I discover the following email in my inbox:

EMAIL
Subject: Emma Adrienne Wilson and UFT
Date: 9/6/2001
From: Dr. Marco

UFT is in the same family of 5-FU and Xeloda, therefore I am not surprised to find out that there is evidence of efficacy. Xeloda and UFT are both derivatives of 5-FU and both given in an oral form.

I don't understand why one is legal and one is not [perhaps]— marketing and FDA regulations.

I am not sure about their differences, if any [maybe in] marketing.

Overall 5-FU and its derivatives have not demonstrated in the past a tremendous response on HCC patients, therefore, its major benefit is ease of administration since it is an oral medicine. Like many other agents, these are small series or case reports, and we have to be cautious on how to interpret their results. That does not mean that one should not consider using these agents when appropriate.

I appreciate that Dr. Marco replied to me, especially considering Adrienne is no longer his patient, but I notice he doesn't sign the email. His response regarding UFT leaves me frustrated, encouraged, and enraged. I want him to be more hopeful about the PubMed studies I found, those few people who survived HCC. Yet, I feel better about Adrienne starting Xeloda tomorrow. I know UFT is derived from the same drug, but hearing it again or in this case reading it, gives me reassurance that a different type of chemo is necessary to continue this fight. However, I am livid marketing may be the reason UFT is not available in the U.S. In her email, Sofia wrote that foreign manufacturers find it too expensive to obtain FDA approval. I know drug companies want to make a profit, but at what cost? UFT has cured liver cancer, and yet, it is unavailable in America, one of the richest countries in the world.

The following day UCLA faxes over copies of Adrienne's lab and test results. I scan the papers looking for the words that match what I heard yesterday. Adrienne's white blood cell count is normal. Her hemoglobin is 10.7, but UCLA has different ranges than Children's Hospital so she is close enough to the low end of normal and does not need a blood transfusion. Her platelets have recovered as of yesterday, little risk of bleeding now. The chem panel shows Adrienne's liver and kidney function are good; even one of her liver enzymes is back within normal range. The brain scan results come a few days later, they read, "The cerebellum and brain stem are normal in appearance. The bones are normal."

Normal. What an inane word. I would have thought the medical field would use words like routine or standard to describe the ordinary. I know

I should be grateful for how well Adrienne is doing, especially considering how much she has endured, but when I read about the change Dr. Fenn referred to, I feel hollow. Not only have the tumors in her liver grown, but her "spleen is enlarged and gallbladder is decompressed and not visualized upon this examination." A CT scan cannot see Adrienne's gallbladder now due to the immense size of her liver and her spleen.

I read more: "Multiple bilateral nodular metastatic lesions that are too numerous to count on the examination and a large subcarinal lymph node mass." *Too numerous to count. Lymph node mass.* Those sneaky bastards have spread into Adrienne's lymph nodes? Why didn't Dr. Fenn say anything? Because he knew I would read the report. Her lymph node tumors are nothing compared to the ones, too numerous to count, already in her lungs. There is nothing he can do or say to make it better.

I read the last report, the results of a chest X-ray to check on Adrienne's central line. "The lung fields contain too numerous to count nodules and masses in every segment of every lobe." *Every segment of every lobe.* How many segments are there? What about lobes? I remember when Adrienne called them "dots of light" and how they looked like snowflakes to me on the film. They seemed . . . harmless. I don't understand how this happened. I grasp the actual progression of the disease, but what I don't know is why. Why Adrienne?

EMAIL
Subject: Emma Adrienne Wilson and UFT
Date: 9/7/2001
From: Dr. Aquino

There is probably not much difference in efficacy between these two drugs. They are both oral fluorouracil-like drugs that target the same cell pathways through different mechanisms. Patients that are sensitive to one are likely to be sensitive to the other and the same goes for resistance. As to why UFT is not approved in the US, the right research has not been done in the US; normally studies done by American institutions are required for FDA approval.
In general, I like to see Japanese results of cancer trials validated before accepting them, but it does seem that UFT has some activity (although marginal) in hepatocellular carcinoma.

I read Dr. Aquino's email and wonder why he fails to mention the difference between Xeloda and UFT: the amino acid Uracil. I guess for him the point is moot because UFT is not an option for his patients. I appreciate his response though and like how he communicates by email. I hope Xeloda can replicate the results of UFT, but without the amino acid, I don't see how it's possible to do so. We have no choice though; we have to try something new.

Before starting Xeloda tomorrow, we begin with interferon, which I will give as a shot in Adrienne's arm on Mondays, Wednesdays, and Fridays at noon. A biologic response modifier, interferon should stimulate Adrienne's immune system, but its side effects include flu-like symptoms such as fever, chills, fatigue, headache, nausea, decreased appetite, and bone/muscle aches. Since Adrienne may still suffer from neuropathic pain, I tell her the shot's side effects resemble the flu, but I don't say what they are. We allow her body to inform us of its reaction to interferon.

Despite administering a Neupogen shot to Adrienne every day, giving her a new injection in another location fills me with dread. I'm afraid I'll mess it up. Wiping Adrienne's arm with alcohol, she winces when I expose the needle, which is slightly larger than the one used for her other shots.

"Don't look," I tell her in my most commanding voice. "On three. One. Two. Three."

I insert the needle at the proper angle and push the interferon feeling . . . it can't be. Resistance?

"Ooo. It feels like syrup," says Adrienne. "Yuck."

So I'm not imagining the difference in consistency between the two medications.

"All done."

A few seconds and a Band-Aid later, we forget about the interferon for a while. I wait in anticipation to see how she handles the drug. If she can make it to dinner, she should be fine. The side effects should present themselves immediately if at all.

No such luck.

Within three hours, Adrienne says, "I don't feel good, Sissy."

She complains her head hurts, her body aches, and she feels nauseated. Her chest also feels tight. I have no idea what that could be. Her temperature is 99.4 degrees, and her heart rate is 110 bpm. I tell her to hold on. The flulike symptoms can dissipate within hours. At 4 p.m., I give her 4 mg of Dilaudid for the joint pain. Her temperature increases to 100.1 degrees but then decreases to 99.8 after a dose of Tylenol. We wait for John to come home.

Adrienne remains stable but when her fever hits 101.4, the highest it has ever been, John and I agree to call UCLA. The doctor on-call believes Adrienne is having a negative reaction to the interferon, but he wants a blood culture to be sure there is no infection. Unlike Children's, UCLA does not insist we drive across town to their emergency room; we go to our local hospital, St. Jo's, instead.

John speeds through Burbank as if his Honda Accord is going to win a local drag race. I wonder if it occurs to him getting a ticket will slow us down. I watch Adrienne sitting in the back seat, wrapped in a blanket, her body shaking. I've made a huge mistake; she has never been this sick before. I mean, before cancer. I suppose this is what the flu looks like, but Adrienne and I don't get the flu. Sure, we catch colds like everybody else. We've had our share of food poisoning. Odd things happen to Adrienne and me like Grave's disease, a ruptured appendix, hepatitis, liver cancer. *Odd is not the word.* We don't get the typical achy-feverish-nauseated-chilly flu that knocks most people on their asses for two weeks. Is that why Adrienne is having such an extreme reaction to interferon? *Great. The shot made her sicker.*

As we walk through the parking lot, Adrienne vomits nonstop for almost a minute. I look at John in panic. I've never seen her like this before. He rushes into the ER to get towels. Feeling helpless, I rub her back as she retches even more. She wipes her mouth with one of the white towels John hands her. Even in the low light, I can see the yellow.

"Bile," says John shaking his head, "all bile."

"Yeah," Adrienne nods her head, "there's nothing left in there."

She motions toward her tummy.

John grabs a wheelchair and insists Adrienne sit down as we enter the ER. I think the worst of it is over.

Then Adrienne says, "Oh no . . ."

I yell, "I need a bucket."

No one acts quickly enough. Adrienne leans over the wheelchair, and a stream of pus-colored bile pours out of her mouth like someone popped a giant zit in her stomach. People look away as the staff cleans up the mess.

Adrienne says, "I guess I was wrong."

The three of us laugh. We are beyond the point where we can be embarrassed about this stuff. I want to say to the waiting room—so my child spews uncontrollable yellow waterfalls and is as hot and clammy as a summer day in the South. Why are you here?

The word cancer grants us a bump to the front of the line, like Disney's fast pass. Dr. Lin, the man who said those fateful words, "she has tumors in her liver and lungs" greets us. We haven't seen him since the initial diagnosis. Though he recognizes us, he maintains his distance. However, he gives Adrienne something to curtail the vomiting and tells me to continue Tylenol at home until her fever subsides. He promises to send the blood culture to UCLA though he agrees the symptoms are probably a strong reaction to the interferon, not an infection. Though he isn't overfriendly, Dr. Lin expedites Adrienne's discharge as best he can, which I guess is his way of saying he cares. We spent less than ninety minutes at St. Jo's that evening.

The following morning Adrienne has no fever, no chills, and no vomiting. All effects of interferon seem to have disappeared in time for her first dose of Xeloda, which will be given orally every twelve hours for fourteen days straight followed by a seven-day break. Known side effects of Xeloda include: diarrhea, nausea, vomiting, mouth sores, hand/foot syndrome (itchy, dry, red, peeling skin), mucositis, abdominal pain, heartburn, headache, dizziness, and decreased blood counts. The most significant ones we are supposed to watch out for, although they won't happen right away, are the mouth sores and hand/foot syndrome because any open wounds leave Adrienne susceptible to infection.

For the moment though, she doesn't seem to mind the possible risks. She has stopped puking and she is doing her chemo outpatient now, which allows her to begin home school tomorrow. I meet with her World History teacher in his home to pick up the materials even though the school district has not approved Adrienne's IEP. I buy math and French software at Comp USA to help Adrienne with her studies. I am determined to give her as much of a normal school routine as possible. *Normal.* There's that word again. If we had a normal life, would Adrienne have cancer?

As I predicted, even our closest friends stopped visiting Adrienne except for Anya and Alex, who are our rocks. I am too tired to be angry and too busy to be disappointed. I'm not sure I would have done anything at all, but Adrienne kept asking where is so-and-so and why won't they come see me?

So I email Adrienne's posse:

EMAIL
Subject: Adrienne
Date: 9/8/2001
To: our closest friends

Hey guys,

I know you are very busy, but you are getting this email because Adrienne has been wondering why she hasn't seen you lately. I'm not trying to make you feel guilty, but some of you haven't seen her since the first time she was in the hospital, and that was almost four months ago! If you were not some of our closest friends, I wouldn't even bother to email you. But <u>you are</u> and Adrienne wants (and needs) to see you! Please understand her "visitors" dropped off significantly after May. She's still sick and she's still here. Now, I know you are still thinking about her, but please visit soon. Her chemo is outpatient now so there should be no hospital visits for a while.

Thank you!

Days 118–123

MONDAY–SATURDAY, SEPTEMBER 10–15, 2001

☺☺☺☺☺

School is very important to me. Ever since I was six, I have wanted to go to college and get straight A's. I'm close to that second goal.

—Adrienne's journal entry dated 12/17/00

Last night, Adrienne felt that same tightness in her chest again. She had difficulty breathing. Using our stethoscope, John heard congestion in her lungs and suggested a hot bath to loosen it up, but it didn't work. Even a two-hour nap after dinner didn't make Adrienne feel any better. Her heart rate remained between 120–130 bpm. She said it burned every time she breathed in. I wanted it to be a side effect of the Xeloda, but listening to Adrienne wheeze while she slept, I remembered the recent test results: tumors too numerous to count in every segment of every lobe. The oxygen has no place to go. She doesn't have enough room left in her lungs. *She doesn't have a lot of time left either.* The Xeloda has to work, but just in case, I order *An Alternative Medicine Definitive Guide to Cancer* on Amazon. I have to make Adrienne better.

Since Adrienne receives her dose of Epogen on Mondays, her second injection of interferon is delayed until the evening. She spends the day tackling her World History assignments; the class is studying Ancient Greece. Adrienne must read several chapters, define the key terms, and answer the questions. Her teacher gave her permission to type her work because writing has become more time-consuming. Every assignment takes her twice as long to do as it used to. Excluding the times she had to stop to see her nurse, to receive medication, to eat lunch, or to lie down due to fatigue, Adrienne spends more than eight hours 'in school' that first day.

However, by six o'clock I declare school over because I have to give Adrienne her interferon shot. John, Adrienne, and I wait in anticipation. An hour passes. No fever—a good sign. Another hour—still no fever or chills. Almost three hours after I administer the injection, Adrienne throws up like last time, only now she has something in her stomach: blue Powerade. After the three ounces of her favorite drink leaves her body, Adrienne vomits intermittently for more than two hours until nothing but bile comes up. The doctor on-call at UCLA suggests giving 8 mg of Zofran to settle Adrienne's stomach. I give it and she throws up one last time ten minutes later. After that, her body seems too worn out to react anymore. I give Adrienne most of her evening medications except for the most important one, Xeloda. She takes one look at the giant pills, and says I can't Sissy. I just can't. I don't argue with her because skipping one dose won't make a difference. I know she won't be able to keep them down. She has a hard enough time taking Xeloda when she feels fine. By 3 a.m., Adrienne falls asleep.

Exhausted, but determined to do schoolwork, Adrienne studies the words in the vocabulary skills book I gave her. It focuses on learning the Latin roots, and I hope it will help her prep for the PSAT. I don't have any formal English assignments for her, but I don't want to wait so I make a school schedule that includes World History, English, and Algebra II lessons on the computer, and French lessons with Anya. Physics is no longer Adrienne's science class because the math is too advanced. Her counselor and I agreed she will take Computer Science and Algebra II with the same teacher, if the district approves it.

While Adrienne works on her assignment, I turn on the television. I have this strange desire to see the news, which I never watch because nothing good ever happens. I switch channels until I realize the same thing is on every channel: the Twin Towers in New York City are on fire. I read the ticker at the bottom of the screen. Terrorist attacks? In America? Then, the network shows a replay of what appears to be an earlier event. A plane collided into the South Tower causing a burst of flames followed by an explosion. Oh no. The time listed on the frame is 9:02 a.m. Eastern Standard Time, but it's noon already in New York. This colossal event occurred three hours ago, and I knew nothing about it.

"Adrienne, you need to see this."

"But Sissy, I have so much work to do."

"Take a break. Now. Consider this a history lesson."

Adrienne sighs as she gets up from the kitchen table. As soon as she turns around and can see the TV, she gasps.

"What happened?"

"I don't know, kiddo. Let's find out."

We sit together and watch as the events of the morning replay themselves. We discover another plane hit the Pentagon although fewer casualties are expected there. A fourth plane—believed to be on its way to the White House—was diverted by the passengers who attacked the hijackers; the plane crashed somewhere in Pennsylvania. Adrienne recalls her friend Sharon is staying with her father in a town near Philadelphia, and she insists I contact Sharon to make sure she is okay. Her concern makes me think about people I know in Manhattan, one person in particular, and I wonder if he is alive.

Just when we think it cannot get much worse, the news replays the South Tower collapse. Adrienne and I watch with our mouths agape.

"How could this happen, Sissy?" she asks.

I wonder if she remembers asking me that same question about the outcome of the O.J. Simpson trial, and I feel inadequate that six years later my answer is the same.

"I don't know."

I use the attacks on America to begin a dialogue with her about Ancient Greece. I ask her what's she read so far and what she has learned. As I listen, Adrienne speaks in detail about democracy and how the Greeks influenced our government. Her eyes are alert and the more she talks the faster her speech gets, like she used to be before the drugs slowed her down. She defends an individual's right to freedom, and analyzes what the terrorists hoped to gain by attacking the United States. I finally stop our discussion because she has a lot of work to do. As I turn off the television, I make a mental note of all the people I need to contact. Beyond saying a silent apology to the victims and their families, I'm too busy fighting a war in my own home to comprehend what has happened.

✷ ✷ ✷

I wonder what childhood experts would think if I told them I have many fond memories of Adrienne and me watching TV together. Some of the best ones occurred when we lived in the small studio apartment where we met John and Adam. Every morning before school, Adrienne would turn on the television to watch the cartoon *Sailor Moon*—excuse me, animated series—while she got ready for school. She would explain the plot as I raced around preparing for my own workday, then she would accuse me of not listening to her. She would quiz me in the car to see if I was paying attention and pretend to pout when I got the answers wrong and act surprised when I got the answers right.

Another time I cherish is when we watched the 1996 Academy Awards together. Things were going along as usual—various awards, long speeches, dance numbers—when Christopher Reeve appeared on stage in a wheelchair, one of his first public appearances since his devastating accident the year before that had caused quadriplegia. The camera scanned the standing, clapping, and crying audience. As Adrienne and I listened to Reeve speak, I patted her thigh thinking how lucky we were. She grabbed my hand. Even at nine years old, she understood. In a few seconds, Superman's life had changed forever. *I get it now—how fast life can change.*

Many people remember the moment in 1996 when the 'Magnificent Seven' made history, becoming the first American gymnastics team to win a gold medal. Adrienne and I were sitting on the edge of our bed, sweating in the summer heat, watching the events on TV, as the Summer Olympics took place in Atlanta. I was Adrienne's gymnastics teacher at her summer camp so the Olympics held a special meaning for us. We were invested in those girls; they had to win. We analyzed every move and cringed at the slightest mistake. We shook our heads when Dominique Moceanu fell on both landings of her two vaults.

Last in rotation, the American team had the advantage and the pressure of knowing what they had to score to be the Olympic champions. With Moceanu's mistakes, the responsibility to pull off the perfect vault lay on the last contender Kerri Strug. Adrienne and I held our breath. Strug fell short after her first vault, scoring a disappointing 9.162. Adrienne squealed, "No!"

I watched as Strug limped back to do her second vault. She was obviously hurt, but shaking it off. Knowing too many dancers who had performed in pain, I had a feeling Strug could do it, win the gold for her team and for her country.

"Hold on," I said to Adrienne, "and watch this girl. She's about to get her fifteen minutes of fame."

Adrienne and I held hands and leaned forward. I swear we didn't breathe during the six seconds it took for Strug to run, jump, leap, twist, turn, and land on one foot. Adrienne and I screamed. We didn't have to wait for the score—9.712—to know Strug's near perfect vault had secured American gold. Adrienne and I jumped up and down, danced around, sharing not only pride in our country, but also the joy in knowing dreams do come true. I took Adrienne to see Strug perform while she was on tour with *Disney's World on Ice*. With her leg still wrapped, Strug executed a flawless balance beam routine. We were fortunate to see her since she retired from gymnastics not long after that tour. I read somewhere she teaches elementary school in the Bay area. I bet the kids love her.

* * *

Wary of giving Adrienne her interferon shot tomorrow, I call Dr. Aquino and ask him what we can do about the vomiting. When I describe what has happened, he says Adrienne's extreme reaction is not normal, and it must be stopped. He prescribes two medications: Decadron and Kytril. Adrienne will receive both one hour prior to the shot, and the Kytril again whenever she feels nauseous. He suggests not giving her interferon again until the prescription for the pre-meds is ready. I don't intend to. Making Adrienne better, not sicker, is the goal.

As promised, one of Dr. Aquino's colleagues contacts me about a clinical trial involving dendritic cell therapy. After reading a folder full of information, I discover many reasons why this vaccine is not a good idea even if I don't understand the research behind the theory. After a previous phase I trial, six HCC patients showed no decrease in tumor size or AFP levels, no increase in their immune systems, but they suffered no side effects either. What a waste of time. Adrienne cannot be on any other therapies if she were in this clinical trial. She just started Xeloda and interferon; it's too soon to quit. She would also have to be at the hospital all the time for constant monitoring which I already know she will refuse to do. A final email from Kirsten, our resident expert in clinical research, solidifies my opinion, "This type of technology has been around for decades and has proven to have little effect over the years. I would NOT consider Adrienne for any phase I clinical trial." I turn down the offer, but reiterate my desire to find a clinical trial involving UFT.

FAX
To: Burbank Unified School District, Hal Jackson

From: Andrea J. Wilson
cc: Rick Carlton (Adrienne's counselor)
Date: Wednesday, September 12, 2001 @ 1 p.m.
Subject: 504 Hearing

My sister Emma Adrienne Wilson was diagnosed with liver cancer
this past May. She is currently a sophomore at Burbank High. Due
to the effects of chemotherapy, she is unable to attend school at
this time. I am aware that the home school program provided by
the district only pays for five hours of school per week. Considering the average student at Burbank High attends school thirty
hours per week, I think five hours is insufficient (not to mention
unfair) in meeting her educational needs.

Adrienne is an honor student with a 4.0 average. She is extremely
self-motivated and is eager to go back to school even if it has to be
at home. I have already arranged for a French tutor three hours per
week since I was told the district would be unable to find anyone
who can teach that subject. Her other subjects include Honors
World History, English 10, Computer Science, and Algebra 2.

I am asking for an immediate 504 Hearing (504 being the section of the Rehabilitation Act that covers educational programs).
Schools must make reasonable (five hours is not reasonable)
accommodations to ensure full, meaningful access to educational
programs for eligible, handicapped persons. As a cancer patient,
Adrienne is protected under the Rehabilitation Act.

I expect this hearing to occur as soon as possible. Adrienne de-
serves the same education as her peers; she should not be punished
for having cancer.

Thank you.

Sincerely,
Andrea J. Wilson

The same day I fax the 504 Hearing request to the school district, Adrienne has a rough twenty-four hours. Though she eats breakfast, she doesn't feel well due to a chronic yeast infection as well as her period starting the night before. She sleeps from 9 a.m.–12 p.m., wakes up to eat a light lunch, and takes her Xeloda before doing her schoolwork. When I go out to run errands around 2:30 p.m., she calls me, something she never does, to tell me she doesn't feel good. I rush home to find her running a low-grade fever, feeling nauseated, and complaining her stomach burns. I give her Tums for what I assume is heartburn and Zofran for the nausea along with Ginger Ale and toast. I skip the interferon that evening because the pre-meds were not ready at the pharmacy. She wakes up at two o'clock in the morning because her liver hurts for the first time in ages. I give her 4 mg of Dilaudid, and she soon falls back asleep. I never question my decision to request a 504 hearing because even on a bad day, like today, Adrienne works on school in between naps and meals, even in bed if she must. School gives her a sense of purpose, a reason to get out of bed, and I will not let Burbank Unified, my former employer, take that away from her.

Adrienne's liver continues to hurt, or sting as she likes to say. When we go to her appointment at the UCLA clinic on Friday, I mention the pain right away because I know it is a clinical sign she is not doing well. The lab results reflect the same thing. While Adrienne's main blood counts are fine, the chem panel reveals her cholesterol is 375 when it should be less than 170. Since her diet hasn't changed, she eats so little anyway, the only explanation is her liver's ability to metabolize fat has been compromised. For the first time, her liver is unable to perform some of its basic functions. One of her liver enzymes has increased from 135 to 164 in five days, but the other has decreased from 24 to 21 so they balance each other out. Her bilirubin, another indication of her liver function, remains within normal range. After conferring with Dr. Aquino, Dr. Fenn increases Adrienne' daily dosage of Pravachol to 30 mg, the cholesterol-lowering drug that was originally prescribed as part of her cancer treatment, now needs to do its original job, lower her cholesterol. At least we know she can tolerate Pravachol.

We pick up Decadron and Kytril at the pharmacy. For once, Adrienne doesn't mind taking more pills if they will prevent her from vomiting.

She surprises me at the clinic by expressing how sad she is; she usually keeps those feelings to herself.

"I'm depressed, Sissy."

"Oh."

I don't know how to respond so I wait for her to continue.

"I miss school. I fall asleep all the time. I can't do anything without feeling tired. I can't walk down the street. I can't talk on the phone. I can't even finish a chapter in *Lord of the Rings*."

"I know, sweetie."

She frowns.

"I mean, I don't know how it feels, but I see you and . . ."

I'd give anything to change it. Before I can come up with something positive to say, Adrienne interrupts me.

"I need help. Maybe medication."

I gulp and nod. Even when she was suicidal, Adrienne was never on antidepressants. I look into her eyes, her gorgeous, olive eyes, and I see how exhausted she is. I wonder if she has given up, but then she wouldn't ask for help if she had. I speak to Dr. Fenn who suggests a psychiatric referral for Adrienne's depression, a common reaction he reminds me as he touches my arm. I nod but can't stop my eyes from watering. *Accept the things you cannot change.* I can't make everything better for Adrienne all the time. But I can try.

When we arrive home, we find a letter in the mail from Burbank Unified; a formal 504 hearing is scheduled for September 24 at 3 p.m. I make a mental note of it and think nine days should be plenty of time to prepare for it. Though Adrienne wants to continue school, she takes little interest in the actual proceedings that are necessary to make it happen. When I show her the notice, she yawns and says she's tired. After napping for about ninety minutes, she wakes up, and I give her the pre-meds, which must be taken one hour prior to the interferon shot.

While we wait for the Decadron and Kytril to work their protective magic, Adrienne reads a stack of get-well letters from a sixth-grade class taught by one of our friends. She is still reading when I administer the shot. Though she appears not to be paying attention, she says without glancing away from the cards, you better bring the bucket, just in case Sissy. I know she's right, but I was hoping for more optimism. I leave the makeshift bucket, a recycled Country Crock plastic margarine bowl, next to her chair.

I make dinner, clean the kitchen, and wait for John to come home. I do my best not to watch the clock. If she's going to vomit, it will start by 8 p.m.—three hours after I gave the shot. Adrienne coughs within thirty minutes, and I rush to grab the bowl, but she shakes her head. It is only a cough so I give her OTC cough medicine. She eats a small dinner; it stays down. She watches television with John. Soon the eight o'clock hour passes, then the nine o'clock, and I exhale. My shoulders release themselves and drop a few inches. When Adrienne says she is experiencing joint pain at 9:30, I feel relief because I know what to do. I give her 4 mg of Dilaudid before helping her into a bath. Right before bedtime, she needs another milligram of Kytril for acute nausea, but overall the pre-meds worked wonders. *Why didn't Dr. Aquino prescribe them after the first time she threw up last week?*

Adrienne with her favorite dog Sophie in Arizona
© Labor Day weekend 2000

Days 124-130

As far as being 'lost' in a way about what career to stick with, I can sort of understand. There are too many careers I want, to, um, do in one lifetime and I just can't choose one.

—Adrienne's email to a friend dated 9/4/01

Adrienne's career list 2000–present:

1. Professor of religion
2. Zoologist
3. Forensic psychologist
4. Full-time artist—painter (gallery) or digital art
5. Webcam star
6. Fashion designer
7. Computer programmer
8. Studio musician

We have to leave our home on Sunday, September 30. For the first time in my life, I am hiring a moving company instead of renting a U-Haul truck and bribing friends with pizza and beer. Even though our new residence is only 3.84 miles across town, I don't have the time or the energy to pack up everything in the house. John refuses to pay for the movers because he thinks they are a waste of money. He doesn't see how much time it will save us, or how important it is to get Adrienne's bedroom set up in the new house as quickly as possible. I save up $1000 from working at picnics and look in the yellow pages under movers.

I randomly call companies to obtain quotes. At the third place I call, an employee named Geena answers my questions and concerns about hiring strangers to handle my things. I feel comfortable telling her in detail why we need movers and why they must work fast, but be careful too. I tell her how Adrienne was diagnosed with hepatocellular carcinoma, how particular Adrienne is about her stuff, and how Adrienne is doing home school now. Then, Geena reveals to me her son was diagnosed with hepatoblastoma[15] when he was two years old. The doctors gave him six months to live, but her son managed to survive for another two years.

I feel as though I've swallowed a licorice stick composed of hope and terror all twisted together. Hope, because her son beat the odds; terror, because he died anyway.

"He's been gone for three years now," she says.

I can hear an echo in her voice, and I know it's not our phone connection. She has other kids though, so she pulled herself together. Raised Catholic, she confides she lost her faith for a few years, couldn't even walk into a church. I imagine her shaking her head remembering the pain, and maybe bitterness.

"I went back awhile ago. Had to forgive."

Geena never pushes her religious beliefs on me or says inappropriate things such as god only gives you what you can handle. Like Adrienne, her son's disease is a horrible, unexplainable thing that should never happen to a child. When I hang up the phone, I realize three things: I forgot to write down the quote, we talked for forty-five minutes, and despite the hope-terror licorice knot in my stomach—I feel better.

Adrienne works on her literature assignments for Honors English 10. The honors classes are often paired together so students study the same culture for two classes. Adrienne has been learning about Ancient Greece: its history, government, and culture. She is also reading about Greek myths, their history, and their relevance in today's society. An English teacher at Burbank High works with me to determine Adrienne's assignments, and her first essay has to be about a myth she creates from any of the following topics: creation, love, heroism, law, or death. Each topic has subsequent sub-categories. She spends three days thinking about which topic to choose.

"What do you think, Sissy?" she asks.

I notice she has one star next to "the function of gods," "sex roles," and "reincarnation." She has two stars next to the "world of the dead and its permanent inhabitants."

"Why did you rule out a creation myth about man?"

15 An aggressive malignant tumor of the liver, typically found in children age three or younger. Unlike HCC, hepatoblastoma is considered a childhood cancer and its cause is unknown.

"Because everybody writes about creation, and I can't think of a myth about life."

"What about heroism? That's what I would choose."

The minute I say it, I know she won't consider it. Adrienne works hard to be her own person. If I would write an essay about heroism, she will do the exact opposite.

"I'm going to think about it some more."

"Well, you better get started. It's due in less than two weeks."

"Yeah, I know."

The next day I find her working on a brainstorm for the essay. Unlike most brainstorms I saw when I was teaching, Adrienne practically writes a rough draft. She fills up three pages, single-spaced, with complete sentences and a diagram of the order of the paragraphs. I don't read it; she never lets me read anything until she has a real first draft, but I ask her which topic she chose.

"Death and the afterlife," she replies.

"Oh," I say.

I don't ask why she picked that topic; I don't want to know. I chalk it up to teen angst, but I know it's not. The licorice knot in my stomach becomes all terror and no hope, and I feel this shot of pain like cramps from food poisoning. Saliva evaporates from my mouth—where did it go I wonder—and I think maybe my appendix is bursting again, but no that already happened. Last year. Last summer. I need to sit down. I grab a kitchen chair, and gravity pulls me into it. I breathe. *Why is she writing an essay about death?* I can't think about it. Adrienne would have chosen the same topic even if she were not sick. *The lies we tell ourselves to survive.*

EMAIL
Subject: Recent events
Date: 9/16/2001
To: my address book
Dear everyone,

I have been getting so many emails regarding the tragedy that occurred in our country this past Tuesday. Since everyone has an opinion on what happened, I am going to be a bit presumptuous and share mine.

Today is significant for me. You see, my world came crumbling down four months ago. It was Wednesday, May 16 @ 3:30 p.m. when I came home from work, and Adrienne said, "I don't feel good." Six hours later, we were told she had tumors in her lungs and liver. Two days later, she was diagnosed with hepatocellular carcinoma, a rare (in this country) and serious type of liver cancer. According to the doctors, there is no cure.

But like me, Adrienne is stubborn and determined. She is fighting and fighting hard. Her liver is still functioning normally. And although the tumors in her lungs have gotten worse, she is still able to breathe on her own. She has started home school and strives to maintain her 4.0 GPA, even though she is always tired from the chemotherapy.

I'm not saying the events last Tuesday didn't affect me; it's just that our world (Adrienne, John, and mine + other family/friends) already fell apart some time ago, and we are struggling every day to rebuild it. I keep hearing people say that the terrible events in our country have reminded them how fragile life is. Trust me, I know. Every day I watch this incredible, amazing fifteen year old fight this nasty disease in her body. Some days you have hope; other days you wonder why she has to go through this. But I know one thing not fighting was simply not an option. I realize terrorism and cancer don't really compare. And I understand violence begets violence. But for our country, I don't think not fighting back is an option any longer. I may not have a lot of faith in our president, but I do have faith in this country and its people.

We will rebuild those structures, we will resume our lives, and like Adrienne, we will beat this thing no matter what it takes. It is a fight worth fighting. Take care everyone.

Love always, Andrea
Adrienne's website (for updates & stuff)

After more than a week of the oral chemotherapy Xeloda, I notice its effects on Adrienne. Though the pre-meds stopped the vomiting, she hardly eats because when she does, she experiences heartburn pain that radiates throughout her digestive tract causing her stomach to ache for hours. The clinic recommends Zantac, Mylanta, and Tums, but nothing relieves the burning in Adrienne's body. I believe the sheer lack of food has weakened Adrienne and caused her to lose more weight. She looks like a walking skeleton. She's so exhausted she naps more than half the day. I often catch her falling asleep at the kitchen table with a pencil in her hand. She coughs constantly, maybe from mucositis, another side effect of Xeloda. The pain seems to move around her body: from her shoulder, to her liver, to her back, to her joints, to her head, until it starts all over again.

The one positive thing is she is at home, and her immune system seems to be intact. Her cholesterol has dropped from 375 to 358, far from normal, but a small improvement is better than none at all. Her liver enzymes continue to fluctuate; one has risen to 230, but the other has lowered to 18. Since the doctors expect her liver enzymes to be abnormal, they pay little attention to these numbers. However, I see a pattern emerging, and I wonder if I should be worried about it.

I email Adrienne's doctors about my concerns. Dr. Aquino suggests a medicine that suppresses stomach acid, like Prilosec, to alleviate the heartburn. While he does attribute Adrienne's exhaustion to the chemo-therapy, he says the cough is unlikely to be related to Xeloda. If mucositis isn't causing the cough, then what is? His omission confirms my fear. The tumors are irritating Adrienne's lungs so much they are creating the cough, which has made her ribs sore and sensitive to the touch. Even though it feels like an exercise in futility, I continue giving Adrienne cough syrup, and even though she must know it's not helping her, she accepts it. I hope the Prilosec will make a difference; Adrienne has to eat. I can't let her starve to death.[16]

* * *

"Sissy, you have no school spirit whatsoever!" said Adrienne as I walked away from the television.

---

16 20–40 percent of all cancer patients die from cachexia—a state of ill health, malnu-trition, and wasting.

She forced me to watch the USC vs. UCLA football game. She doesn't even like football, but every year Adrienne insisted we watch my alma mater play its biggest rival. She followed me into the kitchen.

"I can't believe you're not going to watch the rest of the game."

"SC is winning Adrienne. I don't need to watch the rest."

"But, but, this is huge! Come on, you're always saying how they sucked when you were in school. When was the last time they beat UCLA?"

"I dunno. When I was a freshman, I think."

"That was nine years ago. You should be proud of your Trojans."

"I am, but right now, I'm also hungry."

"Humph."

She made a big show of stomping off, throwing herself onto the floor, and watching the rest of the game. I laughed and ate my sandwich.

I don't know when Adrienne began watching football, maybe when John came into our lives. He doesn't follow college much, but he loves the pros. I also don't know how or when she became a bigger 'SC fan than I am. Since she is already thinking about college, I am always pushing her to consider top schools outside of Los Angeles such as Harvard, Princeton, Yale, Stanford, or Berkeley. I want her to be on her own, free to make her own decisions, good and bad, without me looking over her shoulder. Moving 2,000 miles away from home was one of the best things I ever did. I don't understand those parents who can afford to send their children away to any university in the world, but instead insist they go to a local college, live at home rent-free, and have their expenses paid.

The irony is though I encourage Adrienne to think beyond Southern California, I think she has every intention of staying in LA and applying to USC. She will get in, of course. Her counselor confirmed college acceptance should not be an issue if she maintains her GPA and scores high on the SATs. Adrienne does well on standardized tests, ranking in the 90th percentile on her reading and language skills. She already passed the California High School Exit Exam although according to her, it's a joke and everyone she knows passed. I don't care everyone passed; I'm proud of her. If she can get through this year, this month, this day, she can get into college. *She's always wanted to go to college. Please don't take that away from her too.*

✳ ✳ ✳

Adrienne's feet chap, the beginning signs of hand/foot syndrome. Kirsten recommends Bag Balm Cream.

"Look for the green can," she says, "you can't miss it."

I find the cream at the pharmacy. Even on the shelf, the cube-shaped tin looks like something sold by a street corner apothecary during the 19th century. Looking closer, I read "Vermont's Original, Since 1899" and I laugh. Adrienne's going to love this stuff.

When I show her the tin, she likes it until she reads the small print.

"Did you see this, Sissy? 'For use on cows, thoroughly wash treated teats and udders with separate towels before each milking.' This stuff is for animals."

"Last time I checked, we were mammals, which counts. Kirsten said it works great. Now give me a foot."

Adrienne groans but acquiesces. I apply a generous amount of the Bag Balm, which looks and feels like Vaseline—only thicker, to Adrienne's foot. Then I put a sock over the protective layer and repeat the process on her other foot.

"This feels gross, but sort of better."

"Good. We'll do it every night to prevent your feet from peeling."

Kirsten warned me stopping hand/foot syndrome before it got out of control was the best way to prevent it from hurting Adrienne's quality of life. She told me horror stories of people who couldn't walk on their feet or use their hands at all. I didn't repeat these tales to Adrienne.

"Let me see your hands."

"They're fine, Sissy."

"Let me see."

Her hands show no signs of being chapped, but I massage Bag Balm into them to be sure.

Adrienne frowns.

"Are you done?"

"Yeah, I'm finished."

On my pager, the outgoing voicemail, which I usually update every week, gives information about Adrienne's condition. People leave messages for me there because I don't give our home number out to anyone except close friends. One day, I am surprised to hear a pleasant female stranger's voice.

"Hi, I'm Loreen from the Montel Williams Show. I'm calling to speak to Andrea Wilson. We're interested in doing a show about you and your sister. Can you call me?" she asks.

I grab Adrienne's spiral medical notebook and jot down the number. "Adrienne!"

She looks up from her history assignment.

"What?"

"Guess who called? Montel Williams! Well, not him personally, but the show."

For a moment, the sleepiness leaves her eyes; she sits up straighter. "Really?"

"Yep. They finally called."

What the hell took them so long?

"Call them back, Sissy."

"Okay, I will."

"Now."

"Alright."

After a brief game of phone tag, I talk to Loreen, one of the show's producers, who asks me questions about Adrienne. When she asks me what the angle of the show would be, I feel like saying—isn't it your job to figure that stuff out?—but I don't. Adrienne wants to meet Montel so I reach in the back of my brain for the biggest bullshit answer possible. I tell her Adrienne and I want to educate America about the link between hepatitis and liver cancer as well as share her experience about being a teenager with a serious disease and how it affects her life. All of which is partially true. I want people to know about liver cancer, but I doubt Adrienne cares if the world understands her problems. I can tell Loreen likes it because she talks about the logistics of developing the idea, bringing us to New York, and that's when I stop her.

I didn't think she meant now. The show took so long to contact us, I assumed she was discussing a possible appearance in the future, when Adrienne feels better. Every day this week, Adrienne has experienced pain, heartburn, nausea, exhaustion, and coughing fits. When she isn't sleeping, she struggles to keep up with her schoolwork. We don't have time to fly to New York, and Adrienne doesn't have the energy either. I don't bother hiding the disappointment or frustration in my voice.

"Loreen, Adrienne is too weak to travel. You waited too long." *You should have called last month. She was stronger then.* I don't blame the show producer who is only doing her job, I just . . . damn. Adrienne wanted to meet Montel.

Loreen rushes to get off the phone. Perhaps I made her uncomfortable, or maybe she is moving onto the next story. She says things she doesn't mean.

"Please call us when she gets better; we would love to have her on."

I say things I don't mean.

"Of course, I will. We look forward to meeting Montel one day."

I will never speak to her again.

I tell myself these white lies because my heart can't handle the truth. I feel like my intellect is protecting my heart. Like Jack Nicholson in the film *A Few Good Men*, I hear a voice in my head screaming *you can't handle the truth*.

I need my intellect. She allows me to live in a healthy state of denial so I can get up every morning and take care of Adrienne. She makes sure I don't cry in front of her. I don't know what I would do without her, but sometimes, my intellect lets her guard down like at the end of that phone conversation with Loreen. Adrienne will never meet Montel; my acknowledgment of this truth causes my heart to feel heavy as if it's full of stones. The pain spreads through my lungs, up my throat, which begins closing until I feel myself gasping for air. *Stop. Breathe. Everything will be okay. Take it one minute at a time.*

I tell Adrienne about the conversation with Loreen leaving out what my intellect forced my heart to see. She seems disappointed but not surprised. I try to read what's going on behind her olive-green eyes, and if I'm not mistaken, Adrienne speaks the truth to herself. She knows she will not meet Montel. She has done a lot during these past four months, experienced so much life, I hate I can't make this one thing happen for her. *Has it only been four months?*

"Sissy . . . John . . . I . . . can't . . . breathe."

John rushes to Adrienne's side, asking her what's wrong. She coughs long and hard as she points to her chest.

"It hurts."

"Okay, kiddo," he says, "let's go."

"Where?" I ask.

He gives me his famous are-you-an-idiot look.

"We're taking her to St. Jo's."

"Do you think that's necessary?"

I regret the words as soon as they come out of my mouth. Adrienne's eyes widen; John's eyes narrow; they stare at me. I feel horrible but it's midnight, I'm tired, and I know there's little the ER doctors can do. If Adrienne's oncologists can't stop her cough—what can they do?

During the ten-minute ride to St. Jo's, Adrienne's wheezing makes me realize the hospital can help her, and I am selfish for wanting to stay at home. In the ER waiting room, the staff recognizes us immediately. I guess we left quite an impression two weeks ago when Adrienne couldn't stop vomiting from the adverse reaction to interferon. Wide awake now and ready to be here, I tell them.

"My sister needs oxygen."

After reviewing Adrienne's chart, the doctor on-call orders a chest X-ray and blood panel, starts Adrienne on fluids, and tests her oxygen level; it has dropped to 94 percent. Between coughs, Adrienne lets him know she prefers a mask instead of a nasal tube. *That's my girl.* To dull the pain, Adrienne receives one milligram of Dilaudid through an IV attached to her central line. Soon the coughing ceases, and her breathing relaxes. The chest X-ray, as expected, is normal (except for the tumors); Adrienne does not have pneumonia. She receives a total of 350 mL of fluid to hydrate her, which is good because her daily liquid intake for this week has fallen below fifty-five ounces per day. The CBC is normal except for a below average hemoglobin level, but Adrienne's chronic anemia is not unusual anymore. The doctor discharges Adrienne at 3:08 a.m.; thirty minutes later, we are home and sound asleep.

Adrienne dressed as Ozzy Osbourne at her sister Andrea's
70s-themed birthday party © August 1999

Days 131–138

SUNDAY–SUNDAY, SEPTEMBER 23–30, 2001
☺☺☺☺☺☺☺

I'm tired of people calling me "strong" or telling me that I should be happy to be able to walk. I know I should, but you live in this situation for four months and feel like the ability to walk (which isn't always there) can override the bone aches, the nausea, the headaches, the bruises, the weight loss, the pain of your tailbone DIGGING INTO YOUR CHAIR. Even when those aches and pains aren't there, I look like a goddamn freak and everyone lies through their teeth about it hoping it will make me feel better. Whatever. I'm tired of this. I have no hope no matter what Sissy says. At this point, it feels as though all is lost. I miss home, wherever it is . . .

—Adrienne's journal entry dated 9/3/01

I didn't expect any response to my 9/11 email, but most of the replies were positive. My favorites include: "We must fight to preserve our way of life or Adrienne's struggle would be meaningless." "You have put what's happening in your life in a perspective that most can understand." "You are right, we need to keep fighting. We will rebuild, and Adrienne will beat this cancer."

However, a former college friend misunderstood my point. He sends me numerous emails about bombing Afghanistan. The one that puts me over the edge comes with an attachment that is a picture of a stealth bomber with the words, "If you can read this you're fucked!!" on its wings. We need to defend ourselves, but I'm not a pro-Nazi nut who wants to wipe out an entire population. All I can think when I see that picture is, we're killing innocent people the way chemo kills the good cells, but we have no choice.

I send my friend an email asking him to refrain from forwarding me anything else related to the situation in Afghanistan. I don't judge him, but I explain my position on the matter. He responds to my nine sentences with an eight-paragraph tirade about how I dare accuse him of being a war-monger. I read his email twice and shake my head.

Less than five months ago, I would have gone off half-cocked, called him up, railed at him, and apologized later. However, cancer has taught me a few things. Don't waste time. Pick your battles.

I think about Adrienne's world yesterday. She slept most of the day, took ten milligrams of Dilaudid, and swallowed multiple tablespoons of cough medicine. I save his email, but I don't reply. His friendship isn't worth the fight.

I gather all my materials for the 504 meeting at Burbank High today. John left work early so he could attend. We asked several people, but no one can stay with Adrienne from 3 p.m.–5 p.m. so we opt to leave her alone; however, my pager and our cell phone are on in case she needs us. My goal is to get the school district to provide Adrienne with ten hours of instruction per week and possibly another computer; ours is too slow. They are currently giving her five hours, which does not cover all her subjects. I am prepared for a battle because many sources have told me the district has never provided more than five hours of home-school instruction in the past, no matter what the circumstances were. Part of me can't believe I'm fighting my former employer for what seems like a small request; the other part of me wonders if they have any idea who they are up against.

John and I walk into a large classroom in Burbank High. Someone set up chairs in a circle. I see familiar faces: Diana, Adrienne's therapist; Rick Carlton, Adrienne's high school counselor; and Adrienne's current teachers for World History, English, and Algebra II/Computer Science who agreed to do and/or assist me with the home-school instruction. The Burbank High School AP guidance counselor and the program specialist introduce themselves, and finally I meet the man who will present our case to the district: Hal Jackson, director of pupil services.

I begin by thanking the teachers who have already given their time even before the district has made a decision. Then I state again why five hours is not enough, when the average student goes to school thirty hours per week. Mr. Jackson's face is inscrutable. I remind him I'm not being asked to be paid for my time even though I do have a substitute credential and years of experience. No reaction. I look at him and say Burbank High couldn't find a French teacher so I had to hire someone.

I feel like I'm talking to President Roosevelt's face on Mt. Rushmore. I resort to the law hoping to prompt a response.

"Under Section 504 of the Rehabilitation Act of 1973, 'A recipient that operates a public elementary or secondary education program shall provide a free appropriate public education to each qualified handicapped person who is in the recipient's jurisdiction, regardless of the nature or severity of the person's handicap.' The district is required by law to provide Adrienne with an appropriate education."

All the teachers as well as John nod in support of my statement.

"Adrienne qualifies, Mr. Jackson," I say, "because an individual with a disability is 'anyone who has a physical or mental impairment that substantially limits a major life activity. Major life activities include caring for one's self, performing manual tasks, walking, seeing, hearing, speaking, breathing, learning, and working.'"

I look at him, daring him to argue with me.

He smiles and says, "The problem with Section 504, Miss Wilson, is it is a federal statute, but the federal government does not provide funding for it. Now, most disabled children fall under Special Education, which are separate funds."

A slow burn smolders in my torso. I bite my lip.

"You know Adrienne can't possibly qualify for Special Education due to her grades and test scores."

"I am aware of that," he replies.

Even though the teachers jump in stating we can work something out and John backs up everything I say, I feel as though I'm fighting Jackson alone, perhaps, because we are sitting opposite each other. I picture us in a boxing ring, both of us dancing around, feeling the other one out.

I grit my teeth.

"You are required to provide Adrienne with an education. You can't opt out and punish her for being smart."

Jackson leans back.

"Is she really capable of doing schoolwork? I mean, what's her prognosis?"

His words are gasoline, causing the burn in my stomach, to blow up into a blaze of fire. I lurch forward and realize if he had been closer, I would have hit him. I feel heat around me and see John, too, is ablaze with anger. I grab his arm to restrain him knowing he will walk across the room and punch this man for his insensitive, cruel remark. Unable to control the level of my voice or the tears streaming down my face, I launch into a tirade.

"You don't know my sister or our family. Well, let me tell you something. We don't believe in numbers so there's your prognosis. As far as doing her work, ask her teachers. She is more than capable. School is one of the few things that gives her pleasure now. It brings some normality back into her life. She wants to do the work she would be doing if she could attend school. She doesn't want to be babied. Why are you punishing an honor student? You don't have the funds? Tough shit. Find them! It's the law."

Seeing a crack in his face, I take a breath.

"Maybe you read that front page story in the *Burbank Leader* in July about Adrienne and her illness. She said she wants to go to college and study religion and zoology. How do you think the community will react when they find out you, I mean the district, denied Adrienne her fundamental right to an education?"

Silence. Someone shuffles papers. Jackson clears his throat.

"I will take all of this information to the district, and someone will contact you with their decision."

In the meantime, the teachers volunteer their services for free because they will be compensated retroactively. Whether it's for five or ten hours total per week that will be split amongst them, they don't care, and I am grateful for their commitment to Adrienne.

When John and I get home, we find Adrienne half-asleep, curled under a blanket watching TV. She tells us our wish coordinator Becca dropped off pictures from her Make-a-Wish day. She motions toward a manila envelope on the kitchen table. The 504 meeting temporarily forgotten, I grab the envelope eager to see proof of a happier day. I am disappointed to find most of the professional black and white photographs are too dark because the lighting in the studio was poor. However, one picture stands out—an 8 × 10 the photographer blew up from the original.

Adrienne is sitting next to Dave Navarro, and they are both looking into the camera. The picture is off-center, yet it maintains an odd sense of symmetry: the sparkle from Adrienne's sequined wristband counteracts the shine from Dave's wristwatch; the light shown in the folds of her satin dress mimics the reflection of a coffee mug in the mirror behind them; and their smiles—hers with teeth, his without—hold the same elusive expression. Both Dave and Adrienne seem to possess a serene confidence.

She is better off bald, I think to myself. I don't mean she's better off sick, that would imply all bald people are ill. Adrienne used her hair as a means of self-expression, from red to purple to blue, even shaved; it made a statement. Without her hair, she is stripped bare and her inner beauty, which was always there, shines through like never before; it is no longer hidden under thick bangs or bright colors. I know she hates it when strangers stare. What she doesn't realize is, like that busboy in the restaurant, they don't think she is a freak. Like the goddess Athena, Adrienne radiates wisdom and strength, and people want to be close to her. To know her.

I hate it when I forget to say something in a conversation, but then remember it hours, days, or even weeks later. Before the 504 meeting, Adrienne took her World History Chapter 5 test. I should have told Jackson; maybe that information would have proven Adrienne was capable. I would have left out the part about how she spent two hours taking the exam and how she stopped several times due to coughing fits, sleepiness, and general pain. Despite the delays, I'm sure she did well, but her teacher will grade it, not me. Watching Adrienne plow through fifty-two short-answer and multiple-choice questions, often stopping to reread them, I could only imagine her frustration and admire her perseverance. I said she could stop at any time, but her response was no, I'll finish it today.

With a major test out of the way, Adrienne spends the next few days focusing on her Algebra II and French II assignments. I think she is still working on her death myth essay for English, but I haven't seen a rough draft yet. In the math and foreign language subjects, I feel useless, which is another reason I requested more home-school hours for Adrienne. At one time, I understood Algebra, but now it looks like gibberish to me. Adrienne knows asking me a question is pointless, and she refuses to ask John because he makes math more enigmatic than it already is. She emails her teacher, who drops by once a week to tutor her and pick up her homework.

For French class, we go to Anya's house, where we often have dinner beforehand making it an especially enjoyable experience for John and me because we get to socialize with our closest friends. Anya and Alex cook wonderful, cholesterol-laden meals full of butter and fat, and they always make a side vegetarian dish for me. Despite a low-grade fever and pain in her liver and shoulder, we don't cancel our plans with Anya and Alex on Thursday evening because Adrienne wants to see them, and she doesn't want to get behind in her French assignments.

Adrienne tries to eat, but her appetite has diminished. She struggles to stay awake; the four milligrams of Dilaudid I gave her before we left the house has made her sleepy. She manages to do her French lesson with Anya after dinner. The exercise is about weather, dates, and seasons. Most of the first unit of the book is a review of French I. For Adrienne's next assignment, she will work on 'question' words.

One of the things I notice when we leave Anya and Alex's place is how Adrienne's gait has changed. She shuffles her feet like an old woman. She doesn't ask for help, though John remains next to her in case she needs it. From behind, I can see how hesitant each step is, how much effort it takes her even though we parked the car right outside the building. John takes her elbow and guides her into the back seat. Last month, Adrienne argued with me for more time on the treadmill. Holding her school-books, I tell myself she will get her strength back, she has future French lessons, and we have plenty of fights left. *She's just having a bad week.*

Even though Adrienne's cholesterol continues to decrease, one of her liver enzymes has risen from 230 to 259, and her bilirubin has shot up from 0.9 to 1.9—officially out of normal range. Excessive bilirubin in the body can lead to jaundice[17] so I check her nails, eyes, and skin, but Adrienne does not appear yellow. I email Dr. Aquino with my concerns, hoping the test results are a side effect of chemo, yet knowing they are signs her liver is working harder to perform its basic functions.

I thought Adrienne would feel better because this week she is off Xeloda, but only the heartburn has improved. She coughs every day and suffers from mild diarrhea and dry skin, which I counteract with Kaopectate and Bag Balm cream. We fend off the occasional fever with Tylenol and continue Dilaudid for pain, Ativan for anxiety, and Valium

---

17 A condition marked by yellow staining of body tissues and fluids, a result of excessive level of bilirubin in the bloodstream; jaundice is not usually visible until the total bilirubin level rises above 3 mg/dl.

at bedtime. All of Adrienne's medications are memorized in my head: the name, amount given, how often, purpose served. Dilaudid—2–4 mg—Q4 or PRN—stop pain. At our follow-up appointment tomorrow to discuss the first round of Xeloda, which is the fifth round of chemo, Dr. Fenn will add another pill to the pile.

In the meantime, Dr. Aquino replies Adrienne's overall state of health may represent disease progression or drug toxicity. I don't know which conclusion sounds worse. I guess disease progression, although if Adrienne's body cannot handle these drugs, we are running out of options. Dr. Aquino suggests I stop giving Adrienne interferon this week and to have the tests repeated a week later. If Adrienne's liver test results worsen, he recommends stopping the interferon altogether and lowering the dosage of Xeloda. He reminds me Adrienne has qualified for a different study, an alpha-fetoprotein vaccine protocol, but the FDA would have to make an exception for her since she is underage. He also says to get Dr. Fenn's input when we see him this week. Though I appreciate Dr. Aquino's speedy response, one thing strikes me as odd. He never tells me to do anything; he only suggests. I don't know if that is his way of being polite or protecting himself from a future lawsuit.

On Friday afternoon, I push Adrienne in a wheelchair toward the pediatric clinic at UCLA Children's Hospital. Like Children's Hospital Los Angeles, they are undergoing renovations too. Signs everywhere state the hospital will soon be the "Mattel Children's Hospital at UCLA." I wonder if they will give out free Barbie dolls to the cancer kids. Adrienne attempts to do homework while we wait, but instead she falls asleep despite all the noise—parents talking, children laughing, and computers humming—around her.

A nurse draws blood because Dr. Fenn ordered a standard CBC and chem panel. He also prescribes a cough medicine although he isn't sure if it will help Adrienne. He wants me to increase the amount of Boost Adrienne drinks per day so she can maintain her weight; he also believes it will help with her exhaustion. The psych referral resulted in a prescription for Celexa, which Adrienne will start in the morning. Dr. Fenn concurs with Dr. Aquino's suggestions about Adrienne's treatment. We will wait and see what the test results reveal. Until then, Adrienne will continue Xeloda. She begins her sixth round of chemo tomorrow.

I spend most of Saturday packing boxes. John takes his musical equipment to our new home because he doesn't want the movers to touch it. Our friend Jonathan offers to watch Adrienne and to pack up her room because she is afraid the movers will break her stuff. Just when I think Adrienne is like me, she turns around and acts like John. Sometimes, I feel left out of their tight twosome: we're going to watch *South Park*; we're going to Guitar Center; we're going to a concert; we're going to do something you don't like to do, Sissy. Funny how biology may technically make you a mother or father, but it doesn't make you a parent. *Johnnee*, as Adrienne likes to call him, and I, her Sissy, are Adrienne's parents. I think about this stuff as I put videotapes, DVDs, CDs, and books into boxes. I smile when I come across movies John and Adrienne like or books she and I love. Though she is her own person, Adrienne carries a piece of us inside of her.

On Sunday, Adrienne stays with Anya at her place while John and I work with the movers. After four years of living in this house, we finally meet the owner, an attractive, petite, Asian woman.

She says, "If you had wanted the house, you could have taken over the payments."

My jaw drops. *Does she mean it? Did she tell the management company? We could have stayed?!?* I don't know how to respond. It's too late now. The house is sold, we signed a new lease, and the movers are here. *Shit.*

In less than five hours, we pack up the rest of the house, move across town, and set up Adrienne's bedroom. When we pick her up, Adrienne appears weak and groggy. Anya says she would only sip chicken broth, making Adrienne's total liquid intake for the day less than forty-four ounces. By late afternoon, her gums are bleeding; yesterday she was coughing up blood. Adrienne swishes out her mouth with water and baking soda, and John and I keep a close eye on her the rest of the evening.

The lab results from Friday's tests showed Adrienne's AST—the liver enzyme that keeps increasing—is now 298 and her bilirubin is 2.0. *Disease progression or drug toxicity—which is it?* I also notice for the first time her BUN count—20—is at the high end of normal. I remember BUN indicates kidney function and low is better than high, but I don't know what being high means so I look it up. According to my medical dictionary, "blood urea nitrogen levels may be increased in the presence of dehydration." Adrienne's kidneys are working harder because she is not taking in enough fluids. I don't know how to fix that; I can't force her to drink.

Though she has not had a significant amount of Dilaudid today, Adrienne acts incoherent a few hours later when we are watching television. I check her temperature—99.5 degrees—usually nothing to worry about. Three hours pass and Adrienne's fever rises to 100 and despite her best efforts, she seems unable to communicate because she garbles her words. John and I sit with her trying our best to understand what she is saying to us. I fear something has happened, and we're missing it. What has changed? Think, I tell myself. Is there anything new? Celexa! Adrienne took the antidepressant yesterday. I call her therapist Diana.

I've never woken up Diana in the middle of the night before so she knows something must be wrong with Adrienne. I tell her what has happened over the past few hours. She explains to me an allergic reaction to Celexa is unlikely because it takes weeks for your body to absorb it, but anything is possible. However, Diana is concerned about Adrienne's speech because it's possible her brain is not receiving enough oxygen. She wants me to test Adrienne.

"Have her write down current information like her name, address, date. Anything she should know."

Then she advises me to call Adrienne's doctor with the results.

I hand Adrienne our spiral notebook that doubles as our medical journal.

"Sweetie, write down your name and our address."

She nods and writes:

The writing is messy, even for her, and she hesitates after the city then scribbles through part of it. She doesn't write our entire address, but that makes sense because we just moved.

"Try again."

She slows down this time and seems happier with the result.

"Now, kiddo, who is our president?"

She attempts to speak, but I motion for her to write her answer on the page.

George W Bush

Relief washes over me. Despite her labored handwriting, Adrienne knows where she is and what year it is. Her brain function has not been compromised—yet.

I call UCLA and talk to the doctor on-call who agrees Adrienne may not be getting enough oxygen.

He suggests, "Go to the nearest ER—immediately."

cars pass by
in their pretty coats of paint
but i'm okay!
(fumes, fumes)
i'm slowly being burned
i won't leave, though
(cause everything is
A-OK!)
incinerate

cancer

Days 139–141

I stare at the boxes lying everywhere and wonder where my stuff is. I was so focused on preparing Adrienne's room and getting her things in order, it never occurred to me to put aside clothes for myself in case we had to leave the house on a moment's notice. I give up and grab my purse in hopes we will be back by morning. I can't believe we are not spending the first night in our new home; instead, we will be at St. Jo's ER surrounded by white walls, whirring machines, and the absence of smell.

John, Adrienne, and I arrive in the early hours of Monday morning though Adrienne has no concept of time. She continues to slur her speech and struggles to breathe. A nurse weighs Adrienne—110 pounds and takes her vital signs: blood pressure—140/95; pulse—150 bpm; and oxygen level—88 percent. The doctor explains Adrienne is in an altered level of consciousness, most likely due to the tumors in her lungs blocking the ability to deliver oxygen to her brain. Besides giving her oxygen, the doctor orders the standard chest X-ray and a brain scan to rule out pneumonia and impaired mental capacity. However, he cannot read the X-ray due to the lung metastasis, but the brain scan is normal. I try to appreciate this bit of good news, but I can't get past the 88 percent oxygen intake. *There's been another change. Adrienne needs oxygen.*

Knowing there is little else they can do, the staff at St. Jo's arranges for a transfer to UCLA. I ride with Adrienne in the ambulance while John follows in his car. I ask him to go home first and get Adrienne's tackle box, which contains all her medicines. I think we're going to need them. I call Anya and Alex to let them know what's going on, and they promise to visit us later that day when Adrienne has a room. I do these tasks with such ease it frightens me.

Upon arrival at UCLA's emergency room, we discover here 'cancer' is not a magic password that bumps you to the front of the line. They are swamped and we must wait our turn like everyone else. Of course, a nurse takes Adrienne's vital signs. Her oxygen intake has decreased to

87 percent. Someone gives Adrienne a room so she can lie down and be more comfortable. We wait several hours because there are no beds available on the pediatric floor. Until some patients are discharged, we are stuck in a small white room in the ER, and we are bored, tired, hungry, and most of all—scared.

At 8 a.m., I give Adrienne 5 mg of Marinol and 4 mg of Dilaudid. Except for the oxygen, the ER doctor has given Adrienne nothing for pain, and I don't see why she should suffer while we wait for an official prescription when she already has one. I write down what I gave her in our notebook so I can tell her doctor later. By mid-morning, Adrienne is assigned a room. John and I move like zombies as he pushes her wheelchair, and I carry our few belongings toward the elevator. I don't know how much longer I can go without sleep. I cross my fingers for a private room.

A bright yellow sign hangs over Adrienne's bed; it reads "Emma's allergies: Benadryl, Morphine, Bactrim." I love it because this way a nurse cannot accidentally give Adrienne the wrong medication, an incident that happened one time at Children's Hospital. The room is large and for now, we have it to ourselves. The pediatric oncology unit is much smaller at UCLA compared to Children's; it is one wing of a floor instead of a floor unto itself. I wonder if it's easier for the nurses to have fewer patients with cancer or if it's more difficult because there are many factors involved when dealing with oncology patients. Either way the staff seems to know what they're doing, and they don't mind when I ask if I can give Adrienne the rest of her 8 a.m. meds even though it's almost noon.

We meet Dr. Donne, another pediatric oncologist who works with Dr. Fenn. He starts Adrienne on Zithromax, an antibiotic, in case she has an infection. He schedules Adrienne for a spiral CT scan of her chest to check for any potential blood clots, which would explain the lack of oxygen. By mid-afternoon, Adrienne's oxygen level has increased to 90 percent. She always keeps the mask on, except when she wants to carry on a conversation, which she tries to do when Anya and Alex visit. They bring me clothes and toiletries they found after opening many unmarked boxes. While they spend time with Adrienne, I go to the nearest bathroom to clean myself up. Dr. Aquino is meeting with John, Adrienne, and me this evening to discuss Adrienne's treatment options.

"Shissy," Adrienne calls me.

Her words are muffled beneath the oxygen mask. She gestures toward the water pitcher. I pour her a glass and stick a bendy straw in it. She removes the mask, opens her mouth, and sips the water. Leaning over her, I notice a yellow film glazed across her eyes, and my stomach drops as if I'm on a roller coaster.

"What's wrong?" asks Adrienne.

I can't lie. John and I have been honest with her through this whole ordeal.

"You seem to have jaundice."

"Oh. How can you tell?"

"Your eyes, kiddo, there is yellow where it should be white."

"Oh. I didn't notice."

I chuckle because she's making a joke and because I don't want to think about what being jaundiced means, but I can't help myself. Her liver is failing.

With his no-nonsense stride, Dr. Aquino walks into Adrienne's room like he's about to preside over a corporate board meeting instead of a medical consultation with a family. He examines Adrienne—notes the jaundice—appears unsurprised and proceeds to discuss Adrienne's test results, which concern him. While her basic blood work looks good, in the past three days, Adrienne's bilirubin has increased to 2.8. Since last week, her cholesterol, which we thought was under control, has gone from 346 to 400. The Pravachol isn't working so Dr. Aquino wants to stop it immediately. In fact, he wants to stop all drugs that are either doing more harm than good or not helping Adrienne at all because the less medication her liver has to process the better.

Together we review Adrienne's list of prescriptions. Xeloda and any other types of chemotherapy or experimental treatments are on hold until Adrienne's CT scan results tomorrow. Dr. Aquino stops the interferon because it can increase liver function. He nixes the antidepressant Celexa, too, even though he doesn't believe Adrienne had any allergic reaction to it. He replaces the antifungal mouthwash Nystatin with the antifungal pill fluconazole because either the tumors or a possible fungal infection are causing Adrienne's cough. Fluconazole is stronger than Nystatin and will be easier to administer, once per day instead of four times per day. Then he prescribes a lidocaine wash to coat Adrienne's esophagus, which may have sores due to the extensive coughing. Dr. Aquino says to continue the Boost drink, Elavil, and Dilaudid although he may try a different pain reliever with a longer half-life so Adrienne can take less medication, but receive the same impact. He cuts out Magnesium, Lo/Ovral, Prilosec, and the Peridex mouthwash, but we may still use Marinol, Valium, Zantac, Zofran, and Milk of Magnesia as needed.

Although I listen and write everything down, I have my own agenda as well. Kirsten gave me a list of therapies to discuss with Dr. Aquino, and I won't be deterred from my mission. Before asking him about other possible treatments, I decide to address other issues that worry me.

I ask him, "Adrienne continues to lose weight. Can't she have a feeding tube? Doesn't she qualify for TPN?"[18]

I use the word qualify because Adrienne must be eligible for her health insurance to pay for it.

Dr. Aquino explains, "TPN is not effective in most cancer patients, especially in your sister's case because the liver cannot metabolize the amino acids. I don't recommend it."

I cross that option off my list. Adrienne listens but she doesn't say anything.

"I think she could eat more if the heartburn was gone. Dr. Donne believes Adrienne's liver pressing on her stomach is causing it. What do you think?"

"I believe it's the Xeloda so the heartburn should subside if we decide to stop the treatment."

"What about trying Thalidomide?"

Dr. Marco at Children's Hospital and Kirsten think it's a possibility for Adrienne, but I don't tell Dr. Aquino what others have said about the drug.

"I don't think it's a good option. I stopped using it in most of my patients because the amount of dosage needed to produce results is too toxic."

Anya's mother Sofia is a champion of thymosin alpha I, an experimental drug that treats hepatitis B; it may or may not help Adrienne, but it won't hurt her. Dr. Aquino, however, dismisses the drug. So I ask

---

18 Total parental nutrition, or TPN, is the intravenous provision of dextrose, amino acids, emulsified fats, trace elements, vitamins, and minerals to patients who are unable to assimilate adequate nutrition by mouth.

again about what I believe is Adrienne's personal savior—UFT. If Kirsten gets Adrienne access to the investigational drug, Dr. Aquino agrees to administer it and to track Adrienne's progress even though his lack of enthusiasm is palpable.

Dr. Aquino informs us Adrienne qualifies for home oxygen because her previous disorientation and slurred speech was due to lack of oxygen, and her condition has improved since she has been hospitalized and on oxygen around the clock. I know he means well, and we should be grateful Adrienne will receive the care she needs at home, but seeing her with that mask on—knowing she needs it now—terrifies me.

As Dr. Aquino walks out the door, I hear Adrienne mumble.

"Fok uf."

I know she means fuck off, but her words don't have the impact she desires because the oxygen mask muffles them. I don't think Dr. Aquino heard her, not that I care. John and I go to Adrienne's bed to comfort her. I think about the conversation from her point of view. How many times did Dr. Aquino say no to a suggestion I made? He has all but said he will stop Xeloda unless the CT scan results show improvement. Adrienne is angry because her doctor is giving up on her. I remember Dr. Aquino's email to Kirsten, which she forwarded to me. His last words were I'm sorry I can't offer her much help. If I were Adrienne lying in that bed, listening to him, I would have said fuck off too. We are fighters and if Dr. Aquino wants to give up, we'll find another ally.

I don't wait for permission to give Adrienne her 8 p.m. dosage of Dilaudid and Marinol. When I tell a nurse, she shrugs and notes it on Adrienne's chart. Here, the staff doesn't seem to mind I'm on top of things, and for the most part, they leave us alone unless we need something. I request mashed potatoes for Adrienne's dinner, but when I try to feed her, she shakes her head.

"Just one bite, kiddo—one."

Too tired to argue, she opens her mouth and swallows the small portion on the spoon.

"Sis . . . sy."

I wince as Adrienne struggles to find the strength to speak.

"When can I . . . go back to school?"

I press my lips together to maintain my emotions. One week ago, I was fighting for Adrienne's right to a suitable public education, and now . . . *Damn you, Jackson. Her mind is capable; her body isn't cooperating at the moment.*

"Don't worry about school right now. You'll catch up later. You have to focus on getting well—okay?"

I bet Adrienne never thought I would dismiss school in such a manner. I mean what I say though I tell myself she can catch up. Later. *You can't handle the truth.*

Adrienne looks at me and says, "Okay."

Her disappointment fills the room. She puts her mask back on; she's done talking for now. I look at the monitor above her head. Her blood pressure remains about the same at 144/95, but her oxygen intake has increased to 93 percent. I watch her breathe with her eyes closed, though she isn't asleep yet, and I want to blame someone or something for this . . . mess. Catastrophe? Disaster? I am searching for one word that describes this experience. Journey sounds too positive, and despite what Adrienne believes, I don't think cancer is her fate. If it is her destiny, then I cannot change it. *Accept the things I cannot change.* No, there has to be a way to alter the outcome; I just don't know what it is yet.

The CT scan shows the tumors in Adrienne's lungs have multiplied in the last month. I knew with the coughing, wheezing, increased pain, and decreased appetite the cancer had gotten worse; it was the only logical explanation for all of Adrienne's symptoms. I thought I was prepared after Dr. Aquino's discussion yesterday about stopping chemo, but when I hear the bad news, I feel as though Dr. Donne delivered his best right hook into my gut. Adrienne has little reaction, but John looks like he received the left hook. The wind knocked out of us, John and I listen as Dr. Donne keeps talking.

Despite the increased bilirubin in her system, Adrienne has none in her urine; the test was negative. Dr. Donne has ordered a blood transfusion for tomorrow since her hemoglobin continues to hover around 9.2. To improve her red blood cell count, he also increases her dosage of Epogen, from 34,500 units once per week to 37,500 units spread over three times per week. Besides receiving oxygen at home, Adrienne qualifies for IV fluid, which will help her stay hydrated. Dr. Donne changes Adrienne's home labs from a CBC every Monday and Thursday to a CBC and chem panel every Monday. He decides to continue the Zithromax, although no infection has been detected.

We don't know if we can go home tomorrow because Adrienne's oxygen intake drops to 83 percent at one point. Dr. Donne explains Adrienne is not taking enough breaths per minute to get enough oxygen in her body; her respiratory rate is too low. However, throughout the day, Adrienne improves until her oxygen is back up to 92 percent. I am not sure what caused the change, maybe it was Adrienne's sheer will, or the device a nurse attached to her mask to help her retain the flow of air. Either way, Dr. Donne prepares Adrienne's discharge orders.

The next challenge is figuring out the at-home oxygen situation. In the hospital, the concentration of pure oxygen Adrienne receives is 70 percent, but at home, she cannot go above 45 percent. I'm not sure why; it has to do with the tanks. She will have, however, what is considered a 'high-liter flow' because Dr. Donne is prescribing five liters per minute. Over the next twenty-four hours, the staff weans Adrienne off the higher percentage of oxygen until she can maintain an intake of 96 percent with only 45 percent pure oxygen. As Dr. Aquino suggested, Dr. Donne changes Adrienne's pain medication from Dilaudid to methadone, and it seems to work much better and last longer. He also replaces Prilosec with pantoprazole.

When I sign the discharge papers, I can't believe how short the medication list is. Excluding Epogen, which I don't count because it's given through Adrienne's central line, Adrienne has five drugs now: methadone for pain; pantoprazole for heartburn; Elavil for anxiety/depression; fluconazole to prevent fungal infections, and Zithromax to prevent other infections. Funny how I thought when she had fewer drugs, it would be a sign Adrienne was getting better. Since Adrienne's doctors stopped chemo, I wonder what we will talk about at the follow-up clinic appointment on October 12. Will they consider other options?

I spoke to Kirsten last night, and after doing more research, she agrees with Dr. Aquino and Dr. Marco. UFT is essentially Xeloda, and it will metabolize the same way in Adrienne's body. She believes arsenic trioxide is a possibility. Last year the FDA approved this chemotherapy drug for the treatment of acute promyelocytic leukemia, but only preliminary studies have been done in China regarding treatment of liver cancer. Dr. Aquino is not optimistic.

I'm not giving up though. I've been researching what the FDA calls 'compassionate use': the treatment of a seriously ill person with new, unapproved drugs when no other options are available or satisfactory. Since Adrienne qualifies, I could fight Bristol-Myers Squibb to grant compassionate use for UFT. With Sofia rooting for thymosin alpha I, Kirsten for arsenic trioxide, and me for UFT, I feel as though something will come through for Adrienne. I may have to fight a big pharmaceutical company because our three choices right now are all experimental.

I think about all these things as I follow John through the maze of the parking structure. He pushes Adrienne in a wheelchair, and I see the small oxygen tank attached to its rear. As we walk down endless corridors, I realize we have crossed a threshold, entered new territory. I no longer have to worry about the side effects of chemo or if Adrienne's white blood cell count is high enough for her to go out in public. Now she needs oxygen 24/7, and I . . . well I must find a miracle because that is what we need to keep her alive. *Shit. Maybe I can handle the truth.*

Days 142–144

Our living room resembles a nuclear power plant. Three tall cylindrical steel tanks containing oxygen stand against the back wall next to the television set. Each holds twelve hours of compressed oxygen. The Continental Hospital Supply company will deliver three new tanks every thirty-six hours. I have already memorized their phone number in case there's a problem. With a height of 54 inches and a diameter of 8.5 inches, the tanks are not very portable. Thin tubing from one tank runs along the carpet, across the hallway, and into Adrienne's bedroom, where it connects to her oxygen mask. I set an alarm to remind me when I need to switch the tubing to the next tank. I shoo Adrienne's kitten Marinol away when he plays with the tubing.

I call American Home Health to ask someone how to administer the IV fluid. John and I gave Adrienne almost one liter last night before the IV stopped working. We must have done something wrong; the box of supplies that arrived at our door last night didn't come with instructions. When I explain to the woman what happened, she chastises me for attempting to give the fluid without speaking to someone first. I defend myself by saying the discharge orders state give one liter of fluid via IV over eight to ten hours at night, but the stranger on the phone doesn't care. She acts as though I've done permanent damage by over-hydrating Adrienne.

"You were supposed to start tonight," she says because Adrienne was well hydrated after leaving the hospital.

"No one told us that. How were we supposed to know to start on Thursday?"

The woman sighs and asks, "How do her ankles look?"

Adrienne is drinking apple juice and watching TV. I inspect her ankles; they are puffy.

Great.

"Um . . . they're swollen."

"Uh huh. Skip the IV fluid tonight. Call tomorrow if the swelling doesn't go down. Elevate her legs at all times. Start the fluid again tomorrow night. Do you understand?"

I grit my teeth. I remind myself this woman is only doing her job.

"Yes. Thank you."

I hang up the phone and explain to Adrienne how John and I gave her too much fluid.

She shrugs and removes her mask.

"Am I going to pee a lot?" she asks with one eyebrow cocked.

I smile but I don't laugh.

"Yeah, kiddo. Probably."

"Okay."

"Hey guys, it's Adrienne. Umm . . . if you want updates on how I'm doing, please call my sister's voicemail at 213-941-0617, and sorry I haven't been returning messages, but I'm really either too busy or too tired to get on the phone so yeah. And for those of you who know my website, I usually update that. But if not, then just call the number. Thank you. Bye."

After listening to Adrienne's outgoing answering machine message, a high school friend of hers, Mick calls me. Even though he never visited her in the hospital and she hasn't talked about him all summer, I return his call because he sounds worried, and I always liked him.

The first time I met Mick was when Adrienne and I ran into him at the local Sears store at the Burbank mall earlier this year. Adrienne had done a presentation at school that day; she had twisted her blue hair up into a knot for the occasion, which made her appear older and elegant. I could tell from Mick's body language how much he liked Adrienne: his quick glances, his broad smile, and his witty jokes were a direct response to his interaction with her.

After he left, I said something to Adrienne, but she blew me off.

"Right Sissy, he's just a friend."

He's just a friend meant she didn't think he was boyfriend material. However, I know Adrienne likes Mick, so I speak to him and then relay the conversation to Adrienne.

According to Mick, he called Adrienne's answering machine many times during the summer. What frightened him was how young

Adrienne sounded on her outgoing message; she didn't sound like herself, he said.

"What does he expect?" Adrienne responds, "I have cancer."

The slight sarcasm in her voice tells me she's disappointed he waited so long to call her. I'm not sure he left messages those other times. I didn't tell Mick what I told the producer from the Montel Williams show even though my point is the same: you waited too long; you should have called sooner. Adrienne can't, or in this case, won't see you now.

Through Sofia's connections at the NIH, she has found a clinical trial for Adrienne. Located in San Mateo, California, Sciclone Pharmaceuticals makes Zadaxin, the trade name for thymosin alpha I. The company will allow us to have the drug without charge, and they will ship the medication to our house. Adrienne is sort of a one-woman clinical trial since Zadaxin is meant to treat hepatitis; its efficacy on liver cancer is unknown. Previously unenthusiastic about this drug, Dr. Aquino agrees to oversee and track the results since Zadaxin cannot hurt Adrienne. Sciclone promises to push the paperwork through with the FDA as fast as possible. I believe they have to file for compassionate use. Sofia, Dr. Aquino, and a Sciclone representative reiterate to me Zadaxin is not a cure; it is another type of immunotherapy drug, and Adrienne may have the same reaction to it as she did to interferon.

Nothing they say can quell my renewed faith that maybe a miracle can happen. Even if it only slows down the tumors' growth, Zadaxin could buy us more time to find a cure. Like a piece of driftwood in a vast ocean, I cling to this drug. *Help Adrienne, Zadaxin, you're her only hope.*

* * *

"What do you want to be for Halloween this year, kiddo?"

Adrienne smiles and then shakes her head.

"I dunno. Sumthin' diffrint."

I thought bringing up her favorite holiday might cheer her up, but she didn't take off the mask when she answered my question. Talking takes too much effort, but I can see from her fuddled brow she is thinking about her costume now.

Adrienne's first Halloween in Los Angeles was quite memorable. On that cold, wet night in 1995, we walked through puddles and mud as torrents of rain poured down on us. Shivering, we continued trick-or-treating in Beverly Hills determined to get the best candy possible; however, many people were not home. Maybe the rich have better things to do on Halloween then sitting around waiting to give out candy to children; I guess they go to parties. Dressed as a dead prom queen, with pale makeup on her face and fake blood splattered across her pink formal dress wearing a sash that read "Prom Queen 1985," Adrienne was disappointed no one got her costume. Door after door, people laughed at her and said oh look, it's Carrie! I explained to Adrienne that Carrie, a scary prom queen with telekinetic powers, was a fictional character from a book, but until I let her read the Stephen King novel for herself many years later, she didn't think anyone understood her Halloween costume that year.

Looking older than her ten years, Adrienne became Cleopatra for our first and only Halloween with John's son Adam, who had to be the world's smallest Incredible Hulk. Covered in green body paint and wearing torn clothes, four-year-old Adam growled instead of saying trick-or-treat at each door. John, Adrienne, and I pretended to be scared, but stifling our laughter was difficult, especially when a neighbor thought Adam was an elf. I remember spotting a dead cat on the street, and John and I turned the kids away before they could see it. We had only known each other two months, but the four of us already felt like a family.

Adrienne and I began our pumpkin-carving tradition that year. She created the designs, and I carved the pumpkins. We made our pumpkins look like characters from the cartoon *Space Monkeys* because Anya worked on the show. Adrienne and Adam loved it.

Without Adam the following year, John and I stayed at home while Adrienne went trick-or-treating with a new friend from middle school. Adrienne returned to being as dark and scary as possible on Halloween. She resurrected the dead prom queen costume, but this time she wore a different dress, less blood, and added a fake bullet on her forehead for more dramatic flair.

John and I threw a Halloween party in 1998, and we allowed Adrienne to invite her friends. I dressed as Scully from the TV show *The X-Files*, and as usual, John refused to wear a costume because it's stupid. Adrienne found a weird witchy outfit in a Halloween shop so she donned black and purple for the occasion. Our *South Park* pumpkins were a big hit at the party, especially the fat one we picked out for the character Cartman.

Dressed in a black gown with a hood, Adrienne transformed herself into the Grim Reaper for the next Halloween. She even wore the costume to school that day. I didn't know whether to be happy she was covered from head to toe, or to be worried she seemed attracted to death. She had only been in therapy with Diana for one year, but I thought making a big deal about it was the worst thing to do. All I said was it's a little dark, don't you think, which prompted an immediate eye roll from Adrienne.

Throughout that year, however, Adrienne sometimes called herself Persephone, a reference to the Greek goddess of the underworld, but then again, she often gave herself nicknames. In elementary school, she was Adrienne Cherry Wilson—a tribute to the Pink Ladies in the film *Grease*. Her live journal name is Xio, and she will sign things Dazzled Xio. She even named her hamster Xiola. Anyway, I work hard at letting her have her space because I know what a control freak I am. Regarding the Halloween costumes, I don't think I have anything to worry about because last year, Adrienne dressed as herself.

⁂ ⁂ ⁂

On Friday, I cannot get Adrienne to eat much—a cracker here, a bite of toast there, but she drinks water, apple juice, and grape soda. I forget to keep track of the exact amount of ounces she is drinking because a more pressing matter arises: Adrienne's urine turns sunset orange, which could be a result of the jaundice or possible dehydration. The home health care nurse on the phone, a nicer woman this time, recommends starting Adrienne back on the IV fluids tonight even though her ankles are still swollen.

After taking her first bath in days, Adrienne lies down in her bed in our new home, and I hook up the IV, which will dispense one liter of fluid over ten hours. I place one of the baby monitors Anya and Alex bought us on one of the built-in shelves above Adrienne's bed. She hates the idea we need to listen to her sleep, but we should have gotten the monitors a long time ago in case something happens in the middle of the night. For example, with all the IV fluid dripping into her body, Adrienne will need my assistance if she has to go to the bathroom even though her bed is ten steps away from the toilet. She hasn't had a bowel movement in days, but since she is hardly ingesting solid food that's to be expected. I take the other baby monitor into our bedroom, which is full of unpacked boxes, and put it on my nightstand. I turn it on and the quiet static lulls me to sleep.

I stare at the parking ticket on the kitchen table. While we were at UCLA for three days, my car was parked on the wrong side of the street during the city's weekly street cleaning—something we never had to worry about at our old house because we had a driveway. I doubt I will ever forget on Wednesdays from 10 a.m.–12 p.m., I cannot park on the opposite side of the street. I will remember because the date on the thirty-five dollar parking ticket marks the day Adrienne came home on oxygen. Receiving the ticket is a nuisance, but it doesn't bother me like it would have before. Paying the fine means nothing.

I used to think having loads of money would make me successful and thus happy. How foolish of me. However, wealth does buy freedom and access according to Warren Beatty. As I apply Neosporin to Adrienne's recent bedsore, I think how money cannot make her well. It could give us access to other drugs and the freedom to fly to other countries, but wealth in and of itself is no guarantee of good health.

When I was a kid, I read this book about a young boy who wished for all the money in the world, but in doing so, he caused other nations to go bankrupt. Soon he discovered he couldn't spend or give the money back. As bills and coins piled up on his family's property and the world economy collapsed, he had to figure out how to outsmart the leprechaun who granted his foolish wish. I remembered thinking how if the boy had phrased his wish differently, things would have turned out okay. I understood the point the book was making, but I ignored it.

Now twenty-nine years old, rubbing lotion on Adrienne's arms and legs as she lies in bed half-asleep, dependent on oxygen, I get it. The Publishers Clearing House Sweepstakes could knock on our door right now, and I would tell them to go away. Cancer doesn't respond to cash.

By Saturday afternoon, Adrienne's ankles almost look normal; keeping them elevated alleviated the swelling. From sunset to maize, the color of her urine has improved, so I believe she is more hydrated although I cannot be sure. However, after checking her vital signs, I discover her temperature is 100.5 degrees. Five hundred milligrams of Tylenol and ninety minutes later, her fever climbs to 101, but after twenty minutes, it drops down to 100.5. Despite the descent, I call UCLA and the doctor on-call urges us to go to St. Jo's ER right away for a blood culture, a CBC, and a urine analysis.

At the time when most people are sitting down to dinner, John and I are rushing Adrienne to the hospital. Her body remains warm and although she appears lethargic, Adrienne knows where she is as she lies on a gurney in the ER. Urgency runs like a current through the air as more than one doctor treats Adrienne; she has never received this amount of attention before. Though I notice Adrienne's short gasps as she breathes, I do not count how many breaths she is taking. When a doctor informs us her oxygen intake has dropped to 93 percent—with the mask on—and her respiratory rate is less than ten breaths per minute, I listen for the time between each breath.

Uunnnn/hhh . . . One . . . Two . . . Three . . . Four . . . Five . . . Six. Each hollow inhale is followed by a quick exhale.

Uunnnn/hhh . . . One . . . Two . . . Three . . . Four . . . Five . . . Six . . . Seven.

Uunnnn/hhh.

I feel like I'm in two dimensions: a slow-spacey one where time stops until I hear Adrienne breathe again, and a fast-blurry one where people connect tubes, draw blood, and run tests while machines beep, hum, and shudder. I look on the monitor and see Adrienne's blood pressure is 90/50; it's never been that low. Mine once dropped to 80/50 after my emergency appendectomy, and even though I felt okay, my surgeon was worried.

Not wanting to disturb Adrienne, a nurse takes her temperature under her armpit. The result is 101.5 degrees. She shakes her head and runs to get the doctor. When the nurse returns, I ask her to explain the difference between readings under the armpit versus in the mouth. She says the axillary result is typically .5 degrees lower than the mouth's temperature, which is a more accurate representation of the body's heat level. To be sure, she removes the oxygen mask and coaxes a thermometer into Adrienne's mouth. Adrienne's fever has risen to 102.3 degrees. Within an hour, the doctor lowers Adrienne's body temperature to 101.5 by giving her medication through her central line.

Finally, the doctor has test results that explain why Adrienne's body fell apart. The chest X-ray is inconclusive; the doctors cannot read it because of the numerous tumors. I didn't want them to waste time doing the X-ray, but I knew they had to rule out pneumonia. Adrienne's CBC looks good except she's anemic. So far, these results are normal for her. The urine analysis, however, shows Adrienne has a serious urinary tract infection. *Dammit—those bright colors.* I tell the doctor about the last two days, and hear myself saying, she has never had a UTI before. The results from the blood culture are not back yet, but Adrienne's blood sugar has dropped to 19 when the normal range is 70–110.[19] After giving her dextrose (essentially sugar) in her IV, the doctor raises Adrienne's sugar level to 147—too high, but he seems to prefer it that way.

Concerned about Adrienne's breathing, the doctor introduces a test I've never heard of: a blood gas; it analyzes the pH, carbon dioxide (PCO_2), and oxygen (PO_2) concentration levels in the blood. Adrienne's pH is 7.1, which is on the low side considering the range is 7.35–7.45. I don't need to know what the norms are when the doctor says Adrienne's PCO_2 is 80 and her PO_2 is 70. I understand her blood has more carbon dioxide than oxygen. She can't sustain that much longer, but no one offers a solution.[20]

Instead, the staff expresses their concern about her pain level. Adrienne missed her 8 p.m. dose of methadone. After reviewing her medical records, the ER doctor in charge decides giving Adrienne two milligrams of Dilaudid through her IV makes more sense than having her swallow a pill. I agree except two milligrams intravenously seems excessive, but I can't remember how much that would translate into pill form so I can't be sure. Hell, I can't remember the last time I ate; therefore, I don't trust my memory regarding the milligram conversion. I never ask why methadone, her new pain medication, is not an option.

As Adrienne drifts off to sleep, John urges me to get a Diet Coke. He sees I'm fading. I go to the lobby where the vending machines are and find Anya and Alex who have been there for hours waiting for an update on Adrienne. I remember calling them. Or did John call? I don't think either one of us ever came out to see if they were here. I recall everything

---

19 This is the normal range for a fasting glucose value according to *Taber's Cyclopedic Medical Dictionary.*
20 The normal ranges for PCO_2 and PO_2 are 35–45 and 75–100 (while breathing room air) respectively.

that's happened, especially the numbers. Blood pressure, blood sugar, respiratory rate, pH, and oxygen are too low. Carbon dioxide and body temperature are too high. Oh and now the blood sugar too, but don't worry about it. What else? Adrienne has a UTI, and she is resting after they gave her Dilaudid. Anya and Alex promise to stay there as long as we need them, and then, they push me toward the double doors, where a nightmare awaits.

The doctors don't use words such as overdose or coma; instead, they tell John and me they might have given Adrienne too much Dilaudid—more than her body can handle. Even though the dosage seemed high to me, Adrienne appears to be in a deep sleep, nothing more. I don't think they did anything wrong, but their creased brows and strained faces tell me they believe otherwise. To cover their asses, they want to wake Adrienne up by reversing the effects of all opiates in her system with a drug called Narcan.

I don't know why Narcan sounds familiar to me; our mother never undid the drugs she ingested. Maybe I heard about it on television or in the movies. In the film *Pulp Fiction*, John Travolta plunges a syringe into Uma Thurman's chest to save her from a heroin overdose. Was he injecting Narcan into her body? Of course, these thoughts flit through my mind in mere seconds, and I don't say them aloud. I listen as the doctors caution us: any pain medication Adrienne has received will be neutralized, and she will probably have a strong reaction to Narcan, most people do. Despite their warning, I am not prepared for what happens next.

"AAAHHHHH . . ."

Adrienne pops up like a jack-in-the-box. Her shrieks are coherent despite the mask. Thrashing her thin arms in midair, she pushes doctors and nurses away as they grab her limbs. She spots John and me.

"SISSSYYY! STOP. MAKE—STOP," she yells.

Oh my god! What have they done?

"You have to give her something for the pain. NOW."

The doctor nods.

"We will. We have to calm her down first. She's just scared and confused."

Goddamn asshole. She's alive. You didn't kill her; instead, you're torturing her.

Now lying down, her limbs at her side, but still raising her voice, Adrienne cries out.

"BATHROOM. Have to go now."

I look at the nurses and then the doctors. I realize no one thinks she should get out of bed.

She's going to be humiliated. I show Adrienne the bedpan.

"Okay, sweetie. We're going to slide this underneath you, and you try to go—okay?"

Adrienne nods but after a few minutes, she can't or won't go. I remove the bedpan.

"Forget it," I tell the nurses.

Underneath that oxygen mask, through the yellow glaze over her eyes and despite the wet face of frustrated tears, I see my Adrienne—stubborn, strong, and still fighting. I squeeze one hand; John squeezes the other.

"What now?" I ask.

The doctor gives Adrienne Haldol to decrease her anxiety, and she soon falls back into a sound sleep. Up, down, riding the seesaw, finding that perfect balance, seems to have eluded this doctor. I don't blame him, but I regret putting Adrienne through the Narcan nightmare because it wasn't necessary. I tell myself Adrienne is getting some much-needed rest. However, my shoulders tighten as the seconds go by between Adrienne's breaths, until they relax when I hear her exhale, only to tighten again.

The St. Jo's staff recommends Adrienne be transferred to UCLA as soon as possible so her regular doctors can monitor her care. In the meantime, the doctor orders two strong antibiotics to fight the UTI. Nurses continue to monitor Adrienne's vital signs, and by midnight, her temperature is 101 degrees. Another blood gas shows Adrienne's blood sugar remains high at 143, but her PCO_2 has dropped to 44, a vast improvement and now within normal range. Her pH level is still low though. An hour later, Adrienne's fever drops to 100.7 degrees so the antibiotics must be helping. However, her blood sugar rises to 156, and her PCO_2 increases to 52.

I write the numbers down feeling with every step forward, we take two steps backward. What's worse? A high fever or high carbon dioxide? The answer: neither is worse; they both suck. John and I wait and watch in silence except when we talk to Adrienne. The transfer is delayed because UCLA decides Adrienne needs a special cardiac/pediatric care team to escort her to the hospital. They are sending over their own people:

one doctor, two nurses, and another specialist. The ambulance with the team arrives around 3:30 a.m. They speak in hushed tones with St. Jo's ER doctors. I don't understand their somber faces with sympathy oozing out of their pores. As I climb into the ambulance to ride with Adrienne, I get it. No one thinks she is going to make it across town. *They don't know my Adrienne.*

Days 145–146

I miss life so much. You have no idea how lucky you are. Appreciate your youth and your ability to do shit, ok? Live and have fun for me.

—Adrienne's email to a friend dated 8/11/01

When we arrive at UCLA, we bypass the ER and go to the pediatric floor, where a private room has been assigned to Adrienne. Dr. Fenn, Adrienne's pediatric oncologist, is there waiting to speak to us. Anya and Alex, who followed in their car, stay with Adrienne while John and I step outside the room. Dr. Fenn motions for a nurse to grab some folding chairs. We sit across from him. I hug myself to hold in the pain, but I can't stop myself from crying because I see it in Dr. Fenn's eyes: Adrienne is dying. *No, no, no, no, no.*

"Do you want to put your sister on a respirator?" he asks.

I look at John, not for his approval, but for support. His vacant eyes look through me, but I feel him touch my arm. I don't know what to do. Ask questions. Need more information.

"Can she come off the respirator at some point?"

Dr. Fenn shakes his head and replies, "No, most likely not."

Think. What would Adrienne want? "Can she come home on the respirator?"

"No."

A nurse hands Dr. Fenn a form; I see the letters DNR—do not resuscitate.

For once, I am grateful John always touts how important it is to be rational. I solve the problem with as much logic as I can muster under the circumstances:

1. Adrienne would not want a machine breathing for her.
2. Adrienne hates hospitals. I must get her home.
3. I would never be able to turn off the respirator.

My hand shaking, I reach for the DNR.

"Give it to me."

I scan it reading, "If my heart stops beating or if I stop breathing, no medical procedure to restart breathing or heart functioning will be instituted."

I sign on the line that reads "signature of patient's representative or parent if patient is a minor" and with every loop of my print/cursive letters, I question my decision.

I'm not giving up on you, kiddo—not yet.

On the line "relationship to patient," I write "Guardian/sister."

I swear I'm not.

"I'm going to call a hospice facility now," says Dr. Fenn.

I nod, stand up, and go back into Adrienne's room. John follows. When I tell Anya and Alex I signed a DNR, the words sound surreal to me. The four of us gather around Adrienne—two people on each side of the bed. I count the time between her breaths again.

One . . . Two . . . Three . . . Four . . . Five . . . Six . . . Seven . . . Eight . . . *Oh my god—breathe!* . . . Nine . . . Ten . . . Eleven . . . Twelve . . . Thirteen . . . Fourteen . . . Fifteen . . . Nnnn/hhhhhhh.

With a shorter and quieter inhale, yet longer exhale, Adrienne's breathing has slowed to four breaths per minute.

Despite her slow respiratory rate, Adrienne seems to be in a deep sleep like a princess in a fairytale. Maybe I'm kidding myself, but as I stand on her left side, squeezing her left hand, I feel her spirit—alive—in her body, but I don't know how to reach it. I never read Adrienne's English essay about death, but I saw the title: Summerland. We are saying our goodbyes—Anya, Alex, even John. So I tell Adrienne,

"Go to Summerland. It's okay. I'll be okay. We love you so much. I love you."

I lay my head gingerly on her stomach; her hospital gown absorbs my tears. I don't mean anything I say, except for the part about love. I don't want Adrienne to go to a mythical place called Summerland. It's not going to be okay; I'm not going to be okay. Nothing about this feels right. I can't let her d . . . *don't say it* . . . here. I have to get her home.

Dr. Fenn and his staff want Adrienne to remain in the hospital because she is too unstable to travel. He says she could die in the ambulance on the way home.

They don't know my girl.

When Dr. Fenn finds a hospice nurse at five o'clock in the morning, he sends her into the room to convince me to change my mind. An attractive blonde woman of medium stature walks in and introduces herself as Casey Cline from Trinity Hospice Care. I lean forward and drape my arms across Adrienne's body as if this hospice nurse intends to do physical harm. Before Casey can argue for keeping Adrienne here, I cut her off.

"We are taking Adrienne home. She wouldn't want to be here. I understand the risks. You can't talk me out of it, so don't try. Now let's do what needs to be done and get her home as soon as possible."

Without flinching, Casey nods and says, "Okay."

Later, she tells me upon that first impression, her nickname for me was "Andrea Don't-fuck-with-my-family Wilson."

I can't believe it's only been four days since Adrienne came home on oxygen. That event alone felt like we had entered a foreign country without knowing the language or customs. Now we have even more things to learn and to do, as we prepare to take her home in what I call a deep-sleep state, and what the doctors won't label a coma.

The first step is to put a catheter into Adrienne's bladder. Two nurses ask everyone to leave the room except for me. I scoot over to the other side of the bed, where I stroke Adrienne's forehead and squeeze her right hand. I watch as the nurses bend her legs so her knees are facing up, and I think how Adrienne has never had a pelvic exam. One nurse spreads Adrienne's legs apart, as the other one attempts to insert the catheter. Adrienne's eyes flutter open. She lifts her head, clamps her legs together, and looks at me.

"Make them stop, Sissy."

I laugh even as the tears flow because the nurses look like they have seen a ghost. *Who knew it would take a catheter to wake the sleeping beauty.*

"I have to go to the bathroom," says Adrienne.

I help her sit up. She stands on her legs, holds her IV pole, and pushes me away, as she walks to the bathroom located next to the bed.

"Shut the door," she tells me and I do.

Her voice sounds strong through the mask, and I can understand every word. The toilet flushes, and she pushes the door open. She allows me to assist her as she climbs back into bed. I throw the sheets over Adrienne. The nurses look at me, and I nod. They open the door.

I don't know what they were able to hear, but John, Anya, and Alex rush in. Anya has been crying, and John and Alex look like they've been fighting tears. The nurses' eyes are becoming moist. The best part though is when Dr. Fenn walks in and sees Adrienne. He stops at the door and weeps without making a sound. I look at him. *I made the right decision about the respirator, about taking Adrienne home.*

Smiling, Casey says, "Hi Adrienne. I'm Casey, your hospice nurse."

Adrienne replies, "Oh. Hi."

She looks around. Adrienne realizes her awakening has raised the humidity in the room. She shakes her head.

"I don't know what all the fuss is about. I was just dreaming."

Even as we all laugh and maybe some believe they have seen a miracle, I think to myself—*I know, kiddo. I knew you were still with us.*

Compared to the excitement in the hospital, the ambulance ride home seems dull. No one fears Adrienne will die although a medic monitors her vital signs. Adrienne talks in spurts, asking questions: how long was I at St. Jo's, when did I go to UCLA, and what is the time now. As we travel northeast—almost into the sunrise, I say a silent thank you for another day with my sister.

Because Adrienne's respiratory rate is only six–eight breaths per minute, the oxygen order was increased from five to fifteen liters per minute. Dr. Fenn also sent Adrienne home with a reservoir bag that attaches to her mask. When Adrienne inhales, she draws in 100 percent oxygen from the reservoir bag. A one-way valve separates her exhaled air, which is released into the air through ports on the mask.

Because of Adrienne's decreased respiration and the increased prescription, the compressed oxygen tanks in our living room are no longer a viable option because they won't last. Instead, Continental Hospital Supply installs a larger stationary tank, about one foot in diameter, filled with liquid oxygen. Before doing so, a man on the phone asks me three times if we have a dryer in our garage, and I assure him we do not. After two delivery men set the tank in its place and show me how it works, they attach twenty-five feet of tubing, which we run from the garage, through John's bathroom, down the hallway, and into Adrienne's room.

I make sure it reaches into the living room as well before they leave. When I ask how long this tank will last, one of the men replies hopefully five days because that thing is heavy.

Adrienne stays in the living room drinking water and juice throughout the morning. A few days ago, we had an over-bed table custom-made for her. John rolls it over next to the chair in front of the television; then he adjusts the height making it taller. We place a pillow between Adrienne's head, which she cannot keep upright, and the table. I urge her to swallow liquid Tylenol for her ongoing fever, but according to Adrienne, it tastes nasty. John tries to convince her to lie down, but she refuses to. Anya and Alex offer to watch Adrienne so John and I can sleep, and I want to protest, but exhaustion overwhelms me. I climb into bed, close my eyes, and sleep approximately three hours.

Later that afternoon, our hospice nurse Casey drops by to check on Adrienne. I find it strange we—and it feels like we, not only Adrienne— have been on hospice now for ten hours. No one tries to cure your disease when you are on hospice; you receive palliative care such as pain medication and supportive services like oxygen therapy. I want to dislike Casey because she represents failure. Adrienne and I don't give up a fight just because we're losing. We play to win; we always have. I taught her to be strong, to be a winner. Then I realize Adrienne woke up, I brought her home, and she is where she wants to be. Maybe I need to redefine what it means to win.

I balance Adrienne's pain against her fever for the rest of the evening, as she lies on her bed. The methadone is easy to give her in its liquid form, and she swallows it without hesitation. However, even as her body temperature climbs to 101.4 degrees, Adrienne refuses the liquid Tylenol. She pretends to take it and then lets it dribble out of her mouth. Someone might argue she had an involuntary response, but she knows what she is doing. Adrienne hates the taste, and she won't swallow it even when I implore her to. Finally, I soak washcloths in a bucket of ice water. Putting them on her head and neck and re-dipping the cloths into the ice as soon as they absorb the heat, I cool her body down to 100.9 within an hour. I figure that is the best I can do without using medicine.

For the first time ever, John and I decide to sleep in Adrienne's room. We huddle in blankets on the floor, careful not to lie on the tubing that leads to the oxygen tank. In the middle of the night, we hear Adrienne whispering our names.

"Sisssy. Johnnee."

Our bodies stir then jerk until we realize she is okay. She wants to talk to us. We climb in bed with her. Pulling her oxygen mask down around her neck, Adrienne reaches for John. She hugs him.

"I love you guys."

John replies but I can't hear him for I focus on how clear Adrienne sounds. *She's doing this on purpose.* Then she turns toward me. With unexpected strength, she pulls me into her body with her thin arms and hugs me as if she is absorbing my essence.

Holding me, she says, "I love you, Sissy."

Please don't let these be her last words.

Not wanting to let go, afraid of what will happen if I do, I respond.

"I love you too, kiddo. I love you so much."

Her body relaxes and she lies back down. I put her oxygen mask on her face. Although light peeps through the blinds from the streetlamp outside, I can't quite see John's face. I wonder what he is thinking. Is he afraid like I am? I listen to Adrienne breathe, and I count again. I remember something she said ten years ago. I liked it so much I wrote it down.

"I love you bigger than the ocean, Sissy. I love you deeper than the ocean."

I love you so much Adrienne—I wish it could be me.

Casey arrives in the morning to guide us through this new stage with Adrienne. I worry about Adrienne's fever, which hovers around 101 degrees. Casey assures me if the heat bothered Adrienne, she would let us know. The first time Adrienne loses control of her bladder, John leaves the room so Casey and I can change the sheets and clean Adrienne up. When she urinates two more times, I realize we have to consider other options. Casey suggests adult diapers, but John points out how embarrassed Adrienne would be. I think a catheter would be worse considering her reaction yesterday. Then, Casey tells us to keep in mind Adrienne could be in this condition for days, weeks, or even months. I finally agree a catheter might be the best way to go; it's less humiliating than a diaper and easy to clean, but I'm still not sure. Casey says we can use adult diapers until John and I make a decision.

This morning, someone from Dish Network is supposed to install our satellite dishes. When the Dish guy shows up, I explain to him he needs to put one of the dishes into Adrienne's room, but she is very ill. I watch his eyes as he takes in the scene: the plastic tubing on the floor, the overbed table covered with medical necessities, and Adrienne lying on her bed looking like a thin, pale version of her former self. The Dish guy stops before walking into Adrienne's room.

"Are you sure it's okay?" he asks.

"Yes. She's resting. Look my sister has always wanted MTV2, which is why we chose Dish instead of cable when we moved. Please install it so we can turn it on for her."

"Okay," he says.

He works as fast as he can, and when he finishes, he stops and looks at Adrienne. Then he speaks to John and me.

"I hope she . . . um . . . gets better."

"Thank you so much."

I usher him out the door wondering if he has children and knowing if he does, they will get a special hug from their daddy tonight.

Not long after the Dish guy leaves, Adrienne sits up and begins throwing her body around as if she is boxing someone in her sleep. She's even talking although all we can hear are gurgling noises. Afraid she will fall out of bed, I attempt to hold Adrienne's arms down to calm her.

"Don't restrain her," Casey tells me, "Rock her. Soothe her like you did when she was a baby."

Casey reminds John and me Adrienne's brain never lost its ability to function, so she is completely aware of her surroundings. Adrienne is fighting her illness. She's fighting hard.

John helps me scoot Adrienne over toward the center of her bed, so I have room to sit next to her. I cradle her in my arms as best I can and whisper in her ear.

"Sweetie, I'm going to sing to you—don't laugh."

I allow Adrienne to lead rocking forward and back in time with her. I begin singing "Goodnight Sweetheart Goodnight." When I get to the line about it's time to go, I think *no, it's not. Please don't go.*

Adrienne's arms relax, and she says something, but I can't understand her.

"Yeah kiddo, I changed the lyrics, you know I do that all the time."

Casey smiles, "Keep doing what you're doing. It's working."
Our motion now one movement, I sing another song to Adrienne.

"Hush, Lil' Adrienne, don't say a word,
Sissy's gonna buy you a mockingbird—or a hamster, or a cat, or whatever
*   you want*
If that mockingbird don't sing,
Sissy's gonna buy you a diamond ring—'cause that's your birthstone
If that diamond ring turns brass—'cause we bought it at the thrift store
Sissy's gonna buy you a looking glass
If that looking glass gets broke—and that's seven years bad luck
Sissy's gonna buy you a billy goat
If that billy goat runs away
Sissy's gonna buy you a brand, new day."

I wish it were that simple, kiddo. We are buying you more time. You've been approved for a special clinical trial, but you have to hang in there. I keep these thoughts to myself as I lower a now serene Adrienne to her pillow. Throughout the day, she pops up whenever her brain decides to go another round with her body. Every time, I rock with her and sing silly lullabies or tell funny stories until she quiets down. I want to tell her to stop fighting, but I don't.

People visit throughout the day, but John and I only allow them into Adrienne's room when she isn't flailing her body around. Our home health care nurse Tess, who spent almost every Monday and Thursday morning this summer drawing Adrienne's blood, visits Adrienne. The English teacher at Burbank High who assisted and graded all of Adrienne's papers brings a gift, but doesn't go into Adrienne's room. Anya and Alex are at our house throughout the day whenever they can get away from work.

Jesse, John's childhood friend, ends his vacation early and drives all night from Northern California. He last saw Adrienne a week ago when we were moving. He was one of the people included in that email I sent a month ago today begging people to visit Adrienne more often. Like most of our friends, Jesse has his own relationship with Adrienne. He has taken her to *The Rocky Horror Picture Show* even though she forgot to tell him it started at midnight. When he tried to back out, she reminded him he had promised it as a birthday present. One Halloween, in an attempt to embarrass her, he dressed up like a nun to take Adrienne and her friends trick-or-treating. Standing over six feet tall, wearing his glasses and sporting a goatee, Adrienne laughed when she saw him. Sometimes, she earns extra money helping Jesse grade papers; he is a sixth-grade teacher. When Jesse walks in, he finds me rocking Adrienne.

"We told her you were coming," I say, "She can't respond, but she can hear you and understand you."

I leave him alone so they can talk.

At 5:45 p.m., I squeeze the dropper and watch the methadone drip into Adrienne's mouth. She swallows but then she spits half of it out. As I wipe her upper lip, I smile. Something about her refusal makes me feel better. *Because she's still in there—as stubborn as ever.* She moves her lips, but again the words are garbled.

"It's okay, kiddo. You don't have to take it all if you don't want to."

Three hours later, Casey who had left and then returned, recommends liquid Ativan to relax Adrienne, even though she accepted her subsequent dose of methadone. I don't understand why Casey appears unconcerned about Adrienne's fever, which has spiked to 101.7. She reiterates if the temperature bothered Adrienne, we would see it. All I can think is, doesn't your brain fry after a certain point?

Thinking along the same lines, Anya and I become determined to reduce Adrienne's fever after Casey leaves for the evening. I fill the bucket with ice water and grab even more rags than the night before. Anya and I put cloths under Adrienne's armpits, between her thighs, and on her forehead. However, the minute they touch her skin, they seem to ignite as if Adrienne's body exudes the thermal energy of the superhero Firebird, a woman capable of pyrokinesis. Undeterred, Anya and I continue the get-her-fever-down cycle: place cloths on Adrienne's body, allow heat to zap coldness, redip cloths into bucket, and repeat. After a while we notice we can leave the rags on longer; Firebird is losing this fight. Ninety minutes later, Adrienne's temperature is 99.6 degrees, the lowest it has been in days. Exhausted, but relieved, Anya and I grin. We did something useful.

Casey explained to John and me Adrienne's heart rate is another sign of how hard she is fighting to stay alive. After I give Adrienne her 11 p.m. dose of methadone, I use the fingertip pulse oximeter to test her pulse, which is 155 bpm and her oxygen, which is 98 percent. She's hanging on. *Stop being so selfish—tell her she can go.* I know those people visiting today are saying goodbye to Adrienne. I know it but I cannot allow myself to accept it. I refuse to. Casey said it might be weeks or even months. I can do this for as long as it takes. *But is that what Adrienne would want?* I lean over and kiss Adrienne on the forehead.

"Whatever you want, kiddo. I'll never leave you, no matter what."

IN RECENT
HOURS I
HAVE:
loved ✓
ater ✓
slept ✓

died.

alonealonealonealonealonealonealonealonealone

happy to
meet you

~~sedate me~~
happy!

everything
is A-okay!

~~go away~~

friends!

Day 147

Cancer adds to the story of my individual life; it adds to my unique
character and sense of humor. John, in my eyes, has never seemed more
like a father, and Sissy has never seemed untrapped and free from
time and stress. I know that she's stressed right now, I can see it hiding
beneath her smile, but her soul and spirit have never seemed so bright to
me before. Me, John, and Sissy are one now. This has made us a family,
a support center, and a library of information on the liver. Hehe . . .
Cancer blessed me with these wonderful people and healers; it hasn't
cursed me with the end of a life.

—Adrienne's journal entry dated 5/28/01

Adrienne has been crying in her sleep. Her face is wet, yet she appears
to be . . . smiling. With her legs turned out, knees bent, and the soles
of her feet together, she is in what yogis and dancers call the butterfly
pose. My mind flashes to when a nurse put Adrienne's legs in that same
position when she was a few minutes old. Is this what people mean by
things coming full circle? From birth to . . . *no, no, no.* Adrienne does not
attempt to speak; she does not lash out with her body. I do not need to
rock her today, and I do not have to beg her to take her medicine. Every
time I give her methadone, she swallows it.

Her vital signs reflect her calm demeanor. Before dawn, Adrienne's
fever spikes to 103.3 degrees, and her heart rate reaches 152 bpm. Then
as the sun rises, her temperature drops: 102.7 at 12 p.m., 102.2 at 1 p.m.,
until it is 101.4 at 2:40 p.m. Her heart rate mirrors her fever. At 10:30
a.m., Adrienne's pulse is 140 bpm; by mid-afternoon, it drops to 135 bpm.

I don't know what John thinks, but I am thrilled Adrienne is improving. I refuse to look beneath the surface. I ignore how Casey's
eyes pop when she sees Adrienne today. I close my ears when she says
Adrienne is no longer fighting—she has made peace with herself. I know
she's right of course; I knew it the minute I saw Adrienne this morning

in that position looking happier and more relaxed than she has in weeks. Adrienne has made a choice. She is going to die on her own terms, whatever they are.

More friends visit today to say goodbye to Adrienne. I tell her who is coming, and although she doesn't talk, I feel as though she understands because she murmurs in response. Jared and Joyce spend time alone with Adrienne. Marilyn and Justin drive up from Orange County; I am happy to see them because they haven't seen Adrienne in a while. They, too, were included in the "I'm begging you to visit Adrienne" email from last month. Adrienne's therapist Diana arrives around mid-afternoon. Even Marilyn's father Donald, who once tried to convince Adrienne Santa Claus did exist (he failed), drops by to spend time with his 'niece.' Anya and Alex are our constant support system, as they are with us most of the day and even coordinate the visitations so John and I can speak to Casey.

When I ask again about the fever (I can't let it go), she explains it is a result of both dehydration and the UTI. She assures me the methadone is working, and Adrienne is not bothered by her temperature or in pain. Casey may, however, test Adrienne's kidneys to assess her fluid intake. Then she says she needs to teach John and me some new things since Adrienne is in a different state.

"Remember the five senses and the part of the body that coordinates with each one," says Casey as she ticks off eyes, ears, nose, mouth, and hands.

She tells us we will have to put lotion on Adrienne's body every day to prevent her skin from drying out. Then, we should check her ears daily and clean them with Q-tips if necessary. Inspect her nose to ensure there is no blockage.

"However, the most important things are her eyes and mouth."

Because Adrienne is not blinking enough, we will have to put drops in her eyes every four to six hours so they won't dry out. We also have to swab a special ointment on her teeth every four to six hours to keep them clean.

Even as I write these things down, I think how much Adrienne hated brushing her teeth until I bought her that silly cheap electric toothbrush. I wonder where it is, probably in a box somewhere. Anything we didn't need right away, I haven't unpacked. We moved into this house nine days ago, and we have spent five nights here. We have gone from three compressed oxygen tanks in our living room to one liquid oxygen tank in our garage. Adrienne was on chemo when we moved here; now she is on hospice and expected to live weeks. *Maybe.*

Casey repeats, "If you forget everything else, remember eyes, mouth, and meds."

I write down "EYES, MOUTH, MEDS" in our spiral notebook.

Donald rushes out of Adrienne's bedroom and gestures with his arms as he tries to talk through his tears.

"She . . . Adrienne looked right at me. She opened her eyes and blinked twice. I'm supposed to get you . . . she wants you now."

John and I nod, and as we walk one direction, Donald runs the other— out the front door of our house. Casey, Anya, Alex, and Diana follow us into Adrienne's bedroom.

Casey looks at Adrienne.

"It won't be long now," she says. "Her blood pressure has dropped."

To confirm her assumption, Casey takes Adrienne's blood pressure, and it is 94/60. Her heart rate is 125 bpm. She tells me I should go ahead and give Adrienne her pain medication, but we should not give her any more fluids since there is gurgling in her lungs and swelling in her legs. I watch the .75 mL of methadone slide around Adrienne's mouth; however, I'm not sure if she consumes any of it. She swallows but the action seems like a reflex.

"She's not in pain, I promise you," Casey says.

I nod. Casey explains when someone stops breathing in this situation, the lungs have an involuntary response as they lose oxygen.

"It sounds awful, but Adrienne won't be hurting."

I lie next to Adrienne on her right side. I alternate between stroking her face and holding her hand. John sits on the other side; he holds Adrienne's left hand. Anya and Alex are kneeling next to him while Diana and Casey are sitting at the foot of Adrienne's bed. Little Bit keeps a vigil from her perch on the windowsill where she has been sitting for almost an hour. I know Adrienne wants it this way—at home, in her bed, surrounded by the people who love her most with her cat watching over her. She could have hung on for months, but she would never want to be a burden on me even if I don't see it that way. I think the most important thing though is for Adrienne, wasting away in a room—unable to speak, to walk, or to eat—would be a loss. This way, she wins. I understand because I would make the same choice, but lying next to her, every selfish cell of my being screams for her to stay. *Please don't leave me. Please. Not yet.*

Then Little Bit stretches and jumps down, walking out of the room. *No, animals know.* Adrienne takes in a huge breath as if she is about to go underwater for a long time. Casey pats my leg.

"Remember, it's normal. There's no pain."

Casey leaves. I don't hear the exhale.

Minutes or maybe a minute goes by. Adrienne inhales again, only deeper this time. Diana chokes on a sob as she walks out. I wonder how Adrienne orchestrated this event . . . her dying. How is it people seem to be moving on cue?

Between each breath, more time passes. This time, minutes pass before we hear one again—that familiar *uunnnn/hhh* sound. Under their umbrella of tears, Anya and Alex exit together. I keep stroking Adrienne's face with my left hand, but I put my right hand on her wrist.

Without warning, Adrienne breathes again, sooner than expected. As the *uunnnn/hhh* leaves her lips, John moans and runs out of Adrienne's bedroom. *What the hell is he doing? Where is he going?*

I yell, "John, come back. PLEASE."

I listen as Anya or Alex goes after him.

I know Adrienne is still with us even before I feel her pulse throbbing beneath my fingers.

"Hold on. Just one more minute, baby. Johnnee left, but he's coming back. He'll be back. Hold on. Just hold on."

I squeeze her hand, and I feel the life in it. She hears me.

I sense John's presence, but I don't look at him. Instead, my eyes dart back and forth from Adrienne's face to her chest, and I feel her pulse.

"Johnnee's back. I love you, baby. We're here with you. We're both here. I love you."

Adrienne inhales—deep and long—*uunnnnnnn.* I can almost hear the air whistling through her teeth. Then she exhales a sigh of relief—hh-hhhhhhhhhhhhh. Her chest stops moving. There is no more breath. My world slips away, I grasp for it—check for a pulse. Nothing. I remove the oxygen mask. With my ear to her lips, I strain to hear a sound, a lost breath. Nothing. Adrienne is gone.

John and I spend time alone with Adrienne until her lips turn gray. We tell Casey, who says we need to clean Adrienne up. John leaves and

Anya offers to help us. John closes the door behind him. Casey walks us through the whole thing. Even though Adrienne weighs less than 110 pounds, the three of us have a difficult time moving her because we don't want to be rough with her body. We remove Adrienne's clothes to give her a sponge bath. Anya and I find clean sheets when the fluids, which Casey warned us about, pour out of Adrienne's body.

I notice how hairless Adrienne is, which shouldn't surprise me, but it does. I remember Adrienne saying chemo was the cure for shaving legs. Adrienne hates body hair. *Hated. She can't hate anything anymore.* Last year, she used my Nad's natural hair removal gel to remove the hair on her arms. Funny how when you get what you want, it's never the way you pictured it. Adrienne always wanted to lose weight, too, until chemo ate her muscles. I have no ass meat, Sissy. *I'm going to miss her voice. Her wit. Her everything.*

Casey says Adrienne can wear anything she wants to the mortuary so I select a pair of new Victoria's Secret panties, her blue tie-dyed shirt she wore to Medieval Times, her new studded belt she wore to the ballet, and her favorite pair of jeans. Together, we dress Adrienne. After putting on her jeans, I slide the belt through the loops as Casey and Anya maneuver Adrienne's body. Then something strange happens, but none of us want to acknowledge it. I think, maybe I'm going crazy. Casey looks at me. I glance at Anya, and she turns to Casey.

"She must really like those jeans," she says.

We laugh because we are not imagining what we see—Adrienne is smiling. Her entire expression changed as soon as we finished dressing her. I feel good because Adrienne's soul is here in this room. I don't know for how long, but she's here for now.

"I have to get John," I say, "he has to see her."

We don't have to tell John and Alex what happened because they see it for themselves. Anya and I explain and we laugh again as we repeat Casey's comment. Diana has left so she doesn't see Adrienne smiling in her jeans. Casey goes to the drugstore to buy a disposable camera. She suggests we take pictures. We may want them someday. I don't think we will, but if we can capture Adrienne's spirit on camera that would be worth the pain of looking at the picture.

Casey says we can have as much time as we want with Adrienne. She explains how we need to straighten Adrienne's body including her hands and feet before rigor mortis occurs. As a hospice nurse, she has the responsibility of removing all the 'hard' drugs from the premises when a patient dies at home. Going through Adrienne's tackle box, she takes out methadone, Marinol, Valium, Ativan, Xeloda, Dilaudid, and Elavil. However, if we suffer from constipation, infection, or acid reflux, we have plenty of medicine leftover to relieve those maladies. Casey assures John and me we can call her anytime we're ready, and she will arrange for someone to pick up Adrienne.

I want to make Adrienne as beautiful as possible so I decide to give her a manicure and pedicure. She always cared about the way her nails looked, more than I ever did. I select her favorite shade, blue satin and set to work. After cutting her nails and trimming her cuticles, I file and buff before I polish. After I sweep the final coat on the last nail, I survey my work. I think Adrienne would be proud.

Out of nowhere, Little Bit leaps into the bed, curls up next to Adrienne's foot, and falls asleep. She knows—I think to myself—because Little Bit hasn't been in Adrienne's bed since she became ill. After she scratched Adrienne, Little Bit became more cautious. Now she realizes she can lie next to her owner again. Casey told us stories about other pets, especially cats, acting strange or protective around dying children. You couldn't pay me enough to be a pediatric hospice nurse. I don't know how Casey does her job. Even though we've known her less than seventy-two hours, she helps children die with dignity. I lean over and pet Little Bit. She's purring.

Anya and Alex suggest we order dinner from a place they like called Mo's. John and I have never eaten there before, but it is less than three miles from our house, so Mo's will deliver. I think I order a turkey burger or maybe the shrimp pesto pizza, but I'm not sure. The four of us gather in Adrienne's room with her, and we turn on her TV. I find MTV2 and unfortunately, the channel is having an all-night special on rap, Adrienne's least favorite genre of music. We apologize to Adrienne about the rap, but leave the TV on anyway for background noise.

Judging by the way we eat our food and talk to Adrienne, the atmosphere feels almost festive. I suppose we are in shock. Adrienne's body looks like a life-size porcelain doll dressed up in blue, but her soul fills the room; it has grown beyond the smile now. I want to talk to her, read to her, sleep by her, and most of all, laugh with her. I don't want to send her away, but I know Anya, Alex, and John are waiting for me to give the okay to make that call. I don't like the idea of strangers touching Adrienne. Of course, I would make up any excuse to keep her with me. *One more hour, okay? Well, maybe another.* I can't let her go yet.

Around three o'clock in the morning, I telephone Casey and she answers the phone.

"What mortuary?" she asks.

"Well, Adrienne always liked Forest Lawn."

If cemeteries didn't fascinate Adrienne, I don't know what I would have said. Casey says not to worry, she will deal with the funeral home. After I hang up the phone, I want to call her back and tell her I changed my mind. Please don't take Adrienne away. Why can't she stay with me? The energy in her room right now, what some would call her soul, emanates from her body; without it, that vitality will vanish. I know it. *God, please don't take her.* Twenty minutes later, the doorbell rings.

Two large men stand on our front porch. I think John comes up with the idea for them to drive around the back of our house so our new neighbors won't see, not that anyone is awake at this hour, but I want to protect Adrienne's privacy too. The men drive down the alley that runs parallel to our house. From there, we open the gates to allow the van into our backyard. The plan is for the men to remove Adrienne through Adam's bedroom, which is located at the back of the house and has a patio door. The men walk into the house, but stop when they see the hallway that leads to the front of the house where Adrienne's bedroom is. They look at each other and then at Alex and John. I don't understand their hesitation until I follow their eyes staring at our narrow, 26-inch wide, not-up-to-code hallway. The men won't fit. *Kiddo if you had something to do with this—thank you.* John and Alex offer to bring Adrienne to the van. The men's faces relax, they nod, and then they wait outside.

Alex and John carry Adrienne on a sheet. Holding each corner, they lift Adrienne's body, maneuver through the hallway, walk down three stairs outside, and place her on the waiting gurney. I watch as one man places a band around Adrienne's ankle. In black sharpie, he has written, "WILSON, EMMA." I want to correct him. We call her Adrienne, but I know it will create confusion later. I touch the plastic anklet and trace the letters. *It's not a toe tag like you see on crime shows.* I straighten the bottom of Adrienne's jeans so they appear smooth. I feel the blue satin nail polish as I brush my fingers over her toenails. *How did I end up by your feet and not your face, kiddo?* The nice, yet portly, men give me papers to sign releasing Adrienne's body to Forest Lawn. With the last sweep on the "n" at the end of "Wilson," I'm letting Adrienne go.

I watch the men, whose names I've already forgotten, load Adrienne into the van. I stand there as they drive away. John closes the gate. Amidst hugs and tears, Anya and Alex go home. I climb into bed and lie there, unable to comprehend Adrienne is gone. I tell myself she's no longer in pain, but that fact doesn't fill the void, the emptiness I feel. *Goddammit, I want her back. Bring her back. How could you do that to her? How could you take away the best part of my life? Karma is bullshit.* I continue to vent my silent fury until the anger weighs down my eyelids. As I drift off to sleep, I wonder . . . who is listening to me?

Adrienne and Andrea © August 2001

Days 1–7– Without Adrienne

"Children leave you, so do husbands and lovers but your sisters—they are the only ones with you from crib till death."

—Unknown

I wake up laughing. I look at the clock—7 a.m. Only three hours have passed since the men took Adrienne away. Yet, I feel calm because Adrienne visited me in a dream. *Or maybe it was real? Maybe if I close my eyes, she will return.* As unbelievable as it seems, I know Adrienne sought me out for a purpose: to make me smile on the first day of the rest of my life without her. Adrienne could always make me laugh, and she's not going to let her own death stop her from doing so.

During Adrienne's first visit to Los Angeles, I took her to the Winnetka Drive-In movie theater, when such things existed, in the San Fernando Valley. We saw two movies: *Prelude to a Kiss* and *Death Becomes Her*. Both films were too adult for a then six-year-old Adrienne, but I didn't know any better. We dangled our feet over the edge of the bumper as we watched from the trunk of my car. We consumed a huge tub of popcorn, two sodas, and candy. The actors' voices materializing from the speaker next to the car fascinated Adrienne. She loved the idea of lying down and seeing movies on a giant screen. Looking back, the experience itself was more important than the actual films, but the second picture became one of our personal favorites.

A black comedy, *Death Becomes Her* tells the story of two bitter rivals who attempt to kill each other multiple times, but they fail because each woman has drunk an elixir that gives her eternal life. However, the women discover staying young has its price. While they cannot die, their bodies suffer tremendous tolls, but they soon learn how to cover the wounds they inflict on each other. Every time the movie aired on television, Adrienne and I sat down and watched it together. We giggled as the women covered their graying, dead skin with makeup. I always meant to buy the movie on VHS, but I never did.

When Adrienne appeared before me, she was wearing her blue dress, the same one she wore for Dave on her Make-a-Wish day. I could hear people whispering in the background, but I couldn't see them or make out what they were saying. The faceless crowd seemed to form a semi-circle around Adrienne, who stepped toward me. Initially smirking, Adrienne broke into a full smile when she peeled back some skin from her left shoulder. It was gray underneath.

"See Sissy, it's true," she said.

I laughed immediately. Adrienne didn't need to say another word. The best part about inside jokes is they require no explanation. Adrienne lingered a few seconds longer, and then she disappeared, her mission accomplished.

John wakes up, startled by my laughing, which has dissolved into a choked, wheezing sound, as I fight a cascade of tears. The hug we give each other feels lost and empty like a broken shell washed ashore, its other half lost at sea. We don't say anything, but the best part of us is gone. We may be in shock, but I know our relationship cannot survive without Adrienne. *Does he know it too?*

A few hours later, John and I drive to Forest Lawn in Hollywood Hills. When Casey asked me to name a funeral home last night, I said Forest Lawn because Adrienne liked visiting that cemetery, and it's close to our house. When we arrive, I notice the lush rolling green hills are mysteriously devoid of any tombstones. John wonders where they are too. We decide to ask after we discuss the arrangements. Adrienne likes tombstones. *No, liked. She liked tombstones.* We arrive at the front desk.

"I'm sorry for your loss," a woman says.

The sentence sounds sincere yet rehearsed.

"Name of the deceased?"

She seems puzzled by my answer. Her sympathetic smile tightens.

"Hold on."

She calls someone and speaks in a hushed tone. John and I are unprepared for her response.

"I'm sorry. She's not here."

"What?" we reply in unison.

After I yell at the woman and tell her she has made a mistake and to look again, I stare in disbelief at John.

"They lost Adrienne?"

He assures me they have not and we will find her.

The woman returns with no answer, only another question.

"Perhaps your sister is at another one of our facilities?"

Facility? Call it what it is. You work in a funeral home. A cemetery. You are surrounded by dead people. And somehow, you morons lost my child!

John ushers me outside where we call Casey, who apologizes for the terrible mistake. She called Forest Lawn in Glendale because she thought it was the closest one. I don't know whether to feel relieved or more frustrated. That cemetery is farther from our house.

John speeds toward the other facility, a mere seven miles away. With morning traffic past its peak, the drive takes ten minutes, but it feels much longer because I picture Adrienne's body drifting in limbo, lost by the stupidity of a mediocre society, as John would say. Eventually, we get there. In the parking lot, my legs are numb with pain, but I force myself to walk. *Must find Adrienne.*

A cheerful, yet somber, receptionist confirms Adrienne is here. Now we wait to meet with an advisor, who will guide us through the process. Professional and crisp, Melinda apologizes for the confusion and for our loss. I stop her before she can begin her spiel.

"Where are the tombstones?" I ask.

"Oh, the founder didn't believe in them," she replies.

I frown.

Melinda explains every person has the same small plate for a uniform look. I have this vision of strangers stepping on Adrienne. My dislike of one of the most beautiful and popular cemeteries in the Los Angeles area mystifies Melinda.

"Look, I cannot let people walk on my sister. And she loves—loved headstones."

Melinda's jaw tightens but her smile remains fixed.

"This isn't right," I say. "We need to go somewhere else."

John nods in agreement. Perplexed, but helpful, Melinda leaves to see what she can do. I walk outside and sit on the concrete steps while John calls Casey. We wait, hoping an answer will fall out of the sky. We don't know where to go from here.

Then, I hear the click-click of Melinda's heels as she approaches us. John's cell phone rings, and I answer it. I listen to Casey with one ear while the other one tries to catch Melinda's words. Melinda speaks to John.

"I found another facility."

Casey says, "I think I found the perfect place."

"The name is Hollywood Forever," says Melinda.

"It's called Hollywood Forever," says Casey.

I look at John and repeat Casey's words. Melinda smiles. I imagine that's something she doesn't do often in her line of work. John and I smile too. *Feels like fate.* Somehow, Adrienne made the decision for us. Melinda offers to transfer Adrienne's body at no charge. I thank her and watch as she walks away, wondering if she will remember us.

I don't realize how hungry I am until my stomach growls. Amid the chaos, I forgot to eat today. John and I pick up food on the way home. We call Hollywood Forever and make an appointment for later that afternoon. At four o'clock, we will figure out the details. For now, we eat.

Located at 6000 Santa Monica Boulevard between Gower and Vine, the Hollywood Forever cemetery has an unassuming entrance: a tall, palm tree and a short sign designate the driveway. When I think about how often I drive down this road, I can't believe I never noticed it before. This place feels right; Adrienne belongs here. Her body, one with the Earth, buried near famous movie stars in the heart of Hollywood.

We meet Ilka, a nice older woman, perhaps Slovenian, whose job is to determine how much money we can or will spend on the arrangements. Arrangements? I believe there are more euphemisms in this environment than there are in the medical community. One of Ilka's jobs as our Forever Counselor is to drive us around the cemetery in a golf cart. Of course, she tells us how sorry she is for our loss and Adrienne has arrived safely from Forest Lawn before the three of us go in search of the perfect property for interment purposes.

With my armor intact, I calmly listen as she talks about various types of plots and points out different locations. I consider a double plot. I could be buried on top of Adrienne, but that option loses its appeal when I imagine suffocating Adrienne's soul. I also know now, without a doubt, I want my body cremated. My decision has nothing to do with any belief system; cremation is simply cheaper and easier. No one will have to ride around in a golf cart and decide where to lay me to rest. My ashes will share the same ground with Adrienne's body. We will rest there—together—forever. Now, I must figure out where 'there' is.

Since we already told her we can't afford much, Ilka shows us the cheapest plots in the cemetery, an area bordering Paramount Studios. Even the glamour of a movie studio cannot make this section attractive. The weather-stained, rusted, corrugated tin wall of Paramount along with the overgrown weeds dotting the graves make this block of land feel worn and used. I shake my head. Adrienne may have worn secondhand clothes from thrift stores, but I'm not going to bury her in the discount aisle.

Sensing my building frustration, John squeezes my hand as Ilka drives us to the oldest part of the cemetery. Like the land next to Paramount, this area is less expensive; however, it doesn't appear cheap. Lush grass, fewer weeds, and colorful flowers tell me the living actually visit the dead here. The Garden of Ancestors contains markers from the early twentieth century. Many of our friends view Adrienne as an old soul; she would fit right in here. As we walk toward a plot aligned with the edge of the cemetery's property, I stop in my tracks.

"John, look."

I point toward the sky. We can see the Hollywood Sign, one of the most famous architectural monuments of Los Angeles. Then I look to my right, and see the word school in large white letters. The Santa Monica Boulevard Community Charter School resides across the street from Hollywood Forever. Everything about this land feels perfect. Adrienne loved the Hollywood Sign; she liked school, and she was wise beyond her years.

"This is it," I say to Ilka, "it's perfect."

Ilka embraces our decision with such sincere enthusiasm we almost miss the most important thing she says during her barrage of supportive comments.

"Lot 1-C. Grave 13."

"What did you just say?" asks John.

"Oh. For the paperwork. Lot 1-C. Gra—um—plot 13."

John looks at me. His birthday. The first initial of his last name. All these years he saw the numbers of his birthday—1:13—everywhere. He tried to convince me it meant something, but I never believed him. Not until now. *Maybe another sign of Adrienne's destiny? No, I can't believe that, even if she did.*

Ilka watches us. "Is everything okay?"

"Fine," I reply. "The numbers. They happen to be John's birthday . . . that's all."

My casual tone has the desired effect; Ilka nods politely and asks no further questions.

With the plot selected, Ilka ushers us into her office, where we discuss costs and options, her real job as our counselor. Her polite businesslike demeanor eases me: I slip into my armor, shield my feelings, and prepare to negotiate. John, however, has the opposite reaction. His body shakes as he struggles to speak until he lapses into silent weeping. I don't know if the realization of Adrienne being gone is hitting him or if the birthday-grave site thing is blowing his mind. I can't comfort him right now; there are too many decisions to make. *I doubt I'll ever be able to comfort him.*

Like any business deal, it all comes down to dollars. Scratching numbers on a legal pad, I calculate I have $2,500, the total sum of Adrienne's personal savings from working last summer as well as her leftover Social Security money. The bare minimum for a coffin, plot, and memorial service is approximately $8,000; we are short $5,500. Ilka suggests a personal loan; the cemetery has the MBNA Family Advantage program available for situations like ours. *For poor people.* Knowing I have horrible credit, I ask John if he will apply for a loan. He nods. As he fills out the application, I read the fine print: the maximum amount available is $5,500. *Perfect.* The interest rate is 23.99 percent. *Awful.* No interest accumulates for three months. *Fine.* Without any collateral, the loan is approved, and we have a budget of $8,000.

That evening I remember all the life insurance solicitations I used to get in the mail. They were addressed "Dear Parent" or "Dear Mrs. Wilson." When I became Adrienne's legal guardian, I ended up on a mailing list of companies that insure the lives of children. I maybe read one letter in its entirety. The thought of insuring Adrienne's life seemed like a ludicrous and morbid notion to me at the time. Parents were supposed to have life insurance, not their children. The more I read, the more upset I got. "Free Quote! No Medical Exam! $1 buys 30,000!" I began recognizing the company logos on the envelopes and tearing them up without even opening them.

What if I had bought life insurance? Would Adrienne have cheated death, if only for a few more years? The insurance industry exemplifies Murphy's Law. If you have it, you never seem to use it. When you don't have it, you need it. My reasoning doesn't make sense though because Adrienne had medical insurance, and god knows we used it. I suspect I will swim in a sea of 'What ifs?' for many years to come.

EMAIL
Subject: Adrienne's funeral
Date: 10/11/2001 1:58:36 AM Pacific Daylight

There will be a **public** **Remembrance service** for Adrienne on Tuesday, October 16 from 4 p.m.–6 p.m. at the Hollywood Forever Cemetery located at 6000 Santa Monica Blvd. between Gower & Vine Sts.

(Please note: this is not a come and go type of thing so be prompt.)

Please note the following requests (again!):
1. Do not wear black. Please wear a shade of blue in honor of Adrienne.
2. No matter what your religious beliefs may be, please do not mention god at any time during the service.
3. If you would like to share a story about how Adrienne personally affected your life, please write it down on paper so it can be collected later. Don't hesitate to share; she touched everyone.
4. If you would like to contribute something, please make a donation to the address listed below. Although finger foods and flowers are welcome, we really need monetary donations. This funeral is costing a tremendous amount of money and that fifty dollars you might spend on flowers can be put to better use to help us pay for everything (to put it bluntly).

A private burial service will follow the next day; it will be by invitation only.

Love, Adrienne's Sissy

The next day, Ilka drives us around again with a new objective: find tombstones I like so I can decide what I want for Adrienne. With Ilka's Polaroid camera, I take pictures of Ruth Pines and Jennie Raingold. I almost feel as though I am violating these women in some way, so I say a silent thank you to them. Part of me wants to scream I don't know what shape, size, or color Adrienne's marker should be; who cares about the font, or whether the letters are polished or unpolished. The number of decisions I have to make seems endless, but figuring out the details grounds me. I have to stay in control and make sure everything is perfect for Adrienne.

We gather in a conference room to discuss the memorial service with Ilka and Sean, the funeral director. I sketch Adrienne's tombstone on a piece of paper while Sean discusses other options: the casket, the flowers, and the service itself. I finish my rough drawing, a combination of different elements from the Ruth and Jennie markers.

Ilka asks, "What's that?"

She points to a small brown spherical ball smaller than a tack. I look up and see it rolling across the top of the page. *No way.* John and I glance at one another.

"Where did it come from?"

I hear Ilka's question, but I am too busy examining the ball, feeling its smooth surface slide across my fingertips.

"It's Marinol," I answer.

"No, it can't be," says John.

"But it is. Feel it."

I hand the pill to John. For one moment, no one speaks; we are too stunned. I explain what it is to Sean, who appears doubtful and to Ilka, who smiles as if marijuana pills drop out of the sky every day.

Maybe it fell out of the vial during a hospital visit, lay at the bottom of my bag all this time, and attached itself to my notebook at this precise moment? Even the most logical explanation sounds absurd in my head.

"Maybe, it's Adrienne," I say wondering if I'm reaching, hoping for too much.

"I've seen a lot of strange things happen around here," says Ilka. "Could be your sister. It was rolling across the paper as you were drawing on it."

"Yeah. She likes her tombstone," I reply.

I can tell John wants to believe me; he has no other explanation either. I put the pill in my pocket, satisfied Adrienne is pleased with the marker I designed. I also remind myself only sane people question their own insanity. *I'm not crazy. She was here.*

With most of our budget spent on the plot and tombstone, we have little money left for the remaining costs. John and I have no choice, but to select the cheapest casket, a plain box with gray felt lining. I am not even sure if it's made from real wood. *The plot and tombstone are more important. The coffin will only make a brief appearance.* We barely have enough for flowers, but somehow we manage to purchase one giant bouquet that costs hundreds of dollars. Ilka and Sean must have fudged the numbers, but they don't say anything.

Hollywood Forever offers a unique service with their funeral packages: the Forever Lifestory, which includes the Forever Album and Chapel Tribute. Alana, our assigned Lifestory biographer, arrives at our home the following morning. I must choose ten photographs for the album. Each picture will be accompanied by a voiceover explaining the occasion. Alana brings all her recording equipment with her, and she promises to return the pictures as soon as she completes Adrienne's Lifestory. I select another twenty-five pictures for the Chapel Tribute, a montage with music that will be shown at the end of the memorial service next week. I leave the music up to John. In that department, he knows Adrienne's tastes better than anyone does. Alana also agrees to include video footage from Adrienne's spring dance performance, so we can show it during the service.

Later that afternoon, I argue with a reporter from the local newspaper the *Burbank Leader.* After a brief interview for Adrienne's obituary, the reporter asks about other surviving relatives besides me. I mention John, of course, but the paper cannot legally list him as Adrienne's father. I offer Aidan, our brother, even though Adrienne had not had a relationship with him for years. The reporter keeps pressing me.

"What about her real father?" he asks.

"Dead."

"And her mother?"

I hesitate and stupidly tell the truth.

"She's alive. Lives out of state. Lost custody a long time ago. Don't mention her."

The reporter insists upon listing our mother and wants her name. The more he pressures me, the louder my voice gets until I decide to take the call outside. Soon I'm shouting.

"Look, if you insist on mentioning our mother, you might as well not write the damn thing at all. My sister wouldn't have wanted that. Don't you get it? Our mother lost custody! She doesn't deserve to be listed as a surviving relative; she's not even invited to the funeral."

My tirade silences him. We exchange polite goodbyes and hang up. The next day, the *Burbank Leader* prints Adrienne's obituary. There is no mention of our mother.

The next few days become a blur of activity. John and I meet Anya for lunch at the Glendale Galleria, where I shop for the perfect funeral outfit. John buys a tie to match my shimmery blue full-length dress. I buy a sleeveless, blue sweater for the burial service and blue Sketchers sneakers as well. I decide on a whim to wear Adrienne's blue slippers with my new dress. Even Anya gets into the blue theme with a matching suit from her favorite store Talbots. *If I stop moving, I won't make it through this week. I have to keep going.*

Tuesday morning, I go to the funeral home early to do Adrienne's makeup myself. I don't want her looking like a freak. I remember our grandparents lying in their open caskets at their double funeral in 1990. Papa looked like he had spent too much time in a tanning booth, and To-Mama resembled Bette Davis's character in the movie *What Ever Happened to Baby Jane?* Appalled by their unnatural appearance and unable to control a screaming four-year-old Adrienne, I walked out of the service.

The embalmer, Virgil Wilson, no relation, dressed Adrienne in her blue satin gown with her blue monarch butterfly wings spread underneath her. He warned me in advance the embalming process causes the body to bloat. When he shows me Adrienne in the coffin, she appears as if she has gained ten pounds. However, what disturbs me the most is her smile—it's gone.

"What happened to her smile?"

"I closed her mouth. Is something wrong?"

I feel the tickle in my ears, the precursor to tears. *It's not his fault. He didn't know.*

"No. I just miss her smile, that's all."

Virgil nods.

"Let me know if you need anything."

He leaves me alone with Adrienne in the empty chapel. Shivering, I focus on her face and not the stillness of her body. Remembering the foundation fiasco before the ballet, I only dust light powder over Adrienne's face to combat the pallor of her once olive skin.

Sweeping shimmery eye shadow on her forever-closed lids, I notice how her eyebrows were thinning out, but her eyelashes were growing back. *Don't stop. Don't think. Just keep going.*

I dab color on her lips and realize I will never see her mouth open again, her full-teeth smile again. *Why did he have to close her mouth?*

Finally, I spread body glitter all over Adrienne's bald head, the way she wore it to the benefit in July. I tie her blue scarf around her neck and arrange it so it hides the marks left by her central line. Slipping her favorite blue flip-flops on her feet, I do my best to cover the embalming marks too—Virgil's suggestion.

With her head, makeup, and clothes complete, Adrienne only needs her jewelry; she never left home without it. I slip on her blue-gel bracelets along with Dave's blue-sequined wristbands. I adorn her fingers with her Celtic-knot ring, her amber ring, and during the service, I will give her my college ring. Without moving her head, I clasp three necklaces around her neck: her favorite fairy amulet, the amber pendant that matches the ring, and the diamond necklace Anya and Alex gave her for her thirteenth birthday. She never wore it because she was afraid of losing it.

I stand back and look at Adrienne in the open casket. I see a blue fairy, but only her body. Her soul is gone.

I know Adrienne wants me to be strong for John, for Adam, for her friends, even our adult friends, many of whom arrive early to help us set up. Anya and I notice the dust particles in the air; they seem like fine glitter, something out of a Disney movie. Others see it too.

"Adrienne's in the house!" we say. *So many signs. Is this another one?*

Between my obsessive organization, the detailed program, and Hollywood Forever's fine staff, the actual memorial service goes well with only a few hitches. So many people show up, the crowd tumbles outside and listens through speakers as friends and family tell stories about Adrienne. The battery in the videotape recorder dies after two hours so some speeches are not captured for posterity. Afterward, the line of people paying their respects seems infinite, but I continue to shake hands, accept condolences, receive hugs, and in some cases give hugs. I stand alone though next to Adrienne's open casket, because John took Adam outside to get some air. He doesn't return until the masses leave.

John brings Adam back inside the chapel once the crowd has dissipated. Adam puts a picture he drew especially for Adrienne in the coffin and says goodbye. Then, John ushers him back outside, asking one of our friends to keep an eye on him. They know not to come back into the chapel. What needs to happen next is a private matter.

Brightening our somber mood, Sean says, "I've never seen a service like that one. There must have been over 150 people. It was incredible."

"Really? You think so?"

I beam with pride. *Keep the small talk going so we do not have to do it. I can't say goodbye.* Sean, John, and I stand by Adrienne's coffin staring at her body.

"Remember what we talked about?"

We nod. One of the many disadvantages to buying the cheapest casket is it does not lock down the way expensive ones do.

"Ready?"

John and I shake our heads. I allow the salty tears to fall down my face. No one can see me now. I don't need to be strong anymore. I stroke Adrienne's arm. John squeezes her hand.

"I love you, kiddo," he says.

I kiss the top of her sparkly head.

"I love you sweetie."

Sean slides the lid of the coffin into place.

"We'll secure it, later, but here you go."

He gives John a long nail and a hammer and points to a precise location. John's hand shakes as he puts the nail in position. THUNK! John chips away at my heart. THUNK! Pieces of me fall to the ground. THUNK! Reality seeps into the empty spaces. THUNK! Adrienne isn't coming back.

I grab the edge of the gray felt box for support. John drops the hammer and holds me. *We are nothing without her. I—am—nothing.*

Fewer than thirty people attend the private burial service the next morning. Under a canopy, next to a large hole in the ground, we sit in metal folding chairs, the ones closest to Adrienne, we who love her the most. On this perfect, sunny autumn day in Southern California, we form a cloud composed of many broken hearts. Most of us share our grief by standing up and saying a few words.

I have no written speech, created no program for today. I talk but I don't know where the words come from. They seem to belong to someone else. The pain obscures any logical thoughts I may possess. My blood has turned to razor blades; it pumps, it cuts, and the faster my heart beats, the more the pain increases until my razor-blade blood reaches my heart, which shreds to bits.

Men bring the casket, sealed inside of a larger cement container, closer to the hole. *Getting the expensive coffin wouldn't have mattered anyway.* Two large bouquets of flowers rest atop the concrete, as if the bright colors will make us forget Adrienne's body lies inside that cold chamber. I watch as the men use ropes to lower the cement box into the ground. *Manual labor? In the movies, it's automated.* At one point, they almost drop her, and I hear a collective gasp behind me.

I want to go with Adrienne. I want to push those flowers aside and throw my body on that modern-day version of a tomb. *Bury me with her! Please!* If no one else were here right now, I would do it. The two idiots who cannot balance a coffin with ropes wouldn't be able to stop me. I would hold on so tight my body heat would melt the concrete, and then, I could hug Adrienne again. *Throw dirt on me! I don't care. Nothing matters now. Don't you see?*

I lean forward as the flowers disappear. *Last chance to go for it—jump right in!* The sound of someone sniffling pulls me back, and I see Adam, crying, yet trying not to. He wants to be a brave young man. In that moment, I gain clarity. Not only would I be unsuccessful if I leaped into the hole because our friends would insist on rescuing me, but I might also damage my tenuous relationship with Adam. I walk away from the hole in the ground.

I stay with our friends long enough to release blue balloons in honor of Adrienne. One by one, each person lets a balloon go. We all tilt our heads up to watch as they float through the air. Fueled by a light breeze, they soon become blue dots against a lighter blue sky, far away from us but perhaps closer now to an airplane full of passengers traveling to an exotic island or a flock of birds flying to a warmer climate. I shuffle away, shunning our friends, not bothering to say goodbye.

I find an unmarked gray granite bench facing the lake and lie down, curling my body in a fetal position, much like the one I found Adrienne in five months ago. The pain feels slower now; instead of tearing through my body, it moves with great effort, weighed down by the unknown. Ducks waddle over and form a circle around me, my own white ring. *Adrienne never finished reading The Fellowship of the Ring.* They nestle in the grass, tuck their beaks under their wings, and fall asleep. I feel as though someone sent them to protect me. *Maybe Adrienne?*

I close my eyes. I feel as though my life is over, and in a way, it is. My life with Adrienne is over. All three of my premonitions came true: cancer appeared in my life, I have already outlived my sister, and I will never see her grow up. Why Adrienne? I don't understand. Nothing makes sense. As I lie here, wishing my body could deteriorate in the dirt with Adrienne, I ask myself did I give her a good life? Did Adrienne ever feel . . . happy? And how will I . . . live my life—without her?

I will spend the next ten years seeking the answer to that question.

View of the Hollywood Sign from Adrienne's grave at Hollywood Forever Cemetery

In 2002, Andrea found this sketch of the Hollywood Sign drawn by Adrienne. She titled it "Future."

After Adrienne

Adrienne's hospital roommates/friends lived longer than she did. Eight-year-old **Veronica** (neuroblastoma) died about one year after her diagnosis. Fifteen-year-old **Whitney** (rhabdomyosarcoma) died on her eighteenth birthday, almost three years after her diagnosis. We never saw the unforgettable nineteen-year-old **LaQuisha** (sickle cell anemia) again. Five-year-old **Janelle** (leukemia) is alive and cancer-free as far as I know.

Adrienne's boyfriend **Eli** graduated from John Burroughs High School in 2003. He married in his early twenties and moved to London where he works as a Video/Post-Production Editor. Adrienne died on his 16th birthday.

Though **Anya** and **Alex** lived ten minutes away from my house in Burbank, we are no longer friends. I know they have two beautiful sons, and they visit Adrienne's grave twice a year.

John quit his job at Bank of America and fulfilled his lifelong dream of becoming a rock star. He is the lead singer of the band When in Rome. John is also a Post Audio Engineer at Modern Video Film. We ended our relationship two years after Adrienne passed away. We are not friends.

I have not seen **Adam** since his twelfth birthday in February 2004. He lives in Southern California and pursues a career in music. He and his father John now have a close relationship.

After several years of investigation, our mother **Myra Wilson** pled guilty to one count of theft of government money and two counts of Social Security fraud. I flew to Alabama to speak at her sentencing hearing in March 2006. She received the maximum possible sentence of ten months, which she served in a federal prison in Florida. She stole $51,834 from my sister Adrienne. For many years, our mother stopped receiving disability benefits until she had paid off her debt to the government. Had Adrienne been alive, that money would have gone to her. Though I saw our mother in court, I have not spoken to her since November 2001.

As for me, time moved forward, but I couldn't move on. Part of me died with Adrienne, leaving a void so vast that nothing will ever be able to fill it. For years, I tried to relieve my grief.

- I started a nonprofit to fight liver cancer, Blue Faery: The Adrienne Wilson Liver Cancer Association. For more information, go to www.bluefaery.org.
- I got the dog I always wanted, and as Adrienne predicted, he was an overgrown slobber machine. My 200-pound English Mastiff named Winston was with me from December 2002 until his death in May 2013. He was the best dog ever.
- Despite suffering from feline lower urinary tract disease and diabetes later in life, Marinol was the sweetest cat ever. He lived for thirteen-and-a-half years, dying in November 2014, just one month before I left Los Angeles. Little Bit lived for eleven years; she died on Christmas Eve 2007. Both cats napped in Adrienne's bedroom every day.
- I took antidepressants, saw several therapists, switched careers numerous times, went back to school, lost old friends, and gained new ones. I got married and I got divorced.
- After living in Los Angeles for over twenty years, I returned to Birmingham, Alabama, in December 2014. Adrienne was born in Birmingham and it seemed like a good place to start over.

What people don't tell you is . . . there is no cure for death. Grief doesn't go away. It gets better over time, but I'll never get over the loss of the most important person in my life.

Author's Note

We declared war on cancer, and we—Adrienne's family, friends, peers, teachers, hell the world—lost because we no longer have her. It took me years to appreciate what Anya's mother said, "You will win if you measure winning in terms of good days and good hours." We lost Adrienne, but did she lose?

Adrienne never let cancer take away her spirit no matter how hard it tried. Even when she had no strength left, she kept fighting. I'll never forget her muffled "Fuck off" when she thought her doctor had given up on her. She had her dark moments: I witnessed frustration, fear, anger, and sadness, but I never saw an ounce of self-pity. I never heard Adrienne ask, "Why me?" when all I did was ask, "Why her?" Whether she was eating buttery crab legs or watching ballet dancers glide across a stage, Adrienne savored every experience. She met Jay Leno. She met Dave Navarro—twice. I can still hear her voice, "DAVE Navarro KNOWS who I am!" She not only lived her life to its fullest, but also took control. "I'd rather be dead than deaf, Sissy." She was never on a respirator. She didn't waste away in a hospital. She died at home surrounded by people who loved her.

Adrienne didn't beat cancer, but cancer didn't beat her either. Her prophetic journal entry will always haunt me: "Cancer blessed me . . . it hasn't cursed me with the end of a life." Adrienne was right. Cancer didn't stop her from living the life she had left. She lived more in 147 days than most people do in a lifetime. *Fuck you no change and your friend change.* We lost. But my sister Adrienne—she kicked cancer's ass. Adrienne won.

Thank you for reading my memoir. If you enjoyed it, **please leave a review on Amazon.**

Acknowledgments

I have many people to thank; my apologies if I miss someone.

To everyone who listened to the Better Off Bald podcast/video series in 2017, your feedback and encouragement reassured me that there was an audience for this book.

To my mentors Samantha Dunn, M.G. Lord, Noel Riley Fitch, and Madelyn Cain, you lead by example and I am awed by your beauty and talent. Thank you for reading early drafts of this book, providing constructive feedback, being my champion, and understanding what one classmate called a 'controversial' title for a memoir. Sam, I remember the aha! moment I experienced after your class. The structure of the book hit me in the face like a blast of cold air. M.G., thank you for being a kickass thesis advisor (and you were right about the cats). Noel and Madelyn, you taught me the ingredients of a book proposal and an essay respectively. Those first-semester grad school assignments won national awards from the National Writer's Association and *Writer's Digest* magazine.

To my peers in the University of Southern California's MPW program, especially the nonfiction writers who graduated with me in 2008, your insight made a difference.

To the Independent Writers of Southern California, thank you for giving me opportunities to do readings of this book at Vroman's Bookstore in Pasadena and Barnes & Noble in Santa Monica.

To the outside readers/editors—Alan, James, Lauren, and Sally—your constructive criticism pushed me to improve with every draft.

To Corey: I married you too soon after Adrienne's death; for that I am sorry. Thank you for supporting my writing, reading the first draft of this book, and for giving me a divorce that was more amicable than our marriage.

To the dozens if not hundreds of doctors, nurses, case managers, social workers, and staff at Empire Medical Clinic, Providence Saint Joseph Medical Center, Children's Hospital Los Angeles, and UCLA Medical Center, I appreciate everything you did for Adrienne. May you always remember the beautiful blue-haired fifteen year old who insisted on wearing blue nail polish and metal jewelry to the hospital.

To Dave Navarro and Jay Leno, you brought light into our lives and made some of Adrienne's dreams come true. I will always cherish Days 35 and 105.

To my father and stepmother for treating Adrienne like the granddaughter they never had, for helping me get legal custody, and for helping us out financially so I could quit my job and become Adrienne's full-time caregiver.

To my 2 a.m. friends for loving me for who I am, not what I do. To my soul sister Elizabeth for her encouragement, support, and our shared love of woo-woo.

To the 'aunts and uncles' whose names have been changed in this book, you were so special to Adrienne. You took her to Olvera Street, *The Rocky Horror Picture Show*, Raging Waters, the Psychic Eye Bookstore, and anywhere else she convinced you to take her. (Adrienne was the master of persuasion.) You taught her how to sew and make Matzo Ball soup. You introduced her to yoga before it was cool. You gave her your blood. Literally. Unlike me, most of you shared Adrienne's blood type. I know you would have given Adrienne a piece of your liver if it would have saved her life. My gratitude for you is deeper than you can imagine.

To Adam, Adrienne loved you like a brother. I hope you still remember her.

To John, you were the only father Adrienne ever had. She loved you from the moment she met you and that's how I knew you were different. Thank you for being there when we needed you the most. You were right about your birthday.

To Edward, you are the second-best thing that has ever happened to me. Thank you for loving me for who I am and for being my partner in business and life.

To Adrienne, you are my hero. During a time when most people would have been swimming in a pool of pity, you displayed courage, grace, dignity, and humor. Raising you was and will always be the best thing I have ever done in my life. I miss you every damn day. #bestkidever

To Cancer University's patients, caregivers, members, volunteers, backers, Medical Advisory and Patient & Caregiver Advocate Board Members. To our angel investors, brand ambassadors, corporate partners, nonprofit alliances, pilot campuses, affiliates, employees, freelancers, VAs, and founding team. Thank you for seeing and sharing my vision.

To Blue Faery's donors, supporters, volunteers, contractors, board directors, corporate council, and community members. To the oncologists, hepatologists, surgeons, nurses, and other healthcare providers who treat HCC. To the patients, caregivers, and survivors. Let us work together to find a cure for Hepatocellular Carcinoma in our lifetime. This book is for you.

About the Author

ANDREA WILSON WOODS is a writer who loves to tell stories, and a patient advocate who founded the nonprofit Blue Faery: The Adrienne Wilson Liver Cancer Association. Andrea is the CEO and co-founder of Cancer University, a for-profit, social benefit, digital health company. With Cancer U, Andrea synergizes her talents of coaching, writing, teaching, and advocacy. For over ten years, Andrea worked in the education field as a teacher and professor for public and private schools as well as universities. Andrea obtained her master's degree in professional writing from the University of Southern California; her nonfiction writing has won national awards.

Connect with Andrea on her website andreawilsonwoods.com and follow her on social media:

- Facebook: AuthorAndreaWilsonWoods
- LinkedIn and YouTube: AndreaWilsonWoods
- Twitter and Instagram: AndreaWilWoods

Made in the USA
Monee, IL
19 May 2022

96671816R00229